The Primal Screen

The Primal Screen

A History of Science Fiction Film

JOHN BROSNAN

ORBIT

An Orbit Book

First published in Great Britain in 1991 by Orbit Books
a Division of Macdonald & Co (Publishers) London & Sydney

A CIP catalogue record for this book is available from the British Library

ISBN 0 356 20222 4

Typeset in Baskerville by ⚡ Tek Art Ltd., Addiscombe, Croydon, Surrey
Printed and bound in Great Britain by
BPCC Hazell Books
Aylesbury, Bucks, England
Member of BPCC Ltd.

Orbit Books
a Division of
Macdonald & Co (Publishers) Ltd
165 Great Dover Street
London SE1 4YA

A member of Maxwell Macmillan Publishing Corporation

Contents

Acknowledgements

Where do I start? Well, I guess I'll round up the usual suspects: like my mother, who took me to see my first science fiction movies all those years ago; my bank manager, who kept me financially afloat while I was writing this book; my agent, John Parker, who sold the book; and John Jarrold, my editor, who bought it. Then there's John Baxter, without whom etc. etc., Alan Jones (who provided invaluable help with the illustrations), Alan McKenzie, Tise Vahimagi, David Wingrove, and, finally I'd like to thank my collections of *Cinefantastique* magazine (editor Frederick S. Clarke) and *Starburst* magazine (editor Stephen Payne) which were both very useful. Black-and-white photographs courtesy of the author. Colour photographs courtesy of the Alan McKensie collection.

'The golden age of science fiction is twelve'
Terry Carr

Introduction

To the casual observer I don't appear to have much in common with George Lucas and Steven Spielberg. I am not a successful film-maker responsible for some of the most profitable movies ever made — I am not even a film-maker. Also I am not an American (I did attend Hollywood High School but that was in Australia), yet Lucas and Spielberg and I do have a great deal in common. We, and other American film-makers in our age group, were imprinted by the Hollywood science fiction films of the fifties. They received their cultural imprinting in America and I received mine in a small and remote outpost of the American Cultural Empire, Perth, Western Australia.

Films other than science fiction also had a profound effect on me during this crucial period. I recall Disney's *Peter Pan* (Spielberg is finally making his long-awaited version of this), and *Scaramouche* which later led me to take up, somewhat hilariously, fencing, but it was the science fiction movies that influenced me most strongly. I liked all movies, of course, but the sf ones lodged deepest in my psyche and my earliest cinematic memories are of scenes from *The Day the Earth Stood Still*.

And apart from the films there was the science fiction in the comic books — *American* comic books, of course. In those days they were reprinted in Australia, in black and white, and Australian publishers attempted to create the impression in their young readers that these were Australian products. Hence in a panel showing the towering Manhattan skyline you would find the caption above saying, in shaky printing: SYDNEY. Sometimes it would say MELBOURNE. I was never fooled. Even more pathetic were the occasions when Australian illustrators would alter the original artwork to again try and create the impression these were true-blue Australian comics. When showing the Earth from a viewpoint in space, American artists had the habit of always putting America, north and south, slap-bang in the middle of the shot, suggesting that it was the centre of the world and all other countries were merely peripheral to it. I tell you, it was a sad and sorry sight after an Australian artist, miffed at what effect this could have had on an Aussie child, had got through removing all trace of America and had substituted poor little Australia in the centre of the globe. The result was bizarre to say the least. This silliness came to an end in 1960 when trade restrictions were lifted and it was possible to import the original American comics, in all their glorious colour, directly into the country.

Apart from the sf-orientated comics like *Superman*, I collected Disney comics. These too were then reprinted by an Australian company but, thankfully, in colour. My favourite titles were *Uncle Scrooge* and *Walt Disney Comics*. There was something about the drawing and writing of *Uncle Scrooge* and the lead Donald Duck and his Nephews story in *Walt Disney Comics* that, as I grew older, I realized was a higher quality than the other Disney strips. I had, of course, discovered the magic of the late, great Carl Barks, known as 'the good artist' to kids of my generation in America. Years later I interviewed Gary Kurtz, producer of *Star Wars* and *The Empire Strikes Back*, and though he was pleasant enough, he remained steadfastly dour throughout the interview until, near the end, I mentioned Carl Barks in the knowledge that he was also a fan. As he described a special edition of the collected works of Barks that he was publishing, he became positively animated for the one and only time during the interview.

Science fiction, not to mention fantasy and mythology, featured strongly in Barks's stories, especially in the full-length *Uncle Scrooge* adventures which often had the plucky ducks going on long journeys to remote parts and in discovery of lost worlds. Barks was a great draughtsman and he generated a true 'sense of wonder' with his beautifully illustrated stories. He certainly reinforced my love of the fantastic that had been sparked off by my early exposure to science fiction movies. But here is where I suspect

I began to part company with Messrs Lucas, Kurtz, Spielberg, Dante etc., with whom I had shared a similar cultural imprinting, because apart from lapping up science fiction in films and comics I also started to read science fiction *books* . . .

I began with the 'juveniles', such as the *Kemlo* series by E.C. Elliot (actually William Temple, I am told), and the books by Capt. W.E. Johns, creator of *Biggles*, that began with *Kings of Space*. But from a relatively early age I was also reading 'adult' science fiction, thanks to my mother. She was very keen on the stuff (she was the one, after all, who had taken me to see all those sf films in the first place), and she was also an avid reader of comic books, which made her rather unusual as far as mothers went in my neighbourhood. None of my schoolfriends' mothers showed any interest in comic books — except in getting rid of them at the earliest opportunity — much less read sf books (or probably any kind of book for that matter), but then my mother was also different in that she was separated from my father and had a full-time job as a secretary.

Anyway, thanks to my mother's reading habits I was exposed to the likes of Robert Sheckley (I clearly remember a dog-eared copy of his collection of stories, *Pilgrimage to Earth*), Clifford Simak, Frederic Brown, and A.E. Van Vogt, among others. Then, branching out on my own, I discovered the sf magazines in around 1960 and began haunting second-hand bookshops to increase my collection of back issues of *Amazing Stories* and *Fantastic* (this was the period when both magazines were under the inspired editorship of Cele Goldsmith), *Galaxy*, *If*, and *The Magazine of Fantasy and Science Fiction*. And, of course, I was also buying sf novels in paperback. Not that I had abandoned comic books. On the contrary, with the influx of American editions my interest had increased and, after a letter of mine was printed in an issue of *Green Lantern* in 1961, I had become involved with American comics fandom and was introduced to the delights of comic 'fanzines'. Interaction with this sub-culture later led me into contact with science fiction fandom, which even had branches in Australia, and eventually launched me on my writing career.

To digress a moment before I actually reach the point of all this — a word about puberty and how it is related to special effects. 1960 must have been the year I hit puberty because it was around this time that I suddenly became aware of special effects in movies. Yes, of course I knew, well before that, that a lot of stuff in movies was faked but I couldn't spot the fakery. Yes, I knew perfectly well that Godzilla wasn't really a three hundred foot tall dinosaur but it *looked* like a three hundred foot tall dinosaur to me . . . until puberty arrived and suddenly Godzilla looked like a man in a rubber suit. Suddenly all manner of special effects became apparent to me — I could spot rear projection, travelling mattes, matte paintings, stop-motion photography and miniatures, things that previously my eyes and brain had accepted without question. Talk about loss of innocence! But this led me into an intense interest in movie special effects, which resulted in *Movie Magic*, my second book on the cinema. Incidentally, I'm not sure of the significance of this development, but these days I'm finding it harder and harder to detect special effects in movies; it's probably because the techniques are becoming so sophisticated but it could also be a sign of severe regression on my part.

Back to the main theme: science fiction. By reading the real stuff over the years, I became increasingly annoyed with sf movies because they seemed to ignore most of the potential offered by science fiction. At the same time I'd also picked up a smattering of science — astronomy had been a personal obsession from a very early age — and was further annoyed at how scientifically inaccurate most sf movies tended to be. John Baxter (see Chapter Eighteen, Space, Time and the Nerd Factor) maintains that the gulf between literary sf and sf cinema is inevitable and that they are two entirely different animals, but I find the tension between the two mediums both interesting and irritating, because I think the gulf can be overcome, and, very occasionally, has been. The contrast between written sf and sf cinema provided the source of my first book on sf movies, *Future Tense* and this one, *The Primal Screen*. Bits of the first book are incorporated into this one but they are two completely different works. For one thing, I have tried not to be such a pedant over scientific inaccuracies in sf movies, though I still find such things annoying. Also, this book is much more personal in style — very much my personal response to the sf movies I love — and hate — and should in no way be regarded as a serious reference book though I do hope it will be informative about sf movies and movie-making in general.

This book does not pretend to be a comprehensive survey of the entire sf cinema, but I do think I have touched all the important bases along the way. For reasons of space I decided not to include certain categories of sf films, such as those that could be described as deliberately comedic sf films as opposed to unintentionally comedic (this decision meant I was spared having to try and write about movies like *Morons from Outer Space* and *Earth Girls Are Easy*). Also I haven't included sf movies that have been released only on video, mainly because I've never caught up with so much of this material (this, alas, meant I couldn't write about one of my favourite sf video movies, *Hell Comes to Frogtown*). And I'm sure some purists will complain about my not including *King Kong* in the volume . . . it's a great movie but it's definitely fantasy, not sf (well, it is in *my* book).

In 1978, I ended the Introduction to *Future Tense* by writing that there were signs that sf cinema was catching up with literary sf and hoped that in the eighties we would see sf movies based on the works of some of our top sf writers. Well, we didn't, with the exception of *Blade Runner* and *Total Recall*, two movies loosely based on the work of Philip K. Dick which I liked a lot, with reservations; John Varley's misfire with *Millennium*; and the disastrous *Dune* — so I won't repeat that prediction for the nineties. In fact I won't make any prediction about the future of sf films, except to say that, hopefully, I will go on finding them equally delighting and irritating.

When nobody could hear you scream: science fiction films of the silent era

Strictly speaking, none of the films covered in this chapter are science fiction films. In retrospect, yes, they are, but at the time many of them were made the term 'science fiction' didn't exist. True, the term 'scientific fiction' was first used by pulp-magazine publisher Hugo Gernsback back in 1923, and the following year he proposed a magazine to be called *Scientifiction* before finally, in 1926, publishing *Amazing Stories*, the first true sf magazine (in English at least), but science fiction, and the term itself, remained in its pulp ghetto until after the Second World War. Therefore the film-makers included in this chapter had no idea at the time that they were making sf films, just as H.G. Wells was unaware he was writing sf in the 1890s, as was Aldous Huxley when he wrote *Brave New World* in 1932.

Like the Mormons who convert dead people rectrospectively to Mormonism, we can categorize as sf any film that even slightly fits the definition of sf. And we can shove the chosen film, screaming and protesting, into the box because the definition of sf is pretty flexible. In this particular situation an sf film is any film I *say* is an sf film. Good, I'm glad that's settled. So now we can properly begin.

It's traditional to point the finger at poor George Meliès, stage magician and pioneer in trick photography, and describe him as the earliest sf filmmaker. I myself have been guilty of such rude behaviour in the past but now I'm doubtful. Admittedly, a few of his short, cinematic confections were based on the work of an sf writer, Jules Verne (not that Verne *knew* he was an sf author, of course) but I think it's stretching things to describe Meliès as an sf film-maker. But he did possess one trait shared by most subsequent sf film-makers — he didn't show much respect for the source material. One wonders what Verne thought of the 1895 *Le Voyage dans la Lune* which was vaguely inspired by his novel *De la Terre à la Lune*. If I remember correctly the projectile in the novel was not loaded into the giant cannon by a line of grinning chorus girls.

Leaving Meliès safely behind us we move on to an American film based on what is now widely considered to be the first true science fiction novel, Mary Shelley's *Frankenstein* (not that Mary Shelley *knew . . .*). This is the 1910 production *Frankenstein*, directed by J. Searle Dawley for the Edison Company and starring Charles Ogle as the monster. I had the opportunity of viewing a print of this rare movie at an sf convention and thus can remember little about it. But I do know that it is closer in spirit to Shelley's novel than the later 1931 Universal production.

I suppose we can lay the blame for the 'mad scientist' cliché at Shelley's feet as well; *Frankenstein* appears to have offered the template from which countless movie scientists would be fashioned. Meddling about, like Dr Frankenstein, with things that should be left alone, they inevitably produce all kinds of trouble and get their come-uppance as a result. The scientist in Abel Gance's 1914 film *La Folie du Dr Tube* is typical; his dubious experiments with light waves drive him insane. And in a later French film, René Clair's *Paris Qui Dort* (also known as *The Crazy Ray*), a mad scientist paralyses all of Paris with a mysterious ray. The few people not to succumb to the ray wake up to find the city and most of its inhabitants frozen in a single second of time (this might have been inspired by the H.G. Wells short story 'The New Accelerator' in which a scientist invents a serum that speeds up the human metabolism several thousand times so that, to the serum-taker, the surrounding world seems frozen in time).

A mad scientist was also at the root of the trouble in the 1915 German production *Homunculus* (also known as *Homunculus Der Führer*). A six-part serial directed by Otto Rippert, it was based on a novel by Robert Reinert and concerns the successful attempt by a scientist to create an artificial man whose mind consists of pure reason uncluttered by emotion. Lacking a soul, however, the creature automatically becomes evil. After establishing himself as dictator of a large but unnamed country, he plans to conquer

Brigitte Helm and Paul Wegener in the 1928 version of Alraune, *a warning against the use of artificial insemination.*

Some of the cast and scenery that appeared in Georges Meliès's A Trip to the Moon *in 1902; a pre-science fiction science fiction film.*

Olaf Fonss as the star of Homunculus, *a 1915 German movie about an artificial man who becomes the 'Führer' and tries to conquer the world.*

the world but is struck dead by a bolt of lightning, presumably sent by an offended God. The idea that unnatural birth processes produce spiritually damaged goods spawned another German film, *Alraune*, made in 1918, based on a novel by Hanns Heinz Ewers which had stirred up controversy in the German-speaking world in the early 1900s. Artificial insemination is the 'unnatural' process used here; a scientist impregnates a prostitute with the semen of a convicted murderer and adopts the resulting baby girl. He raises her himself as an experiment to test his theories on the relationship between character and the environment. But as the girl is irredeemably tainted both by the nature of her true parents and by the 'soulless' way in which she was conceived, it all ends in tears. She grows up into an 'evil' woman who uses her charms to drive poor, innocent men to suicide. This theme, seemingly based on a mixture of superstition and pseudo-science, has proved surprisingly persistent — the 1976 film *Embryo* concerns a scientist who brings a female foetus to maturity in an artificial womb at rapid speed. She seems perfect (she's played by Barbara Carrera) but proves to be 'tainted' by the unnatural birth process and the bodies soon start to pile up. Even more recently, in 1988 there was the BBC-TV serial 'First Born' which suggested that the half-ape, half-human protagonist, created by genetic engineering, was a brick short of a full spiritual load.

Alraune was remade in 1928, starring Brigitte Helm (the star of *Metropolis*) as the beautiful Alraune. In Britain it was released as *Daughter of Destiny* where it greatly confused audiences. This is because the British film censor removed all references to artificial insemination, so what remained was an odd story about a girl who, for no apparent reason, acts very badly towards her loving foster father.

A mad scientist and reflections on the nature of human evil both featured in the 1920 version of *Dr Jekyll and Mr Hyde*, starring John Barrymore. The short novel on which it was based, *The Strange Case of Dr Jekyll and Mr Hyde* by Robert Louis Stevenson, was published in 1886 and clearly belongs in the early sf canon. Stevenson's suggestion that civilization is only skin deep prefigures the theme that would dominate the work of H.G. Wells, who later admitted the influence of Stevenson. Subsequent film versions of the novel picked up the novel's implication that Jekyll wasn't merely taken over by the 'evil' side of his personality but was regressing back to a more primitive state. This was especially obvious in the 1931 version in which Frederic March's make-up makes him look like a Neanderthal man, though in the 1920 version Barrymore, with plenty of absurd leers, plays him simply as a caricature of evil. Furthermore, the whole experience turns out to have been a dream — a common device in American fantasy films of that period.

A couple of years later H.G. Wells provided the uncredited inspiration for a film called *A Blind Bargain*, a Sam Goldwyn production directed by Wallace Worsley. Though ostensibly based on a novel called *The Octave of Claudius* by Barry Pain, it obviously owes much to Wells's *The Island of Dr Moreau* with its story of a scientist experimenting with a combination of man and beast. Lon Chaney plays the mad scientist, Dr Lamb, who is trying to create a new race by grafting monkey glands onto humans. Inevitably, he is killed by one of his own creations. Amusingly, the following advice was given to potential exhibitors in a trade magazine at the time: 'Talk a story of unusual strength with a topical flavour. The newspapers lately have been giving prominence to gland grafting.'[1]

Conan Doyle's mad, and very idiosyncratic scientist, Professor Challenger, was brought to the screen (played by a miscast Wallace Beery) in the 1925 version of *The Lost World*. This slow-moving film is relatively faithful to the novel for about two-thirds of the way: an expedition to South America, led by Challenger, discovers a remote plateau which is still inhabited by dinosaurs and other prehistoric creatures. In the last third the film goes its own way with the plot and ends with the plateau being destroyed by a volcanic eruption and a surviving brontosaurus being transported to London. (In the novel a small pterodactyl escaped.) The creature breaks out of its cage while being unloaded from the ship and rampages through the city (thus setting the trend for subsequent prehistoric visitors to large cities). It then attempts to walk across Tower Bridge but the structure collapses under its weight and the dinosaur is last seen swimming out to sea.

These final sequences were technically the most ambitious in the film and Willis O'Brien, the pioneer model animator, produced some major innovations in his model-animating technique. They also required the construction of a huge set representing two London streets, peopled with two thousand extras together with two hundred cars and six London buses. Well, that's what the press handout at the time claimed; exaggeration had

(Top) *One of Willis H. O'Brien's camera set-ups for a stop-motion photography shot in* The Lost World, *complete with glass painting, miniature scenery and model dinosaur.*

(Bottom) *The same shot as seen through the camera.*

already become the Hollywood norm by 1925, but it does remain a spectacular piece of film. Years later O'Brien would top it with his model animation masterpiece, *King Kong*.

Also in 1925, Fritz Lang was making his masterpiece *Metropolis* over in Germany. Now I don't strictly classify this film as science fiction. It does feature a robot (though one created by magic rather than science, but then most scientists in early sf films were magicians disguised in white coats) and it is presumably set in the future (though there is hardly anything futuristic about the city), but it would be unthinkable to leave it out as so many people do regard it as a classic early sf movie. And I do admire it, despite its flaws — such as the plot. To say that the plot is both naive and downright ridiculous is to state the obvious, but this does not detract from the film's undeniable visual power. As a piece of pure cinema it remains an extraordinary achievement and one which is still appreciated by audiences today, as was witnessed by the success albeit limited of Giorgio Moroder's reconstructed 1984 version complete with disco soundtrack (it's difficult to imagine such an approach working with the ossified *Things to Come*).

The screenplay for *Metropolis* was written jointly by the film's director, Fritz Lang, and his current wife, Thea von Harbou, who had written the original novel (something I've never had any desire to read). The action is set in a vast Gothic city neatly divided into a ruling elite and a mass of *very* downtrodden workers. Just how the workers are kept so downtrodden is never very clear, as there are no police or guards in evidence and the elite are a pretty wimpish lot. Wimpiest of all is Freder (Gustav Froehlich), hedonistic son of the city's grim ruler, John Frederson (Alfred Abel). Freder spends most of his time running about in absurd white knicker-bockers with his frivolous friends and is completely oblivious to the workers' existence until he meets the beautiful Maria (Brigitte Helm) and a group of ragged children from 'down below'.

Freder follows Maria back down into the bowels of the city and has an eye-opening experience in a nightmare world where men work unceasingly as they tend huge machines which totally dominate them. He finds Maria in a church where she is preaching to the workers on the subject of good worker-employer relationships. The gist of her message seems to be that the two parties should at least meet occasionally. Hardly Marxist ideology but it alarms John Frederson who is also spying on the meeting. He instructs an evil scientist/magician, Rotwang (Rudolph Klein-Rogge), to create a robot double of Maria, and they test out her effectiveness in a night-club where, dressed in a scanty costume, she performs an erotic dance. The test is successful — not one rivet shows in her convincing layer of human flesh — and the male patrons are driven into a frenzy of lust (interesting to look at this twin protrayal of Maria in feminist terms; she is the classic case of woman seen as either saint or whore).

Then, in the clothes of the saintly Maria, the wicked robot leads the workers in a violent revolt. The workers go beserk and smash up all the machines, causing a flood. The real Maria, who has been imprisoned by Rotwang, escapes and saves the workers' children from the flood. All ends happily for everyone except for Rotwang and his lovely robot (Rotwang has a fatal flaw, the robot is incinerated). Freder gets Maria and the workers get a vague promise from Frederson that he'll be nicer in future. The central absurdity, of course, is why Frederson would want to engineer a revolution that would destroy the city in the first place. Surely all his energies would be towards preventing a revolution. Maybe it all makes sense in the novel.

But forget the plot, it's the visuals that count. Fritz Lang originally trained as an architect then became a graphic artist and for a time supported himself selling cartoons and caricatures. As a result of wounds sustained in the First World War he turned to writing and began selling melodramatic thrillers. Then he entered the film industry and began making films on similar subjects. One of his first was *The Spiders (Die Spinnen)*, made in 1919 about a group of men who attempt to take over the world using Inca gold, and later he made the first of the famous *Dr Mabuse* films about an evil genius who also plans to conquer the world. (Many of his films during this period contained elements of sf.) When the Nazis came to power Goebbels asked Lang to head the National Socialist film industry, telling him that Hitler had been enormously impressed by *Metropolis*. Lang's response was to leave the country. After a spell in France he emigrated to America and Hollywood and continued to make films.

Edgar C. Ulmer, another German director who later worked in America, had been Lang's assistant on many of his German productions, including *Metropolis*. He described the working methods of those days: 'At that time, up to the coming of sound, there were *two* directors in each picture: a

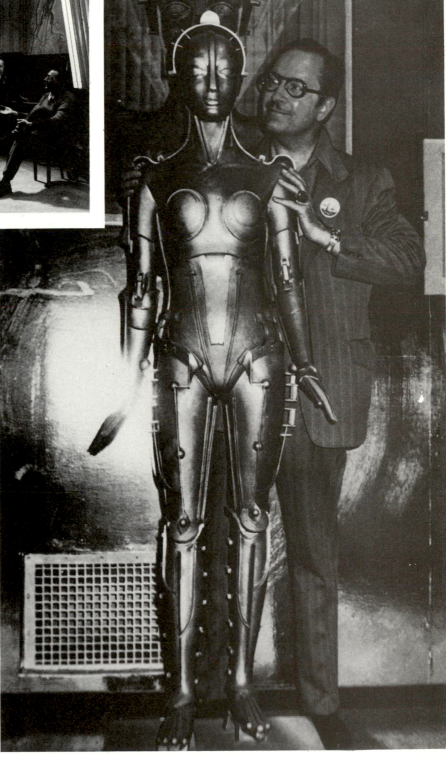

Fritz Lang (right with monocle), rehearses Brigitte Helm, (centre) in her erotic dance for the sequence where the evil robot incites the populace of Metropolis to riot.

A replica of the robot from Metropolis — without her covering of Brigitte Helm. Posing with her is Forrest Ackerman, Mr 'Sci-fi' himself.

A key image from
Metropolis. *Fritz Lang,
its director, later said of it,
'It's really too much, isn't
it?'*

director for the dramatic action and the actors, and a director for the
picture itself who established the camera angles, camera movements etc.
There had to be teamwork. Our sets were built in perspective with rising
or sloping floors. Everything was constructed through the viewfinder. So
what happened was that you could take one shot of that set if you had, say,
a room. If there were to be ten different shots in that room then you built
ten sets of that room. Because the one eye was the point of perspective,
the furniture was built in perspective. That's where the great visual flair
of those pictures came from. It gave you, of course, a completely controlled
style. When you look at the old UFA [Germany's famous pre-war film
studio that produced *Metropolis*] pictures today, you're startled at how
precise every shot is. Because a set was built for each one. Fritz Lang was
a designer too, and he had unbelievable energy and stick-to-it-iveness; you
could never stop him. He saw what he wanted in the picture. Nothing could
distract him, he would do it fifty times.' Ulmer, however, did not get on
with Lang. 'Not at all. Because on the set he was the incarnation of the
Austrian who became the Prussian general. A sadist of the worst order you
can imagine.'[2]

Metropolis took over nine months to shoot and put UFA heavily into debt. It did well in its initial European release but not well enough to recover its costs. It was re-edited for its American release in 1927 and lost several reels. When Paramount later bought out the bankrupt UFA studio it decreed that only the American version of the film should be circulated and had the negative of the three-hour original destroyed; the later American version was shortened even further. Moroder located copies of the longer American version and though his version is only 83 minutes long it contains scenes that have been missing from prints since the twenties.

It was not a popular success in America but it had a great impact on American film-makers, who were impressed by its huge sets, its imaginative design and its visual effects. Lang's directing style also impressed the American directors; his ability to manipulate huge crowds of extras so that they formed giant, fluid sculptures was particularly admired, and imitated (Cecil B. De Mille adopted many of Lang's techniques). The film's influence, in terms of design, persists to this day as *Blade Runner* and *Batman* testify. Lang himself became dismissive of *Metropolis* in later years. In a 1967 interview he said he thought it was pretty bad — 'That shot of Eric Masterman holding back the man-sized hands of the clock is really too much, isn't it?' — and he doubted whether a new *Metropolis* could be made, whether there was anything new to say on the subject. 'All right, so man has to live with the machine – is that a message today? He still has to live with himself first.'[3]

Space travel, nowadays synonymous with the term science fiction, was rare in the silent era. Two notable exceptions were *The First Men in the Moon* (1919), and *Die Frau Im Mond* (*Woman in the Moon*) made by Fritz Lang in 1928. The former was a British production based on the novel by H.G. Wells. It was directed by J.V. Leigh and by the sound of it wasn't very faithful to the book, mainly concerning itself with a triangular love affair and a scheming villain. I've never seen it, and, in fact, doubt if a print still exists but this is what one contemporary reviewer wrote: 'Primarily perhaps the film is a notable feat of studio-craft. The scenes on the moon, which naturally constitute the outstanding feature of the production, have been staged with genuine skill and imagination, which do great credit to Mr J.V. Leigh and his technical staff. The landing of the two explorers amidst the wild and desolate lunar mountains, which tower mysteriously in the chill and eerie twilight, is a situation of altogether novel power and suggestiveness. In the picture of the Grand Lunar's glittering palace Mr Leigh strikes an almost poetic note. In their grotesque beauty and originality some of these settings are worthy of the fantastic art of the Russian ballet.'[4] Weren't film reviewers awfully *polite* in those far-off days?

Woman in the Moon was the nearest thing to a straight sf film that Fritz Lang ever made. The melodramatic story (by Thea Von Harbou, natch), involving a hunt for 'pure' gold on the moon's surface, is weak but the film is technically interesting. It was the first film to attempt to portray realistically the mechanics of space travel. The technical advisers on the film were the German rocket experts Hermann Oberth and Willy Ley (Oberth later worked on rocket designs for the Nazis) and their spaceship design was remarkably prophetic (too much so for Hitler who later had all prints of the films seized). Not only was the rocket multi-staged but the scene where it is moved on its tracks out of its vast hangar towards the launching pad is similar to later true-life scenes at Cape Canaveral. The film even included the first use of the now-traditional countdown before the rocket's launch. But once the rocket lands safely on the moon scientific authenticity comes to an end. Complete with an atmosphere, the lunar landscape resembles the Swiss Alps.

Space travel, of a kind, featured in the 1924 Russian film *Aelita*, set mainly on Mars. A young Russian engineer, dissatisfied with life on Earth, builds a 'machine' which takes him to the Red Planet (I've never found out how exactly) where he becomes romantically involved with the Queen of Mars, Aelita. It was clearly more of a political allegory than science fiction, with the engineer learning that a good communist should never trust an aristocrat. And, of course, it all turns out to have been a dream. I have never seen it but from the surviving stills it was strikingly designed.

Around the same time, in America, J. Ernest Williamson was trying to get a lavish project off the ground — a film of Jules Verne's *Mysterious Island*. Back in 1916 Williamson had been involved in the making of a successful version of *Twenty Thousand Leagues Under the Sea*. With his brother George, he had developed the first effective technique for filming underwater. They build a spherical chamber of thick steel with a single porthole. It was suspended from a barge by a long tube made of removable

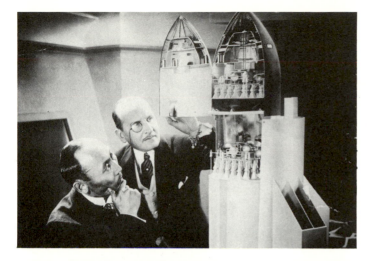

(Above left) Scientists in the 1928 Woman in the Moon *study a model of the only prophetic aspect of an otherwise silly movie, a multi-staged rocket.*

(Above) The full-scale rocket in Woman in the Moon *(well, another model really).*

A gaggle of Martian slaves in the visually inventive 1924 Russian sf movie, Aelita.

The Nautilus *and its crew
as they appeared in the
1916 version of* Twenty
Thousand Leagues
Under the Sea.

metal sections wide enough for a man to climb through. Air was pumped
down the tube from the barge, and the whole structure was strong enough
to be lowered to a depth of 80 feet.

When Universal decided to film Verne's novel the Williamson brothers
were hired to handle the sea footage. The director, Stuart Paton, had
concocted some absurd additions to the Verne original, including the
discovery of a pretty young woman on a desert island, but J. Ernest
Williamson, as he wrote in his autobiography, was determined to remain
as faithful as possible to the novel as far as his part of the production was
concerned. 'To vindicate Verne the dreamer was my problem — to make
Jules Verne's dream come true, but where were the unique and
extraordinary props?' Failing to obtain a real submarine, he built his own.
In his autobiography he claimed it was a hundred feet long and could be
operated by one man. But on the first trial run, watched by the Governor
of the Bahamas, things went wrong. 'I knew it could be submerged but I
was not so confident that it could be raised to the surface with entire success
at the first attempt.' Bit of a handicap for a submarine. 'Ordinarily I
planned to handle the Nautilus myself but on this occasion I entrusted it
to an assistant who was clad in a diving suit as a precaution. All was going
well, up came the railed platform, up came the rounded cigar-shaped hull.
And then! Cries of dismay from the spectators. Wildly the craft rolled. It
heeled from side to side in imminent danger of turning turtle and

drowning the man inside. And then slowly, smoothly, the Nautilus rolled back and came to rest on an even keel. I saw the Governor slap the Chief of Police on the back and heard him exclaim: "By Jove, these motion picture fellows — you can't baffle them, you know." '[5]

The film's release coincided with the news that a German U-boat had slipped through the blockades and sunk a dozen British ships outside New York. With this sudden new public interest in submarines the film was assured of success but Williamson had a great deal of difficulty in interesting anyone in the sequel. Finally MGM bought his scenario of *Mysterious Island* but then he encountered a problem familiar to writers who get caught up in the Hollywood machine: 'I was to learn that Jules Verne hadn't written a story big enough for this Hollywood crowd. The powers had definitely decided they would not film his romantic adventure story which my version followed closely. It must be something more than that, something larger, something "Big!" And the Abraham Lincoln atmosphere with its Civil War characters was definitely *out*. For technical reasons the story was now to be laid in Russia. Captain Nemo was to be Russian, the whole cast were to be Russian.' (Interestingly, Verne had revealed in the novel that Nemo was actually an Indian Prince with a big grudge against the British Empire.)[6]

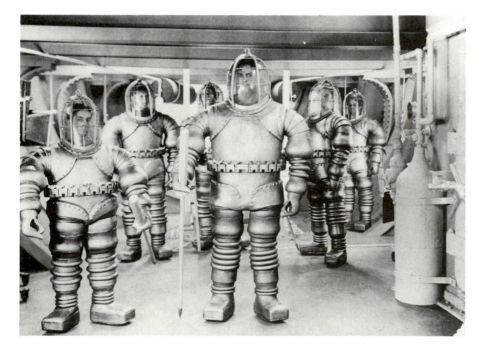

No one involved with the making of the ill-fated Mysterious Island *(1928) had much to laugh about, as this shot testifies.*

Williamson finally got the go-ahead to start shooting the location material in 1926, but faced a series of major obstacles, most of them originating back in Hollywood. The MGM executives couldn't make up their minds about the film's basic content and kept changing things around. Directors came and went, as did leading members of the cast, which meant that material had to be reshot endlessly. Altogether it took four years and a million dollars to complete the film, and the result was visually spectacular but hardly something that Jules Verne would have recognized (Nemo was now called Count Dakkar and was played by Lionel Barrymore). It might have been a popular success if it hadn't been rammed by a technological innovation as deadly to silent films as Nemo's Nautilus had been to conventional shipping. Because, by the time the film was finished, sound had arrived.

Sound effects were hastily added to the film (the final version directed by Lucien Hubbard) but *Mysterious Island*, despite a favourable critical reaction, sank almost without trace. And films based on 'scientific romances' acquired a bad reputation in Hollywood that was to last a considerable time.

Things that never came

If *Mysterious Island* made Hollywood dubious about the fledgling genre of science fiction cinema then *Just Imagine* (1930) completed the job by strangling the genre in its crib. A would-be musical comedy, *Just Imagine* was directed by David Butler, whose first film was *Fox Movietone Follies* (1929) and who later went on to make Shirley Temple vehicles. Lavish and very expensive, it centred on the experiences of a character played by comedian El Brendel (whose speciality was playing a fake Swede with a problem with the English language) who is struck by lightning in 1930 and wakes up in New York in 1980, or rather the 1930 version of 1980. The film's huge model set of the city cost, it was claimed, a quarter of a million dollars, and is definitely the most interesting aspect of the production. Obviously inspired by the city in *Metropolis* it was much more elaborate in detail and included such touches as a canal network for ocean liners.

The film is a wishy-washy satire on contemporary fashions and trends of the late twenties and as a result has dated very severely. A typical example of the in-jokes that pepper the film is that all the cars have Jewish names, a reference to Henry Ford's then well-known anti-Semitism. Not a lot of laughs there for modern audiences. The musical numbers don't help either. Such classics as 'The Romance of Elmer Stremingway' and 'Never Swat a Fly' (the latter being about the love life of a blow fly) don't stand the test of time.

It's interesting to speculate on what provided the inspiration for *Just Imagine*, as it has all the visual trappings of pulp sf. Most likely it was the highly popular *Buck Rogers* newspaper strip which had begun in 1929. More than anything else the comic strip was the most important disseminator of the prime visual trappings of pulp sf to a wider public — futuristic cities, spaceships, spacesuits, ray guns, flying belts, the common stage scenery of pulp sf still in use today. (Another important sf comic strip which later performed a similar function was *Flash Gordon*, which started in 1934.) The influence of the comic strip was so pervasive that until the end of the forties the 'man in the street' usually referred to sf as 'that crazy Buck Rogers stuff'.

The *Buck Rogers* strip was based on two stories by Phillip Francis Nowlan, 'Armageddon 2419' and 'The Airlords of Han', published in *Amazing Stories* in 1928 and 1929. They concerned the adventures of a lieutenant in the US Air Force, Anthony 'Buck' Rogers, who is put into a state of suspended animation by a mysterious gas he encounters in a cave and wakes up 500 years later. He finds that America is under the heel of the evil Han, an Oriental race of decadent technocrats (it is later discovered that the Han are the product of Chinese interbreeding with creatures from outer space and therefore 'have no souls'). While the Han dominate the land with their huge flying ships and destructor rays, the surviving Americans are a plucky band of freedom fighters who live in secret underground bases and only emerge to carry out hit-and-run (or rather, hit-and-fly, as they have flying belts) attacks on the Han. Buck joins the rebels and by the end of 'The Airlords of Han', the Han have been virtually wiped out. The comic strip, written by Nowlan and illustrated by Dick Calkins (a rather crude stylist), roughly followed the down-to-earth setting of the original two magazine stories (though the Han were now called 'Red Mongols') and were later extended into outer space to become a bona fide 'space opera'.

The Fox studio, which made *Just Imagine*, was surprised when the movie failed badly at the box office. It seems likely that the Fox executives put the blame not on the weak script or the lousy musical numbers, but on the 'crazy Buck Rogers stuff'. In any case, pulp sf, with its ingrained optimism about the future and technology, didn't make a return to the screen until the juvenile-orientated *Flash Gordon* and *Buck Rogers* serials were made in

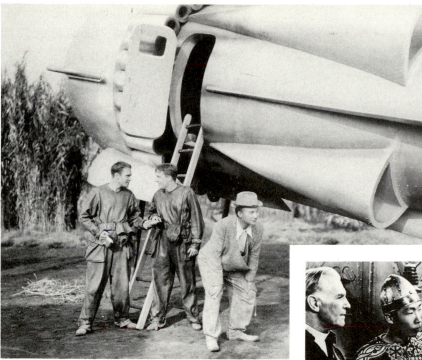

The influence of the Buck Rogers *comic strip is clearly seen in the design of the rocketship in this shot from* Just Imagine.

Buster Crabbe as the man who personified science fiction in the thirties — Buck Rogers.

the latter half of the decade. (It's probably significant that, while Hollywood snapped up Edgar Rice Burroughs's Tarzan character, they never filmed any of his space fantasies, such as the John Carter series of novels set on Mars). Instead, cinema sf became associated with the darker, more pessimistic Gothic cinema, thanks to the success, in 1931, of a second version of Mary Shelley's *Frankenstein*. It was to renew the trend of men in white coats tinkering with things that 'man was not meant to know' and would firmly establish the link between science fiction and horror.

Frankenstein was directed by a young Englishman, James Whale, who had originally been brought to Hollywood to direct the film version of R.C. Sherriff's famous First World War play *Journey's End*. Whale had trained as a commercial artist and also worked as a scenery designer in the theatre.

He brought a definite visual flair to his filming of *Frankenstein* with atmospheric lighting, smooth tracking shots and numerous low angle shots that made effective use of the high-ceiling sets. He succeeded in making a film that is still visually interesting today (unlike the static 1930 version of *Dracula*) but the problem lies with the script which was written by Garrett Fort, Edward Faragoh and Robert Florey.

Shelley's basic theme centred on metaphysics; her creature was intelligent and articulate, and able to voice his existentialist anguish over the way he had been brought to life. He *knew* he had been made a monster with no place in the human world and was thus able to articulately confront Frankenstein with the enormity of what he had done, yet the problems of the film monster, though elegantly played by Boris Karloff, seem to arise simply because of a mix-up of brains, one from a dead criminal being used by mistake. This device, which was one of Florey's contributions to the script (Florey, a Frenchman, was to have directed *Frankenstein* with Bela Lugosi as the monster, but the two test reels he shot were rejected by the studio), effectively clouds and confuses Shelley's theme. It also shows that screenwriters of the period had curious ideas about the nature of the human brain; no attempt is made to keep the brain alive and the problem of degeneration is completely ignored. In addition there is no suggestion that the personality of the criminal survives in the revived brain; instead the creature is treated as a totally *new* being. Even the brain's criminal 'taint' is forgotten along the way since most of the monster's actions arise from fear and confusion rather than evil intent.

After Dr Frankenstein, mad and seriously irate scientists poured out of Hollywood. The following year, 1932, saw the release of *Dr Jekyll and Mr Hyde*, *Doctor X*, *Island of Lost Souls* and *The Mask of Fu Manchu*, all of which featured scientists who were very disturbed indeed. Most interesting of the batch was *Island of Lost Souls*. It was based on H.G. Wells's *Island of Dr Moreau* and marked the first time that one of his works received the Hollywood treatment. In 1925 Cecil B. De Mille had purchased the rights to *The War of the Worlds* for Paramount but the obvious problems involved in transferring the story to the screen caused De Mille to abandon the project. In 1930 Paramount offered it to the Russian film-maker Eisenstein, and though it reached the script stage he also withdrew from the project. Paramount tried again in 1932 but it was twenty years before it was finally filmed (by George Pal and Byron Haskin).

Boris Karloff as the Monster takes a snack break during the filming of the 1931 version of Mary Shelley's Frankenstein.

Directed by Erle C. Kenton, the script of *Island of Lost Souls* was written by Waldemar Young and Philip Wylie, the latter being a science fiction writer himself (ironically, his novel *When Worlds Collide*, co-written with Edwin Balmer, was bought by Paramount in 1934 as a possible project for Cecil B. De Mille but once again it was George Pal who finally brought it to the screen in 1951). Young and Wylie diluted much of the impact of Wells's book and inserted a typical Hollywood love story, but for all their alterations the film remains relatively faithful to Wells's theme. As the evil vivisectionist Dr Moreau, who is attempting to transform animals into men by crude and painful surgery, Charles Laughton gives a marvellous performance. A leering, whip-cracking monster, he is much more disturbing than his hapless creations, but he isn't really mad — he knows

Another mad scientist, Dr Moreau (Charles Laughton), gets his come-uppance at the hands of his aggrieved creations.

what he's doing, which makes him even more disturbing. Of course, he has nothing to do with Wells's character whose cruelty sprang from a scientific zeal that made him oblivious to the suffering of his victims. Laughton's Moreau is simply an evil sadist who relishes every moment of their distress. It is a memorable film that is still fun to watch today, thanks to Laughton's performance, along with the help of a better-than-average script and the atmospheric setting — the exteriors were real exteriors on Catalina Island instead of a shot in a studio, which was unusual for an early talkie). Wells, incidentally, didn't like it at all and disowned the picture.

Apparently he also disapproved of *The Invisible Man* which was made by James Whale for Universal the following year. It's true that most of the more interesting elements in his novel were discarded by Whale and R.C. Sherriff, who wrote the script, but it still remains an impressive film. While Whale and Sherriff may have diluted some of the horror in their adaptation, they do retain the strong streak of black humour that runs through the novel and the comedy in the movie is more than a shade sick. There's also a great deal of gleeful anarchy in it, and one feels that both director and writer had more sympathy with Claude Rains's invisible man, who has been turned into a raving megalomaniac by a side effect of his invisibility drug, than with his victims; they certainly seem to derive pleasure from making the British policemen look ridiculous.

While a British director and writer were shooting H.G. Wells in Hollywood, and creating a studio version of England while doing so, what was happening back in the real England as far as sf cinema was concerned? The answer: not a lot. Back in 1929 the very po-faced *High Treason* was based on a play that reflected the pacifist movement strong in Europe in the twenties and early thirties. It is set in a 1940 where the two most powerful political alliances in the world are called the United Atlantic States and the Federated States of Europe. As war between them seems imminent twenty-five million people of all nationalities have formed a Peace League. The President of the League is obliged to assassinate the President of the Federated States of Europe to prevent him from declaring war, and then makes a broadcast to the world which calms down the tension. The film ends with him bravely facing execution for the murder of the European leader. A rather bizarre championing of pacifism when the chief pacifist has to commit murder!

Directed by Maurice Elvey, who later directed the British version of *Der Tunnel*, it attracted favourable critical comment, particularly in Britain where one reviewer wrote: 'It confirms the impression that the talking picture is the medium in which Britain is qualified to lead the world. Comparisons with the great German film *Metropolis* will naturally arise but as popular entertainment such comparisons must be in favour of the British film . . . The forecast of London and New York in the future shows imagination of design within the bounds of possibility, and steers clear of the exaggerated phantasy of *Metropolis*. Neither has Mr Elvey relied overmuch on tricks of the camera. The lighting is effective and the sensational scenes of the flooding of the Channel Tunnel and the destruction by bombs of the Peace League buildings are most realistic and impressive.'[1] All of which reads like embarrassing chauvinism today since *High Treason* has been all but forgotten while *Metropolis* continues to impress new audiences.

German film-makers of the early thirties were also concerned with maintaining world peace. This was the reason given in *Der Tunnel* (1933) for building the transatlantic tunnel that would link Europe with the

The transport of the future as seen in the 1934 film The Tunnel.

United States. Directed by Kurt Bernhardt and scripted by Kurt Siodmak (who was soon to emigrate to America himself), it is said to be a very spectacular film, with realistically staged cave-ins, explosions and floods as the tunnel is excavated (so much so that the film's associate producer was killed during the shooting of one such sequence). I have never seen it but I have seen the British version made two years later — *The Tunnel*, directed by Maurice Elvey and scripted by Clemence Dane and L. du Garde Peach from Siodmak's own adaptation of his German screenplay. Though it lacks the spectacle of the German version it is said to roughly follow the same plot, one big difference being that the European end of the tunnel is now in England, which makes the new reason for building the tunnel — 'to establish a permanent peace between the English-speaking nations' — even more tenuous. Or did some people really believe there was a chance of war between the United States and Britain in the thirties? Maybe they did.

Despite the British direction, script and actors, the film remains a very German production of the period — all blood, steel, and self-sacrifice . . . and it's very dreary. As always with old films that attempted to depict a future which is already in our past, a chief source of interest is in seeing how far off the mark the film-makers were. The protagonist, McAllan the engineer, is said to have built the Channel Tunnel in 1960 so the film itself presumably begins in the late sixties and then spans two decades, yet apart from some TV phones and some quaintly modernistic cars the film seems firmly set in the thirties. And despite the long period of time that the film covers, women's clothing fashions remain unchanged throughout. Critics of the time also commented on this lapse.

In 1932 another German movie concerned itself with making transport between Germany and America somewhat easier. As it was based on a novel by *Der Tunnel*'s Kurt Siodmak this should come as no surprise. Called *F.P.1. Antwortet Nicht (F.P.1. Doesn't Answer)*, it is ostensibly about the construction of a huge floating runway for planes to be moored in the middle of the Atlantic but is actually more concerned with a tedious love triangle. The central character is an egotistical aviator (played by Hans Alber acting as if he's wandered in from a bad opera) who helps his best friend, a designer, to convince a shipyard to build the platform. The sister of the shipyard owner (Sybille Schmitz) falls in love with the aviator but he leaves her to fly non-stop around the world. He doesn't return for two-and-a-half years — it transpires that he had crash-landed in Australia and was too embarrassed to emerge from the bush (that must rank pretty highly in the 'most audacious plot devices of all time' stakes). By the time he returns F.P.1. has been completed and is in position in the Atlantic, and the woman has switched her affections to the designer who is now in command of the platform. A saboteur attempts to sink F.P.1. but all ends happily. The designer gets the girl and the aviator flies off to try to capture a giant South American condor. On the level of a mediocre pulp novel the movie has none of the vitality, slickness or humour of a similar Hollywood production of the period. Even the model work, which is sparse, isn't very

While some tunnelled under the Atlantic in the thirties, others built giant floating platforms on top of it, as in this movie, F.P.1. Doesn't Answer.

convincing. The only real source of entertainment is the overacting of Hans Alber and the languid posing of the statuesque Sybille Schmitz. Some have described the film as being in the tradition of *Metropolis* and *Die Frau Im Mond* but don't believe them.

In 1934 Karl Hartl, the director of *F.P.1. Antwortet Nicht*, directed *Gold*, which was a bit better but not much. It's about an evil Englishman who builds a giant machine capable of turning lead into gold — the old dream of the alchemists. Hans Alber, the posturing hero from *F.P.I.*, plays a German engineer who is hired to work on the machine. Basically, it's a mediocre adventure film, though it's a bit more entertaining than the lumpen *F.P.1.*; its climactic scenes showing the machine running out of control are mildly spectacular. Some people have suggested that the English villain, who is rat-faced and has a tendency to rant wildly, was Hartl's sly dig at Hitler, but if this was so it must have been too subtle for the Führer as Hartl was one German film-maker who did not depart hastily for America.

In 1934 Hungarian film-maker Alexander Korda persuaded H.G. Wells to adapt his book *The Shape of Things to Come* for the screen. Wells had always been interested in the cinema, and as he was more than dissatisfied with Hollywood's versions of his works, the offer must have seemed very attractive. It would provide him with a new medium — and one of mass popularity — to spread his message to the world. Unfortunately, by that time messages were about the only things he *was* producing. Nearing 70, the writer who had once presented his ideas in stories and novels that were innovatory, daring and exciting had been replaced by an impatient polemicist, now giving his ideas more or less undiluted to the world in books such as *The Shape of Things to Come* (yes, the book is fiction but it's hardly a novel). And, worse, he was also supplying his *answers* to the world's problems — a danger for any artist, since answers have the embarrassing habit of looking irrelevant in a very short time while the original questions retain their relevance.

In the thirties, most of his answers to mankind's plight seemed to depend on a touching faith in technology — a technology in the hands of the 'right people', a group of enlightened, beneficient technocrats (not unlike Wells himself) who would use rationality to enable the human race to overcome the grubby, emotional and aggressive beast that dwells within. This is the message he promoted in a screenplay that was to undergo many transformations before it reached the screen.

It begins in a city centre captioned 'Everytown', which closely resembles Piccadilly Circus, in '1940'. War is imminent and from John Cabal (Raymond Massey), the film's central character and Wells's main mouthpiece, comes the first of many messages: 'If we don't end war, war will end us.' (Well, you can't argue with *that*.) But war does begin, and, in the film's most successful piece of prophecy, Everytown is blitzed into ruins. Wells's Second World War lasts until the mid-sixties when Everytown has been reduced to a feudal state and is ruled by a warlord called the Chief (Ralph Richardson, giving the liveliest performance in the movie). Then John Cabal arrives in a mysterious aeroplane and tells the Chief that he is part of a society of scientists called the Airmen who intend to reform the world. The Airmen are Wells's deus ex machina, his cavalry who arrive from nowhere to save the day. The Chief and his kind are overthrown and Everytown is rebuilt.

By 2036 it is a vast, gleaming, underground complex with all the appeal of a shopping mall. John Cabal's grandson (Massey again) is in charge (which suggests a dynastic form of government) but he has problems with a reactionary artist, Theotocopulous (Cedric Hardwicke), who heads a band of twenty-first century Luddites; they want to wreck a planned Moonshot involving a manned projectile being fired from a huge cannon. Despite the Luddite uprising, the gun is fired, the laws of physics are ignored, and Wells, through Cabal, delivers his final message to the audience which ends with: '. . . All the Universe or nothingness? Which shall it be . . . ?' In other words, Wells was telling the world to pull its finger out and pay attention to him or go up in smoke. As we know, the world didn't listen and he died understandably depressed in 1946.

The film stands like a great monument on the landscape of sf cinema: huge and impressive in some ways but basically a cold and lifeless memorial to H.G. Wells's obsolete ideas about how the world should be. It has many flaws — the dialogue is ponderous and pompous (we can't entirely blame Wells for this as a Hungarian writer called Lajos Biro assisted him on the screenplay), and the characterization is dismal (the characters are little more than symbols). But the film is also cinematically disapppointing, thanks mainly to Korda's choice of director, William Cameron Menzies. He

Raymond Massey, representing 'law and sanity', looms over the defeated Ralph Richardson in Things to Come's *version of life in 1970.*

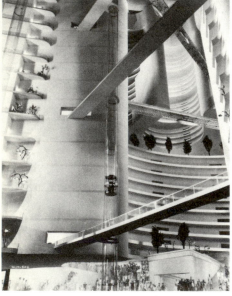

The only aspect of the 'future' that the film-makers got right in the thirties — that there would be giant, shiny shopping malls.

The giant 'space gun' featured in the climax of Things to Come, *which should now be retitled* Things That Didn't Come.

was a former set designer and had never directed a complete feature film by himself before. This lack of experience is revealed not only in the uninteresting treatment of the actors but also in the lack of continuity between various camera set-ups, thus making an already episodic film appear even more disjointed. Despite all the effort and expertise that went into them, even the much-lauded special effects in *Things to Come* are disappointing. Much of the model work is particularly unconvincing.

At the time of its release in 1936, it received many favourable critical responses but the film did quite badly at the box office. Wells's technology-based Utopia was plainly not attractive to audiences of the time; they preferred the fantasy Utopia of Frank Capra's film version of James Hilton's novel *Lost Horizon*, which was a big hit the same year. *Things to Come*, being pro-technology and pro-space travel, was a rarity among sf films in the thirties as it reflected the themes promoted in the pulp sf magazines of the time (which surely would have horrified Wells). People who considered manned space travel a serious possibility were definitely a minority, especially in established scientific circles, and most of the enthusiasts for the idea were to be found in the sf community.

The only other sf films of the thirties that took space travel for granted were the serials such as *Flash Gordon*, *Buck Rogers* and *Brick Bradford*, which, as mentioned earlier, were all based on newspaper comic strips which in turn had drawn their inspiration from the sf pulp magazines. Science and technology (or rather, pseudo-science and technology) were not regarded as evil in themselves, they were simply tools to be used by either the hero or the villain to gain the upper hand. Flash Gordon's loyal helper, Dr Zarkov, certainly wasn't evil or mad in the traditional movie fashion, though he was pretty eccentric to begin with. The serials, though hindered by low budgets and juvenile scripts, were the nearest thing to the space opera genre that flourished in the sf magazines and it would be many years before film-makers would attempt to exploit that genre again.

The failure of *Things to Come*, like the failure of *Just Imagine* six years earlier, served to deter Hollywood from taking further chances with more ambitious (and more expensive) sf movies. So with very few exceptions it was back to the mad scientists playing around with things that man was not meant to know. Dr X returned in the guise of Humphrey Bogart in *The Return of Dr X*; Frankenstein returned in *The Son of Frankenstein*; and even

A crucial moment in the
highly symbolic Dr
Cyclops.

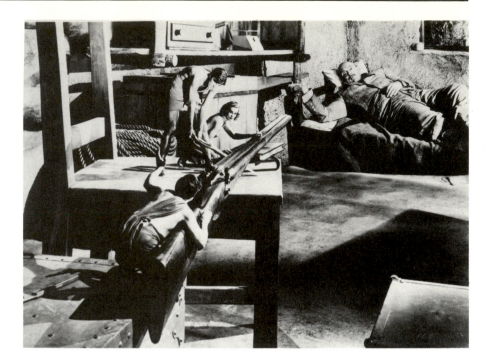

Boris Karloff was back in the familiar role of resuscitated corpse in *The Man They Could Not Hang*, all made in 1939. One mad scientist movie of that year is of some interest. *Dr Cyclops*, directed by one of the makers of *King Kong*, Ernest B. Schoedsack, is about evil Dr Thorkel who lures a group of scientists to his remote laboratory in Peru and then shrinks them to an average height of twelve inches. They escape into the jungle but the doctor hunts them down. Three survivors creep back into his lab, steal his spectacles and lure him to an open mine-shaft where he falls to his death. It's a fast-paced, inventive film though the dialogue is awful and the acting is undistinguished with the exception of Albert Dekker's portrayal of Dr Thorkel. As with Laughton's version of Dr Moreau his evil is not a by-product of scientific zeal but a deliberate choice of action. The special effects deserve a mention, being ingeniously contrived and rather convincing, but the film is also noteworthy for its two unintentional references to the war that was about to engulf the world and end with the prospect of a nuclear apocalypse — Thorkel draws the power for his device from a 'radium mine'; and, with his shaven head and thick, round glasses, he resembles the wartime caricature of the 'beastly Jap'.

The Second World War created the conditions for a future boom in science fiction, but during the war itself sf cinema reached its lowest ebb and remained there until the end of the decade. While real-life scientists, mad or otherwise, were working on weapons far beyond the imagination of Hollywood scriptwriters (though not beyond that of the sf writers), the cinema's collection of mad scientists were still concentrating on such innocuous goals as making people invisible or turning them into apes. If the situation could have been reversed the world might have remained a much less disturbing place.

3

Big bangs and small bangs

H. G. Wells first described atomic warfare back in 1914 in *The World Set Free*. True, his pilots dropped their atomic bombs by hand after activating the fuses with their teeth but Wells was pretty accurate about their destructive power and even mentioned 'poisonous radiation' created by the bombs. Thirty years later, *Astounding* magazine published a story by Cleve Carmill called 'Deadline' — about an atomic bomb, it actually mentioned Uranium U-235 which prompted a visit to the editor's office by the FBI who thought there had been a leak from the Manhattan Project. But the world at large didn't become aware of the possibility of such an awesome bomb until Hiroshima and Nagasaki. The atomic bomb was no longer something out of science fiction. And that wasn't all — another science fiction device, the rocket ship, entered the real world in the form of the V2 and promptly flattened large sections of it in London. Maybe all that 'crazy Buck Rogers' stuff wasn't so crazy after all . . .

While the war years saw a dearth of science fiction movies, the sf publishing scene in America flourished. In spite of paper shortages new magazines appeared (though sometimes they didn't last for very long) and the period also marked the rise of a new generation of sf writers who had been fans of the pulps in the thirties, including Isaac Asimov, A.E. Van Vogt, James Blish, Damon Knight, C.M. Kornbluth and Frederik Pohl. In the postwar years sf began to achieve a little respectability (though not much) with the publication of sf anthologies by 'proper' publishers, such as *Adventures in Time and Space* (1946) by the prestigious Random House. And in 1947–48 new sf magazines began to appear, reflecting the increasing popularity of the genre. Hollywood, with its finger ever firmly placed on the cultural pulse of America, became aware of the trend in a mere matter of years. In 1950 the first sf movie boom began, and it was great fun while it lasted.

As I said in the Introduction, though I certainly enjoyed other genres such as westerns and comedies, the sf films of the fifties imprinted themselves upon me in a way that no other films did (except maybe the Disney full-length cartoons). I suppose they left such a forceful impression because they scared the hell out of me. *It Came from Outer Space, Them, The War of the Worlds, The Day the Earth Stood Still*, and *The Beast from Twenty Thousand Fathoms* — I saw them all in the early fifties when I was very young. I remember I spent almost the entire length of *The War of the Worlds* kneeling on my seat with my back to the screen, much to the discomfiture of the man sitting behind me, and then the following day I pestered my

A primal movie image imprint upon the author: Gort the robot and Klaatu the alien (Michael Rennie) in The Day the Earth Stood Still.

A scene from The War of the Worlds *that I didn't see at the time of its initial release — I was facing the other way throughout most of the movie.*

A scene from the fifties movie that probably disturbed me more than any other sf film: The Quatermass Experiment.

mother for all the gruesome details of the film that I'd heard but not seen — as a result, the film that I'd built up in my imagination, via my mother's description, bore no relation to the film of *The War of the Worlds* that I finally saw again when I was a teenager. Later films such as *Forbidden Planet* (which, like *Twenty Thousand Leagues Under the Sea*, really impressed and influenced but didn't really scare me), *The Quatermass Experiment* (which *did* scare me!) and *Village of the Damned*, among others, made equally strong a mark. I am sure I wouldn't be a writer of horror and sf novels, and books such as this, if my mother hadn't subjected me to those films at such a tender age (this was before film censorship tightened in Australia at the end of the fifties and 'horror' films, with some exceptions, were virtually banned until the late sixties). So if you don't like my books blame my mother, not me.

The horror element that quickly dominated the sf films of the early fifties annoyed the sf enthusiasts who argued that these films didn't reflect contemporary science fiction which had become much more sophisticated. And they had a point; the start of the two truly literary sf magazines, *The Magazine of Fantasy and Science Fiction* and *Galaxy Science Fiction* (which began in 1949 and 1950 respectively) ushered in a rich period of sf writing which bore no resemblance to the sf cinema of the time. And significantly, two sf movies of the early fifties, *The Thing* and *The Day the Earth Stood Still*, were based on magazine stories originally published more than a decade before (John W. Campbell's 'Who Goes There?' in 1938 and Harry Bates's 'Farewell to the Master' in 1940). As for the horror element, well, in the case of *The Thing*, which was a very influential movie and the first in the nasty alien visitor trend, the blame can be placed at the feet of an sf writer (and sf editor) as it was based on his own story. But to me horror and science fiction are intrinsically linked, perhaps because of the cinematic imprinting described above, but also because I feel that both the horror genre and science fiction deal with the unknown, and that one's automatic reaction to the unknown, whether it might be what's lurking in the attic of an old dark house or lurking out among the stars, whether it's the future of the human race or the prospect of death itself, is one of trepidation. It's certainly *my* reaction.

But before we get embroiled in a long and fruitless discussion about the meaning of horror and science fiction let us quickly change tack and look at another reason why much of the sf cinema of the fifties tended to be traditional horror movies dressed up with sf props (apart from the obvious reason that Hollywood knew you could make money out of horror, but more on that later). The observation has been made countless times before but it is worth saying again that the fifties was a very uneasy and paranoid decade and that is reflected in the sf films of the period. And here we must pause while I point out that I'm referring to American society and its cultural colonies, such as Britain and Australia. I'm sure that, for example, Russian society was equally paranoid and uneasy during the fifties but I'm not familiar with either that society or its cinematic output of the period — I am very much a product of American popular culture.

People had good reason to feel uneasy during the fifties; it was, after all, the first post-nuclear decade and an atomic war seemed imminent. There was also the fear of communist infiltration, though this was more of an American phenomenon; it wasn't so prevalent in Britain and Australia (white Australia's particular fear had long been fear of invasion from any one of the over-populated Asian countries to the North, once referred to as the 'Yellow Peril'). Thus film historians say that the sf films dealing with alien invasion, such as *The War of the Worlds* and *Invasion of the Body Snatchers*, reflect fears of world war and communist infiltration. And they probably do so on one level, but it should be remembered just how widespread was the genuine fear of flying saucers. Today there is still much interest in the subject of UFOs but nothing as intense as it was in the fifties. Sightings were rife and a lot of people really believed in them (as many still do today). I know I did.

UFOmania had certainly spread to my home state of Western Australia (a kind of Down Under replica of California which proved to be fertile ground for all manner of American religious cults, from the Plymouth Brethren to Scientology) and everybody I knew took the existence of flying saucers for granted. Friends of my mother worked for an agricultural research unit which entailed frequent trips out into the country where they were continually spotting strange things in the sky while working out there. I even saw a UFO myself when I was very young. I was at the front gate with my mother one evening and we both watched a glowing red sphere hovering over the lake at the bottom of the street for several minutes before it shot up into the sky and vanished. We both believed we'd seen a flying saucer though now, of course, I think it could have been any number of things (most likely incandescent swamp gas). And, of course, many people didn't fear the idea of alien visitors from outer space but instead welcomed it, believing the aliens to be potential saviours of the planet (just like Klaatu in *The Day the Earth Stood Still*). Undoubtedly the new threat of a nuclear apocalypse was directly and indirectly responsible for the growth of such irrationality but it is important to make the point that in many movies flying saucers are actually meant to be flying saucers and are not necessarily metaphors for the H-Bomb.

My affection for sf movies of the fifties is, to be sure, fuelled a good deal by nostalgia but I maintain that the films do possess a special charm all of their own. I have, after all, affection for such movies that I never saw at that time but caught up with much later when I was well past that crucial impressionable age. Ideally, the perfect fifties sf movie should be in black and white, be set in a small American town, have lots of night scenes (preferably in a desert) and have an evocative and spooky sound-track. The doyen of such movies was Jack Arnold, who directed the movie that fulfils all the above requirements, in fact established the above requirements — *It Came from Outer Space*. Thanks to this movie I experienced the delicious

Another primal sf movie image: man versus the Unknown in the form of an alien spaceship in It Came from Outer Space.

thrill, whenever I went on night rides through the bush in the hills above Perth, of expecting to see round the next bend a giant eye sitting in the middle of the road, eerily illuminated by the car's headlights. Alas, it never happened. It was a colleague and friend of mine, John Baxter (see Chapter Eighteen), who first drew attention to Jack Arnold's contribution to fifties sf cinema in his ground-breaking book *Science Fiction in the Cinema*, published in 1970. In his chapter on Arnold he wrote, 'Adopting the pale grey style of sf film, he raised it briefly to the level of high art . . . to tap again, as Whale and Kenton had done, the elemental power of the human subconscious. No imprint lingers so indelibly on the face of modern fantasy as that of this obscure yet brilliant artist.'[1]

Arnold stands out from the general run of fifties sf directors perhaps because most of them were Hollywood hacks just doing a job. I'm not being derogatory here: they were, in the main, very skilled craftsmen but they treated a science fiction assignment in the same way they would have done a western or a crime thriller. It's unlikely that any of them had ever read an sf story in their life or had any particular affinity for the genre, with some exceptions, Jack Arnold being one of them. It was very different in the seventies and eighties when the film-makers producing sf and fantasy movies, people like George Lucas, Steven Spielberg, Joe Dante, John Carpenter, John Landis and James Cameron, had been weaned on the sf movies of the fifties.

This leads me to a complaint I had as a young boy about sf movies — they bore little resemblance to what I thought of as *proper* science fiction. My idea of proper sf had been fashioned by comic books, juvenile sf novels and, in particular, the *Speed Gordon* comic strip that used to run in the weekly magazine *The Broadcaster* (it was really *Flash Gordon* in the period the strip was drawn by the great Mac Raboy but don't ask me why the name changed). It was the sf of visuals inspired by pulp magazines which, as I noted in Chapter Two, featured futuristic cities, spaceships, ray guns and aliens. In short, the visuals of space opera. There were no real space opera sf movies in the fifties (I'm ignoring cheapo things like *Cat Women of the Moon*) until *Forbidden Planet* and *This Island Earth*, and when I saw those two movies, especially *Forbidden Planet*, which remains one of my all-time favourite sf films, I said to myself, Ah, the real thing at last (I'd never seen the old *Flash Gordon* and *Buck Rogers* movie serials). Many years later I told

Kenneth Tobey and his pals find themselves a buried UFO in The Thing.

myself the same thing when watching a preview of *Star Wars*.

If the directors were studio hacks with no prior knowledge of sf, the same thing could be said for the screenwriters. Again, I'm not being derogatory; as with the directors I have a great deal of admiration for Hollywood screenwriters of the studio period, and having read of the conditions they worked under it was amazing that any halfway decent movie ever got made. The better the screenwriter the better, naturally, the finished movie, but this didn't necessarily mean it was a better science fiction movie. For example, the screenplay for *The Thing from Another World* was written by Charles Lederer, one of Hollywood's top screenwriters (he co-wrote the first screen version of *The Front Page* in 1931. *The Thing from Another World* is a great movie, but the key sf idea from Campbell's original story, the fact that the alien can assume the identity of any human being in the camp, was discarded along the way (though that may not have necessarily have been Lederer's decision). Robert Heinlein's involvement with the writing of the script of *Destination Moon* was that rare thing: a script for an sf film being written by a bona fide science fiction writer (though it's doubtful how much he actually contributed). It remains a rare event to this day (one notable exception was Arthur C. Clarke's collaboration with Kubrick on *2001*). Why? There are several reasons, I think, but the main one is the demarcation line that exists between novelists and Hollywood screenwriters; the film industry is very much a closed shop and producers prefer to stick to their own rather than take risks with outsiders, no matter what their literary stature.

Hollywood screenwriters and, more importantly, Hollywood producers, were just as unfamiliar with science as they were with science fiction. To be fair, a few made an effort at first — after all, that postwar period saw a considerable growth in general interest in science and technology. *Destination Moon* made in 1950, was relatively scientifically accurate for its time, and the science and pseudo-science in *The Thing*, *The War of the Worlds*, *The Day the Earth Stood Still*, and, most especially, *Forbidden Planet*, is pretty convincing. But these films represent the cream of the sf film boom in the early fifties and are not typical when compared to the majority of sf movies, which were largely made on a low-budget (even the above movies weren't made as A-movies with A-movie budgets — with the exception of *Forbidden Planet*, which was more by accident than design). Most producers realized that, despite the new interest in science, the general public were just as scientifically illiterate as they were themselves, so why go to the bother of trying for scientific verisimilitude? Who would know the difference? What the public wanted was the monster alien or whatever; they didn't care one way or the other if the events they were watching had a scientific or even a science fiction rationale.

Despite the popularity of the genre, the readers of science fiction literature were still a specialized group and their particular interests in science were not shared by the general mass of film-goers. As John Baxter wrote in his book: 'Sf film sources lie remote from sf and its visual style is likewise drawn from other areas, primarily the semi-visual world of the comic strip. Sf film offers simple plots and one-dimensional characters in settings so familiar as to have the quality of ritual. It relies on a set of visual conventions and a symbolic language, bypassing intellect to make a direct appeal to the senses. Written sf is usually radical in politics and philosophy; sf cinema endorses the political and moral climate of its day.'[2] That was written in 1969 and not much has changed — sf films still, in the main, bypass the intellect.

There certainly weren't many sf films in the fifties (or since, for that matter) that celebrated science and technology. The exceptions include

George Pal's *Destination Moon* and *Conquest of Space*. With Captain Nemo's marvellous inventions set against a Victorian setting, Disney's *Twenty Thousand Leagues Under the Sea* appears to celebrate the potential of technology but everything ends in a mushroom-shaped cloud and the message that humanity is not ready for it yet. There was a similar message at the end of *Forbidden Planet*. Though we spend much of the movie marvelling at the alien Krel technology, it was this technology that released their evil Ids which destroyed them. Again, everything ends with a bang.

In fifties sf movies fear of science was usually represented by atomic radiation, which got the blame for creating a wide variety of menaces. It woke up prehistoric monsters (*The Beast from Twenty Thousand Fathoms*), it caused ants to grow to colossal size (*Them!*), and provoked giant sea

More primal imagery in this shot from Twenty Thousand Leagues Under the Sea.

Giant ants seemed all too plausible to the author when Them! *was released in 1954.*

creatures into committing anti-social acts (*It Came from Beneath the Sea*) though rarely in the movies did radiation actually make anyone radioactive. (One exception was Mickey Rooney — in a film called *The Atomic Kid*, made in 1954, he became highly radioactive after driving by mistake on to an atomic bomb testing range.)

On the other hand, scientists themselves were often treated sympathetically. In *The Beast from Twenty Thousand Fathoms*, *Them!*, and *It Came from Beneath the Sea*, among others, the scientists were the ones who either first detected the menace or were brought in to provide expert advice on how to deal with it — and at the same time give lectures to the audience (and, significantly, many of the scientists in these early movies were women). There were very few of the 'mad' and sinister movie scientists so prevalent in the thirties and forties. Exceptions were Dr Carrington in *The Thing* who admires the dangerous alien for its lack of emotions and thinks the pursuit of scientific truth is more important than saving lives, and the scientist played by Leo G. Carroll in *Tarantula* whose zeal leads to tragic results. But the one most like a mad scientist of the old days was *Forbidden Planet*'s Morbius (Walter Pidgeon) whose arrogance blinds him to the truth of what his meddling with alien technology has produced.

An evocative image from the sf movie that remains one of my all-time favourites: Forbidden Planet.

The Golden Age of fifties sf movies really only lasted from 1950 to 1956 and climaxed with the release of *Forbidden Planet*. If that expensive experiment had proved a huge financial blockbuster then it might have started a trend in big, fairly intelligent sf movies but, while no box office dud, it wasn't successful enough to persuade the studios to continue in that direction. And it does appear that the wider public's appetite for sf movies had waned by 1956. Some worthwhile sf movies did appear after that date, like *The Incredible Shrinking Man*, but in the main the bulk of sf movies made in the rest of the decade were cheap monster movies increasingly aimed at the teenage/drive-in market. I have a fondness for some of those movies (*It — the Terror from Beyond Space*, *Twenty Million Miles to Earth*, *The Monster that Challenged the World*), but in a sense the first sf movie boom came to an end when the star Altair went bang at the climax of *Forbidden Planet*.

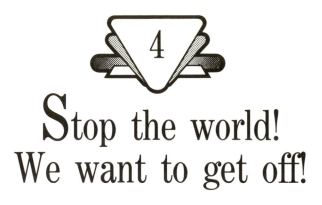

4

Stop the world! We want to get off!

Destination Moon almost launched the fifties sf boom in 1950 — it was the first fifites sf movie to go into production but it was beaten to the box-office launching pad by *Rocketship XM*, a much cheaper production that took less time to make. *Destination Moon* was the much more prestigious of the two, produced by George Pal for Universal, shot in Technicolor, directed by Hollywood veteran Irvin Pichel, drawing on the technical advice of German rocket expert Hermann Oberth and costing $586,000 to make. *Rocketship XM*, on the other hand, cost only $94,000, was shot in black and white and in only three weeks. According to Jack Rabin, the special effects man who came up with the idea, he had planned to make a movie called *Destination Moon* two years before Pal started his version but the deal fell through for a variety of reasons. When he heard about Pal's film he went to Robert Lippert, who specialized in financing and distributing cheap exploitation movies, and suggested they make a quick rocket-to-the-moon movie and beat Pal to the cinemas. Lippert agreed and *Rocketship XM* was hastily put together and shot. To save money the rocket landed on Mars instead of the moon. That way they didn't have to build expensive moon sets but could shoot the Martian exteriors on desert locations around Palm Springs. Other budget short-cuts included using baked potatoes wrapped in tin foil as meteors hurtling past the spaceship.

Written and directed by Murray Lerner, *Rocketship XM* concerned a group of astronauts, headed by Lloyd Bridges, who blast off for the moon but end up on Mars due to a minor navigational problem en route (a small error involving some fifty million miles, assuming that Earth and Mars were in conjunction at the time). On the Red Planet they find the remains of a human civilization that has destroyed itself by atomic warfare. 'From Atom Age to Stone Age! We've got to get back to Earth to tell them!' cries one of the characters. But they are attacked by some of the Martian survivors and only three make it back to the ship. And then, due to a fuel shortage, the ship crashes when it reaches Earth, killing them all. A surprisingly downbeat ending but it was cheaper to shoot a crash than a landing. Despite its obvious cheapness it is more entertaining than the Pal movie, and also a little closer to sf pulp traditions. The special effects, by Rabin and his partner Irving Block, were not bad considering the financial circumstances under which they were shot. The film made money and even attracted some good reviews, prompting Rabin and Block to provide the effects for a whole series of cheap sf movies throughout the fifties (though Block will be remembered mainly for being the one who wrote the original story for *Forbidden Planet*).

Destination Moon was based on *Rocketship Galileo*, a novel by sf author Robert Heinlein published in 1947. A 'juvenile', it was about three boys and their uncle building a spaceship in their backyard, travelling to the moon and discovering a Nazi establishment there. Heinlein himself worked on the screenplay, along with the suspiciously named Rip Van Ronkel (a refugee from the Black List hiding out under a pseudonym, maybe?) and James O'Hanlon. 'For a time,' Heinlein said later, 'we had a version of the script which included dude ranches, cowboys, guitars and hillbilly songs on the moon . . . combined with pseudo-scientific gimmicks that would have puzzled even Flash Gordon.'[1] Actually, that sounds rather more fun than the script they ended up shooting. It begins with inventor Dr Cargraves (Warner Anderson) and General Thayer (Tom Powers) watching their experimental rocket crashing after take-off. The Army orders a halt to their work but when the two men discover that enemy saboteurs were responsible for the crash they decide to continue. As the government won't supply them with further funds they approach a rich industrialist, Jim Barnes (John Archer) and ask for his help, telling him that 'Who controls the moon controls the Earth.' He agrees to help, saying, 'The government always turns to private enterprise when they're in a jam.' (My favourite line in the movie is 'Do we go to lunch or do we go to the moon?!')

The huge rocketship is built in the Mojave desert but after the 'unfriendly foreign power' manipulates public opinion against the project the government bans the take-off. Cargraves, Barnes and Thayer ignore the ban and take-off, accompanied by radio technician Joe Sweeney (Dick Wesson) whose prime function is to provide comic relief — a task he fails at miserably. Unlike the astronauts in *Rocketship XM* they actually land on the moon rather than Mars. Or rather they land on an expensive studio moon set (backgrounds courtesy of artist Chesley Bonestell who specialized in painting astronomical subjects) that bears no resemblance to the real lunar surface that we've since become familiar with. Stepping on to the surface, which resembles a dried-up lake bed, Cargraves says, 'By the grace of God and in the name of the United States of America I take possession of this planet for the benefit of mankind.' Fortunately, nineteen years later, Neil Armstrong had a slightly better screenwriter.

When the time comes to take off they discover that they have only enough fuel to take three people back to Earth and Joe, already established as an idiot, volunteers to stay behind. But by stripping eveything that is non-essential from the rocket they are able to lose enough weight to get Joe off the moon as well. Phew.

Shot in a pseudo-documentary style, as so many movies were in that period, *Destination Moon* is a dull, blandly directed movie. There is little in it that is recognizably the work of Robert Heinlein, apart from the libertarian sub-theme. Perhaps the blame for the disappointing screenplay can be laid at the feet of Rip Van Ronkel.

But *Destination Moon* was a financial success and producer George Pal made another rocket movie the following year, *When Worlds Collide*. Based on the novel by Edwin Balmer and Philip Wylie published in 1934, it had originally been bought by Paramount as a project for Cecil B. DeMille, but as with *The War of the Worlds*, the DeMille passed it by. Maybe he didn't like sf but *When Worlds Collide* (1951) a modern-day Old Testament story, would have made an ideal subject for the great moralizing hypocrite in the thirties. One can just see all those big orgy scenes in the streets as wicked humanity has its last bit of sinful fun before getting its divine come-uppance. As directed by Rudolph Maté, the Polish-born ex-cameraman whose career began back in the silent era, *When Worlds Collide* is a rather

The first moon landing as predicted in the 1950 film, Destination Moon. *Note the 'dry lake bed' appearance of the lunar surface.*

A closer view of the space ark.

The method of take-off for the 'space ark' in When Worlds Collide *was rather unconventional.*

staid affair, though there are suggestions that some people, faced with imminent destruction, are letting go of their inhibitions. It's also a bit old-fashioned: people were more worried about the planet being destroyed by atomic war rather than being hit by another planet, though one can always say that the approaching celestial object was yet another metaphor for the Bomb. No doubt Pal said just that to his financiers.

Scripted by Sydney Boehm, a writer who specialized in crime movies as a rule (he wrote the screenplay for Fritz Lang's *The Big Heat*) the film begins with astronomers discovering that a wandering star, called Bellus, accompanied by its captive planet Zyra, has entered the solar system and will eventually collide with the Earth (the odds of this happening do seem rather, er, astronomical). The world is doomed, but a scientist, Dr Hendron (Larry Keating) has designed a spaceship capable of reaching the habitable Zyra, so that a small number of people have a chance of survival. As in *Destination Moon* the ship is built by private enterprise, the money provided by a bitter, wheelchair-bound billionaire called Stanton (John Hoy), whose motives are purely selfish. A nationwide lottery is held to determine the lucky passengers (only those who are young and capable of breeding need apply, with the exception of Stanton). As the rogue star approaches, there are outbreaks of rioting and sedate riotous living as well as earthquakes and floods, achieved through a mixture of special effects and stock disaster footage. The ship takes off, without the nasty billionaire, of course, and in space the lucky survivors witness the collision between Bellus and the Earth on a TV screen before reaching the safety of Zyra (the landscape of which resembles something out of a Disney cartoon).

Special effects man Gordon Jennings and his team won an Oscar for their work on the movie and true, the shots of model New York streets being flooded, and the take-off of the spaceship — along a ramp rather than straight up — are fine, but one vital effects shot is missing from the film. We never actually see the event which gives the movie its title — we never see the worlds collide. We watch the passengers on the spaceship watching the collision but we never see it. A strange omission. Maybe it was too expensive to shoot, or beyond the technical expertise of Jenning and his people. And another thing, shouldn't the title of the movie have properly been *When Star and Planet Collide?*

In 1955 George Pal made another space movie called *Conquest of Space*, in the same pseudo-documentary vein as *Destination Moon*. It was such a disaster that no one attempted to make a 'serious' space movie until Stanley Kubrick started work on *2001: A Space Odyssey* over a decade later. Based on a non-fiction book, *The Mars Project* by German rocket expert Wernher von Braun, and an illustrated coffee-table book, *The Conquest of Space* by Chesley Bonestell and Willy Ley, what the movie needed was a good screenwriter to create a solid drama incorporating all this technical expertise about the future of space travel. Instead, what it got was someone called James O'Hanlon . . .

Set in the eighties, O'Hanlon's script begins in a space station in orbit around the Earth. Moored nearby is a huge spaceship whose construction has been supervised by the commander of the station, Samuel Merritt (Walter Brooke). Officially, the ship's destination is the moon, but as it's been built with a large pair of wings attached this seems very unlikely. Sam, however, doesn't even seem puzzled about why a ship he's built to go to the moon should require wings, and this is a dead giveaway that Mr O'Hanlon must have given the source material a very quick read indeed. Then Sam gets a curt message from Earth: 'Moon trip cancelled. Your destination is now Mars.' Hey, those wings will come in handy after all! Not that Sam registers much surprise when he receives the message. One wonders how Wernher von Braun, one of those token 'technical advisers' on the film, tried to deal with this technical anomaly: 'Er, George, about those vings on the moon-ship . . . they should not be there. There is no need for them. The moon does not haf an atmosphere.' 'I know that, Wernher. I made *Destination Moon*, remember? But the spaceship is not going to the moon, it's going to Mars. You know that, you read the script. The ship must have wings.' 'Yes, George, I know the ship is going to Mars, but the engineers who haf built the ship believe it is going to the moon, so they would not haf put wings on it. You will haf to alter the script.' 'No, I can't do that, Wernher, but if it will make you feel better, maybe the engineers knew it was wrong to put wings on the ship but they were only following orders.' '*Gott in Himmel!*'

Also on board the space station is Sam's son Barney (Eric Fleming) and a team of 'highly trained' astronauts. The latter are a bunch of sexist cretins whom we first meet as they sit salivating while watching a dance number involving scantily clad women from a movie clearly made back in the fifties.

Another great moment for mankind, this time an awkward landing on the surface of Mars in George Pal's Conquest of Space.

In the fifties space flight caused serious facial problems (Conquest of Space).

This apparently is Mr O'Hanlon's method of establishing that, despite being highly trained, the spacemen are not elitist types but simple, down-to-earth morons like the average working-class joes watching the movie.

Mr O'Hanlon has come up with a pretty clever reason for the trip to Mars. It is presented by a Japanese astronaut, Imoto (Bensong Fong) who, in a bizarre speech, explains that the Japanese attack on America was caused by Japan's lack of steel and good food. The shortage of steel caused the people to live in paper houses and eat with chopsticks, while poor nutrition made them stunted, unhealthy and, consequently, very envious of the rich, healthy and handsome Americans. But, says Imoto, if Japan can obtain all its necessary raw materials from Mars it's extremely unlikely that war between America and Japan will ever occur again.

The director, Byron Haskin, was well aware at the time that he had a dud on his hands. 'The picture was a flop,' he said years later, 'because the personal story was too intrusive [yes, well, that and the script, Mr Haskin]. Our co-producer, Macrea Freeman Jnr, insisted that we have this incredible father and son neurosis — the father loses his cool and his son has to kill him. Also we had another crewman killed earlier on and his body is sent off towards the sun . . . if anything the whole film was a series of impressive funerals.'[2]

As usual with Pal's sf films the effects in *Conquest of Space* were ambitious but they were not as successfully executed as those in either *The War of the Worlds* or *When Worlds Collide*. Early on, for example, there's an elaborate effects set-up showing a space shuttle approaching the space station and then a number of space-suited figures cross from the shuttle to the station while the Earth revolves below them. Unfortunately thick matte lines around the various image components — the spacemen, the shuttle — completely destroy the illusion. The other major flaw is the model work itself. The models are very unrealistic, with none of the surface detail we've bceome so used to post-*2001*, and so badly lit they look no bigger than their actual size; nor are they well-animated, sometimes resembling the space-craft from a *Flash Gordon* serial. There were high spots though, such as the landing on Mars, and the sequence mentioned by Haskin, where Ross Martin's space-suited corpse is pushed off towards the sun, partially eclipsing it as he goes.

In direct contrast to the turgid *Conquest of Space* was a film released the previous year, *This Island Earth*. Along with *Forbidden Planet* it is one of the two *real* space operas of the fifties, though somewhat garish and crude compared to the former. Based on a serial by sf writer Raymond F. Jones that appeared in *Thrilling Wonder Stories* in 1949–50, it was produced by William Alland (who also produced Jack Arnold's sf and horror movies) and directed by Joseph Newman. Rex Reason stars as scientist Cal Meacham who, after his private jet is prevented from crashing by a mysterious green light, receives an equally mysterious electronics catalogue a short time later. This allows him to build a strange device called an 'Interociter' which consists mainly of an inverted triangular TV screen capable of shooting destructive beams from its corners. A strange-looking man (Jeff Morrow), with the sort of high forehead that automatically says 'alien from advanced race' to any sf fan, appears on the screen and congratulates Cal for having passed a kind of intelligence test and asks him to join a secret think-tank of the greatest importance.

He is whisked away by a pilotless plane to a secret establishment in the country where he encounters a number of famous scientists, including Dr Ruth Adams, played by Faith Domergue. She introduces him to the resident cat by saying, 'This is Neutron — we call him that because he's so positive.' Cal doesn't notice this little slip-up, which casts doubts on the scientific qualifications of both of them. But Cal isn't a complete dunce — he does notice that Exeter (Morrow) and his assistant Brack (Lance Fuller) have the same high foreheads and snow white hair. 'Something strange about those two,' he cleverly observes.

The aliens, for that is what they are, have gathered these top Earth brains together in the hope that they will come up with a weapon that will help their planet Metaluna in its war against an implacable enemy. They don't appear to have had much success with the Earth scientists (small wonder if none of them are aware that a neutron doesn't possess an electrical charge). Wily Cal persuades Dr Ruth that escape might be a good idea. Evading the aliens' death ray they reach a plane and take off, but then the alien's flying saucer emerges from behind the hill in which it's been hiding — lovely scene this — and captures their plane.

They are taken to the shattered planet of Metaluna which is clearly on its last legs. The enemy, the Zhagon, is using a fleet of ships to constantly bombard it with guided meteors. Metaluna was protected by a barren outer

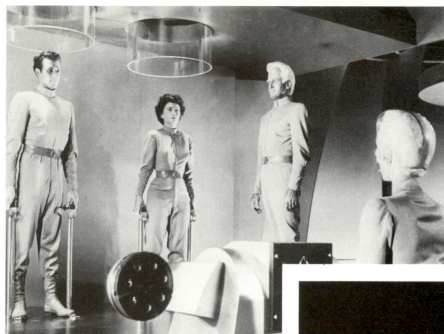

Rex Reason and Faith Domergue prepare, anxiously, to go where no man, or woman, has gone before in This Island Earth.

The aliens' flying saucer glides over the asteroid-blasted surface of Metaluna (a miniature set over 110 feet in length).

shell which served as a shield against the enemy bombardment but is now full of holes. After skimming over the surface the ship descends through one of the holes to the ravaged, inner surface. These are impressive sequences, even though you can see the wires holding up the Zhagon ships and their captive meteors (or asteroids). The panorama was created with a miniature set some one hundred and ten feet long and the meteors (or asteroids) were made of plaster filled with magnesium and slid down blackened piano wires (though not blackened enough). As they hit the set small canisters of petrol were ignited to create the fiery explosions.

The ship lands in the remains of a futuristic city which consists almost entirely of an obvious painting, and a rather crude one at that. Metaluna's population is sparse, numbering at a rough count, one — the planet's ruler, who is called The Monitor — but don't forget the mutant slave who provides the film's necessary monster quotient (actor Eddie Parker in a $24,000 dollar monster suit, if the publicity is to be believed; the publicity also claimed that the movie was two and a half years in the making when in reality it was six months in pre-production and shot in only four weeks).

The Monitor orders our hero and heroine to be mind-zapped, not noticing that they already appear to be in that condition, but a falling meteor (or asteroid) intervenes and with Exeter's assistance they reach the ship and take off. Ah, but the mutant also manages to stagger on board and later makes a pest of himself with Dr Ruth while she is helpless in her 'pressure tube'. But before it can do whatever it has in mind with the Earth woman the mutant collapses and literally fades out of the picture. Exeter, who has been fatally injured by the mutant, does the decent thing by dropping off Cal and Dr Ruth in their plane when they reach Earth before hurtling off in his flaming saucer to finally crash into the sea. All in all, for Cal and Dr Ruth and everyone else concerned, it's been a completely wasted journey.

This Island Earth was Universal's attempt to make an upmarket sf movie but the script, by Franklin Coen and Edward O'Callaghan, considerably coarsened Raymond F. Jones's original, and Joseph Newman's direction was, to put it politely, uninspired. In fact, it was rumoured that producer William Alland had Jack Arnold come in to reshoot all the interior scenes set on Metaluna. The best thing about it is its wildly colourful and spectacular (if entirely unconvincing) special effects sequences. I don't personally rate it very highly among sf movies of the fifties but it deserves recognition as a trendsetter, though the trend it set took a long time to get going. It did well at the box office but apparently not well enough for Universal to continue with bigger budget sf movies in Technicolor. The same thing was to happen in 1956 with MGM and *Forbidden Planet*.

As I've said earlier, *Forbidden Planet* remains one of my favourite sf movies and, like *This Island Earth*, was in the long term a trendsetter (it was, for example, clearly the inspiration for *Star Trek* but even that doesn't dent my affection for the movie). It's far, far better than *This Island Earth* — for one thing, it had a far, far better script. Not many sf films can claim that Shakespeare did the original treatment but *Forbidden Planet* can —it is based on *The Tempest*, which happened to be special effects man Irving Block's favourite play, and it was Block, along with writing collaborator Allen Adler, who wrote the story for the movie (the screenplay was written by Cyril Hume). Block also had a strong interest in mythology and incorporated several basic mythological themes into the story (for example, when Altaira loses her virginity she also loses her power over her wild animals).

The Tempest was set on an island inhabited by the magician Prospero, his daughter Miranda, a hunchbacked witch-child called Caliban and the spirit Ariel; *Forbidden Planet* is set on a distant world in the far future where Prospero has become the scientist Morbius, Miranda turned into Altaira, Caliban into the Monster from the Id, and Ariel is a robot called Robby. Most Shakespearian scholars agree that Shakespeare would have heartily approved of these changes if he had been alive at the time (providing, of course, he got a screen credit and a percentage of the gross).

Directed by Fred McLeod Wilcox (best known previously for directing *Lassie Come Home* in 1943, and for practically nothing else afterwards), *Forbidden Planet* begins with a spectacular display of special effects, foreshadowing similar opening scenes in *Star Wars* two decades later. The credits, accompanied by the evocative and eerie 'electronic' music of Louis and Bebe Barron, are presented against a backdrop of stars from which a flying saucer suddenly appears. But this is no alien craft — it's one of ours. Wow! This ship, a voice solemnly informs us, is United Planets Cruiser C-57D which is on a mission to trace an expedition from Earth that has been missing for years within the planetry system of the star Altair. Yes, as commented earlier, this was indeed the real thing for the first time in the cinema: an sf movie set in the future just as it should be, calmly presenting the fact that the human race would survive long enough not only to develop a highly advanced technology but expand into the stars! Sf fans wept openly in the cinemas. Here, at last, was a sophisticated sf movie. Well, relatively sophisticated. And it's true that it was more in line with the magazine sf of the forties than *This Island Earth*, which, though based on a forties story, had more in common with the lurid pulp sf of the thirties.

When the ship enters the Altair system we are treated to some spectacular special effects that are nearly as convincing as some of those in *2001* and *Star Wars* — particularly memorable is a shot where the enormous sun, Altair, is blocked by a planet, leaving only the ship silhouetted by the corona of the eclipse, the sort of imaginative detail usually found only on the covers of the better sf magazines at that time.

After landing on the planet Altair 4, the Earthmen, led by Commander Adams (a young Leslie Nielsen), discover that only one survivor of the original expedition remains — the coldly aloof Dr Morbius (Walter Pidgeon), a man who clearly has something to hide. Living with him in the luxurious home he built from the wreckage of the ship is his teenage daughter, Altaira (Anne Francis), born just before his wife died. Morbius warns the Earthmen that though the planet is uninhabited a mysterious force killed all the other members of the expedition and warns them that they should leave Altair 4 as soon as possible. But Adams is suspicious. Morbius has a highly sophisticated robot, Robby, which he claims he built himself but, as Adams points out, Morbius was a language expert, not an engineer.

The truth soon comes out. Morbius is sitting on top of a vast underground machine constructed by a long vanished race called the Krel. 'Prepare yourself, gentlemen, for a new scale of scientific values!' he announces before taking Adams and one of his officers on a tour of the local sights. And what sights they are, the most spectacular being a gigantic shaft, full of moving equipment spitting electricity, that is supposed to extend 7,900 levels into the planet and actually looks as if it might. But what's it all for? Morbius doesn't know. And the Krel? All he knows is that whatever happened to them thousands of years ago happened very suddenly.

Meanwhile 'something' has begun to penetrate the defence system of the Earth spaceship. First it only sabotages equipment, then it kills. Adams marshals all his weaponry for its next visit — and discovers that the thing is both invisible and impervious to beams capable of destroying any matter. So he reasons that the creature is being constantly rebuilt from micro-second to micro-second. But what is supplying the energy? There can only be one answer — the Krel supermachine. Adams tries to convince the dubious Morbius of the truth that the Krel built the machine so that they could instantly materialize anything their little hearts desired but they hadn't reckoned on the dark things that lurk in every subconscious. So when they switched on the machine they unleashed monsters from the Id that slaughtered everyone on the planet. Morbius has to face the truth when his own Id monster pays a call, punching a hole through the steel shutters that surround the house.

The climax takes place in a Krel lab where Adams, Morbius and Altaira have retreated. As the Id monster burns its way through a thick door of Krel metal Morbius has to face up to another final awful truth. His jealous rage at losing Altaira to another man, Adams, is what has unleashed his Id monster. He confronts it coming through the door — it disappears and he dies . . .

The underlying Freudian themes of the movie were rather daring though reviewers didn't comment on the intimations of an incestuous relationship between Morbius and his daughter (one interpretation of the Id monster is that it's a manifestation of his sexual desire towards his daughter), and MGM's promotions at the time of the film's release were aimed primarily at the 'kiddie market', so MGM execs clearly didn't pick up on the incest angle either. Block took much of the credit for the Freudian content: 'The idea of a bug-eyed monster is pretty childish,' he

The crew of the United Planets Cruiser C57D confront Robbie the Robot in Forbidden Planet.

said, 'but there are real monsters and demons that exist within us that we know nothing about. We're capable of doing the most horrendous things and we're often shocked at this truism.'[3] Block had originally sold the story of the movie to producer Nicholas Nayflack by playing up the idea of an invisible monster but had always intended that the thing should finally be shown. 'You can't tease an audience forever.'[4] The monster was to appear twice, during the final attack on the spaceship, and at the climax when Morbius confronts it and then is attacked by it in the laboratory. The latter sequence was shot but cut from the movie, apparently because no one could explain why the monster should have become visible at that moment. The monster was created by Joshua Meador, then head of the animation effects studio at Walt Disney and while it has interesting design it persists in looking like an animated cartoon character. In any event, trying to visualize something that one assumes is terryifyng beyond belief is a hopeless task. Ironically, in my first viewing of the movie in Australia in 1956 the monster in its visible form was entirely absent from the movie, thanks to the activities of the ever-zealous film censors of the period. I didn't see the complete version until nearly twenty years later in London, and, as much as I enjoyed the novelty of seeing the animated creature, came to the opinion that, for the one and only time, the Australian film censors had actually improved a film with their butchering.

So why didn't *Forbidden Planet* usher in a whole host of other, intelligent, well-made sf movies? Well, the sad fact is that, as marvellous as it was, it wasn't very popular (but, hey, remember that *The Wizard of Oz* was also a failure when it was first released). It wasn't a box office dud by any means but it didn't make enough money to recover its costs. Originally, despite being made in colour and all the hype of being MGM's first sf movie and thus a major feature, it was supposed to have been a B-movie. It had a B-movie cast, director and so on, and was to cost well under a million dollars. But its production values took on a life of their own: the sets, props, background cycloramas and special effects became more expensive to create than expected (everything had to be designed from scratch — this was the first sf movie to be set entirely in the distant future). Eventually the sets took eight weeks to construct and cost nearly $1,000,000, exceeding the original budget for the entire film. The finished movie cost in the region of $1,900,000, which is nothing these days but was a lot back then for a B-movie. And it seems that, at the time of its release, it only made just over $1,000,000. Much cheaper sf movies, like *Earth vs the Flying Saucers*, made more money than *Forbidden Planet* that same year. So, not surprisingly, Hollywood decided that the expensive space opera type of movie was a waste of space. Why go to all that trouble when you could make more money by giving the public cheapo sf movies with guys in rubber monster suits?

It's also possible that, back in 1956, sf of the *Forbidden Planet* kind (i.e., real sf) simply had yet to catch on with the general public. Science fiction meant something entirely different to mainstream cinema audiences (i.e., guys in rubber monster suits and invading UFOs) and only the relatively small group of hardcore sf readers fully appreciated a movie like *Forbidden Planet*. It was, to use a much-worn cliché, ahead of its time.

The sky is
full of ships

Movie aliens came to Earth for a variety of reasons during the fifties. Some came to drink human blood, some came to set up house with a healthy Earthwoman and breed, some ended up here entirely by accident, some came to take the entire place over, and one or two came to tell us to pull our moral socks up or else. One of the latter was Klaatu (Michael Rennie) in *The Day the Earth Stood Still* (1951). Though I first saw this film when I was very young I can still remember the vivid impression left by the film's key images — the glowing saucer moving through the sky over Washington DC; the huge silver saucer landing in the park, the saucer slowly opening its door; the emergence and shooting of the alien, and then the appearance of the robot, Gort, which, whenever it opened its single eye, vaporized men and machinery; the robot standing motionless beside the saucer at night, and then later coming to life, unnoticed by the two soldiers on guard duty; the robot advancing on the woman (Patricia Neal) before she utters those all-important words ('Klaatu barada nikto!'), the robot appearing outside the barred window of Klaatu's cell . . . yes, that damn robot terrified me.

Seen today *The Day the Earth Stood Still* stands up pretty well though poor Gort, who so scared me when I was five or six, now sadly looks just like a tall man in a rubber suit painted silver, and very crinkly behind the knees. That's what the loss of innocence does for you.

What my younger self missed on that first viewing of the movie was that the plot parallels the story of Jesus Christ. Klaatu comes to Earth to save the planet, adopts the name of Carpenter, is killed and then returns to life. This was deliberate on the part of the screenwriter, Edmund H. North, but, strangely enough, no one noticed the parallel at the time of the film's release, not even the director, Robert Wise. 'I can see now why people would notice it,' he said in an interview in 1976, 'Michael Rennie had that quality in his performance.' (And like many actors who play Jesus Christ, Rennie never seemed to have escaped the role of the holy Klaatu.) It even escaped the notice of the Breen Censorship Office when they were sent a copy of the script, though they did protest at Klaatu being resurrected ('Only God can do that!') and so the script was altered to stress that Klaatu's return to life was only 'temporary'.[1]

The message delivered by the temporarily resurrected Klaatu to the assembled scientists and soliders at the climax of the movie was more Old Testament than New in tone and concludes with the words: 'Soon one of your nations will apply atomic power to rockets. Up to now we have not cared how you solve your petty squabbles but if you threaten to extend your violence this Earth will be reduced to a burnt-out cinder. Your choice is simple. Join us and live in peace. Or pursue your present course and face obliteration.' Film critic Jeff Rovin once memorably described this speech as 'the finest soliloquy [sic] in film history.' In my opinion, it rather undoes all that the film is trying to achieve which, very admirably at the time it was made (with the Cold War hotting up and the McCarthy witch-hunt in full swing among Hollywood writers), was to make a plea for international understanding and an end to war — a call for disarmament, no less. Klaatu's speech suggests that his people are on the same moral level as humanity. It is ironic that he threatens to destroy our planet unless we stop behaving violently.

Nor is Klaatu's solution to our problems very attractive — that we should submit ourselves to the supervision of a group of implacable, authoritarian robots such as Gort. For Gort, we learn, is not Klaatu's servant but his moral minder. These robots have been built to maintain law and order in the galaxy. The gimmick of the robot turning out to be the boss was the raison d'etre of the original story, 'Farewell to the Master' by Harry Bates and published in the magazine *Astounding* in 1940, but what attracted Fox producer Julian Blaustian to the story was the scene where the spacecraft lands and the alien emerges to receive a dose of human hospitality. 'The thing that grabbed my attention,' he said years later, 'was the response of people to the unknown. Klaatu holds his hand up with something that looks unfamiliar to them and he is immediately shot. It was a terribly significant moment for me in terms of story.'[2] Poor Bates, who had been editor of *Astounding* between 1930 and 1933, received only $500 for the film rights of his story.

Shot in black and white by Leo Tover the film is marvellously atmospheric, especially in the night scenes involving the flying saucer and the robot, crinkly knees and all (of course, the visuals receive major help from Bernard Herrmann's eerie, electronic music). The saucer is, as they say, one of the real stars of the movie and a beauty to behold. It consisted of various models, for the flying, landing and take-off sequences, and a full-scale mock-up one hundred feet in diameter and twenty-five feet high. The latter was only three-quarters there — the missing quarter, kept off-camera, was where all the men and machinery, needed to operate moving parts such as the extendable ramp, were located. It cost either $100,000 or $20,000 to build, depending on whether you believe the studio publicity or the special effects man involved in its construction.

For all its sermonizing *The Day the Earth Stood Still* remains a stylish piece of work thanks to a good script, fine direction and a good cast. As with most of the early productions in the fifties sf boom it was made with care and treated by the studio almost as an A-film. *The Thing from Another World* was similarly treated. Produced and co-directed by Howard Hawks for RKO, it was also based on an sf story, 'Who Goes There?' by John W. Campbell (writing as Don A. Stuart) published in *Astounding* magazine in August 1938.

The Thing's motive for visiting Earth is very different from Klaatu's. It hasn't come to lecture but to drink human blood and multiply itself. Though why a plant should need to drink human blood is never made clear. And yes, that's what the alien is — a plant. As one of the scientists says, as he examines a discarded limb from the alien, 'No nerve endings. Porous, unconnected cellular growth . . .' 'It sounds like you're trying to describe a vegetable,' exclaims the reporter, Scotty (Douglas Spencer). The scientist agrees. 'An intellectual carrot!' says Scotty. 'The mind boggles!' It does indeed, but as the chief scientist Dr Carrington (Robert Cornthwaite)

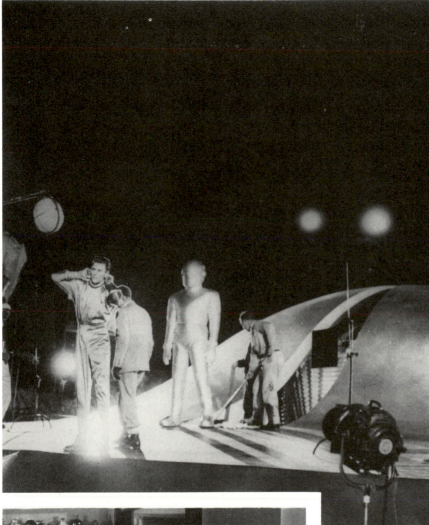

Between takes on a night shoot during the making of The Day the Earth Stood Still.

Scientists watch as lots of little 'Things' flourish on a diet of human blood, while Nikki (Margaret Sheridan) looks doubtful about Dr Carrington's (Robert Cornthwaite) eagerness to be a midwife to aliens.

explains, an intelligent life-form that has evolved from the plant kingdom
has an advantage over us humans: 'Its development was not handicapped
by emotional or sexual factors — it's our superior in every way.' Doc
Carrington clearly admires the alien veggie for its ruthless efficency, in the
same way that, many years later, the science officer on the spaceship
Nostromo was to admire another anti-social alien: 'I admire its . . . *purity*,'
says Ash (Ian Holm) in *Alien*, but then Ash himself is an android, which
kind of prejudices his view on such matters.

As mentioned in Chapter Three, Hawks and his screenwriter, Charles
Lederer, abandoned Campbell's concept of the alien as a shape-changing
organism capable of taking over the personalities of its victims. In the story
he became a multi-organism as he spread among the members of the
Antarctic expedition that had released him from its 20,000,000,000,000-
year-old coffin of ice (over thirty years later John Carpenter would return
to Campbell's original idea for the alien when he made his own version of
The Thing). Hawks and company opt for a much more simple alien threat
— a single humanoid creature which resembles a very large bald man in a
pair of overalls. The bald man, James Arness (later of 'Gunsmoke' fame)
wearing a bulbous headpiece and a pair of claws, is hardly a frightening
creation when you look at him in the publicity stills, but thanks to the skill
of Hawks, his co-director Christian Nyby and the editor Butch Gross, the
'intellectual carrot' comes across as a scary customer in the movie mainly
because he's rarely seen, except in the climax. He inhabits the movie more
as a disturbing presence liable to spring out at any moment. The few
sightings of the alien are well handled, the first occurring when Hendry
(Kenneth Tobey) and his men open the door to the greenhouse and come
face to face with the snarling Thing. It happens so fast it's almost
subliminal, and you don't really expect it because people have opened
doors before and found nothing. After this sequence every time a door
opens — and Hawks ensures that doors are constantly opening without
warning — you flinch. And yet, despite the build-up of tension and
menace, it's a surprisingly mild movie in terms of actual violence. The only
two deaths among the human contingent occur off-screen and it's the alien
himself (despite being described as asexual the Thing is always referred to
as a 'he') who suffers the onscreen violence, first being attacked by sled
dogs and losing an arm in the process, then being doused with paraffin

An embarrassed James Arness poses as the intelligent carrot from outer space in The Thing.

and set alight (a bravura sequence, this!) and finally being electrocuted to death. How different this movie is compared to Carpenter's somewhat more visceral 1982 version.

I never actually saw *The Thing* during my crucial 'imprinting' stage (probably due to my mother having an uncustomary qualm about its suitability for me) and didn't catch up to it until much later when I saw it for the first time on TV. It impressed me immediately as a superior piece of film-making. It is very much a Howard Hawks movie — Nyby, formerly an editor who made his directorial debut with this film, later said: 'Of course it was in Hawks's style. This is a man I studied and wanted to be like. You would certainly emulate and copy the master you're sitting under, which I did.'[3] But according to some of the cast members, Hawks was the one in charge. The film contains all of the Hawks trademarks, in particular the overlapping dialogue. 'We all kind of fell in love with his style,' said Kenneth Tobey years later, 'and, as it happens in dramas, you get a camaraderie and a sense of jollity and fun that comes across very clearly.

Of course, we rehearsed a great deal on that picture. It takes a lot of rehearsal to get that unrehearsed quality.'[4]

Even the inevitable 'love interest', between Hendry and Dr Carrington's assistant, Nikki (Margaret Sheridan), is handled with wit and style, its clichés made painless by the amusing delivery of both Tobey and Sheridan. Nikki is a typically feisty Hawks heroine and is treated as one of the boys by Hendry's men but you do notice that when things are getting desperate it's her job to walk into the room with the line, 'Anyone around here want some coffee?' But she is the one who comes up with the solution on how to deal with the alien. 'Why not do what you usually do with a vegetable — broil it.' The delightful Sheridan was one of Hawks's 'finds'; like Lauren Bacall she had been a model when he spotted her. She rather sank out of sight after *The Thing*, though she did make other movies. She retired early to raise a family and, sadly, died in 1982. Ironically, it was just two months before she was due to attend a *Thing* cast and unit reunion.

Where *The Thing* succeeds on script, direction, acting and sheer style, *The War of the Worlds* (1953) gets by on garish colour, lots of noise and special effects galore. It was George Pal, the former Hungarian puppet animator, destroying the world again. And again, destroying it on the cheap. This was the movie I initially 'saw' looking away from the screen, so I was very pleased when it finally turned up in a Perth cinema years later when I was a teenager. It started out fine — hokey acting, especially from Ann Robinson, but there was a good build-up of tension. Some great moments with the hatch on the Martian cylinder unscrewing itself, the emergence of the cobra-like heat-ray apparatus, the three men approaching it carrying a white flag ('What should we say to it?' 'How about "Welcome to California!"?') before they are abruptly disintegrated in a red blast of light. The tension continues to build as the Army surrounds the crater from which mysterious green light emanates and we wait for the Martian war machines to appear. Then comes the big moment . . . the first machine, shaped like a manta ray with its cobra death-ray projector extended above it, rises above the lip of the crater. Then it is joined by two others. Wow! One of the great moments in sf cinema. There's just one thing wrong with it. The wires. There seem to be millions of the bloody things! Never before, or since, have so many wires been visible in a special effects sequence. Hell, there were even fewer wires in 'Thunderbirds!'.

The War of the Worlds
producer George Pal (left),
with Sir Cedric Hardwicke
who narrated the movie.

Okay, later research on the subject revealed that the models of the Martian war machines were awfully heavy, being packed with equipment, and each required fifteen piano wires, connected to overhead tracks, to support them. Well, fine, but couldn't they have done something about them afterwards? Like, matted them out, for example. Maybe they thought nobody in the audience would notice them? Maybe they didn't notice them themselves? 'Er, George, I'm not sure about those wires.' 'Wires? What wires?' Strangely enough, they're not visible in the final sequences when the machines are razing Los Angeles. At least, I don't think they are — maybe by then you just become accustomed to them and mentally edit them out.

Pal updated H.G. Wells's classic Martian invasion story and also transposed the action from Britain to California. 'With all the talk about flying saucers,' Pal said later, '*War of the Worlds* had become especially timely.'[5] He still faced the technical problem of putting the Martian war

This shot shows the actual size of the models of the Martian war machines, and also shows why they needed all those damned wires to support them.

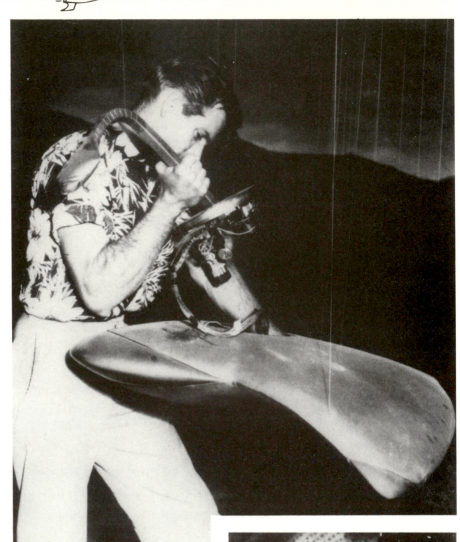

A shot of the only Martian we actually see in The War of the Worlds — apparently this scene inspired Steven Spielberg to later make E.T. *Tsk, tsk . . .*

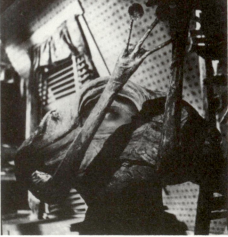

machines on the screen. In the novel they are hooded platforms, complete with tentacles and heat-ray projectors, mounted on three long, mechanical legs, but according to Byron Haskin, the film's director and a former special effects man, the film-makers never considered duplicating this design. 'Although we were afraid to desert the Wells concept entirely we eventually decided anything he may have written about water tanks on towers walking slowly across meadows in rural England was now ridiculous in a film sense.'[6] Their alternative was the copper-coloured manta ray-shaped machine that hovers, sometimes, on three beams of energy. The machines in the Pal film are, in spite of the wires, impressive but I still think you could have made an effective movie version of the machines in the novel. Look, for example, at the machines in the old *Classics Illustrated* comic of 'The War of the Worlds'. And there was a BBC-TV children's series some years ago, called 'The Tripods' — based on novels by John Christopher that were clearly inspired by Wells — that featured three-legged walking machines that were fairly visually effective, despite the usual budget limitations of BBC children's television.

The War of the Worlds is flawed by its script by Barre Lyndon, all those wires, and Ann Robinson's performance (compared to Nikki in *The Thing*, her character is a bit of a wimp and given to screaming a lot, though, like Nikki, she does get to hand out coffee to the men at a crucial moment in the proceedings). But it is tremendous fun and, in the final, apocalyptic sequences, with Gene Barry running through the empty streets looking for Robinson while other survivors huddle in churches listening to the Martians coming ever closer, even quite affecting.

Operating on a much smaller scale were the aliens in *It Came from Outer Space* (1953), one of the all-time greats among fifties sf movies. Not that they were really invaders; they only came to Earth because they were having mechanical problems with their spaceship (alien spacecraft, in those days, had two methods of landing: they either gently touched down or crashed into the ground and buried themselves — the aliens in this film chose the latter option). Harry Essex gets the credit for the screenplay while Ray Bradbury is credited for the original treatment but in reality he wrote much of the actual screenplay. 'Universal had an idea they wanted me to do,' said Bradbury, 'And I said it's not a very good one but I'll do it. On the other hand while I do that I'll write a second version, and you can read them both. Anyway, two weeks later I turned in I don't know how many pages on each one, and they were sensible enough to choose mine. But then they took me off the screenplay because I wasn't a screenwriter. They gave it to someone else. He got the screen credit and I got the story credit. What the hell, there's enough room for everyone, and the movie turned out very nicely.'[7]

It Came from Outer Space concerns the efforts of the aliens to get their ship repaired by impersonating several of the inhabitants of a small Arizona town. This was the first of the 'alien take-over' movies which was followed by *Invasion of the Bodysnatchers*, *I Married a Monster from Outer Space* and *Quatermass 2*, to name but the best of the bunch. *It Came from Outer Space* also set the precedent on how aliens impersonating human beings act — oddly. Lacking human emotions the alien impersonators are handicapped with little giveaways such as blank faces, staring eyes, monotone voices and are often a little stiff in their movements. Ever since *It Came from Outer Space* aliens impersonating humans have almost always followed these ground rules, though there have been notable exceptions.

With his skilful use of the desert setting, director Jack Arnold creates an eerie atmosphere, and in place of the barrage of special effects used in *The War of the Worlds* the aliens here are suggested through visual ingenuity. Much of the time the camera itself plays an alien, gliding through the desert to the accompaniment of Herman Stein's suitably otherworldly music score. The aliens themselves are glimpsed briefly at times, one of the most effective moments being when an alien suddenly moves into the road in front of a car at night and is illuminated by its headlights. The aliens seem to consist of a single large eye surrounded by a lot of cotton wool and little else. It is no wonder that they had to impersonate humans in order to carry out the repairs on their ship as, in their native forms, they appear to be somewhat lacking in the limb department.

Arnold had a good cast, with Richard Carlson in the lead, playing the astronomer who spots the crashing spaceship (and fatally typecasting himself in such roles), and Barbara Rush as his girlfiend. Rush's character, a schoolteacher, is poised and intelligent, but becomes more interesting when she too is taken over by an alien (or, rather, impersonated by one). When Carlson enters the mine shaft that leads to the buried spaceship it is, significantly, the alien in her form who attempts to kill him and whom

It Came from Outer Space, *the first of the sf movies to have aliens impersonating human beings, though the two in this shot have made one small error, giving the game away.*

he kills instead. She/it reverts to her original alien form before toppling down a shaft. There is no offer of coffee here.

The same year saw the release of a strange little movie that was similar in theme if not in execution. It was *Invaders from Mars*, directed by the man who directed *Things to Come*, William Cameron Menzies. It has its admirers but I'm afraid I'm not one of them — Menzies may have been a great designer but as a director he left much to be desired. Scripted by Richard Blake, it was about a little boy (Jimmy Hunt) who sees a flying saucer land on the hill behind his home one night. It burrows into the sand and disappears. Naturally, no one believes him, then people start getting pulled under the sand as well, and when they reappear they are acting oddly. When his parents suffer the same fate he goes to the police and discovers they too are under alien influence, but he does succeed in convincing a lady doctor (Helena Carter). She takes him to see a famous astronomer (Arthur Franz) who happens to be an expert on UFOs and is sympathetic to his story. The military move in and the aliens are routed, but the boy wakes up and finds it was all a dream. Then he looks out of his window and sees the flying saucer landing again . . . (this ending is missing from some versions).

Invaders from Mars has a certain visual charm with its distorted sets reflecting the boy's growing unease but it has dated badly. Apart from the silly script it is seriously hampered by a budget that wouldn't stretch between two lovers (it was a cheapo Republic Pictures production merely distributed by 20th Century Fox). All of Menzies's tricks with forced perspective can't conceal the fact that the hill that the flying saucer burrows into is a very small pile of sand. As the saucer is described as being 250 feet in diameter this is more than stretching things a little.

The most amusing thing about it now is the long 'scientific' discussion in the middle of the movie between the astronomer, the lady doctor and the boy (the lady doctor gets to ask the *really* dumb questions). Never has so much scientific gobbledegook been spoken in one movie for so long. One example: Franz tells them that 'if we could shoot a rocket far enough into space it will simply anchor there and we can use it as a base.' Later he conveniently produces models of the most commonly sighted UFOs and the boy picks one that is the exact replica of the one he saw. The scientist is then totally convinced by his story.

Apparently the original screenplay was written by a couple called John and Rosemary Battle. When they heard what had been done to their project (they particularly disliked the idea of it all being a dream), they refused to go and see the finished movie. Unfortunately as an in-joke they'd used their own phone number for the observatory where Arthur Franz is based. As a result, for years afterwards, every time the film was shown on television they would get phone calls from viewers checking to see if the number was real. A lesson there for budding screenwriters.

Over in Britain one of the best of all alien-possession movies was made in 1955. It was called *The Quatermass Experiment* (US title: *The Creeping Unknown*) and was based on a BBC television serial written by Nigel Kneale, a writer with the uncanny knack of combining contemporary sf themes with both mythology and the traditional elements of the supernatural and the occult. Directed by Val Guest, who had previously directed only comedies, its beginning isn't too promising. We see a young couple giggling inanely as they gambol along a country road at night and then retire behind a haystack for a quick snog. Fortunately at that moment a rocket

More aliens pretending to be Americans, but the kid in this scene from Invaders from Mars *isn't fooled by his erzatz parents.*

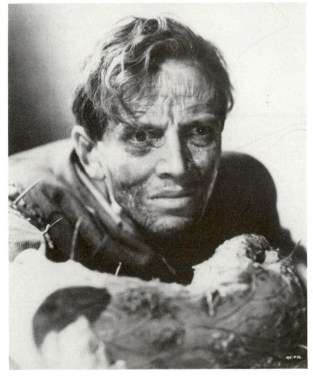

Richard Wordsworth as the tragic astronaut who returns to Earth more alien than human in The Quatermass Experiment.

comes hurtling out of the sky and buries itself nose-first in a nearby field and the moronic couple disappear from the rest of the movie.

The rocket has been launched by Professor Quatermass (Brian Donlevy), head of Britain's space research programme. The rocket went up with three astronauts but has come down with only one, Victor Carroon (Richard Wordsworth) — what has happened to the other two? Carroon isn't saying. The only words he can get out are 'Help me.' He is not the man he used to be, his skin and bone structure are slowly altering. Unwisely, his wife springs him from hospital only to discover, as she drives him away, that his entire right arm has become a spiky, vegetable mass (he had absorbed a potted cactus plant in his hospital room). He staggers off into the darkness while she understandably has hysterics (she too disappears from the movie at that point).

What is Carroon becoming? What has happened out there in space? We last see him in human form when he knocks the head off Jane Asher's dolly in a part of London's dockland. Later, when he attacks a zoo to suck the blood out of various animals all we see of him at first is a pair of eyes peering out of the bushes, and then, when he emerges, only a grey fold of slime that drags behind whatever he has become.

Needless to say, this movie scared the hell out of me when I saw it at the ripe old age of eleven (it didn't reach Perth until 1958) and even today, despite all its creakiness, it still manages to unsettle me. It's got something to do with the pseudo-documentary style of the film: all those grittily realistic London locations, the bomb sites, the docklands lend it an air of realism. And again, of prime importance, is the contribution of the soundtrack, in this case supplied by James Bernard who never wrote a more unnerving, jangly score (he went on to write the music for Hammer's *Dracula*, among many other horror movies). But most of all its effect is achieved through the performance of Richard Wordsworth as the doomed Carroon. Not since Boris Karloff as Frankenstein's monster has an actor managed to create such a memorable, and sympathetic, monster out of mime alone.

'I was the one who cast Richard as the infected astronaut,' Val Guest told me years later. 'He was a very good character actor and he had the right sort of face for the part. He gave an incredible performance, I thought. I don't know why his career never took off after *Quatermass* because he was so good in it. Particularly in his scene with the little girl, Jane Asher, by the canal.'[8]

Carroon, who has been taken over by some sort of space entity that invaded the rocketship, is last seen as a kind of giant octopus oozing across the top of scaffolding inside Westminster Abbey. Not too convincing in long shot (more damn wires) but the close-ups suggest something that is actually alive. 'There were quite a few attempts to construct the monster and eventually it ended up being made mostly out of pieces of tripe and rubber solution. That was all the work of Les Bowie, the special effects man. We didn't have it on the stage at all, it was all shot in the special effects department.' Said Les Bowie defensively, when I interviewed him in the early seventies, 'We did *Quatermass* on a budget so low it wasn't a real budget. I did it for wages really, not as a proper effects man who gets allotted a certain budget for a movie. I think I received only £30 a week.'[9]

Even less money must have been spent on the effects for the climax on the original BBC-TV serial as, according to Nigel Kneale, 'What happened was that somebody went down to Westminster Abbey and bought a guidebook to the place and blew up one of the photographs and cut a couple of holes in it. I stuck my hands through, which were draped with rubber gloves and various bits and pieces, and waggled them about. It looked very good, actually, surprisingly effective.'[10]

As the BBC-TV serial consisted of six episodes, each forty minutes long, the film, running at just over eighty minutes, is a drastic condensation of the story and Nigel Kneale disowned it. He was pretty dismissive of *Quatermass II* (1957) as well. He shares a credit for the screenplay with Val Guest but this is misleading. 'Whether Nigel gave us a draft script I honestly can't remember,' said Guest. 'I think it was probably the case, seeing as he has a credit on the film, but I certainly didn't work with him on the script.'[11] That is true, and as a result Kneale withheld the film rights of *Quatermass and the Pit* for ten years until Hammer agreed to let him write the screenplay. *Quatermass II* isn't as good as the first one, despite a bigger budget. Again the theme is possession (all four Quatermass stories are variations on the same theme) with Kneale again cleverly mixing sf with the supernatural. The alien invasion may be sf but it is presented with the trappings of traditional horror, such as the V-shaped 'mark of the devil' that all the possessed people display.

More alien takeovers of human bodies in Quatermass II, *a film that greatly impressed many young American film-makers-to-be, like John Carpenter and Joe Dante.*

Brian Donlevy again plays Quatermass in this sequel which concerns the Professor's discovery of a coastal establishment which suspiciously resembles his own model of a proposed moon base, right down to the giant 'atmosphere' domes. When he goes back with one of his assistants (Bryan Forbes) to investigate more closely the assistant picks up a missile-shaped object on a hill overlooking the establishment only to have it explode in his face. Quatermass thinks he saw 'something' fly from the object and attach itself to his assistant's face before disappearing (a device later to be used in *Alien*). Anyway, his assistant's a goner even before he's captured by armed men from the establishment (any film that turns Bryan Forbes into an alien zombie already has a lot going for it). Quatermass just manages to escape with his life but, back in London finds that the aliens have already taken over people in positions of high authority and he will have to act on his own to combat the threat. In an action-filled climax, Quatermass and a group of local workers fight it out with the possessed guards at the alien base and finally succeed in blowing up the domes that house the giant aliens (true, the aliens resemble giant duvets covered in barnacles, but in all the excitement one is willing to overlook this). At the same time his own people fire off a rocket that destroys an orbiting asteroid which is the source of the alien invasion. Once again Quatermass has saved the world.

Donlevy's portrayal of the autocratic, single-minded Quatermass was not a sympathetic one and in both movies he's a hard man to like but Donlevy succeeded in communicating the driven quality in Quatermass's personality. For him, only his own scientific goals matter and woe betide anyone who gets in his way, be they human or alien. I asked Guest about Donlevy and he said, 'He was a great guy to work with. He used to like his drink, however, so by after lunch he would come to me and say, "Give me a breakdown of the story so far. Where have I been just before this scene?" We used to feed him black coffee all morning but then we discovered he was lacing it. But he was a very professional actor and very easy to work with.'[12] But in Kneale's opinion: 'The trouble is they were stuck with old Brian Donlevy. He was hitting the bottle rather heavily at the time and frankly wasn't interested in the part at all.'[13]

In 1956 a more subtle story of alien takeover was filmed by Don Siegel back in America, though its title — *Invasion of the Body Snatchers* — was anything but subtle. This is another fifties movie I never saw during my seriously impressionable age so I can be relatively objective about it. Based on a novel by Jack Finney (called merely *The Body Snatchers*) it is probably the most sophisticated of the 'paranoia' movies of the period. Kevin McCarthy plays a doctor, Miles, who returns home to a small town in California and notices that many of the townspeople have changed since he's been away and are now acting oddly. His one-time fiancée, Becky (the cool and beautiful Dana Wynter) has also noticed there is something wrong in the town, and then their mutual friend Jack (King Donovan) finds a large pod growing in his greenhouse. When it opens they find a half-formed duplicate of Jack inside it. The aliens are taking over the town by replacing the original people with replicas when they fall alseep (I've never been able to figure out what happens to the original bodies). Somehow the personality and memories of the victim are absorbed into the duplicate but with a major difference — they lack human emotions.

At one point, Miles and Becky are cornered by the pod people and one of them, formerly a psychiatrist, does a good job of making the idea of becoming a pod person seem pretty attractive: 'There's no pain. Suddenly, when you're asleep, they'll absorb your minds, your memories, and you'll be born into an untroubled world. Tomorrow you'll be one of us. There's no need for love. No emotions, no feelings, only the instinct to survive.' 'You can't love or be loved?' asks Miles. The pod person replies, 'You say that as if it were terrible. Believe me, it isn't. You've been in love before. It didn't last, it never does. Love, desire, ambition, faith. Without them, life is so simple.' But neither Miles nor Becky are convinced and they escape. Finally, Miles and Becky are the only real humans left in the town. They take refuge in a mine and Becky makes the fatal mistake of briefly falling asleep. Miles doesn't notice anything wrong at first; it's only when they kiss that he realizes the terrible truth. Becky has literally gone to seed. (Again, I can't figure out the actual mechanics of the take-over process. What happened to her own body? Where was the pod?) Originally the film ended with Miles vainly trying to warn passing motorists of the danger but the studio considered this too downbeat, after adverse reactions at preview screenings, and insisted that further footage be added showing him convincing the authorities of the truth of his story.

Invasion of the Body Snatchers has been claimed by liberals to be a powerful political allegory attacking McCarthyism and the conformist society of fifties America but I'm not so sure. It seems to me that the film could be seen as playing on fifties fears of communist subversion, as so many other films of the period did. After all, Siegel was the man who later made *Dirty Harry*, hardly a liberal movie. Siegel himself cannily doesn't give much away: 'People are pods. Many of my associates are certainly pods. They have no feelings. They exist, breathe, sleep. To be a pod means you have no passion, no anger, the spark has left you . . . of course there's a very strong case for being a pod. These pods, who get rid of pain, ill health and mental disturbances are, in a sense, doing good. It happens to leave you in a very dull world . . . it's the same as people who welcome going into the army or prison. There's regimentation, a lack of having to make up your mind, face decisions . . . People are becoming vegetables. I don't know what the answer is except an awareness of it. That's what makes a picture like *Invasion of the Body Snatchers* important.'[14] Hmmm, maybe, but I'm not convinced. I still think the pod people are supposed to represent dirty, infiltrating commie Reds.

Human emotions, or rather the lack of them, are at the crux of *I Married a Monster from Outer Space*, made in 1958 (the title was no doubt inspired

5504-48

A fateful moment in the most famous of all alien possession movies, Invasion of the Body Snatchers, *when a kiss reveals to Miles that Becky is no longer the woman she used to be.*

The spectre at the wedding in this publicity shot from I Married a Monster from Outer Space.

by an earlier movie, *I Married a Communist* — spot the subtle connection). Produced and directed by Gene Fowler, a former editor for Fritz Lang, and scripted by Louis Vittes, this low-budget movie has loads of atmosphere to compensate for the lack of money. Gloria Talbot plays Marge who is due to marry handsome hunk Bill (Tom Tryon) but when Bill turns up, late, for the wedding he is acting . . . oddly. Marge clearly hasn't seen either *It Came from Outer Space* or *Invasion of the Body Snatchers* else she would have recognized the tell-tale signs. Yep, Bill is now an alien. Yet even after going to bed with him, let alone kissing him, Marge doesn't work this out. But she does notice that Bill isn't his old self and after the honeymoon writes to her mother that 'He's not the man I fell in love with.'

A year passes and Marge still hasn't picked up on the fact that her husband is a humanoid fungus from outer space. Her main concern is getting pregnant but she can't, despite her doctor (Ken Lynch) assuring her that the problem doesn't lie with her. As a substitute for a baby she buys a puppy on the day of their wedding anniversary but Bill and the puppy don't get on (animals can detect the aliens) and very quickly the puppy meets a grim end. Bill isn't an isolated case. Several of the men in the town have been replaced by aliens, including the police. Marge's growing suspicions about Bill's behaviour finally lead her to follow him when he sneaks out of the house one night (I say night but this movie has the brightest 'night' scenes I've ever seen). In the woods outside of town she sees an alien emerge from Bill's body and enter a spaceship (for budgetary reasons the spaceship is represented by some shrubbery and a hatchway). Alarmed, she tries to spread the word back in town but no one believes her.

Naturally her marriage suffers after this revelation. At the same time, ironically, Bill is starting to develop feelings towards her. Exposure to human emotions can have that effect on some aliens — they pick them up like flu germs and start asking questions like: 'What is this thing you call . . . *love*?' His alien buddies, however, are not similarly affected. 'Personally, I find human beings disgusting,' says one of them as they sit in a bar with their drinks untouched in front of them (they can't tolerate alcohol). Marge later confronts Bill with what she knows about him and he admits the truth. He tells her that the sun in his home system became unstable and they built a fleet of ships to escape. However, while the ships were being built the altered rays from their sun killed all their women. They have come to Earth in order to breed with human women. Admittedly, they haven't had much luck so far but their scientists are working on a way of changing female chromosomes. 'Eventually we will have children with you,' Bill tells an alarmed Marge. 'What kind?' she asks. 'Our kind,' is the reply. It's not the reply that Marge wanted to hear. She asks about the aliens' mating habits. 'Did you love your women?' 'No,' he says. 'We came together for mating purposes only. But I'm learning what love is . . .'

Marge is not impressed and runs to the doctor with this information. He works out that only the men in town who have recently had children can be trusted. He rounds up a posse of new Dads and they head out for the spaceship with guns and dogs. The guns prove useless but the dogs save the day by biting vital bits off the aliens and killing them. The human captives inside the ship are found plugged into strange machines and when they are freed their alien duplicates are reduced to piles of goo, including the fake Bill (who, as he starts to die, tactfully warns Marge 'not to look'). So Marge gets her hunk back and the aliens in the fleet of spaceships orbiting Earth realize that decorating all those nurseries was a complete waste of time and head off into space.

I Married a Monster from Outer Space can now be recognized for what it was — an early feminist work, portraying, as it does, a nightmarish experience shared by many a woman: the discovery that the seemingly attractive man she has married is really a hideous, alien monster underneath it all.

Earth vs the Flying Saucers (1956) was another of those movies I never saw at the time of its release, which is a shame because I sure would have loved it as a kid. It was much closer in tone to comic book sf than the other, darker, films of the time. Here was a movie that lived up to its advertising poster and delivered everything that it promised: huge flying saucers, weird aliens firing disintegrator beams out of their arms, and destruction galore. And all delivered on a very small budget. It was the work of a partnership that was to produce a great many sf and fantasy movies: producer Charles H. Schneer and special effects wizard Ray Harryhausen (it was their second film together, the first being *It Came from Beneath the Sea* — see Chapter Six). Thanks to Harryhausen's skill the low-budget movie ends up looking pretty spectacular. That old standby, stock footage, was used in abundance. For example, a burning oil refinery stands in for a rocket launching field after it's been devastated by an alien attack, but Harryhausen enhances the footage by inserting his saucers into it. And the final alien attack on Washington DC, with the saucers crashing into famous monuments and historic buildings, is a testament to Harryhausen's skill that a small effects budget stretches to almost impossible limits. 'Many shots were of the real buildings in Washington,' Harryhausen told me. 'We, of course, did have model duplications for the destruction sequences but our budget didn't permit high-speed shooting so the collapse of the buildings had to be animated frame by frame. That meant that each brick was suspended with invisible wires and had to change position with every frame of film. Dust and debris were added later. It was something I would never do again.'[15]

Like the aliens in *I Married a Monster . . .* these aliens have a legitimate reason for attacking the world. They are survivors from a 'disintegrated solar system' and want the inhabitants of Earth to surrender quickly, thus avoiding a lengthy war, so that their waiting space fleet can land. We only see an alien's face once; for the rest of the time they are encased in

An alien bites the dust in Earth vs the Flying Saucers, *a cut-price imitation of* The War of the Worlds.

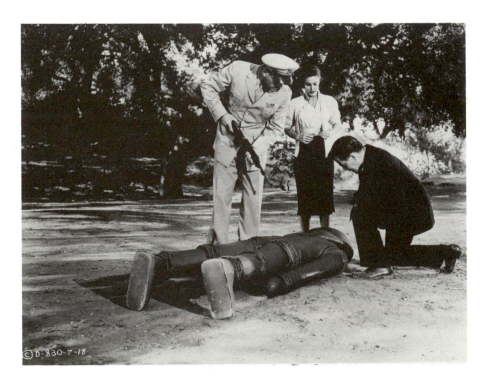

featureles suits which turn out to be, like Darth Vader's suit, mobile life-support systems. The aliens, it seems, are very old and frail. A strange fact to ponder on: the face of the one alien we briefly see bears an uncanny resemblance to the alien on the cover of Whitley Strieber's 'true' account of alien encounters, *Communion*.

Star of the movie is Hugh Marlowe, who played the Judas who shopped Klaatu in *The Day the Earth Stood Still* — and who I still confuse with Richard Carlson to this very day. He plays the scientist who comes up with the means to defeat the aliens: giant transmitters that produce an ultra-sonic beam that disrupts the saucers' electromagnetic anti-gravity fields (?). You can tell he's a genius because during the climactic battle he yells the immortal line to the crews manning the transmitters: 'Keep firing at the saucers!'

Finally, a film that features the most ingenious alien invasion of all, *Village of the Damned*. Technically, this is not a fifties sf movie at all as it was released in 1960 but it very much belongs in that canon, being a low-budget, black and white, unpretentious film. Based on an excellent novel by John Wyndham, *The Midwich Cuckoos*, it was one of the last sf/horror movies I saw during my oft-mentioned impressionable age and gave me that special chill that you can only get from a movie (or TV show) when you are at that age. I guess I was twelve or thirteen when I saw it and was on the edge of the puberty that was to alter my perception of what I saw on the screen, among other things (see Introduction). What really scared me about *Village of the Damned* was the way the kids' eyes glowed when they were using their power to take over people's minds (in some versions their eyes don't glow, which is pretty mean of someone somewhere).

After a small English town is mysteriously cut off from the outside world for several hours by some kind of energy field that puts everyone to sleep within its radius, a number of women in the town discover they are pregnant. Among them is the wife of Dr Gordon Zellaby (George Sanders), Anthea (Barbara Shelley). Twelve children are subsequently born, six boys and six girls, and they develop rapidly. Also they bear an uncanny resemblance to each other with high foreheads, blond hair and large, piercing eyes. And finally, they act . . . oddly. Yep, it's that old lack of human emotions again. A dead giveaway, as usual.

Zellaby's son, David (Martin Stephens), is the spokesman for the group which Zellaby soon realizes is a gestalt, with all their minds telepathically linked to form an 'overmind'. He works out that the children are a form of alien invasion. The aliens, on some distant planet, have invaded the world by proxy; by the use of their energy beam they have fertilized the Earth women, somehow inserting their genetic information into the human eggs to produce hybrid children with human bodies and alien minds. Zellaby is at first prepared to give them the benefit of the doubt but when they start using their powers to destroy any of the villagers who display aggression towards them he realizes they pose an enormous threat and must be stopped before the 'overmind' becomes too powerful. He packs a briefcase full of explosives with a clock as a timer and goes into their isolated classroom. Suspecting something is wrong they try to read his mind but he keeps concentrating on a brick wall. When the brick wall crumbles under their onslaught and they see what's in the case it's too late. Boom.

Village of the Damned succeeds because of its unsensational, low-key approach. Directed by Wolf Rilla and scripted by Rilla, Stirling Silliphant and George Barclay, it was a commercial and critical success. The *New York Times* said, 'One of the trimmest, most original and serenely unnerving little chillers in a long time . . . The picture will get you, we guarantee, and anyone coming upon it cold will exit it colder.'[16] It led to *Children of the Damned*, an unsatisfactory sequel which was more of a remake than a sequel, in which the children were treated sympathetically, thus weakening the whole premise.

Village of the Damned marked the end of the first cycle of alien visitation movies. It was a genre that was out of fashion in the sixties, as proved by the commercial failure of that very good 1968 version of *Quatermass and the Pit* (US title: *Five Million Years to Earth*). Of course, there was *2001: A Space Odyssey*, but that is in a category all of its own. Unless you count *The Andromeda Strain* (1971) as an alien visitation movie, and I suppose it is, the genre remained out of fashion until Spielberg's *Close Encounters of the Third Kind*.

The metaphor that ate Tokyo: monster movies of the fifties

Like the aliens-from-outer-space movies of the fifties, the monster movies of the same decade are commonly regarded as metaphors for the anxieties of the period, namely the H-Bomb and nuclear devastation. It's certainly true that atomic radiation is often the catalyst that either creates or provokes the monster in many of these movies — the 1954 Japanese movie *Godzilla*, about a giant reptile razing Tokyo with its radioactive breath, does seem too close for comfort so soon after Hiroshima and Nagasaki, but the origin of most of these beasties lay with the desire of film producers to jump on the science fiction bandwagon. One such was producer Hal Chester who decided to make a movie about a frozen monster who is released from the Arctic ice by an atomic explosion and goes on the rampage. His intention was to combine *The Thing* with *King Kong*, thus the movie starts in the Arctic Circle (and also features Kenneth Tobey in the cast) and ends with a giant, prehistoric animal loose in New York. This was to lead to the making of the archetypal fifties monster movie, *The Beast from Twenty Thousand Fathoms*.

Chester's other clever idea was to hire Ray Harryhausen, protégé of King Kong's creator, Willis H. O'Brien, to handle the special effects. Harryhausen had worked with O'Brien in the late forties on a smaller version of King Kong which starred in *Mighty Joe Young*. It hadn't been a great success and further projects with O'Brien failed to materialize so Harryhausen returned to his old profession of making animated fairy tales. Then entered Hal Chester with his proposal, which Harryhausen quickly accepted.

The screenplay, originally called *Monster from Beneath the Sea* was written by Lou Morheim and Fred Freiberger, both of whom went on to have careers in television as producers (Morheim later produced 'The Big Valley' and 'Ironside'; Freiberger produced a series of 'Star Trek', 'Space 1999', and 'The Six Million Dollar Man'). Then Chester made a mistake: he asked author Ray Bradbury, and a friend of Ray Harryhausen, to have a look at the screenplay. He did so and pointed out that it had some similarity to a story of his, 'The Beast from Twenty Thousand Fathoms', which had recently been published in *The Saturday Evening Post*. Chester's reaction was to immediately buy the rights to the story and its title. Bradbury received $2,000. His story, later retitled 'The Foghorn', was about a million-year-old sea reptile, the last of its kind, being attracted by the sound of a foghorn coming from a remote lighthouse. The lonely monster woos the lighthouse and, when it doesn't respond to his advances, attacks and destroys it in a fit of lover's pique.

Of the film, Harryhausen said, 'It was the first one where I was in sole charge of the special effects. It was also the film for which I first developed a simplified technique of combining animated models with live backgrounds. The film had a very low budget, only around $200,000, so I couldn't afford the complicated and expensive technique of using glass paintings combined with miniature rear projection as was done in *King Kong* and *Mighty Joe Young*.'[1] (His effects budget was a mere $10,000 plus the necessary photographic equipment.)

The creature, frozen for millions of years in the Arctic Circle, is released from his icy tomb and heads south towards its old breeding grounds, now the site of New York City, pausing en route to knock over a lighthouse as per Bradbury's story. Harryhausen's effects are fine and the final scenes showing his animated reptile stomping through Manhattan before being incinerated in an amusement park are spectacular but the movie takes a long time to get going and the live action sequences, with scientists and military experts speculating on the nature of the beast, are pretty dull. It was directed by Eugène Lourié, a former art director who went on to make a number of genre movies, including *Behemoth* and *Gorgo*.

In the early fifties Japan was anxiously absorbing and imitating

The monster in The Beast from Twenty Thousand Fathoms *led the way for a whole range of giant beasties who rampaged through the fifties.*

American technology in an attempt to rebuild their wartorn economy so one presumes that *Godzilla* was a direct imitation of *The Beast from Twenty Thousand Fathoms*. Made in 1954, it was about a four hundred foot tall prehistoric monster that is roused by an atomic explosion and comes ashore to stamp on Tokyo. Unlike the monster in *The Beast from Twenty Thousand Fathoms*, Godzilla was a man-in-a-suit job (and that man was Tomoyuki Tanaka) created by Toho Studios' resident effects supervisor Eiji Tsuburaya. *Godzilla*, or *Gojira* as he was called at home, was a big success in Japan but in 1956 he became an international star when Joseph E. Levine bought the overseas rights to the movie. He had it recut and inserted new footage featuring an American actor, Raymond Burr (the year before he found steady employment as Perry Mason) and *Godzilla, King of the Monsters*, was a big financial success.

Godzilla was usually portrayed by a man wearing a dinosaur suit but occasionally, as in this case, mechanized miniatures were used. The man in the middle is Eiji Tsuburaya, who used to supervise all the effects at Toho Studios.

Ray Harryhausen's animated, six-tentacled (for reasons of economy), giant octopus in It Came from Beneath the Sea.

Producer Charles H. Schneer and effects wizard Ray Harryhausen, the duo responsible for many creature-related sf films during the fifites.

It Came from Beneath the Sea, in 1955, was a virtual remake of *The Beast from Twenty Thousand Fathoms* — though this time Harryhausen's animated monster was a giant octopus (it was also the first time he worked with producer Charles H. Schneer). Again, atomic testing is the culprit, and again scientists and the military argue as the thing gets ever closer but this time the live action is more interesting with a battle of the sexes between scientist Dr Lesley Joyce (Faith Domergue) and military man Peter Mathews (Kenneth Tobey, yet again). Lesley is a feminist and Pete a male chauvinist pig. He, of course, falls in love with her but is jealous of her professional relationship with her equally modern-thinking colleague, Dr John Carter (Donald Curtis). While hunting for signs of the octopus on a remote Californian beach at night, Lesley reacts to some patronizing comment from Pete by giving a rousing speech about women's rights and the New Woman, and is backed up by John. Alas, all this is undermined when, shortly afterwards, she gets her first glimpse of the monster and lets rip with a very old-fashioned, movie-heroine scream of terror. But she wins in the end. In the final scene, in a restaurant, Pete says to John, 'Say, Doc, you were right about this new breed of woman,' after Lesley has turned down his marriage proposal and suggested that they collaborate on a book instead.

I only have vague memories of seeing *The Beast from Twenty Thousand Fathoms* when I was a child (I never saw *It Came from Beneath the Sea* until many years later) and I don't know why it didn't make a greater impression on me. One monster movie that did was *Them!* (1954) which was about giant ants, mutated by atomic tests, emerging from the desert to attack mankind. A movie about giant ants must have seemed frighteningly feasible to me, as at the time Perth was suffering the great Argentine ant invasion which caused a great deal of chaos and inconvenience until a major extermination campaign got underway (the insecticides that were sprayed indiscriminately all over the city and the suburbs were probably more dangerous than the ants).

Based on a treatment by George Worthing Yates, who also worked on the screenplays for *It Came from Beneath the Sea* and *Earth vs the Flying Saucers*, *Them!* was directed by Gordon Douglas, a former comedy writer and director (his initial reaction on reading the script was to suggest it would make a perfect vehicle for Jerry Lewis and Dean Martin; one presumes he was joking but one can't be certain). Douglas may not have been wholeheartedly committed to making a movie about giant ants (the studio boss, Jack Warner, certainly thought the project was a waste of space) but he did a good, workmanlike job in producing one of the better monster movies of the fifties.

It begins with two cops (James Whitmore and Chris Drake) finding a little girl wandering through the desert clutching a doll and in a state of deep shock. Some distance away they find a caravan and car which obviously belong to her parents, but the entire side of the caravan has been torn out and there is no sign of the parents. As they prepare to send the girl to hospital they hear an eerie, high-pitched squeaking sound being carried by the desert wind. Later, they find a store similarly wrecked and the corpse of the owner in the basement. An autopsy reveals that his body has been pumped full of formic acid. That and the fact that the store's supply of sugar has gone missing should immediately point to giant ants as the culprits, but it's not until the movie's resident experts, Dr Harold Medford (Edmund Gwenn) and his attractive daughter Patricia (Joan Weldon), arrive on the scene that the truth is discovered.

Dr Medford is your typical, elderly eccentric scientist, and Patricia is your typical, feisty lady scientist of the period. When the ants' nest is found she insists, against the wishes of FBI agent Robert Graham (James Arness, glad to have washed off his embarrassing *Thing* make-up), on accompanying the men down into it after they have gassed the ants with cyanide. But, of course, the first shot we have of her is her legs when she gets her skirt caught up while climbing out of a plane (Weldon, a singer, had been put under contract to Warners after being spotted at a party by Jack Warner's son-in-law). Unlike most of the heroines in these movies she doesn't get to have a romantic dalliance with the leading man; there is a hint that something is going to happen between her and the FBI agent but the potential relationship is never developed.

Incidentally, while watching the movie again recently, I was struck by the similarity between the sequence in *Them!* where she and the two men explore the tunnels of the ants' nest as they search for the lair of the Queen (the walls are held together by the ants' saliva, Patricia explains helpfully), and the scenes in *Aliens* set in the underground nest. There's another similarity with *Aliens* at the climax when Whitmore, armed with a

The giant ant in this shot from Them! *was a full-scale model capable of some movement. Well, a bit.*

flamethrower, enters the network of storm drains under Los Angeles, where another nest has been established, to attempt to rescue two missing children from the ants. He rescues the children but, unlike Sigorney Weaver, is killed by one of the monsters in the process.

It's still an enjoyable movie to watch but one has to admit that the ants themselves are a bit wonky by the standards of today's special effects. Unlike the monsters in *The Beast from Twenty Thousand Fathoms* and *It Came from Beneath the Sea*, which were animated models, the ants in *Them!* were full-sized constructs. Actually, there were only two main 'active' ants built for the film, a complete one and another that only consisted of a head and forequarters. The latter was mounted on a boom which gave it some mobility and this one was used for most of the close-ups of the ants' heads. It was capable of moving its head, mandibles and antennae by means of a series of levers and knobs operated by a large group of sweating men off-camera. The complete model was used for long shots as well as a few overhead shots where it appears to be walking but was actually being towed along on a camera dolly. A motor in its body moved its legs back and forth but it was incapable of walking on its own. For all their shortcomings the ants pass muster in most of the shots – they fare better in the early desert sequences where they are partially obscured by a sand storm, but are suitably creepy in the underground scenes. It's a pity more money couldn't have been spent on their construction but the budget was slashed by the studio (originally it was to have been filmed in colour). Jack Warner just didn't like the whole idea. Even when he saw the finished movie he told his staff afterwards that 'Anyone who wants to make any more ant pictures will go to Republic!'[2] Ironically, it was Warner's highest-grossing movie that year. Bet he didn't apologize though.

As with so many of the first wave of fifties sf movies, *Them!* inspired a series of giant insect movies from other studios; or rather, giant 'creepy crawlies' as technically the stars of movies like *Tarantula* and *The Black Scorpion* weren't insects. Incidentally, in my previous book on sf cinema I pedantically pointed out that the giant ants of *Them!* were scientifically impossible as insects can't grow beyond a certain size because of limitations imposed by the nature of their breathing systems. Air enters an insect through a number of holes on each side of the thorax and is circulated through its system by air pressure alone. This is an effective method for a small body but once you pass a certain size air pressure is not enough and you require a pair of lungs. That's why you can't have an insect the size of a rabbit, much less the giants in *Them!* Well, this prompted a well-known horror writer to accost me years later at a convention and accuse me of lacking a 'sense of wonder' for drawing attention to the fact. So to avoid offending anyone else's sense of wonder again, let's assume that the mutations acquired by the ants included lungs as well as giantism.

I have fond memories of the delicious chill I received when initially watching *The Black Scorpion* back in 1957 but viewed again through relatively adult eyes it is revealed as an inferior, cheaper remake of *Them!* The setting is Mexico and this time it is giant scorpions emerging from an underground cavern to cause havoc in the surrounding countryside by eating cattle and stinging hapless individuals to death. The live action sequences are pretty dire and the chief interest lies in the special effects. Unlike the ants in *Them!* the giant scorpions are models animated by stop-motion photography, and the work was supervised by Ray Harryhausen's mentor, Willis H. O'Brien. The effects sequences are darkly lit and moody in atmosphere; the sequence in the cavern, filled with giant creepy-

The giant arachnids that provided the menace in The Black Scorpion *were animated models, filmed by none other than Harryhausen's mentor, Willis H. O'Brien, creator of* King Kong.

The giant arachnid in Tarantula *was an actual live spider, though in this publicity shot he looks suspiciously stiff.*

crawlies, into which our intrepid heroes descend to destroy the monsters on their home ground (mirroring the one in *Them!*) is almost surreal. But the film's effects tour de force occurs at the climax with the battle between the last surviving scorpion and the Mexican Army using tanks and a helicopter in a Mexico City sports stadium. For those interested, the scorpion loses, expiring after finally being shot with an electrified harpoon.

The best of the *Them!* imitations is *Tarantula* (1955), directed by Jack Arnold, the man responsible for *It Came from Outer Space*. As the title suggests, the creepy-crawly star of this movie was a very large spider, the accidental result of a scientist's efforts to increase the size of agricultural produce to solve the world's food shortage. John Agar, who would later star in several of the most inferior, low-budget exploitation movies of the fifties, was the hero and Mara Corday, who also starred in *The Black Scorpion*, was the film's standard-issue lady scientist (well, student scientist, to be exact), while Leo G. Carroll played the scientist who meddled in 'things that Man is not meant to know.' The scenes of the giant spider scuttling over the hills of the desert, attacking a house or creeping up on a herd of horses are very impressive. Neither full-scale model nor animated miniature, the spider was a real one matted into the scenery. Said Arnold, '*Tarantula* was shot in the same desert area where I shot *It Came from Outer Space*, a place ten or fifteen miles north of Hollywood called Dead Man's Curve. There was an outcropping of rocks there that I particularly wanted to use. I would just go out into the desert and look for something that looked eerie. If something gave me the shivers I would say, right, we'll shoot here. What we did was match the miniature rocks in the studio with the actual rocks in the desert and shoot them in perspective. We'd push the spider about with air jets until I got the shot I wanted. I would want, say, a leg to appear over the top of the hill first, then the mandibles and so on. Usually after about ten attempts we got the shot I wanted. We'd shoot the spider against a black background then superimpose it into the scenes with the live actors.'[3] Important bit of trivia here: one of the jet pilots who incinerates the giant spider with Napalm at the climax was played by Clint Eastwood.

Arnold was responsible for probably the most famous movie monster of the fifties, *The Creature from the Black Lagoon* (1954). The creature, later referred to as the Gill Man, is the last surviving member of a pre-human but humanoid species of amphibians that dwells in a small lake (it's certainly no lagoon!) deep in the Amazon river basin. I was not permitted to see this at the time and from what I heard about it from my mother and her friends it seemed to me that it just had to be the most horrific movie of all time. Alas, by the time I did get to see it I was unfortunately capable of recognizing a man in a rubber suit at twenty paces, but the movie still generates a certain tension in the build-up when the monster is mainly an off-screen presence. The underwater scenes retain their power and in

The Gill-Man from The Creature from the Black Lagoon *was a rubber suit with two men in it, though not at the same time. Ben Chapman was the beastie on land while Ricou Browning did it in the water.*

The Creature's director, Jack Arnold (right), with the man in the monster suit, and other members of his crew.

some ways the film can be seen as a prototype for *Jaws*. The sequence where the heroine (Julia Adams) goes for a swim in the lake unaware that the creature is below and watching the movement of her long, vulnerable legs definitely foreshadows similar sequences in *Jaws*. Speaking of this sequence, Arnold said, 'It plays upon a basic fear that people have about what might be lurking below the surface of any body of water. You know the feeling when you are swimming and something brushes against your legs — it scares the hell out of you if you don't know what it is. It's the fear of the unknown. I decided to exploit this fear as much as possible, but I also wanted to create sympathy for the creature — or my little beastie as we called it.'[4]

The original idea was conceived by screen writer Maurice Zimm and the screenplay was by Harry Essex, who had worked on the screenplay for *It Came from Outer Space*, and Arthur Ross. The film proved to be a big financial success for Universal and spawned two sequels, *Revenge of the Creature* in 1955, and *The Creature Walks Among Us* in 1956. There was talk in the early 1980s of Arnold directing a remake of the original with a script by Nigel Kneale and John Landis as the producer, but problems over the screenplay were never sorted out and the project came to nought.

Arnold found himself directing a spider again in *The Incredible Shrinking Man* (1957), generally regarded as his most interesting movie. After passing through a radioactive cloud (what else?) while on a boat with his wife, Scott Carey (Grant Williams) begins to shrink. By the time he's a mere three foot tall both he and his wife (Randy Stuart) realize that their marriage is never going to be the same again unless the doctors can reverse the process. Medical science fails to find a treatment and soon Scott is reduced to living in a doll's house. Now only a few inches tall, a series of accidents leads to him getting lost in the vast wilderness of his own cellar with his wife believing him to have been eaten by the family cat. A leaking boiler seems like Niagara Falls while the spider resembles a Volkswagen on legs to the shrunken Scott. He, er, rises to the challenge and overcomes all the various threats to his survival but continues to shrink and we last see him leaving the cellar through a fly screen to venture into the Great Beyond. His last words are: 'To God there is no zero. I still exist.'

'It's definitely my favourite film among my sf ones,' Arnold told me. 'It was the most challenging because it hadn't been done before. They had

Another hostile arachnid in this publicity shot from Jack Arnold's most famous movie, The Incredible Shrinking Man.

done *Dr Cyclops* with small people but the shrunken people stayed the same size. Neither did that picture have the atmosphere I thought the situation required — the situation of being so small that the commonplace suddenly becomes bizarre and threatening. In *The Incredible Shrinking Man* an ordinary cellar becomes a hell of a place filled with monsters. I wanted to make the audience realize that their own cellars were potential hells, that the familiar could become horrible if the circumstances were changed.' As for the spider: 'It's very hard to direct a spider, I used spurts of air, as I had done in *Tarantula*, to prod him in the direction I wanted him to move. We flew in sixty Panamanian tarantulas because the domestic ones were too small and we couldn't keep a sharp focus on them. They were tremendous beasts — six inches in diameter! We used so many during the shooting because we had to light to such a high intensity they cooked.'[5]

A surprise financial hit in the creepy-crawly genre of the fifties was *The Fly* in 1958. The credit for its success must go to the producer and director, Kurt Neumann. It was the German film-maker's third sf movie after the incredibly low-budget *Rocketship XM* and *Kronos*, but with this movie he changed tack. Having bought the rights to the short story by George Langelaan, he hired a good screenwriter, James Clavell, to do the screenplay and shot the film in wide screen and in colour. It was not an expensive movie to make but it looked expensive. And he also insisted that his cast play it absolutely straight, which must have been difficult at times considering the nature of the story . . .

Patricia Owens plays Helene who, at the start of the film, has been arrested for crushing her husband's head to a pulp in a giant steam press. In a long flashback we learn the reasons for this drastic action. Her husband (Al Hedison who now calls himself David Hedison) was a scientist who was working on a matter-transmitting machine in their basement and one day had a nasty accident. She suspects something is wrong when he won't leave the basement and writes her notes asking for bowls of milk to be left outside the door. When he finally lets her in he is wearing a napkin over his head and won't speak. Yes, something is definitely wrong.

Through notes, he requests that she track down a certain fly that's free in the house; a fly with curious white markings. We learn, as does she, that during an experiment he had become physically mixed up with a fly that had got into one of the transmitter cabinets, with the result that he now has the head and arm of a fly while the fly is sporting his head and arm. But to be annoyingly pedantic again, how is it that the scientist still seems to have his own brain within the fly's head now firmly established upon his shoulders? And at the end of the movie, after his wife has done the job on him with the steam press, there is the famous scene with the fly, complete with Hedison's head and arm, caught in the spider's web crying 'Help me! Help me!' (His brother, played by Vincent Price trying to keep his tongue out of his cheek, promptly crushes him with a rock.) So what happened to the fly's brain? And why doesn't the autopsy on the scientist reveal that there are bits of fly mixed up in his crushed remains? (David Cronenburg, in his 1986 remake, managed to avoid these worrying questions too.)

Neumann's previous movie, *Kronos*, had been very different: a black and white, low, low-budget effort about a giant machine, under the control of aliens, that rises out of the sea off the coast of California and then moves inland, absorbing energy from power stations to transmit it to the energy-starved aliens above. The movie's chief interest lies with Kronos itself, a most unusual-looking robot consisting of two giant cubes joined together. It moves by means of two piston-like legs that stamp up and down beneath it. It had been the idea of effects man Irving Block (who had come up with the original story for *Forbidden Planet*): 'I wanted it to be anthropomorphic, to look like a robot, but at the same time I wanted it to look like a piece of machinery. At one time it looked more like a construction by Picasso but I reduced it down until ultimately it became just a black box.' Block described the problems of making a movie like that with a small budget: 'Some of the big scenes in the desert were done with nothing more than a white sheet with sand thrown on it. There's a scene where a helicopter lands on Kronos; well, we couldn't do anything like that, so we had the helicopter land on top of Hansen Dam, then we just took the dam and everything out of the scene, put Kronos in its place and did a blend with the sky. The actors had no idea what was going on. They were just standing on top of the dam and moving around. Sometimes they'd get very confused.'[6]

No doubt the actors in *Twenty Million Miles to Earth* (1957) were equally confused during its making, as the monster was another of Ray Harryhausen's animated creations that would be inserted into the movie long after the shooting of the live action had been completed. As usual with Harryhausen's films, the special effects are the real star while the human actors are treated as a kind of necessary evil. They don't have much to do in this minor sf movie. It begins with a spaceship, returning from an expedition to Venus, crashing into the sea off the coast of Italy. On board is an alien egg that later hatches out a small creature which is a kind of humanoid dinosaur called, for no particular reason, a Ymir. The Ymir is like the Incredible Shrinking Man in reverse: it grows and grows . . . It is captured and put on display in Rome but, like King Kong, breaks loose and goes on a low-budget rampage through the city. It meets its end on the top of the Coliseum though, unlike King Kong, it is empty-handed at the time.

Strangely enough, when I saw the movie back in 1957, it was the smallest version of the Ymir that I found most disturbing. One rated monsters on their ability to get into your bedroom; man-sized or smaller monsters were the scary ones while monsters the size of a house, or bigger, while impressive, were not personally threatening. I never saw *The Blob* at the time of its release in 1958; if I had I'm sure I would have found it frightening because *The H-Man*, a Japanese movie about a large glob of animated slime, certainly scared me that same year. Its images of the green, pulsating goo sliding up out of drains, slithering under doors and dissolving its victims stayed with me ever afterwards and had me checking my bedroom window at night for several months. I never saw the movie again until a few years ago when film critic and author Kim Newman invited me to a rare screening. As I sat there watching it I wondered what on Earth had happened to the movie I'd seen all those years ago. Surely this collection of old rope wasn't it! Called *Bijo To Ekitain-in-Gen* in Japanese, which, roughly translated, means *Beautiful Women and the Hydro-Man*, it's a pathetic, padded-out, slow-moving exploitation film that is as scary as an episode of 'Sesame Street'. The only memorable thing is a car chase that has to be the slowest car chase in the history of the cinema. If I tell you that *The Blob* is a far, *far* better movie then you'll know just how bad *The H-Man* is. What a pity.

The Blob, about a ball of orange-coloured goo from outer space that eats people, was very much in the mould of the teen-market movies of the late fifties with the teenagers, misunderstood by suspicious adults, finally winning the day. The trouble with the teenagers in *The Blob* is that they seem pretty *old* teenagers. This results from the casting of Steve McQueen in the leading part — as he was 27 at the time the producers had to cast 'around' him. *The Blob* (originally it was going to be called *The Glob That Girdled the Globe*) was an independent production made by a small film company in Chester Springs, Pennsylvania. It was shot in three weeks on a budget of $240,000 and became a surprise hit after Paramount picked it up for distribution. Maybe it was because audiences caught on the fact that you weren't supposed to take it seriously. This was due to the cheery calypso-style title song (written by Burt Bacharach and Hal David) that Paramount stuck over the opening credits. This turned the movie into a camp artifact (long before the term became common) which provided a tremendous boost to its popularity (comedians like Bob Hope and Jack Benny would mention it on their TV shows and get a surefire laugh). Seen today it's still fun, and McQueen's earnest impersonation of a teenager is amusing, though the meagre special effects testify to the low budget. Oddly enough, the big-budget remake in 1988, which had terrific special effects, didn't catch on with audiences. Finally, some interesting trivia: Steve McQueen and his co-star, Aneta Corseaut, mutually loathed each other and the love scene had to be shot last.

Another 1958 monster, and one that I did see at the time, was *The Monster That Challenged the World*. It didn't become a cult film like *The Blob* and, in fact, I rarely encounter anyone else that has seen it (it may turn up regularly on television in the United States but I've never seen it shown on British TV). Directed by Arnold Laven, who went on to become a director primarily of westerns, it was scripted by Pat Fielder and David Duncan (the latter contributed to the screenplays of several sf movies, including *The Black Scorpion*, *The Time Machine* and *Fantastic Voyage*). It begins with a Navy pilot parachuting from his plane and landing in the Salton Sea (a large inland body of water in southern California). When a couple of naval ratings go out in a launch to pick him up they find his body all withered,

No, don't ask what is going on in this scene, it doesn't appear in the actual movie, The Monster That Challenged the World.

as if something has sucked all the liquid out of him. Then, out of the sea, rises a ghastly shape which looms over their boat . . .

As with *The Creature from the Black Lagoon* and *Jaws* it exploits the idea of something monstrous lurking below the surface of the water, and one of the most effective sequences takes place when a couple go for a midnight swim. They disappear and the next day, when two divers are searching the gloomy bed of the sea, there is a sudden close-up of the girl's withered and contorted face amid the flowing underwater reeds (*Jaws* was to repeat this underwater shock in the sequence where Dreyfuss is checking the submerged boat and the head of its dead owner floats into shot). As per usual, atomic radioactivity is the culprit; after an underwater earthquake has let loose the eggs of a giant, prehistoric snail the radioactivity stimulates them into hatching. Yes, that's what the beasties are supposed to be — snails — but they look more like giant caterpillars. Much is made of the threat these creatures will pose to mankind if they make it down a canal to the open sea but even my twelve-year-old self doubted that these things, fearsome as they appeared, would prove much of a problem, let alone challenge the world. I haven't seen *The Monster That Challenged the World* for over thirty years but I have fond memories of it and I thought the monsters themselves were well-executed. I am backed by Bill Warren who, in his book *Keep Watching the Skies*, says of the eleven-foot-tall model built for the film: 'All in all, the monster is one of the most effective low-budget menaces of the period, and one of the best full-sized models ever built.' And of the movie itself, it is 'an exceptional example of a routine exploitation story enlivened by good direction and technical work, and a better-than-average script.'[7]

Another movie that made an impression on me, as it clearly did certain other people of my generation was *It! The Terror from Beyond Space* (1958). This was another low-budget effort with mediocre direction by Edward L. Cahn, a fifty-nine-year-old veteran of undistinguished second features. But it had a fairly good screenplay by sf writer Jerome Bixby, (who will always be remembered for the classic sf short story, 'It's a Good Life'. It was based on a pretty good idea, originally conceived by sf writer A.E. Van Vogt in his 1939 story 'The Black Destroyer' (which was later incorporated into his novel *The Voyage of the Space Beagle*, published in 1950) about an alien creature that invades a spaceship and stores the bodies of its victims

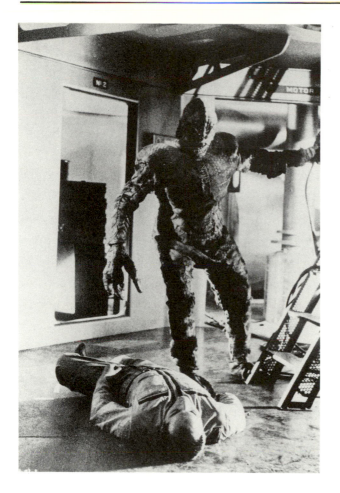

This monster, another man-in-a-rubber-suit job, from It, the Terror from Beyond Space, *later inspired the* Alien *movies.*

in the ship's ventilation system, laying eggs in them as a wasp does with caterpillars. Sounds familiar? The same idea was the basis for a little movie called *Alien* in 1979. In style and budget *It!* and *Alien* are light-years apart but both seem inspired by the same idea. In a 1983 magazine interview Bixby said that his inspiration for his screenplay came from *The Thing*. 'As for the flap over *Alien* and *It!* and Van Vogt's *Voyage of the Space Beagle*, or whom did what in which manner to whom . . . hmmm. In *Alien* and my story, the creature (1) is virtually invulnerable; (2) hides out in the ventilation system — well, that's logical; (3) drives the ship's small crew this way and that as it gobbles them up one by one; (4) is zapped by asphyxiation in space at the end. I understand that a degree of affectionate homage was paid to *It!* during preparation of *Alien* . . . but was I respected in the morning? There are also resemblances to Van Vogt's story, plus

Planet of Blood and *Planet of the Vampires*. I have no particular comment. One amusing thing, speaking of logic in sf — you and I would have thought of letting the air out of the ship in the first five minutes. A part of the commercial writer's art is to conceal the fact that his characters are part-time idiots. Otherwise half the yarns in existence would be one-liners. In *The Thing*, for example: "Okay, guys, we've got plenty of bullets. Rapid-fire at its legs until they're useless!"'[8]

I saw *It!* again not so long ago and in spite of the dud direction and the cheap budget it still works, thanks to Bixby's script and the dark and moody photography by Kenneth Peach. As with *The Thing* the creature, another man in another rubber suit, works best when it is only briefly glimpsed. Incidentally, the women on board the spaceship make a lot of coffee.

The monster movie that imprinted itself most firmly upon me in the early fifties was *Twenty Thousand Leagues Under the Sea*. I was captivated by Nemo and his marvellous, monster-shaped submarine, the *Nautilus*. To a young boy Nemo seemed to have the ideal lifestyle. He was his own boss, had tremendous power at his fingertips and had the exciting hobby of ramming ships with his submarine (though I wasn't too sure about his diet of dubious-sounding seafood). Ever since seeing that movie I became obsessed with mysterious megalomaniacs, submarines, giant squids and the ocean deeps. In 1982 I combined all those obsessions in a novel I wrote called *The Midas Deep*. It was published in 1983 and, alas, sank from sight in the same manner as the *Nautilus* at the end of the movie.

Seen today *Twenty Thousand Leagues Under the Sea* stands up okay. From its first appearance as a sea monster with glowing green eyes cutting through the water, the *Nautilus* is as marvellous to watch as ever, as is James Mason's performance as Nemo. And the giant squid is still impressive, as long as you don't look too closely at it, but one could do without Kirk Douglas's hammy performance as Ned Land, that silly song he sings and the bloody seal (the latter was Uncle Walt's idea, of course).

I once had the pleasure of interviewing the film's director, Richard Fleischer: 'I spent a year preparing the film. I worked on the screenplay with the writer, Earl Fenton, because, to begin with, there was no actual story. You can't make a story out of the book because it doesn't have one. The novel really consists of a series of unrelated incidents with a few clues as to what might be a story about Nemo. There are all sorts of allusions as

The beautifully designed sea monster/submarine, the Nautilus, *from Disney's* Twenty Thousand Leagues Under the Sea.

to what he is doing under the sea and why, allusions to what his politics are and what happened to his family and so on. So Earl Fenton and I found it very interesting to try and construct a story from what was hinted at in Verne's novel. The odd thing is that now *Twenty Thousand Leagues* is always thought of in terms of our story, the story in the film, instead of what is in the actual book. Our trick was to retain the basic ingredients that people always remembered from the book but not necessarily in the same way or the same order. For instance, everybody remembers the underwater burial and the fight with the squid, so we had to include those two incidents, but our motivations for them were quite different from the book. I must say it was Earl Fenton who came up with a way of approaching the whole thing. He decided, and I fully agreed, that the only way you could tell this story, and make it work as far as suspense was concerned, was to make it a jail-break story. And that's basically what we did. The three men were captured by Nemo and kept in the submarine and we treated them as if they were in a prison story — all their time was spent planning an escape, and after making several abortive attempts along the way they finally succeed at the end.

'I loved working with Walt Disney. There were no difficulties at all. One example of working with him: I'd got into the big sequence involving the fight with the squid. It was written to happen at sunset on a calm sea and the special effects people had this giant, mechanical thing which had very little animation to it — it was stuffed with kapok and pulled around with wires, and because the damn kapok kept soaking up water it got heavier and heavier to the point where all the wires kept breaking. The squid got soggier and soggier and would slowly submerge from view. It all looked very artificial and I just couldn't make it work. I tried for about a week and it just looked terrible. In fact, it looked very funny. So Walt came to me and said, "Stop shooting the squid sequence, go and shoot something else. There's something terribly wrong with that thing." I said, "I know there is. The squid is just no good." And he said, "Well, we'll just have to rebuild it." "But it's not just the squid," I said, "there's something basically wrong with the whole sequence."

'So I talked it over with Earl Fenton and again he came up with a solution. He said, "The problem is that you can see everything too clearly. This should be a sequence in a storm at night with big waves, lots of spray, so that you can't see the wires and all the other mechanical deficiencies." He was right but it was going to be very expensive to do — it would mean putting in dozens of wind machines and all kinds of extra effects that we hadn't budgeted for, and it would be much more difficult to shoot. But when I went to Walt and told him Earl's solution he said, "You're absolutely right. That's the way we'll shoot it." Now that cost him a lot of extra money but there was no argument from him about it. Walt knew when things were right — he had a great instinct for that. But the new squid alone must have cost a quarter of a million dollars. Each tentacle of the squid had eight or ten wires attached to it with one man on each wire. We must have had fifty or sixty men in the studio acting like a mammoth crowd of puppeteers moving this thing. Some made the tentacles move up and down and some made them move laterally. The squid, which weighed nearly a ton, also contained complicated pneumatic systems which made the tentacles coil and uncoil as well as moving its beak and eyes.

'I think our *Nautilus* also improved on Verne's description of the submarine in his book. That was the work of Harper Goff who designed the picture as a whole as well as the submarine. He also designed the submarine for me in *Fantastic Voyage*. The idea was to make the *Nautilus* look as menacing as possible, which is why he gave it those big eyes.'[9]

Out of embarrassment I didn't, during our conversation, tell Mr Fleischer of the one big disappointment I received from *Twenty Thousand Leagues* when I first watched it as a young boy. I had been waiting for the moment when the submarine made its great dive, of the title, all the way to the bottom of the sea, but it never came. Yes, I had taken the title to mean twenty thousand leagues straight down.

The monster movies of the fifties ended as they had begun, with a large reptile emerging from the sea and going on a rampage through a modern city. Coincidentally, this film, *Gorgo*, was directed by the same man who had directed *The Beast from Twenty Thousand Fathoms*, Eugène Lourié. The differences between the two movies were that *Gorgo* had a bigger budget, was shot in colour, set in Britain and featured a man-in-a-suit monster rather than an animated model. The other difference was that it had an extra, clever plot device: the monster discovered at the start of the movie,

Gorgo, or rather his mother, does a demolition job on a London landmark in the movie, Gorgo, *inspired by the producers' love for their own mother.*

and subsequently captured and taken to London to be put on display, is only a baby member of its species. Its captors, and the residents of London, learn this when two hundred foot tall Mommy turns up and, in a fit of maternal rage, demolishes many of the city's tourist attractions before rescuing her son and escorting him back into the sea. It was the latter angle that appealed to the film's backers, according to Lourié: 'The idea of the baby and mother came to me from a visual point of view. In fact, the idea seduced the King brothers because they were very devoted to their mother. I believe they had a bit of the mother complex. They were sensitive to the maternal influence, and I think it convinced them that this was indeed a very good idea!'

However the King lads, Frank and Maurice (who used to run a chain of vending machines before forming a film company in 1941) were soon mucking Lourié about, telling him that his original script, set in Japan and called *Kuru Island*, was going to have to be rewritten and relocated to a European country for financial reasons. '*Kuru Island* was a hell of a good script,' said Lourié. 'Although it was set in Japan it had nothing to do with the Godzilla-type of story. I wanted the creature to confront human beings, but there were no scenes of the military shooting artillery at it — that concept is really ridiculous. There was no military confrontation at all and the creature was not supposed to destroy the town.' Two new writers brought in by the King lads changed all that, and when Lourié had finished shooting the movie the brothers even recut it, adding more bangs. 'More and more military action stock shots were added,' Lourié said. 'Depth charges were being dropped, planes criss-crossed the sky, explosions were added! When I expressed my doubts to the King brothers, they assured me that they knew the taste of audiences better than me . . . maybe they did?'[10] Well, they certainly knew what my twelve-year-old self wanted; when I saw *Gorgo* in 1960 I thought it was all bloody wonderful (I will spare it a reassessment). But what I want to know is what dear old Mom thought of this curious tribute from her boys.

Why everyone has stopped worrying about the Bomb... *again*

While the films in the previous chapter tended to be metaphorical representations of the anxiety felt about the Bomb and the possibility of a nuclear war during the fifties, other films addressed the anxiety more directly during that period. However, while some movies were set in the aftermath of a Third World War, very few films actually showed such a war occurring (one exception is *The War of the Worlds* but with that we're back in metaphor land), but budget-limitations are just as likely as any other reason for this.

The first Bomb movie came shortly after the arrival of the Bomb itself. Called *The Beginning or the End* it was a sanitized description of the development of the Bomb. Though executed in a dismal semi-documentary style it wasn't very informative because most of the relevant information was still classified. The US government wouldn't even let the film-makers have a *photograph* of an atomic explosion, which was a problem as they had to simulate such an explosion in the film. All that the effects man, Arnold A. Gillespie, had to guide him was the fact that an atomic explosion formed a 'mushroom-shaped cloud'. Then he remembered an old Tarzan movie he'd worked on where the ape-man had wrestled underwater with a mechanical crocodile. When Tarzan had slashed the reptile's neck with a knife, small sacs beneath the 'skin' had released a dye that looked like blood. Gillespie remembered that the dye had formed a mushroom cloud as it floated upwards so he utilized this effect for his atomic explosion, releasing dye in a glass tank full of water then superimposing over background scenery. Ironically, the shot so impressed the military top brass that they included it in their own instruction films for the Air Force.

The Beginning or the End tried to give the impression that the Bomb was in good hands; i.e., the hands of the American government, but by the end of the decade the Soviets had the Bomb as well and everyone got very worried. By then people had seen footage of actual atomic explosions not to mention footage of devastated Hiroshima and Nagasaki (I still clearly remember the newsreel footage of American atomic tests in the desert where automatic cameras recorded the effects of the explosion's shockwaves and heatwaves on houses and the dummy people inhabiting them.) It was clear that an atomic war between the United States and Russia could mean the end of all human life. This was soon reflected by Hollywood — one of the first of the 'warning' movies was *Five* (1951), written and directed by Arch Oboler who was then famous for his radio plays. It's a talky, moralizing film concerning five survivors of an atomic war who gather in a cliff-top mansion and discuss why 'it all went wrong'. For a time these five symbols of humanity — a pregnant woman, a murderer, an embittered idealist, a dying man and a black man get on peacefully but when they visit a deserted city (apart from a lack of people this post-nuclear war world appears remarkably undamaged), the Fourth World War breaks out, leaving only the girl (who has lost her baby) and the idealist. The film's message is pretty obvious — that people should learn to live in peace together — but as usual with such messages, the how is missing.

One warning movie that did attempt to say how this could be achieved was *The Day the Earth Stood Still*. As I said in Chapter Five, the alien's solution to the problem of human aggression is for us to submit to the supervision of a force of robot policemen as his race has done. Not exactly helpful or even feasible advice back in 1951 and forty years later the same applies. But the screenwriter did at least acknowledge that simply saying that the human race must stop being beastly to itself is not enough. People have been saying that for thousands of years but human nature remains the same.

A rare example of a fifties movie trying to show an atomic war taking place was *Invasion USA* (1952). Unfortunately, it's a very cheap and pretty awful movie. A group of apathetic New Yorkers in a bar suddenly find themselves in the middle of the Third World War, courtesy of stock footage of collapsing buildings and explosions — and die one by one. But, whew, folks, it's okay; it turns out to have been nothing but an illusion created by a hypnotist (Dan O'Herlihy, the Old Man in the *Robocop* movies) in the bar to shake them out of their apathy. They go off to prepare for the real war . . .

Considering how real was the fear of atomic war in that period it's surprising how quickly the down-market film-makers were to exploit it as just another sf gimmick. Heading the pack was Roger Corman who made *The Day the World Ended* (1955), a cheap remake of *Five*. Again, only five people have survived an atomic war and they gather in a house designed by a scientist to withstand radiation. A giant (well, tallish) three-eyed mutant (what did he mutate *from?*) has designs on the scientist's daughter and kidnaps her but before he can do whatever it is that three-eyed mutants do to captive women it starts to rain and he is destroyed. The downpour also washes all the radioactivity away and the hero and the heroine are able to leave the house and go forth into the world, presumably to multiply. Some critics, those who think Corman is an underrated cinematic genius, have had good words to say about this movie but I am not among them.

Almost as tacky was Corman's *Teenage Caveman* (1958) which had poor Robert Vaughn dressed in an animal skin running around waving a club as the teenage caveman of the title (he was twenty-six at the time). The movie's big 'surprise' is that it isn't set in prehistoric times, as it seems to be, but in a post-nuclear holocaust world. But *Variety* liked it, saying: 'somewhat surprisingly, a plea for international co-operation in terms of the dangers of atomic radiation.'[1] Oh, come on.

An intelligent film on the same theme was *The World, the Flesh and the Devil*, also made in 1958. Written and directed by Ranald MacDougall, it was based very loosely on M.P. Shiel's 1901 novel *The Purple Cloud* and concerns three survivors of an atomic war who meet up in an empty New York (again, the city appears remarkably undamaged). Conflict begins when the woman (Inger Stevens), who is white, chooses the black man (Harry Belafonte) instead of the white racist (Mel Ferrer). The two men hunt each other among the empty buildings of Manhattan but, surprisingly, the film ends with all three of them walking off into the sunset together — a rare movie example of rationalism winning out over human nature. A polished, well-crafted piece that is quite subversive for its time.

The major after-the-bomb movie of the fifties came in 1959 — *On the Beach*. Based on the bestselling novel by Nevil Shute, it was a serious attempt by producer/director Stanley Kramer (the David Puttnam of his day) to treat the subject of nuclear war in a realistic and unsensational manner. He doesn't completely succeed. Like all of his films it is marred by ponderousness and an over-developed sense of its own worth, but it does create a convincing picture of a dying world and a mood of utter hopelessness.

Perhaps it's because I'm an Australian that I find the movie so affecting. I remember that when I read the novel in my early teens (I didn't see the movie until much later) it gave me nightmares. It wasn't so much the prospect of nuclear war that upset me as the thought of Australia being the only country left in the world. And being Australian also makes it

Ava Gardner (left) filming On the Beach *in Melbourne, of which she said, to the annoyance of the city's inhabitants, that it was the perfect place to make a movie about the end of the world.*

impossible for me to sit through the picnic sequence when everyone sings 'Waltzing Matilda', first cheerfully and finally as a funeral dirge. When the movie shows on TV I get so embarrassed at that point I have to leave the room.

The scenes showing the people of Melbourne queueing for death pills still have impact though when one of the film's stars, Ava Gardner, said at the time that 'Melbourne is the perfect place to make a film about the end of the world,' the people of Melbourne were not amused. Also impressive are sequences involving the American sub, commanded by Gregory Peck, making a futile journey to California to look for survivors — a window shade blowing against a morse code transmitter is found to be the source of radio signals that prompt the expedition — as well as the film's final shots of the sub heading out to sea to scuttle itself.

Concern about the Bomb naturally continued into the sixties and so did Bomb movies. Roger Corman was still at it — in 1960 he made *The Last Woman on Earth* (well, he would, wouldn't he?) which was a cheap, exploitation version of *The World, the Flesh and the Devil*. The woman in question, played by Betsy Jones-Moreland (where is she now?), and her husband survive the end of the world because they happened to be scuba diving at the time. Another survivor turns up and one thing leads inevitably to another. Amusingly, the screenplay for this mess was written by Robert Towne, who also played the last woman's husband under the pseudonym of Edward Wain.

A much better after-the-Bomb movie is *Panic in the Year Zero* (1962), though its basic message is a distasteful one. A visual handbook for the Survivalist movement, it stars Ray Milland as a man who knows exactly what to do when the Bomb falls. When he and his family witness the destruction of Los Angeles (suggested by flashes from off-screen) from the safety of the hills while on a fishing holiday, he springs into action as if he had been eagerly waiting for this moment all his life. 'It's going to be survival of the fittest,' he tells his shocked family as he breaks into a gunshop. At first they are unwilling to accept his cynical attitude towards other people but when the daughter is kidnapped by a gang of thugs and raped, the family is united in its desire for vengeance. The son (Frankie Avalon, obligatory teenager in so many films back then) happily helps Dad shoot the gang dead while Mom cheers them on from the sidelines.

Directed by Milland himself, the film is saying that the best policy for survival is to shoot first and ask questions later. Still, the film honestly reflected a common attitude of the time — there were many news items in the early sixties about people in the States building bomb shelters and then buying a machine gun to keep the neighbours out on the Big Day.

Britain contributed *The Day the Earth Caught Fire* to the Bomb genre in 1961. Written and directed by Val Guest, who had directed the first two Quatermass movies in the fifties, it had an *On the Beach* feeling of conviction as it showed London dying from the heat after atomic tests had knocked the Earth out of its orbit onto a collision course with the sun. The film ends on an ambiguous note. Four nuclear bombs are to be exploded simultaneously in different parts of the world with the intention of pushing the planet back into its orbit. The final shot in the film shows two newspaper headlines already prepared: one reads 'World Saved!', the other 'World Doomed'. 'Actually I wrote the treatment seven years before anyone would let me make it,' Guest told me. 'Whenever I had a successful film the company concerned would ask me what I wanted to do next and I would show them the treatment. The reaction would be, "No one wants to know about the Bomb." And so the treatment got pushed aside and pushed aside. Eventually I found a producer here called Steven Pallos who was interested and between us we rustled up the money. I'd made a lot of money from *Expresso Bongo*, a film I'd made in 1960, so I ploughed it into the movie and Pallos and I became production partners. Then I went to Wolf Mankowitz and said, "Do you want to come in on this? We can't afford to pay you anything yet but you'll get a share of the profits." He agreed and we wrote the script together, based on my treatment, and we both made an enormous amount of money on it, along with Steven Pallos. The money is still coming in.'[2] That was in 1976. Presumably it still is.

Back in 1959, Ian Fleming, Kevin McClory and Jack Whittingham hoped to make a lot of money out of a film treatment they'd devised about the hijacking of two H-Bombs by a sinister organization who planned to use them to blackmail NATO. It was to have been the first James Bond movie, *Thunderball*, but the project failed to get off the ground and Fleming went off to write a novel based on the treatment. The legal chaos that resulted (Fleming had failed to mention McClory's and Whittingham's contribution) meant that the two film producers, Cubby Broccoli and Harry Saltzman, who had subsequently bought the rights to the Bond novels, couldn't make *Thunderball* first as planned so instead made *Dr No*.

I consider *Dr No* to be one of the most significant films in the 1960s, not because it's a great movie but because it had tremendous influence on popular cinema as a whole. But more on that in the next chapter. There are no H-bombs in *Dr No* but there is an atomic reactor (depicted with a great deal of artistic licence) in the villain's stronghold that goes critical at the end of the movie and blows up. Dr No himself (in the film, at least) symbolizes science's uneasy relationship with nuclear power. He is arrogantly confident that he can control it even though radiation poisoning has cost him his hands.

The half-German Dr No obviously provided Stanley Kubrick with part of the inspiration for the title character in *Dr Strangelove or How I Learned to Stop Worrying and Love the Bomb* (1964). But though Peter Sellers's marvellous mad doctor has a Dr No-like mechanical hand, and has been similarly poisoned by his close association with radioactive material, Strangelove was also inspired by the real-life German scientist Wernher Von Braun (Strangelove also bears an uncanny resemblance to Henry Kissinger but that must be a pure coincidence as the movie was made years before Dr K became a public figure). Von Braun had been instrumental

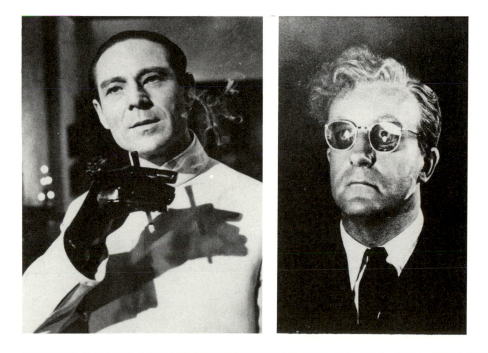

Joseph Wiseman as Dr No (left), a character who, along with people like Wernher Von Braun, clearly inspired Peter Sellers's Dr Strangelove (right).

Slim Pickens, dwarfed by two H-Bombs, is about to take a ride to the very core of the apocalypse in the best of the Bomb movies, Dr Strangelove.

in the development of the V2 rocket that did so much damage to London but at the end of the war he quickly offered his services to the United States (Dr No had done the same but his offer had been refused). He and his rocket designs became very important to the US space programme and in 1960 an awful movie about his life was made starring Curt Jurgens (who was to end up playing a Bond villain). It was called *I Aim at the Stars.* Someone suggested a better title would have been *I Aim at the Stars But Keep Hitting London.*

Dr Strangelove remains the best of the anti-bomb movies. Kubrick's approach, which seemed rather shocking at the time, was to treat the infinitely serious subject matter in a farcical way. In retrospect it seems the only way to treat it. What better way to show the innate lunacy of politicians and military men who can so easily come to terms with the unthinkable and the unspeakable? Originally, though, Kubrick had planned to film Peter George's novel *Red Alert* as a straight suspense novel. Said Kubrick: 'As I tried to build the detail for a scene I found myself tossing away what seemed to be very truthful insights because I was afraid the audience would laugh. After a few weeks I realized that these incongruous bits of reality were closer to the truth than anything else I was able to imagine. And it was at this point I decided to treat the story as nightmare comedy.'[3]

To prove that Kubrick's approach was the right one Sidney Lumet gave us *Fail Safe* the same year. Based on a novel by Eugene Burdick and Harvey Wheeler, it also concerned an American bomber penetrating Soviet airspace, thanks to a mechanical malfunction. Moscow is destroyed and to placate the understandably miffed Russians the American government obligingly nukes New York on their behalf. It is an absurd movie, despite fine acting by a good cast (Henry Fonda, Walter Matthau, Fritz Weaver and Dan O'Herlihy), and as Julian Smith pointed out in his book *Looking Away: Hollywood and Vietnam*, there is something intrinsically unhealthy about it too. '*Fail Safe*, a far more "serious" film than *Dr Strangelove*, is ultimately weaker and shabbier because it turns disaster into an excuse for national pride. The disaster itself is blamed on a machine instead of on the men who put so much trust and pride in their toys; the hero of the piece becomes the American President who does what must be done, and the tragedy is that the Empire State Building becomes ground zero. The novel refers to the President's sacrifice of New York as "the most sweeping and incredible decision any man has ever made" and ends on a patriotic and upbeat note as the President orders a Medal of Honour citation to be prepared for the general who bombed New York.'[4] Still, I bet that President had a hell of a time getting re-elected. Imagine his campaign trip; visiting every city and town in the United States and assuring the citizens of each one that if there's another foul-up it won't be their patch that gets incinerated as a goodwill gesture to the Russians.

One of the few films to try and show what it would be like during and immediately after a nuclear war was Peter Watkins's *The War Game* (1965). Though crudely made, and on a tiny budget — it was a BBC-TV production — it is full of truly harrowing images, including the glare and concussion of the falling bombs, the raging fire storms, the hideously disfigured casualties, mass cremations, buckets of wedding rings gathered from the dead, and execution squads of British policemen shooting looters. So harrowing that the BBC refused to show it. 'It might disturb audiences,' said a BBC spokesman at the time. Kind of ironic, seeing as it was *supposed* to disturb people. But it did get a theatrical release and attracted a great deal of critical praise.

But the mid-sixties saw the temporary end of the serious Bomb movie. More typical of the cinema's approach to the Bomb was *Thunderball*, which

The 'War Room' set for Dr Strangelove *that Ken Adam designed.*

Another conference room also designed by Ken Adam, but for a very different kind of Bomb movie, Thunderball.

finally got made in 1965. In it the Bomb is just one more technological toy within the movie's huge arsenal of technological toys. Even the prospect of nuclear war itself was diminished in the next Bond movie *You Only Live Twice* (1967) when SPECTRE, apparently on behalf of the Chinese, attempts to provoke a nuclear war between the United States and the Soviet Union. And it was the same in the virtual remake of that film in 1977, *The*

In You Only Live Twice *S.P.E.C.T.R.E. was still trying to provoke a Third World War but by then no one cared much.*

Spy Who Loved Me. Despite all the grim paraphernalia that featured in the film — the nuclear submarines, the missiles, the nuclear warheads — and the last-second prevention of a nuclear holocaust, there is no sense of real threat. The potential end of the world has been reduced to a colourful plot device in an escapist fantasy.

Atomic war was nothing but a gimmick in the overrated *Planet of the Apes* (1968) when it was used to provide a predictable frisson at the end of the movie when the astronaut (Charlton Heston) finds the remains of the Statue of Liberty and realizes he's been on Earth all the time (surely the fact that the apes speak English should have given him a clue that he wasn't on an alien planet).

The Bomb theme was more ambiguously exploited in the sequel, *Beneath the Planet of the Apes* (1970). The hero (James Franciscus) is captured by mutants who live in the ruins of a New York destroyed by an atomic war two thousand years in the past. In their subterranean church the mutants worship a nuclear missile — the Doomsday Bomb — which rises up in the altar. They chant 'Glory be to the Bomb and the Holy Fall-Out; As it was in the beginning and always shall be . . .' and they sing 'All things bright

In Planet of the Apes *a Third World War not only led to the takeover of the world by apes but also screwed up the Statue of Liberty.*

and beautiful, the Lord Bomb made us all.' In a surprisingly downbeat ending the bomb actually goes off and a voice dolefully informs us that the planet Earth is no more. Despite this, it was a financial success and its British screenwriter, Paul Dehn, received an urgent telegram from the producers saying: 'Apes exist. Sequel required.' Dehn, incidentally, co-wrote with the film composer James Bernard the original treatment for one of the earliest British Bomb movies, *Seven Days to Noon* (1950) which was about a guilt-ridden scientist who has created a suitcase-sized atom bomb and hides it in London in order to blackmail the government to end their nuclear bomb programme.

Probably the last 'serious' Bomb movie for some time was Richard Lester's post-apocalyptic black comedy *The Bedsitting Room* in 1969. Based on a Spike Milligan play the goonishness sits uncomfortably with the bleak reality of the settings, such as the shattered dome of St Paul's protruding from a swamp, the line of wrecked cars stuck in a permanent traffic jam on a fragment of a motorway, the grim expanses of landscape dominated by piles of sludge and the heaps of discarded boots, broken crockery and false teeth. 'The really awful thing,' said Lester, 'is that we were able to film most of those things in England without faking it. All that garbage is real . . .'[5]

In 1977, when I was working on my previous book on sf cinema, I wrote: 'Over the years the fear of an imminent atomic doom has receded from the minds of most people . . .' But no sooner had I written those words it seemed that the Bomb was suddenly back in the public consciousness with

In The Bedsitting Room *the dome of St Paul's performed a similar function to the wrecked Statue of Liberty in* Planet of the Apes.

a bang and the nuclear disarmament movement was soon flourishing again. Why this ten- to fifteen-year hiatus when everyone appeared to stop worrying about the Bomb? I think it's because the war in Vietnam acted as a distraction from the mid-sixties onwards but with its end the 'demonstrating classes' slowly switched their concern back to the Bomb. Also the late seventies saw public unrest grow about all things nuclear in general, sparked off by the Three Mile Island incident and the almost simultaneous release of Jane Fonda's movie *The China Syndrome* (1979). Or maybe a whole new younger generation had simply got around to discovering the potential menace of the Bomb for themselves while their parents' generation had sunk into apathy about it.

Anyway, for whatever reason, there was a revival of the Bomb movie. One of the first was *Damnation Alley* in 1979, a truly terrible film (it's a shame that the makers didn't stick to the Roger Zelazny novel on which it was supposed to be based as they would have had something as innovative, cinematically, as *Mad Max 2*). It does have one memorable sequence though, at the beginning when the nuclear war is in progress: in an underground control bunker a huge illuminated map is showing the cities of America disappearing one by one and the air force personnel are watching this with a matter-of-fact calmness that is chilling.

The Bomb movie that created the most interest and controversy and really led the new wave of Bomb movies was *The Day After* (1983), directed by Nicholas Meyer. The American equivalent of *The War Game*, it was actually a TV movie and was originally four hours long, but Meyer cut it down to 195 minutes. The British critics, right-wing politicians and other pundits of the Right heaped abuse upon it when it was televised here in Britain; it was called a 'second-rate disaster movie' and a 'badly made soap opera' and while it's true that the first half is pretty feeble as Meyer introduces us to his cast of Kansas small-town characters who are so bland they make the Waltons seem interesting, the second half is quite powerful. Unusually for an American TV movie it is resolvedly bleak. There is no last-minute happy ending, no sudden miracle cure for the survivors; instead it finishes on a note of true despair. It's this uncompromising approach that, in the final analysis, elevates *The Day After* out of the status of 'mere American disaster movie' to something rather important. Its stark pessimism was undoubtedly the reason it caused such a fuss in both the United States and Britain and irritated politicians of a hawkish persuasion in both countries. After all, the year before had seen the transmission of a two-part TV movie called *World War III*, starring Rock Hudson and David Soul, in which a Russian and American military confrontation in Alaska all ends peaceably, and there was not the slightest murmur of dissent.

Just as bleak as *The Day After* was an American feature movie released the same year called *Testament*, though its characters had far greater depth. Directed by Lynne Littman, it is set in a small town north of San Francisco and relentlessly depicts the slow death by radiation sickness of its inhabitants after a nuclear war. It stars Jane Alexander as Carol Wetherby, a mother of three children who conveys a sense of tragic dignity as she is obliged to watch everything she holds dear die around her. Another film that showed ordinary people trying to carry on after the unthinkable has occurred was *Where the Wind Blows* (1987), the animated feature based on the illustrated book by Raymond Briggs. The two central characters, a retired, English country couple, at first treat the nuclear war as a minor inconvenience and believe that the government — which no longer exists

— will get things back to normal. Even when they're mortally ill from the radiation they are unable, or rather, incapable, of facing the truth.

Other movies of the early eighties that touched on the Bomb included David Cronenberg's *The Dead Zone* (1983), which had its hero sacrificing his life to prevent a psycho with an Armageddon complex from becoming President (how unlike real life), and *Dreamscape* (1984), which had a President (Eddie Albert) driven by his nightmares of a post-nuclear war world to enter into a disarmament pact with the Soviets. But in terms of popularity, the most successful Bomb movie of the period was *War Games* in 1983. Despite the similarity in titles it bore no resemblance to Watkins's *The War Game*; on the contrary it was a slick, juvenile-orientated entertainment directed by John Badham (who had previously given us *Saturday Night Fever*) about a young computer hacker (Matthew Broderick) who hacks into the government computer that controls America's military response to a nuclear attack, and plays war games with it. The computer takes the games seriously and when the hacker realizes this he attempts to warn the authorities of what's happening. They don't believe him, of course, but needless to say the world is saved in the nick of time. Yes, the film has a serious message — that the more sophisticated the technology becomes the more likely it is that a nuclear war will happen by accident — but it's still a Disneyfied Bomb movie designed not to upset the kiddies too much.

Before I write off the Bomb movie completely, I should at least mention Steve DeJarnett's *Miracle Mile* (1990) in which the protagonist, Harry (Anthony Edwards), gets a crossed line in Los Angeles and overhears a panic-stricken Army man phoning his parents to warn them that the Third World War is underway and that the first wave of missiles will hit LA in fifty minutes. The rest of the movie concerns Harry's efforts to get himself, his girlfriend and her grandparents across the panic-stricken city to a rooftop helicopter pad, their only means of escape, before the missiles hit. And the sequel to *The Terminator* features a vividly realized nuclear holocaust that wipes out three billion people. The film's title says it all: *Terminator 2: Judgement Day*.

It seemed that the Bomb movie was back in vogue and here to stay this time but once again everyone seems to have stopped worrying about the Bomb. The apparent end of the Cold War is the most obvious reason; it really doesn't seem likely that war between the Soviet Union (if there is still such an entity by the time this sees print) and the United States will occur. But the Bomb itself hasn't disappeared. On the contrary, it's proliferating like crazy and the likelihood of a nuclear war is increasing all the time. It may not be the one between the Soviet Union and the United States that would undoubtedly end the world but a 'small' nuclear war between two other countries. Of course, there is no such thing as a 'small' nuclear war, which is the main trouble with the bloody things. No doubt some Hollywood screenwriter is working on a treatment about the first such war at this moment.

The swinging years: the sixties

We all know that decades are arbitrary, man-made creations, but it does seem true that a sixties sf movie is a very different animal from a fifties one. You can describe a typical fifties sf movie but there's no such thing as a typical sixties sf movie. Thematically, sf cinema diversified during this period and examined as a whole presents an eclectic range of subjects. It had also escaped, to some extent, from its B-movie status and many important directors tackled sf subjects during the sixties, including Hitchcock, Kubrick, Godard, Frankenheimer, Truffaut, Losey, Lumet, Schaffner and Sturges, though often there would be a defensive announcement from the film-maker concerned that his movie was not really science fiction but something, well, more important; this still goes on today.

Sf had become trendy in the early sixties and one of the main causes of this was, I believe, the success of *Dr No*. I said in the last chapter that I thought this was one of the most influential commercial movies of the period. Its influences pervaded many areas; for example, it heralded the so-called 'permissive era' with a promiscuous hero who isn't punished for his lifestyle by the end of the story, as would have been the case in a straight, dramatic piece of the time. It also influenced the visual style and pace of commercial cinema and television. Truffaut rightly described it, disapprovingly, as the first truly decadent movie. He wasn't referring to its subject matter but the way it flaunted the rules of cinema as they had existed up until then — it changed the relationship between what was happening on the screen and the audience. *Dr No* was committing an act of 'submerged complicity' (as originally described by the critic Alexander Walker) with its audience, making them aware that it was aware they were watching a movie. Comedies had done that in the past — *Hellzapoppin*, the *Road* movies, for example — but never a movie that appeared to be, on the surface, a straight adventure movie. And this was what Truffaut resented, this loss of cinematic innocence. (And who is to disagree with him? This trend quickly led from submerged complicity to open complicity and then things like the 'Batman' TV series.) *Dr No* was the first deliberately *camp* movie.

Questions of cinematic purity aside, *Dr No* was a hit and the first of the very successful and long-running series of Bond movies. James Bond and his world suddenly became very fashionable and prompted imitations in both the cinema and literature. However, *Dr No* was, among other things, an sf movie. Like several of Ian Fleming's other novels (*Moonraker, Thunderball, On Her Majesty's Secret Service*), the novel was sort of sf, but the

The high-tech gloss in Dr No *quickly became fashionable in sf and non-sf movies in the sixties.*

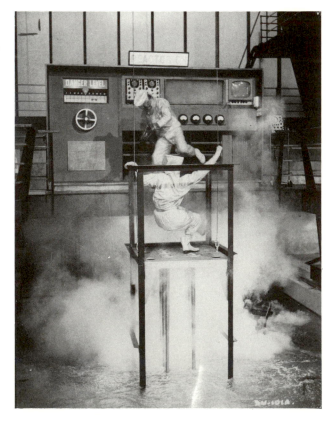

film-makers made it more so by adding the atomic reactor, and the high-tech, almost surreal, Ken Adam sets. If, say, *From Russia with Love* had been the first Bond movie the outcome might have been different but from the beginning, thanks to *Dr No*, the James Bond films have been associated with the paraphernalia and visual trimmings of science fiction. So, as a result, science fiction itself attained a patina of fashionability in the sixties purely by association with Bond.

Well, it's a theory . . .

A moment's digression here while I describe the impact *Dr No* had on me personally. I was sixteen when I first saw it and I was at the stage where I had reluctantly decided I would have to grow up. It was time, I told myself sternly, to put aside childish things, such as my cherished comic book collection, and think about improving my mind. Then *Dr No* came along. It was a revelation in more ways than one. For example, I couldn't get over the fact it was a *British* movie. I'd never seen a British movie like this before — it was in colour for a start — and the hero didn't act like any hero I'd ever seen in a British movie before, or an American one, come to that. And the way the movie turned into science fiction two-thirds of the way through, and the villain, Dr No (marvellously played by Joseph Wiseman), was straight out of a Marvel comic book! And yet this was an adult movie. It had to be, I mean the hero went to bed with a woman, on-screen (well, almost). So I came to the obvious conclusion — I wouldn't have to put away my childish things after all. It was okay to like comic books even when you were adult! This adult movie proved it. So, yes, *Dr No* saved me from having to grow up, not to mention all that mind-improving stuff.

Another thing that struck me while watching the movie — was that it featured a strong element of Disney's *Twenty Thousand Leagues Under the Sea*. Dr No was like Captain Nemo (as you may notice, their names are very similar), they shared an interest in the sea, both had island strongholds from which they flouted international law, and both exploited atomic power. When I got around to reading the novel I saw yet another connection which the movie didn't utilize (no doubt for budgetary reasons) — a giant squid! Years later, while reading an extract from one of Evelyn Waugh's numerous diaries, I came across a mention of his going to see *Twenty Thousand Leagues Under the Sea* in the company of the Flemings.

The inspiration for Dr No, Captain Nemo, returned in the form of Herbert Lom in a 1961 version of Mysterious Island.

Waugh himself was dismissive of the movie but clearly Fleming was impressed enough to borrow extensively from it in his novel.

But enough of *Dr No*, a film that clearly left an indelible mark, if not stain, upon me. What of other sf movies of the same period? While sf would attract a number of prestigious film-makers in the second half of the decade, the first half saw several of the sf film-makers from the fifties trying to find a new and successful formula for the genre. On the whole, they failed. George Pal, for example, got it right with his version of H.G. Wells's *The Time Machine* (see Chapter Fifteen) in 1960, but it marked his last real success. Certainly his next film, *Atlantis, the Lost Continent* (1961), which, as with *The Time Machine*, he directed himself, was an absolute disaster (though I must admit I enjoyed it at the time of its release). Its amazingly loony plot involves a lost Greek fisherman forced into slavery after falling in love with an Atlantan Princess and a mad dictator who provokes the wrath of the gods when he lets loose with a disintegrator ray projector powered by sacred crystals. Even the destruction of Atlantis at the end is a disappointment. It's clear that MGM had provided him with a ridiculously low budget for a movie that was designed as a spectacle (the climax had to be padded out with footage of Rome burning from *Quo Vadis?*) but the script and direction, not to mention the cast, must take a large share of the blame.

Stock footage played an important part in *Master of the World* (1961), a cheapo production from AIP, who gave us so many cheapo productions, usually directed by Roger Corman, in the fifties. In fact, you could call this movie a collection of stock footage with some new bits added on. I found it a terrible disappointment back in 1961 because I already had in my possession the comic of the movie and it promised many wonderful visual treats, treats that the artist could easily produce but that were far from the ability of an AIP effects budget to create on the screen. Based on two novels by Jules Verne, about the mystery man Robur who has built a huge flying machine, the *Albatross*, made of compressed paper and kept aloft with a forest of small helicopter rotors, *Master of the World* is an aerial version of the Disney *Twenty Thousand Leagues*. A group of people, including Charles Bronson in the Kirk Douglas role (though, mercifully, he doesn't sing and there isn't a seal), are captured by the mad genius (Vincent Price) and kept prisoner in his flying machine while he flies around bombing the hell out of everyone in an effort to get the nations of the world to renounce war. In the end Bronson and his pals succeed in escaping, leaving a bomb on board the *Albatross*. As the flying machine hurtles towards the sea Price has time to give his loyal crew a lecture about the future of mankind along much the same lines as the one Mason delivered to the crew of the *Nautilus*.

The model of the *Albatross* is fine but all the battle sequences have been lifted from other movies, and not necessarily ones even in colour. The lowest point of all is when the *Albatross* bombs London. It's supposed to be the mid-nineteenth century but the London we see in the movie looks a little, well, earlier than that. Medieval, in fact. This is not surprising as the footage comes from Olivier's 1944 production of *Henry V*.

That same year there was another version of *Twenty Thousand Leagues*, updated to modern times. It was called *Voyage to the Bottom of the Sea* and was made by the dreaded Irwin Allen, the man who has done more than anyone to knee science fiction in the groin. A former literary agent, which explains a lot, he came to prominence in 1953 when he won an Academy Award for his pseudo-documentary, *The Sea Around Us*, based on Rachel Carson's bestselling book warning of pollution of the oceans. If he had stayed in this area of activity I would gladly be singing his praises today but no, in 1960, after making some bizarre movies like *The Story of Mankind* (1957), he discovered sf. In 1960 he gave us his version of *The Lost World* and we sincerely wish he hadn't. Then came *Voyage* in which Allen packed a group of hackneyed characters into a glass-nosed submarine called the *Seaview* (what else?), loaded them up with every plot cliché known to hack writing and sent them off to save the world. Well, you see, the Van Allen Belt had caught on fire and the sub's inventor, Admiral (oh God) Nelson, thinks the way to put the fire out is to shoot an atomic missile into the Belt from a specific point on the Equator. Why? Well, it doesn't pay to ask. Allen's approach to sf is to ignore anything approaching logic, much less a scientific fact, and simply concentrate on action and lots of flashing lights (plus lots of stock footage). It's a formula that has served him well over the years. *Voyage* proved a financial success and led to a long-running TV series of the same name. He also produced other sf TV series that were even more inane, such as 'The Time Tunnel', 'Lost in Space' and 'Land of the Giants'. Eventually he left sf for the disaster movie genre and again enjoyed great success — with virtually the same formula — until he met his nemesis, a movie about killer bees called *The Swarm*.

Two veterans from the fifties were Ray Harryhausen and Charles H. Schneer: after having a big success with a fantasy movie in 1958, *The Seventh Voyage of Sinbad*, they returned to sf in 1961 with *Mysterious Island*, vaguely based on Verne's sequel to *Twenty Thousand Leagues*. Confederate prisoners escape from a Yankee prison by balloon and end up on an island inhabited by giant animals and two shipwrecked ladies. After the castaways cope with a giant crab, giant bees, a giant bird ('It was a prehistoric Phorohacos,' said Harryhausen, 'but most reviewers and audiences assumed it to be an overgrown chicken.') they encounter Captain Nemo (Herbert Lom) and his submarine. It turns out that Nemo has been breeding the giant beasties in an attempt to solve the world's food problems but his work is terminated by the obligatory volcanic eruption. The castaways escape but once again Nemo goes down with his ship.

This okay movie was not a big financial success and neither was their next movie, *First Men in the Moon* (1964), based on the H.G. Wells novel. Despite a script by Nigel Kneale and good effects this has never been a favourite of mine; it is all done strictly for laughs and seems aimed very

Nemo was trying to solve the problem of the world's food shortages but people just weren't ready for his giant crab.

much at the kiddie market, with Lionel Jeffries going over the top as Professor Cavor. Wells's fascinating depiction of Selenite society, which clearly inspired Huxley's *Brave New World*, is absent. Two interesting touches are the prologue and epilogue set in modern times. In the prologue a United Nations spaceship lands on the moon and the astronauts discover a British flag planted there. Back on Earth a very old man (Edward Judd) tells us that he put the Union Jack there in 1899, then there's a flashback to the main story. In the epilogue the astronauts discover that the underground Selenite city is deserted and in a state of decay. The old man remembers that Cavor had a cold when on the moon and deduces that his germs must have wiped out the Selenite civilization. This black joke, a play on the ending in *The War of the Worlds*, was one of Nigel Kneale's contributions.

A rare example of a fifties-style monster movie in the sixties was *Reptilicus* in 1961. Made and set in Denmark, it was produced and directed by American Sidney Pink, who co-wrote the screenplay with Ib Melchior, the Danish-born screenwriter who has long worked in Hollywood. He wrote scripts for several low-budget sf movies, such as *Angry Red Planet* (1959) and *The Time Travellers* (1964), both of which he directed, and he co-wrote the screenplay for the more upmarket (but not much) *Robinson Crusoe on Mars* (1964). *Reptilicus* begins promisingly enough: a team of oil surveyors finds that their drill bit is full of flesh and blood, which has come from something buried hundreds of feet below the ground. They excavate what turns out to be the tail of a dinosaur but then the film gets silly. The tail gets hit by lightning and grows a new body. And the body it grows is nothing to write home about. Reptilicus has to be the most ludicrous-looking giant reptile to ever draw artillery fire from stock footage. Actually, it looked more like a dragon than a dinosaur and even had a pair of tiny wings that enabled it to soar shakily into the air. This movie is certainly no advertisement for Danish special effects.

But *Reptilicus* is probably more fun to watch than Joseph Losey's *The Damned* (1961). Losey made some great movies (*The Servant, King and Country, Accident*) but he also made some real duds and this is one of them. A Hammer production, it was based on the novel *The Children of the Light* by H.L. Lawrence (of whom little has been heard of since) and was scripted by Evan Jones. Hammer probably thought they were going to get an exploitation movie that would cash in on the success of *Village of the Damned* but what they got was a slow and pretentious little number which they were understandably reluctant to release. For reasons too tedious to recount (let's just say that Oliver Reed is involved), Macdonald Carey and Shirley Anne Field (winning the Ann Robinson Award for Terrible Acting in an sf Movie) are obliged to take refuge in a cave under a military base and discover a group of children living there. It turns out that the children are the product of an experiment to produce a race of humans that can survive an atomic war. The drawback is that they themselves are highly radioactive and will fatally contaminate anyone they come into contact with. Mac and Shirl, not realizing this, help the children to escape and it all ends on a downbeat note with Mac and Shirl slowly dying of radiation poisoning in a boat while a sinister helicopter hovers overhead waiting for them to die. (Losey later inflated that image into a whole movie, *Figures in a Landscape*, which consisted of ninety-five minutes of two men being pursued by a helicopter. That was a dud too.) But to be fair, a lot of critics thought this movie was pretty damned good. *Films and Filming* magazine, for example, said: 'This is undoubtedly one of the most important British films of the year, even, perhaps of the 60s.'

No one made that claim for the 1963 *Day of the Triffids*. John Wyndham, who had been well served by the makers of *Village of the Damned*, got well and truly shafted by the makers of this movie. Wyndham's classic sf novel, first published in 1951, about ambulatory plants who take over the world, was turned into a very patchy and disjointed movie by American writer/producer Philip Yordan. It is disjointed as extra footage had to be shot, by Freddie Francis, and inserted into the original version, directed by Steve Sekely, which couldn't be stretched to feature length. Howard Keel, star of the Sekely section, said that the dialogue was so sparse in the script that he had to write his own in order to have something to say. The Triffids themselves are a droopy, variable bunch that could do with a good pruning. They were better realized in a BBC-TV serial version of the novel made in 1981.

Roger Corman finally made a goodish sf movie in 1963, *The Man with the X-Ray Eyes*. It starred Ray Milland as a doctor who invents a serum that

No, not a scene from that classic Ray Milland movie, The Lost Weekend, *but a shot of Milland in another film, Roger Corman's* The Man with the X-Ray Eyes.

enables him to see through solid objects. His motives are purely altruistic — he intends to use it as a diagnostic tool — but, of course, this act of hubris leads to tragedy in the grand tradition of scientists meddling with Things That Man Was Not Meant to Know, though here it's a case of Things That Man Was Not Meant to See. It's visually inventive but the small budget prevents the movie from realizing the full potential of the central idea. As usual Corman seems determined to spend as little money as possible and one suspects his personal motto is: 'Budget? I don't need no feelthy budget!' (A day after I wrote those words I happened to see a review of his just-published autobiography entitled *How I Made a Hundred Movies in Hollywood and Never Lost a Dime.*)

That same year Alfred Hitchcock made his only sf movie, *The Birds* (back in the thirties Hitchcock had wanted to make *The War of the Worlds* but nothing came of it). Based on the story by Daphne du Maurier and scripted by Evan Hunter (also known as Ed McBain, both pseudonyms of S.A. Lombino who used to write sf in the fifties), it is set in Bodega Bay, a small seaside town where the bird-life suddenly turns nasty and starts attacking the locals. Actually, this never struck me as being a science fictional idea as I had grown up being attacked by birds on a regular basis. Magpies, to be exact. It wasn't just me. In Perth the magpies were the size of British crows and would selectively dive-bomb small and not-so-small boys during the nesting period every year. One theory was that they were after hair for their nests but I never saw them attack a girl, they only attacked boys — no doubt because they recognized that only boys posed a threat to their nests and eggs. People in Britain react very doubtfully when I tell them of this but it's true, or was true. I don't know if this tradition persists today. Anyway, I had a great deal of sympathy for the characters in *The Birds* which remains a very watchable movie with great technical effects (I consider it to be Hitchcock's last great movie).

A movie I think is very overrated is *Robinson Crusoe on Mars*, made in 1964. Directed by Byron Haskin, who directed *The War of the Worlds*, it's a thuddingly predictable variation on Defoe's classic with a lone Earthman (Paul Mantee) struggling to survive in the hostile Martian environment. The film becomes more interesting when it starts to get silly. An alien spaceship arrives with a consignment of slaves, one of which escapes to become his Man Friday. They avoid the flying 'drones' sent to kill them by

It's a hard life for both man and monkey on Mars, as can be seen in this shot from Robinson Crusoe on Mars.

the aliens (the drones resemble the Martian war machines from *The War of the Worlds* but minus their cobra-head heat ray projectors) and reach the Martian icecap where they are rescued by an American spaceship. This is what I call a 'fake' sf movie. The sf elements, the things that are really interesting — in this case the aliens themselves (Who are they? Where do they come from? What are they doing in our solar system?) — are merely accoutrements to the central gimmick, which is: Hey, let's do Robinson Crusoe on Mars! Another example of a fake sf movie is *Outland* where the central gimmick is: Hey, let's do *High Noon* on one of the moons of Jupiter!

By the mid-sixties sf was becoming fashionable and sf writers (well, some of them) found that movie producers were sniffing around their works. One such was Robert Sheckley whose story, *The Seventh Victim*, was bought by Carlo Ponti and filmed in 1965 as *The Tenth Victim* (there had been an earlier horror movie called *The Seventh Victim*). What is potentially a nifty idea — a future world where murder has been legalized and turned into a public sport — is buried under its dated pop-art visuals. If it will be

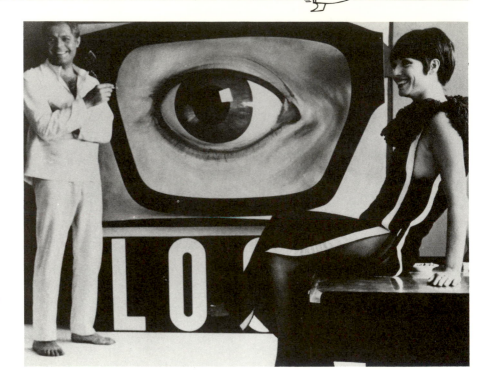

Science fiction gets the Pop Art treatment in this Italian film version of Robert Sheckley's The Tenth Victim.

remembered for anything it will be for the scene where Ursula Andress shoots someone with her bra.

Ray Bradbury, who had been sprung free from the ghetto of sf back in the fifties when Christopher Isherwood announced that he wasn't just an sf writer but a poet, was much better treated by François Truffaut who filmed his novel *Fahrenheit 451* in 1966. The movie is a stylish and evocative, if cold, adaptation of Bradbury's parable about a future world where all books are banned. Montag (Oscar Werner) is a member of the Fire Brigade, an organization that starts fires rather than extinguishes them. The Firemen root out illegal book hordes and incinerate them, but Montag, like the protagonist in *1984*, comes under the influence of a rebellious young woman (Julie Christie) who changes his attitude towards the status quo. Eventually he rebels completely and incinerates the Fire Chief (Cyril Cusak, in a creepy performance) instead of the books. He escapes from the city and joins the Book People community, the members of which are each memorizing an entire book to preserve them (Montag chooses a book by Edgar Allen Poe). The film ends with Montag and the other Book People walking about in the snow-filled woods (the snow was a lucky accident) reciting the words from their respective books. It's a haunting image but a depressing one; the Book People have become robots, living memory banks whose only purpose is to be a store for someone else's words. The books may be preserved in this way but literature as a living artform is plainly dead. (Trivia fact: Oscar Werner caused problems during the making of the movie because he had a powerful phobia about fire.)

Time to put on my philistine's cap again and say that I find another famous French sf movie a pain in the gut. I am referring to *Alphaville* (1965), Jean Luc Godard's allegorical story about a private eye in the future who enters a city (contemporary Paris) to rescue a scientist from the clutches of a malign super-computer. When I first saw this movie at a Perth film festival in 1966 I was unimpressed (admittedly, I didn't understand it) and I remain so. Sure, the movie is beautifully photographed in black and white, and Anna Karina is also beautiful, and it's packed with smart-ass allusions to Hollywood B films, 'sci-fi', comic books, thrillers and cartoons, and, along with *Eraserhead*, is probably J.G. Ballard's favourite movie, but it is not for me.

Another dislike of mine is *Barbarella* (1967). I seem to be in a minority here but this tacky, inept, unfunny, unerotic, unimaginative, self-regarding, smug 'sci-fi' romp has always got up my nose. Okay, it's only

The late, great Francois Truffaut demonstrates the art of pole sliding to his cast during the making of Fahrenheit 451.

meant to be a bit of fun, but for some irrational reason the movie just irritates me. Maybe because I resent it for not being the movie it could have been. The basic idea sounds great: a movie based on the witty and playfully erotic comic strip by Jean Claude Forest but that's not the movie we get. For a start, Jane Fonda is miscast as the dewy-eyed, naive sex kitten who brings sexual salvation to any male she encounters — even back then playing such a role was clearly going against the grain for her. And as for the film's humour content — good grief, it had *eight* writers contributing to the screenplay and if they had contributed just one funny idea each the movie would have been vastly improved, but all the humour is leaden and unfunny, with the exception of the sequence where Barbarbella encounters an inefficient revolutionary (David Hemmings) and they make love via sex-pills and their fingertips. Oh, yes, the special effects are crummy too.

Back in Hollywood, in 1966, a strange thing happened. A lot of money was spent on the making of an sf film, and then another strange thing happened. When it was released this expensive sf movie actually became a big box-office success. This was to have important repercussions for the cinema of science fiction. The movie was *Fantastic Voyage*, directed by Richard Fleischer and made by 20th Century-Fox, a studio that was to have another major success with an sf film, just over a decade later when it made *Star Wars*. *Fantastic Voyage* is a dopey movie but a spectacular one. I certainly enjoyed the special effects when I first saw it but realized it veered dangerously close to Irwin Allen-style daftness. It belongs to the sub-genre of 'shrunken people' movies and, as usual with such movies, totally ignores the problem of mass. I mean, here you have five people and a submarine shrunk to a size where they can be injected into someone's bloodstream but there's no mention of mass. Logically, the combined mass of the people and the submarine concentrated into such a small unit would cause them and the sub to fall through the floor and probably end up in the centre of the Earth. But maybe it's my defective, poverty-stricken sense of wonder at work again. (In the novelization of the film Isaac Asimov tried to rationalize such scientific problems but none too successfully.)

The original treatment was written by Jerome Bixby (of *It!* fame) and Otto Klement and was very different from the final movie. 'We placed the story before the turn-of-century,' said Bixby in a 1983 interview, 'imbuing it with much of the quaint bronze-and-crystal technology flavour of *The*

Suspended by wires, wiped with acid to prevent reflection, high above the studio floor, the cast of Fantastic Voyage *can be excused many things, such as their performances.*

Time Machine. Our characters ventured inward with an innocent sense of wonder, unacquainted with our discoveries of the past hundred years. They saw a virus and debated what it might be. It was a great story and I wish 20th had done it that way. Instead they swung the story to frontal sf, with tons of hard data available to the characters — radioactive tracking tells them where they are, computer maps tell them where they're going, experts tell them what they're seeing, and zip went awe and mystery right into the toilet, save for some mutters about the handiwork of God and the miracle of oxygenation.'[1]

'It was a very hard picture to make,' said Fleischer, 'and a very boring one. We had that big submarine to manipulate and shoot, and we had the problem of wires. As it was all supposed to be happening underwater everybody was flying on wires. It was a big wire job and also a rather dangerous one because sometimes the actors would be twenty or thirty feet above the stage floor and held up by only four wires, and if only two of the wires broke the actor could fall. We broke wires all the time but luckily it was only ever one at a time, never two. Once we heard a wire go we brought them down immediately, of course. They kept breaking because we had to wipe the wires with acid which corrugated their surfaces and prevented them from reflecting back light, but naturally the acid weakened the wires.'[2] This explains some of the performances. I mean, I wouldn't like to be suspended on four acid-wiped wires thirty feet above the floor and be expected to act as well. *Fantastic Voyage* looks a bit creaky today; its special effects still spectacular but not very convincing (just compare the effects in *Honey, I Shrunk the Kids!* to see how the technology has progressed since 1966), but it still has a few memorable moments, notably the one where Raquel Welch is attacked by some stroppy anti-bodies.

An sf movie that didn't make money was *The Power* (1968), produced by George Pal and directed by Byron Haskin, the team that had been so successful with *The War of the Worlds* and so unsuccessful with *Conquest of Space*. The failure of the latter movie ended Pal's relationship with Paramount and he moved to MGM; *The Power* was to be his last movie for MGM (and the second-last of his career). This was based on a novel by a minor sf writer, Frank M. Robinson, and began with a scientist (Arthur O'Connell) alerting his colleagues that among their number is a mutant with powerful mental powers, but before he can reveal the mutant's identity he is murdered. Suspicion falls on biochemist Jim Tanner (George Hamilton) so Tanner desperately tries to find the real culprit. His investigations unearth a mysterious character called Adam Hart who appears to have been a different person to all who ever encountered him. No two descriptions of him are alike and Tanner realizes that Hart has the power to manipulate minds. Surviving various attempts to kill him, Tanner finally unmasks Adam Hart (Michael Rennie) and discovers that he too is a supermind. They have a battle of wills and guess who wins . . . This had the potential of being a fast-moving, and impressive sf thriller but it's let down by a stodgy and confused script and mediocre direction. Haskin blamed the studio: 'The personal friction between MGM and Pal — the hatreds between them you just wouldn't believe — were allowed to operate on that film's economy. It wasn't released with any fanfare. It was grudgingly left to escape because they were trying to get rid of Pal. I don't think the film is too bad although you could get confused unless you paid very close attention. I came onto the project when it was fully prepared. I assisted the writer [John Gay] in polishing one or two points but I had no authority to change anything further. I felt that a few things could have

RETARDATIO
IN WEIGHTLES

George Hamilton is faced with his own corpse in this scene from The Power.

been changed but I didn't go into it because I was just glad to be doing something.'[3]

That same year saw the release of two sf films on the theme of alien manipulation of human evolution. One movie became very famous, the other movie slipped in and out of cinemas almost unnoticed by critics and audiences alike. The former movie is, of course, *2001: A Space Odyssey*. I remember seeing this in a wide-screen cinema in Sydney in, I guess, either late 1968 or early 1969. Needless to say it was a memorable experience, akin to seeing *Forbidden Planet* for the first time back in 1956. I may have been past the truly impressionable age when I saw *2001* but its impact was enormous. 'At last . . . at last,' I told myself as I watched the space shuttle doing its mating dance with the space wheel to the accompaniment of a Strauss waltz, 'someone has done it *right!*' (Pretty much what I said to myself on seeing *Forbidden Planet*.) I just couldn't get over the quality of the special effects. I was so used to being able to spot every effects shot in a movie that this came as a real shock — these effects didn't look like effects! Why had effects never looked this good before? Okay, things did go wonky towards the end — those exploding suns and swirling star clusters do look exactly what they are, greatly magnified spots of coloured

*Scenes from Stanley
Kubrick's masterpiece*
2001: A Space Odyssey.

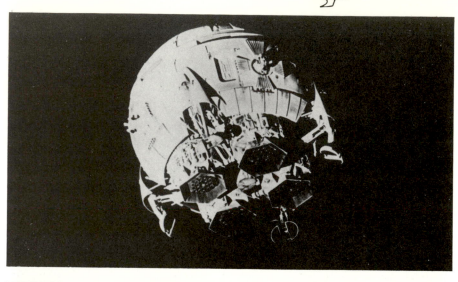

oil — but overall the movie was visually mind-blowing. How had Kubrick pulled off this miracle?

I found out later, of course, and when doing the research for my book on special effects, *Movie Magic*, had the opportunity of interviewing two of the four effects supervisors who worked on the picture, Tom Howard and Wally Veevers. Kubrick's secret, apart from having a lot of time and money to spend on the effects, went back to basics. Eschewing the use of any of the automatic matting processes, such as the blue-screen system, Kubrick and his effects team utilized techniques of trick photography that had been established by cameramen working in the silent era. In those days, as there were no optical printers or automatic matting processes, the cameramen were obliged to combine the various image components in the camera. To elaborate: a silent cameraman wanted a split screen shot to create the illusion of twins using only one actor. First he would shoot the actor on the left side of the set, with a matte in front of the lens masking the right side of the set, then he would wind the film back in the camera and shoot the actor on the right side of the set with matte this time obscuring the left side of the set — the result was two separately filmed images joined on the same piece of film.

This method, using much more sophisticated equipment, was used in the making of *2001*. For example, for the scenes of the huge Jupiter-bound spaceship *Discovery* gliding through space, or of the giant space station revolving against the stars with people visible through the ports or windows, it was necessary to film the models at least twice. First, say, the model of the *Discovery* was filmed moving slowly along a track with its window areas blacked out, then the same movement was repeated, but this time the exterior of the model would be covered with black velvet apart from the window areas which were represented by glossy white cards. On to these cards would be projected footage of the actors. The film would be wound back and the model filmed again, and thus the actors and the spacecraft would be combined on the same piece of film, just like in the silent days. 'The models had to move absolutely smoothly,' Veevers told me. 'When you consider that the model of the space station was nine feet across and we were only moving three-eighths of an inch a minute while shooting it rotating you can appreciate why it had to be smooth. The same applied to the model of the *Discovery* which was fifty-four feet long and moved along a track one hundred and fifty feet in length. It took four and a half hours to reach the end of the track and each time we shot it it had to travel at exactly the same speed.'[4]

To combine the footage of the various models with backgrounds of star fields Kubrick again refused to use any automatic matting systems ('I feel it is impossible to get original-looking quality with travelling mattes,' Kubrick said later.[5]) He insisted that hand-drawn mattes be used. This meant that for a shot of the *Discovery* moving through space, the outline of the spaceship had to be rotascoped frame by frame onto animation cells which were used to produce individual mattes that blanked out the corresponding areas on the star field background on each frame. These methods certainly produced brilliant results (no matte lines, no jiggling between the various image components, no blue glare reflected from a blue screen onto the surface of the models and so on) but they were both time-consuming and very expensive. *2001* took nearly two and a half years to make and $6,500,000 was spent on the effects alone. When, in 1976, George Lucas aimed to recreate such visual conviction in *Star Wars* he was obliged to use cheaper and faster methods: one innovation was to move the camera rather than the model in the model shots, using a computerized camera that could make exactly the same pass over a model again and again. He also used the blue-screen matting process.

But enough about the effects in *2001*, what did I think of its content when I first saw it? Well, to be honest, I was a little disappointed. I think I expected more story, a more event-packed movie. And I wasn't wild about the ending which I didn't really understand. I thought the light show went on far too long and I didn't even pick up on the fact that Bowman, the surviving astronaut, had gone through a 'star gate' and was hurtling through the universe at a terrific speed. I just thought he was having an alien-induced psychedelic acid trip, as did many of the hippies who flocked to the movie and watched it under the influence of various substances. I did like the sequence in the white suite as Bowman rapidly ages, and also the final scene with the foetus surveying Earth. I didn't understand it, mind, but I liked it. And, overall, I liked the movie itself. And I recognized that it was a landmark movie. Thanks to Kubrick, sf movies, special effects and the cinema itself would never be the same again. Well, I was kind of right about that, but also kind of wrong.

Initial critical reaction to *2001* was almost uniformly hostile. It was described as confused, pretentious, disjointed, boring, baffling, dull and banal. The chief complaint was that it was difficult to understand what it was all about, and Kubrick was accused of being deliberately enigmatic in order to disguise the fact that the film wasn't really about anything. And at first it looked as if MGM were going to have a costly cinematic folly on their hands but very quickly word-of-mouth turned it into a very popular movie with younger audiences. By a stroke of luck (or because of Kubrick's canny sense of timing) the movie came out at just the right time — it was a mind-blowing movie when things mind-blowing were all the rage. And, unusually, many of the critics who had originally given it bad reviews, recanted after a second viewing.

Of course, much of *2001* was deliberately ambiguous, revolving as it does around the giant question mark of humanity's relationship with both the Universe and the mysterious entities that have been manipulating the development of the species. It is nothing less than a secular movie about God. Both Arthur C. Clarke, who co-wrote the screenplay (he and Kubrick wrote it first as a novel) and Kubrick are, or were, atheists but postulate the existence of aliens who are so far advanced they have become God-like. But if the nature of these aliens was revealed or explained or shown in the movie then *2001* would have lost its atmosphere of awe and wonder. Yet people persisted in asking Kubrick what the 'message' of the movie was and in an interview in *Playboy* he replied: 'It's not a message that I ever intend to convey in words. *2001* is a non-verbal experience; out of two hours and nineteen minutes of film [he had cut about twenty minutes from the original running time after preview screenings], there are only a little less than forty minutes of dialogue. I tried to create a *visual* experience, one that bypassed verbalized pigeonholing and directly penetrated the subconscious with emotional and philosophic content . . . you're free to speculate as you wish about the philosophical and allegorical meaning of the film . . . but I don't want to spell out a verbal road map of *2001* that every viewer will feel obliged to pursue or else fear that he's missed the point.'

Surprisingly, quite a few sf writers reacted with hostility towards *2001*. Ray Bradbury, for instance, wrote: 'Clarke should have done the screenplay totally on his own and not allowed Kubrick to lay hands on it . . .

the test of the film is whether or not we care when one of the astronauts dies. We do not . . . the freezing touch of Antonioni, whose ghost haunts Kubrick, has turned everything here to ice.'[6] On another occasion Bradbury told an interviewer: 'I think it's a gorgeous film. One of the most beautifully photographed pictures in the history of motion pictures. Unfortunately there are no well-directed scenes, and the dialogue is banal to the point of extinction.'[7]

What upset some of the older, conservative sf writers was Kubrick's treatment of humanity. It had long been a tradition in the *Astounding/ Analog* school of sf writing to present Man as a plucky little creature who faced the Universe with a slide-rule in one hand (no, none of them predicted the pocket calculator) and a blaster in the other and soon has it whipped. Kubrick, however, treats the human race as an impotent, pathetic, helpless pawn of forces beyond its comprehension. To many sf writers this was a philosophical step backwards for an sf movie. Lester Del Rey, who once wrote a short story where mankind declares war on God and wins ('For I Am a Jealous People') was particularly incensed by *2001*.

Gary Lockwood and Keir Dullea, who played the two human astronauts in 2001 *(part of the non-human crew, member Hal 2000 can be seen on the left).*

An even bigger sin committed by Kubrick in the eyes of the sf old guard was his attitude towards technology. In the 'hard' sf produced by the *Astounding/Analog* school, technology was to be the means by which Man conquers the Universe, but when Kubrick jump-cuts from the apeman's bone club flying upwards through the air to the shot of the satellite (actually a weapons platform but that is not made clear in the movie, only in the novel), he seems to be suggesting that for all the advances in technology that lead from the bone to the satellite, fundamentally nothing has changed. Man is still an ape playing with his weapons; the weapons may be more complicated but Man himself hasn't developed one iota in the cosmic sense.

But perhaps I'm reading things into the movie that aren't there. My opinion certainly is not shared by Michael Moorcock, who certainly can't be described as a member of the sf old guard — just the opposite in fact. 'I thought it was barren of ideas,' he said. 'Irony is no substitute for imagination. It struck me that poor Kubrick had innocently got Arthur C. Clarke to do what he thought was going to be a wildly imaginative flight of fancy but Arthur did his usual thing instead. I was on the set twice while they were making it and they'd got technology-heavy: they had all these NASA people around and everything. It's like when you're writing a novel and you start doing the preliminary research — after a while the research becomes the whole thing and you have to finally chuck the whole lot out before you can start writing the fiction. But Kubrick kept everything and got stuck with it.'[8]

I'm still impressed with *2001* but I wonder how it will appear to future audiences. A stuffy, portentous artifact that is very much the product of its era, in much the same way that *Things to Come* appears to us now? Possibly, but I doubt it. I think it will remain a timeless piece of cinema well past its sell-by date of 2001.

As for that other movie in 1968 that also dealt with alien interference in human prehistory, it was called *Five Million Years to Earth*. At least that was the title when I saw it in a Sydney cinema but it wasn't long before I realized I was watching *Quatermass and the Pit*. I'd never seen the BBC-TV original but I knew the plot well enough to recognize it as the film version of the third of Nigel Kneale's 'Quatermass' TV serials which had been transmitted ten years before in 1958. I've since had the opportunity of viewing the

Andrew Keir as Professor Quatermass and James Donald in a scene from Quatermass and the Pit.

original (the BBC have thoughtfully released it on video) and this movie, directed by Roy Ward Baker, faithfully follows it, though, by necessity, the story has been telescoped down to a ninety-seven-minute running time (Nigel Kneale wrote the screenplay). It begins when the remains of an apeman are discovered by workmen excavating for a new Underground station in London. Then, when part of what appears to be a large metallic object buried in the same spot is also found, the Army presume it to be a German rocket from the Second World War and call in Professor Quatermass (Andrew Keir) and his military counterpart, the arrogant and narrow-minded Colonel Breen (Julian Glover).

When the object is excavated Quatermass realizes that it has nothing to do with the Second World War. And when he finds one of the fossil skulls *inside* the metallic object, he knows for certain, because the fossil apemen have been already dated as some five million years old. And above the station site runs a road called Hob's Lane which has a long history of spooky manifestations . . . Then a compartment is found in the front of the object and it contains the bodies of insect-like creatures that promptly begin to rot when removed. Quatermass deduces that the creatures came from Mars when, millions of years ago, they realized their planet was dying. They invaded the Earth by proxy; not being able to live here they kidnapped a number of apemen, took them to Mars where they genetically altered them and turned them into Martians mentally. The apemen were then returned to Earth to breed with others of their species (on this occasion the ship had obviously crash-landed, killing the Martians and their altered captives). The implications stun Quatermass. 'Gentlemen!' he cries. '*We* are the Martians!'

But Colonel Breen thinks it was all part of a Nazi propaganda campaign to lower morale and arranges for a TV crew to come and film the object. Once the power cables have been laid into the excavation the alien spaceship begins to feed off them and comes to life, being a kind of organic construct. As it grows more powerful its baleful influence spreads across London and the people who carry the Martian genes assume psychic powers in order to 'cull the nest' and kill those humans who don't have the Martian streak within them . . .

It's understandable how the original TV serial kept the viewing audience gripped each week in 1958 — with *Quatermass and the Pit* Kneale created one of the most ingenious and unsettling alien-invasion stories of all time. As a condensed version of the serial, the film is fine but the old black-and-white version, though understandably creaky in places and with inferior effects, still works surprisingly well, having more time to build up a disturbing atmosphere. As with Kneale's other works it is the cunning mixture of contemporary sf with mythology and the occult that gives it an extra resonance. In *Quatermass and the Pit* he is exploring themes similar to those of Arthur C. Clarke. The idea of the devil becoming implanted in the human racial memory as a result of a contact with a horned species of aliens figured prominently in Clarke's 1953 novel *Childhood's End*, and the idea of an alien artifact being discovered buried underground was the subject of Clarke's 1950 short story, 'The Sentinel', which, of course, was to form the basis of *2001: A Space Odyssey*.

Movies that had space scenes in them suddenly looked pretty feeble after *2001*. One such was *You Only Live Twice* (1967), the latest Bond movie, and another was *Marooned* (1969) directed by John Sturges. *Marooned* was the first space soap opera. Written by Mayo Simon, it concerned a space mission that goes wrong, trapping three American astronauts in orbit. The scenes involving the three wives waiting anxiously back at the base are particularly mawkish but the dialogue wasn't much better up in the capsule. The exchanges between the astronauts are so trite they make the deliberately banal dialogue in *2001* seem almost scintillating. Each of the three actors involved (Richard Crenna, James Franciscus and Gene Hackman) was saddled with a character consisting of pure stereotype. As for the visuals, the only impressive sequence consists of footage from an actual Saturn rocket launch.

A non-space sf movie made in 1968 was *Charly*, based on the story 'Flowers for Algernon' by Daniel Keyes (later expanded into a novel). Most actors would jump at the chance of playing a character who, within the time-span of one film, ranges from being a subnormal thirty-year-old to a super-genius after being given an experimental brain drug, and then back again to sub-normal (the drug only works temporarily). Cliff Robertson did more than jump, he formed his own production company, optioned the novel and, after various setbacks, raised the money to make the movie. It was a gamble that paid off; the movie was a success and also won him an Oscar as best actor. It stands up okay; Robertson does give a good performance, most notably when he realizes that he is going to regress back to his retarded self, but it is a shade too sentimental and some parts have dated, especially the hippy sequence.

Less successful was the appalling film version of Ray Bradbury's *The Illustrated Man* (1969). It was directed by Jack Smight and the screenplay was written by one of the producers, Howard B. Kreitsek, who should have been kept away from his typewriter at gunpoint. In his book Bradbury used the device of a completely tattooed man whose tattoos come to life and tell a series of stories to a stranger the man encountered at a campsite, but this device doesn't work in the movie. Only three stories from the book are used and all are effectively mangled by the producer turned mad screenwriter. Nor is there any apparent connection between the three stories, apart from the fact that Rod Steiger and Claire Bloom (his wife at the time) star in all of them. An embarrassingly pretentious movie. Ray Bradbury was unhappy with both the movie and the way he was treated

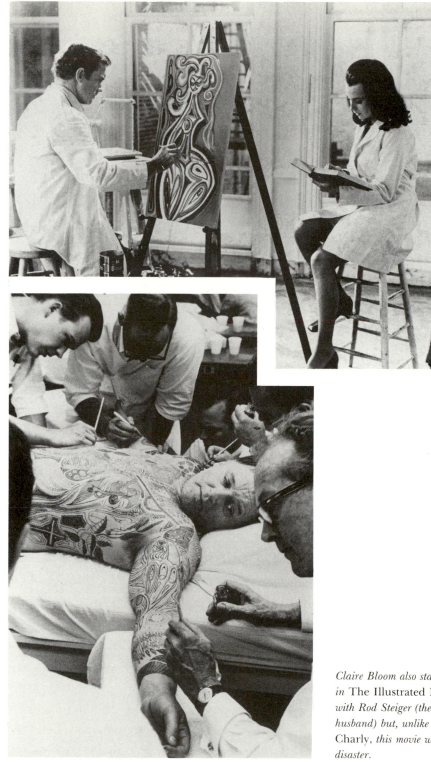

Cliff Robertson, as Charly, was supposed to be in the genius stage of his development in this scene with Claire Bloom from Charly, *though to judge from his painting he still had some way to go.*

Claire Bloom also starred in The Illustrated Man, *with Rod Steiger (then her husband) but, unlike* Charly, *this movie was a disaster.*

Two ape scientists react with astonishment in Planet of the Apes *when they discover that a Hollywood star is capable of speaking English.*

by the film-makers. 'They never talked to me. The screenplay was written by a real-estate man from New Jersey. It really was. I guess he's back there selling real estate. He never read my book, because if he'd read it he would have followed the storyline. A terrible disappointment. There was a wrap party for the movie; Rod Steiger and the director got up and introduced everyone — the cinematographer, the editor, the art director, the composer — but I was never mentioned. But what could I do? Stand up and protest? When the whole thing was over they all went off to separate parties and I wasn't invited.'[9]

Finally, the sf movie that, along with *2001*, was a big success in 1968, though I've never been able to figure out why exactly. I'm referring to *Planet of the Apes*. Based on the novel *La Planète des Singes* by Pierre Boulle, it was directed by Franklin J. Schaffner and scripted by Michael Wilson and Rod Serling. It stars Charlton Heston as an astronaut whose spaceship goes through one of those space warps that spaceships are always going through and hurtles thousands of years into the future. When he and his companions crash land on an 'alien' planet they find it to be ruled by apes while human beings, who can't speak, are treated as lowly animals. As I've pointed out before, the fact that the apes speak English should have alerted our hero to the fact that this planet wasn't an alien one, but no. We're all supposed to be as surprised as big Chuck when he comes across the ruined Statue of Liberty at the film's climax.

Schaffner was a good director and as a plain action adventure movie *Planet of the Apes* works okay. It's often quite exciting, but it wants to be more than that; it wants to be a clever allegory and a satire as well. But the allegorical and satirical elements are so obvious and heavy-handed they set my teeth on edge. Of course, this movie was nothing as bad as the four sequels that followed, not to mention the television series.

But I guess it's mainly because the fact that the apes speak English is so calmly taken for granted that really annoys me. You could say that the film-makers expected you to ignore that for reasons of artistic licence but then they make language a central point of the story by having the apes react with surprise when Charlton Heston first manages to speak (he had lost his voice for much of the movie). But then maybe it's all another side-effect of my defective, poverty-stricken sense of wonder.

From dystopia to Disneyland: the seventies

Science fiction movies continued to proliferate in the early seventies though it couldn't properly be described as a 'boom'. As in the late sixties they covered an eclectic range of subjects but what was unusual was the almost entire absence of movies set in space. One would have thought that *2001* would have been a major influence on film-makers but no doubt they were daunted by the scale of Kubrick's achievement, not to mention its cost. One exception was *Silent Running* (1972), which was directed by one of the effects supervisors on *2001*, Douglas Trumbull, who produced some impressive visuals on a relatively small budget but wasted them on a lousy script (see Chapter Ten). It would take time for *2001*'s influence to percolate through Hollywood, and when it finally manifested itself in 1977 the result was a vastly different kind of space movie, but one that lit the fuse of a real sf movie boom. It was *Star Wars*. The man responsible would be George Lucas but back in 1970 he made a very different kind of sf movie — *THX 1138*.

The one thing that many of the sf movies of the first half of the seventies had in common was that they were set in very bleak future worlds. *THX 1138*, a more futuristic, technology orientated version of Orwell's *1984*, was typical of a trend that included *Colossus: The Forbin Project* (1970 — see Chapter Eleven), *The Omega Man* (1971), *A Clockwork Orange* (1971), the laughable *Zero Population Growth* (1971), the equally laughable *No Blade of Grass* (1970), *Soylent Green* (1973), *Zardoz* (1973), *A Boy and His Dog* (1975),

The young George Lucas, on the 'all-white' set, during the making of THX 1138.

The Final Programme (1975), *Rollerball* (1975) and *Logan's Run* (1976). Even *Silent Running*, an early example of a green sf movie, is set in a grim future world, though we never actually see it. There were a few sf movies made during this period that didn't fit into the dystopian category but not that many: *The Andromeda Strain* (1971) about an invasion by a virus from outer space (see Chapter Thirteen); *Westworld* (1973) concerning rebellious robots (Chapter Eleven); *The Stepford Wives* (1975) about women being replaced by robots (Chapter Eleven); *Dark Star* (1975) a black space comedy (Chapter Ten); *The Man Who Fell to Earth* (1976) in which David Bowie plays a spaced-out E.T. (Chapter Twelve) and *Demon Seed* (1977) about a computer wanting Julie Christie to have his baby (Chapter Eleven).

THX 1138 didn't overly impress me when I first saw it but subsequent viewings have led me to appreciate it more. Even so, for all its technical brilliance, it's still something of a hard slog for much of its running time.

Maggie McOmie as LUH and Robert Duvall as THX have just discovered sex in this scene from THX 1138.

Lucas too effectively creates a grim, emotionless, subterranean world where individuality and sexual intercourse are crimes. It's also interesting that Lucas cannot maintain the grim *1984* tone throughout the movie; two-thirds of the way through it changes gear and almost becomes a comedy-chase movie with the protagonist THX (Robert Duvall) escaping from the 'white prison' with his companion, a black man who is actually a hologram (nice touch, this) and outrunning, outdriving and outwitting his robot pursuers (a precursor to *Star Wars* is the fun Lucas has with the robots). And unlike Winston Smith in *1984* THX succeeds in escaping from the system, though where he escapes to is somewhat unclear. Despite the upbeat mood in the last third and a happy ending, the audiences stayed away in their droves. Lucas, with justification, blamed the studio, Warner Brothers. Francis Ford Coppola had made a deal with Warner where they would back his company, American Zoetrope, for five or six pictures and *THX 1138* was the first project in the package to go into production, but Warner didn't like the rough cut and they didn't like any of the other scripts that were in development, including one called *Apocalypse Now*. They pulled the financial plug on Coppola, making him pay for everything himself (which plunged him into a financial crisis), recut *THX 1138* ('ruining it' in the process, according to Lucas) and sort of let it escape without any publicity or promotion. It was not an auspicious beginning for the film-maker who was to shake Hollywood to its twisted roots.

Another movie that was little seen at the time of its release (and never again since then) is *Zero Population Growth* (also known as *Z.P.G.*), something for which its cast, which includes Oliver Reed, Geraldine Chaplin and Diane Cilento, must be truly thankful. It's set in the twenty-first century where the air pollution is so bad that a yellow smog covers the whole planet (which is a big saving on sets) and so great is the over-population that all births have been banned for thirty years. People who disobey this law are 'publicly' executed by having a glass dome lowered over them. The dome is then sprayed with black paint and those inside are left to die of suffocation. Why the black paint if the execution is supposed to be public? Because it's necessary to the plot, as you'll see.

Ollie Reed and Chaplin play a couple who are dissatisfied with the state-provided alternative to real children — horrible-looking dolls that stagger around croaking 'Momma . . . Dadda . . .' — and decide to have a secret baby. After a DIY course in obstetrics Reed delivers the baby himself and they successfully keep it hidden for a time until a neighbour shops them. Aha, but Ollie cleverly arranges for them to be standing over a manhole cover when their death dome is lowered on them and he and family escape by rubber raft down a sewer to freedom (but where?). Hence the reason for the black paint sprayed on the dome, otherwise someone might have spotted Ollie and Co. escaping. This is what is called clever plotting. The script — we name the guilty men — was by Max Ehrlich and Frank DeFelitta, though DeFelitta put the blame on the director, Michael Campus, claiming that he hired an English screenwriter to rewrite their script with the result that 'their serious story on overpopulation became comedic.'[1] Oh, sure. One other thing, the term 'zero population growth' means the birth rate matches the death rate and the population figures remain stable; by banning all births for thirty years the population would shrink. By rights, the film should have been called *Zero Population*.

An equally inane movie about an ecological disaster is *No Blade of Grass*, directed in 1970 by the former film star Cornel Wilde and based on the excellent novel by John Christopher, *The Death of Grass*. In the novel the catastrophe that wipes out the world's cereal crops is caused by a mutated virus but in the film it is all due to chemical pollution. The film vaguely follows the plot of the novel, concentrating on one family's desperate journey across a Britain that is collapsing into anarchy, led by the quick-thinking father (Nigel Davenport) who had foreseen the disaster. With its suggestion that the fall of civilization tends to bring out the worst in people and that qualities like compassion and altruism had better be put into mothballs until more comfortable times return, the film is similar to *Panic in the Year Zero* (see Chapter Seven). However, Ray Milland, another actor, did a much better job at directing his apocalyptic tale than does Wilde; *No Blade of Grass* is crudely handled and disjointed. Last-minute cuts by the distributor were blamed for this but as one critic observed at the time: 'The mood changes violently from one scene to another, the visual quality and the colour clash from shot to shot as though it had been photographed by different crews, and the actors seem unsure of what kind of film they are supposed to be in.' Exactly. It gives the impression of being a very amateur movie. Wilde's heart may have been in the right place but his cameras weren't.

Stanley Kubrick's contribution to the dystopian trend was *A Clockwork Orange* (1971), his controversial film version of Anthony Burgess's novel. Malcolm McDowell starred as Alex, a teenage thug in a vaguely futuristic Britain, who is turned off his violent way of life by an extreme form of aversion therapy, thus becoming the 'clockwork orange' of the title. The novel is a social, political and religious allegory, Burgess's main point being that everyone must have the freedom to choose between good and evil and that it is an even greater wrong to remove the choice from a person like Alex than it is to let him continue his violent way of life. Burgess, a devout Roman Catholic, is reworking the old Frankenstein theme in warning that Man should not compete with God. He is also saying that it is just as wrong, in God's eyes, to unmake a monster as it is to make one.

'There are some things Man was not meant to know,' is the somewhat less-than-original message of the novel. The message of the movie is less clear, thought it's certain that Kubrick is not endorsing Burgess's Christian tone. It may be doing Kubrick a disservice to suggest that he was attracted to the novel not by its philosophical and theological stance but because he saw the cinematic potential of the story. And no doubt the important part that classical music plays in the novel also attracted him. Alex is obsessed with the music of Beethoven which he associates with images of violence, sadism and sexual lust; later Beethoven becomes linked to his aversion therapy. Just what Kubrick is saying in his movie of *A Clockwork Orange* may not be clear but it is definitely an electrifying visual and emotional experience. As with *2001* many scenes were given greater impact by being juxtaposed with music that contrasted wildly with their visual content, such as Rossini's 'The Thieving Magpie' as the accompanying background for an attempted rape scene and subsequent rumble between two gangs.

The film's violence was the cause of the controversy. The fact that the acts of violence that Alex and his 'droogs' carry out is motiveless is probably the prime reason it created such a furore. Motiveless violence is profoundly unsettling and here was a movie that appeared to be glorifying it. After all, Alex is the protagonist and we end up feeling sympathetic towards him after his aversion treatment. And the film, and we along with it, does celebrate the restoration of Alex's evil ways at the climax. The British tabloid press, in its usual hysterical way, was very quickly producing examples of copy-cat violence committed by teenagers who had seen the movie. And it wasn't just in Britain. 'The trouble for me arose in America where I was living when the film was released,' said Burgess in a 1989 interview. 'I received telephone calls from people who reported mayhem, violence and rape and asking did I feel responsible for this. I said no, I'm not responsible for mankind's inherent sinfulness. All I've just done is reflect it . . . When I first saw the film in private with Kubrick standing behind me I was a bit shocked. I thought some of the violence was a bit overt but it didn't really worry me too much then. When I went to see the film on its first public appearance in New York the people on the door wouldn't let me in . . . they said I was too old. After having to persuade them that I wrote the damn thing I found it really quite frightening because the cinema was full of blacks standing up and shouting "right on man" because they refused to see anything beyond a glorification of violence.'[2]

The movie may not glorify violence but it certainly glamorizes it. Kubrick's defenders during the controversy (as far as I know Kubrick himself didn't make any public statement about the film) said that because the violence was so stylized it was distanced from the viewer. But as Alexander Walker wrote in his book on Kubrick, *Stanley Kubrick Directs*: 'The assaults on the writer and his wife, Mr and Mrs Alexander, are themselves gruesome and believable acts. But Kubrick's rapid-fire editing at once embodies the surprise of each asssault and confines its depiction to fleeting essentials. Again, it is treated like a masque or, perhaps, a plebeian rather than a courtly entertainment this time, since the note is that of vaudeville farce and aggressively Pop. The wife is first stripped of her red jumpsuit. Like the sadistic child he basically is, Alex goes for the mammaries first, slicing off the garment's elasticized material to expose the breasts before cutting the fabric up lengthwise in a Jack-the-Ripper parody. He then launches into a Gene Kelly take-off, soft-shoe shuffling through "Singin in the Rain" while putting a very unsoft boot into the writer's ribs at every cadence. Anyone who winces at the supposedly comic sadism of circus clowns will recognize how, in this scene, Kubrick has turned the frightening realities of domestic invasion, rape and assault into an experience akin to that of "entertainment". The horror of it still comes through — it is one of the most unsettling scenes in modern cinema — and to say it is "distanced" from us is simply to use a fashionable term from the hollow vocabulary of critical hip. But the violence does not gratify; on the contrary, it repels.'[3]

That sequence is indeed repulsive but much of Alex's reign of anarchy is positively exhilarating — I certainly found it so when I first saw the movie nearly twenty years ago. In particular I single out the fight between the two gangs, the joyride along the country road and Alex's slow-motion attack on his rebellious gang members, because it is so impeccably filmed by Kubrick. Does this make the film dangerous? Possibly, but I can only speak for myself and say that my first viewing of the film, and subsequent ones, did not inspire me to go off on sprees of mayhem and murder. No movie ever has, though I admit images of violence — cinema violence, unreal violence — excite me. Advocates of censorship inevitably say that they want a particular film, novel, painting, TV programme or comic book banned because of the effect it will have on *other* people; they presumably consider themselves immune from any exterior influence. I'm no advocate of censorship so, naturally, I don't think *A Clockwork Orange* should be banned. In spite of my ambiguous attiude towards its violence I think it's a great piece of film-making. But alas, in an odd act for a film-maker, Kubrick himself has banned it in the United Kingdom. I believe he should reconsider this decision so that people in this country will no longer have

Malcolm McDowell as Alex in Kubrick's A Clockwork Orange.

to view it on shoddy pirate video copies (as I had to only recently).

And for all his reservations about the media fall-out from the movie and its effect on his life, Anthony Burgess still stands by *A Clockwork Orange*: 'I thought the film was extremely well made; in its own way it's probably a classic, though one which is denied British audiences.'[4]

Author Richard Matheson had no such supportive thoughts for *The Omega Man*, a 1971 movie based on his novel, *I Am Legend*. Much of Matheson's work deals with paranoia and none more so than this novel, which is about one lone man whose fortified house is surrounded by vampires every night. They call him by name and demand he come outside. They know his name because they're all his former neighbours. During the safe daylight hours he emerges from the house and tracks the sleeping vampires to their hiding places and stakes them through the heart. The twist in Matheson's novel is that they're not real vampires, but victims of a post-world war plague that produces vampire-like characteristics. Finally the man is captured by the surviving vampires who tell him that they represent the new race that will inherit the planet and that he is now the aberration in the scheme of things, the 'vampire' who must be destroyed for the common good.

Little of this superior horror novel remains in *The Omega Man*, which was directed by Boris Sagal and scripted by John and Joyce Corrington. The vampire element, so crucial to the novel, is missing and instead the lone man, played by Charlton Heston (in full macho mode) is hounded each night by a group of hooded albinos who appear to be suffering from terminal eczema. This was the second time the novel was filmed, the first being a Robert L. Lippert production made in Italy in 1964 under the title *The Last Man on Earth*. Said Matheson: 'The first one was very poorly done but at least it followed the book. *The Omega Man* bore no resemblance to my book so I can't comment on it. I don't know why they bothered really.'[5]

Science fiction writer Harry Harrison was much happier with Richard Fleischer's version of his grim novel about over-population, *Make Room! Make Room!* Scripted by Stanley R. Greenberg, *Soylent Green* (1973) preserved much of the novel's grimness in its depiction of a horribly overpopulated New York City in 2022 but makes the foreground action determinedly more upbeat and action-packed. Charlton Heston (this was the peak of his sf period) stars as Thorn, the cynical cop who is investigating the death of a government official (Joseph Cotton); Leigh

Harry Harrison's novel Make Room! Make Room! *got the Hollywood treatment when it was turned into the movie* Soylent Green.

Taylor Young is the dead man's paid lover (she is referred to as 'furniture' because she comes with the apartment) who becomes involved with Thorn; and Edward G. Robinson, in his last screen role, plays Thorn's aging room-mate who remembers the way the world used to be. A major difference from the novel was the conspiracy that Thorn uncovers about the true nature of the artificial food known as 'soylent green'. 'Soylent Green is people!' screams the badly wounded Thorn as he's carried away at the end of the movie.

'I heard later,' Harrison said, 'that it was all Heston's doing that the film ever got made. He'd read the book and had been trying for five years to set it up. He got the producer, Walter Seltzer, involved in the project and they both kept trying. The size of the budget was one of the problems — it was almost $4,000,000 — and MGM, the studio they were both working for, would not do it. But they persisted, they invested a good deal of their own money and had a screenplay written and drawings made but the MGM chiefs kept saying that they didn't think the subject of overpopulation was important enough. So when they came up with the plot twist of cannibalism MGM finally decided it was a viable theme for a film — which gives you some idea of how the film industry thinks! Overall, I was happy with the way the film turned out, given the screenplay, and such things as the "furniture" girls, which should have been thrown away because it was just nonsense. The ending was cornball too but everyone likes to see blood so I suppose it was a wise move on their part.'[6]

It is interesting to contrast Harrison's comments with those of the film's director. 'The story of *Soylent Green* concerned one of my favourite topics really — the pollution of the environment, what's happening to us and what will happen to us. It's a look into the future but I don't consider it science fiction — it's science fact [uh oh!]. It was a bit of a commercial risk to show the future as grim and depressing, but I don't think you can honestly show how wonderful the future is going to be when you know how terrible it will be. There are a lot of things in the film that I like — what it has to say about police corruption, for instance, which in the film has been so commonplace it's no longer looked upon as corruption but part of their daily routine. When the Chuck Heston character goes to see his superior he's asked, "What did you take from the apartment?" And he says, "Everything I could lay my hands on." And then he shares out the loot with his chief. Another thing I find interesting about the film is that it presumes a backlash against Women's Lib has taken place in the intervening years as the women in that society no longer have any status or power — they're simply referred to as "furniture". The suggestion is that women are going to have to endure the worst role they've ever had in history due to the overpopulation.[7] Of course, he's referring to Western women here; women in Third World countries were enduring such roles at the time of the film's making and still are. In fact people living in many Third World countries experience a more distressing way of life than that shown in the movie, but this was probably why the movie had such an effect on American audiences — it was the horror of the idea of America turning into a Third World country.

Michael Moorcock was far from happy with the film version of his novel *The Final Programme* (in the US the title was changed to *The Last Days of Man on Earth*, obviously by someone with a knack for devising pithy titles). It was made in 1974 and written and directed by Robert Fuest, a former set designer who is best known for directing the *Dr Phibes* movies, and features one of Moorcock's most famous creations, Jerry Cornelius, the multi-faceted, multi-purpose character who embodies many of the prevalent myths of the late twentieth century. He's rich, he's a rock star, a mercenary, a mystic, a secret agent, a Christ figure and many other things beside. The movie fails totally to capture this essential ambivalence, and while it does occasionally succeed in suggesting a world where reality is crumbling at the edges, and has some nice sets, it is basically incoherent. It does, however, sort of follow the plot of the novel. Cornelius's father has died, leaving behind some hidden microfilm on which is the mysterious 'final programme' which has great significance for humanity. Apart from Cornelius (Jon Finch) there are others hunting for the film, including his evil brother Frank (Derrick O'Connor) who has kidnapped their sister Catharine (whom Cornelius loves in a way that exceeds brotherly affection), and the awesome Miss Brunner (Jenny Runacre) who has a tendency to totally consume her lovers, bones and all. In the novel the 'final programme' serves to combine Cornelius and Miss Brunner into a single creature, a bisexual Messiah who leads the entire population of Europe into the Mediterranean and oblivion but the film's ending is somewhat less ambitious: their combined bodies form a shaggy Neanderthal who winks

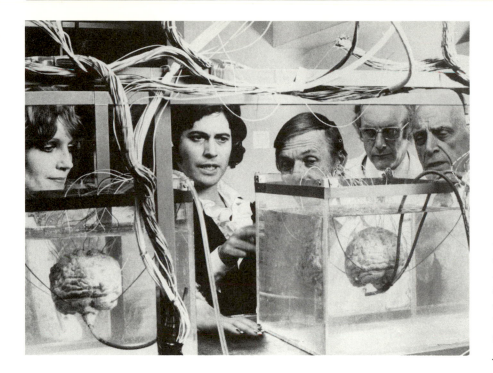

Michael Moorcock would have even preferred the Hollywood treatment rather than what British film-makers did to his novel The Final Programme *in this version that starred Jon Finch (centre).*

into the camera and does a Humphrey Bogart imitation.

Moorcock had rewritten Fuest's script at the behest of the producers but the script that Fuest shot was Fuest's. 'There's something absolutely terrible about a bad version of your stuff,' said Moorcock, 'and it affected me very, very badly and quite fundamentally for a long time. When I saw it I sat there willing it to be better but the strain of watching it was just too much. There were one or two sequences involving scientific explanations which, when I first saw them, I literally laughed aloud, they were so ridiculous. As for the ending, it would have been all right in a TV sketch. There's nothing wrong with the idea but it had nothing to do with the rest of the picture. Fuest was doing his best to shore it all up by sending up everything that had happened before because there was no sort of fundamental logic to the structure of the film.

'I didn't want the film to do well. I knew it wouldn't do well. I mean, my faith in the British public would have been badly shattered if it had done well. So I was glad it did badly but in a way I was also very bitter because they'd bought the rights to the sequels and obviously no one is going to film the sequels after that one was such a disaster. But the thing is that they'd be very different films. It's possible to interpret *The Final Programme* in very trendy, daft terms in the way that Fuest did but you're less and less able to do that with the later books.'[8]

Another sf film made that year ended with two of the characters being transformed into a new form of life that ushers in the apocalypse for the human race. At least, I think that's what happens. The movie, *Phase IV*, looks great but, like *The Final Programme*, is very confusing. It was directed by Saul Bass who had previously specialized in shooting credit sequences (*Walk on the Wild Side* and *Psycho* are two examples), so it's not surprising the movie is visually impressive (the art director was John Barry, who later designed the sets for the first two *Star Wars* movies). But the script, by Mayo Simon (who was involved in the writing of two other sf duds, *Marooned* and *Futureworld*), is a disaster. It's all about a species of ants in the desert of Arizona that has acquired intelligence, presumably because of some alien influence from outer space, and has forced the local human inhabitants to flee. A scientist, Hubbs (Nigel Davenport) and his assistant (Michael Murphy) set up a base in the desert to study the phenomenon. They are later joined by a young girl (played by the future Mrs Peter Sellers, Lynne Frederick, here doing a good imitation of a block of wood). Hubbs turns out to be a typical movie scientist, i.e., he's a test-tube short of a full set and starts acting like Captain Ahab on a bad day. Instead of studying the ants he declares war on them, but they outwit him at every turn and end up eating him. His assistant and the girl undergo some sort of mystical transformation at the hands of the unseen aliens, and at a direct nod to *2001*, the film originally ended with a four-minute long montage of surreal imagery but this was cut by the distributor. I later saw this montage on its own — it wouldn't have helped the movie but it is very pretty. *Phase IV* is one of those science fiction movies, of which there are too many examples, made by people who know nothing about science or sf — the result is a kind of mock-up of a science fiction movie.

And then there are those sf movies that are simply loony. John Boorman made such a movie that same year called *Zardoz*. It is also a very pretentious and po-faced film. Boorman is a good director and when he makes movies based on good novels he makes good movies (*Point Blank*, *Deliverance*), but when he makes movies from ideas of his own he makes movies like *Zardoz*. It is set in the year 2293, years after the Great Collapse of Civilization, and the world is divided into two regions, the Vortex and the Outlands,

A scene from Phase IV, *one of many sf film projects that should never have got past the 'let's have lunch and discuss it' stage.*

Zardoz, *a great-looking sf movie that, alas, had a script of breathtaking banality.*

separated by an impenetrable force-field. Within the Vortex live the Eternals, immortal and decadent, while in the Outlands live the Brutals, who are ruled by the Exterminators who in turn are controlled by a giant, flying stone head which represents their god, Zardoz (Wizard of Oz, geddit?). An Exterminator, Zed (Sean Connery) manages to enter the Vortex where his earthy, macho presence causes consternation among the Immortals, a wishy-washy bunch who spend most of their time running around in coloured underwear. Despite their attempts to tame Zed, he succeeds in destroying the computer, called the Tabernacle, that controls and sustains the Vortex, and brings their society to an end. The

Exterminators swarm in and massacre everyone, leaving Zed to escape with a reformed female Immortal, Consuela (Charlotte Rampling), to a cave where they grow old together at high speed and we last see them sitting together as skeletons (this could be Boorman's nod to the end of *2001*, and then again, maybe not).

Boorman's message in this good-looking (it was shot in Ireland) but inane movie is a familiar one: science is Evil, Nature is Good. Zed represents the Primal Force that brings back to the Immortals basic human experiences such as Fear, Hate, Love, Sex and Death (and, no doubt, Wholemeal Bread as well), thus releasing them from their static, impotent way of life and allowing them to become part of the Natural Order of Things once again; i.e., Dead. Unfortunately for Boorman he overlooked another powerful force — the Audience, which left his movie a pitiful and bleeding thing at the feet of the great god known as the Box Office.

A movie set in another post-apocalyptic setting, *The Ultimate Warrior* (1975) hasn't a pretentious bone in its body. It's a simple tale about the conflict between two groups of survivors in the wreckage of civilization, rather like *Mad Max 2* without the vehicles. One group are the Good Guys (well, goodish) who live in a fortified enclosure in an empty city and try to maintain some civilized standards while the Bad Guys (who are very bad) are a bunch of thugs who keep preying on the Good Guys whenever they leave their refuge to forage for cans of food. So the Good Guys hire Yul Brynner, a kind of super-samurai character, to act as their protector. He's so good at knocking off Bad Guys that several of the Good Guys get nervous and turn against him. When the leader of the Good Guys, the Baron (Max Von Sydow), is killed by his own people, Yul heads off, with the Baron's pregnant daughter in tow, in an attempt to escape via the city's subway tunnels. They are pursued by the surviving Bad Guys, but despite the girl choosing an awkward moment to give birth, and Yul having to chop off his own hand to avoid being dragged to his death, they survive and reach an island sanctuary. Apparently Warner Brothers had big plans for this movie — it was originally called *The Baron* — but something went wrong along the way. If it was intended to be a serious and prestigious project it seems odd that Warner hired the director of the Bruce Lee epic *Enter the Dragon* to write and direct it. It's not surprising they ended up with the first and only kung fu sf movie. I must admit I enjoyed it when

I first saw it but I suppose it's really only a mediocre piece of work.

A similar, but more successful, world of chaos, anarchy and violence, and another movie that clearly inspired the makers of the *Mad Max* series, is featured in *A Boy and His Dog* (1975), written and directed by L.Q. Jones and based on the novella by Harlon Ellison, science fiction's shyest writer. Set in 2024 after a nuclear war has done the usual job on the environment, it concerns the adventures of a young man, Vic (Don Johnson) and his dog, Blood (Tiger). Blood is a mutation and at least as intelligent as the average human. He's certainly more intelligent than Vic with whom he has a telepathic link. Much of the entertainment in the earlier sections of the movie is the telepathic conversations between thick Vic and the laconic and cynical Blood as they search the desolate landscape for food and women, two commodities in short supply. At a makeshift cinema Blood picks up the scent of a woman disguised as a man . . .

They pursue her, Vic's intention being rape but when she is cornered she offers herself to him freely. In reality she is bait from an underground community who desperately need a fertile stud. Against Blood's advice Vic follows the girl, Quilla (Susanne Benton), down below and the movie makes a sudden change in gears. Compared to the gritty realism of life on the surface the underground community is presented in a very stylized way. There's a whole town down there, complete with houses and parks and the people, acting as if the old world still exists, maintain lives of exaggerated gentility. It doesn't work very well and Ellison admitted as much: 'It's my fault, it's not an inadequacy on L.Q. Jones's part. I didn't really create a down-under section that was realistic. I did a kind of papier-mâché Disneyland because I wanted to poke fun at the middle classes.'[9] This section also suffers from the absence of Blood because he's obviously the best thing in the movie. Anyway, when Vic learns that he's going to be hooked up to a milking machine instead of getting to service the town's young ladies in person he's less than happy. After a change of heart Quilla helps him to escape and they return to the surface where the faithful Blood has almost starved to death.

Cut. Blood is eating. There's no sign of Quilla. Says Blood, 'You haven't eaten a bite . . . I really appreciate this . . . if not a particularly good taste . . .' Then Vic and Blood stroll off into the sunset together, with Vic telling the audience that, '. . . after all, a dog is a boy's best friend.' Yup,

Quilla has become pet-food. Feminists have called this ending ideologically unsound, and some have gone as far as to say that both novella and film are misogynistic, an accusation Ellison hotly denies. Anyway, *A Boy and His Dog* is a rare example of a faithful movie version of an sf writer's work.

Rollerball (1975) is an example of a short story (by William Harrison) stretched out to feature film length. The strain shows in Norman Jewison's slick but empty production. As usual with sf films based around a single idea, much of the two hours of *Rollerball*'s running time consists of padding and fake profundity. The single idea, which is not new, is to transport the gladiatorial arena of ancient Rome to the future. Instead of men fighting each other with swords, tridents or spiked gloves we have men fighting each other with just spiked gloves while on *roller-skates*. Wow. The Corporations which rule this typically over-simplified future world have devised the game as a means of keeping the population under control, the belief being that if people can watch men on skates beating each other up on television then they won't want to indulge in any awkward political activity. The scheme goes wrong when one of the rollerball champs, Jonathon (James Caan), is so successful at the game that he becomes a cult hero throughout the world. Fearful of this dangerous display of individual-

James Caan (left) as a roller-skating gladiator in Rollerball.

ity the Corporations attempt to eliminate him by making the game increasingly dangerous by abolishing the rules. He survives, however, and the film ends with him alone and triumphant on a body-littered track while the Corporations, represented by a haughty John Houseman, gnash their corporate teeth in frustration.

The rollerball sequences are well-staged and exciting to watch but off the track the film is slow and pretentious. We learn very little of this future world apart from the fact that the Corporations have abolished all individual nations (neat trick) and that war, poverty and disease no longer exist (more neat tricks). Jonathan's token effort for information about the past only leads him to Sir Ralph Richardson doing an amusing cameo as the caretaker of a broken-down computer in which all historical records have been stored. The computer, called Zero, keeps wiping its memory banks by mistake and isn't much help. ('We've just lost the thirteenth century,' murmurs Richardson. 'Oh well, there was only Dante and a few corrupt Popes.') As a result the events in the film are left suspended in a cultural and social limbo. According to Jewison his intention with the movie was to issue a warning about the growing violence in spectator sports and how this caters to the baser instincts of the spectators. Seems to have worked, Norm, we're a decade and a half further on and the level of violence in spectator sports doesn't seem to have risen by any appreciable amount. Guess this proves that sf movies do serve a positive social purpose.

By 1976 the sf community was abuzz with the news that a real boom in sf movies was about to break as it seemed that every film producer and his cousin had an sf project in development. Then, surrounded with hype, came *Logan's Run*, a joint production between MGM and United Artists, and as *Cinefantastique* magazine commented, 'The science fiction boom begins with a bomb.'[10] A bomb indeed. It was based on the 1967 novel by William F. Nolan and George Clayton Johnson which, unusual for an sf novel in those days, got a lot of critical praise from mainstream critics and was a bestseller. This was because Bantam didn't publish it as an sf book but as a kind of literary 'event'. Nolan and Johnson had planned it that way, and also, from the start, planned it to be a movie. 'We wrote the whole book almost as a scenario for a movie,' said Johnson at the time of the film's release, 'because that was our goal, to sell the story as a book first, as a lever to get it made into a movie later. So we planned from the outset to sell it as a literary work, not genre sf. We subtitled it a "Pop-Op" novel, which capitalized on the trend for Pop Art at the time.'[11] Stage two seemed to be working back in 1968 when MGM bought the rights on the advice of George Pal who intended to make the movie. But management shake-ups at the studio caused the project to be put on hold for several years. Ironically, the producer who was finally put in charge of it, Saul David (producer of *Fantastic Voyage*), had rejected the novel when he had been an executive at Bantam Books! Not surprisingly, the movie he wanted to make was not the movie of the novel. As the screenwriter, David Zelag Goodman, said, 'Saul David had a vision of the film which was quite specific . . . the material was shaped to fit us, rather than we to the material.'[12] And is the reason why they ended up with a crappy movie.

The novel was a celebration of sf and its clichés. Though set in a dystopia where the young rule the world and everyone at the age of twenty-one must enter a Sleepshop to die, it's bascially a romp, a fast-moving chase adventure that moves from one outlandish set-piece to another. Okay, it may have dated now, as it was very much a sixties artefact, but when I read it at the time it was great fun. You can't say this about the movie. It is not fun. It is not a romp. It does not celebrate the clichés of sf but presents them as new inventions, proudly trotting them out to amaze us with their cleverness. Maybe to Saul David and David Z. Goodman they did appear to be new ideas. To quote from *Cinefantastique* magazine again on the movie, 'Science fiction gets raped again.'[13]

In the novel the action roves right across the world but in the movie is mainly localized within a domed city. It is 2274 and this is all that remains of the human race after nuclear war. As natural resources are scarce the inevitable super-computer running the place has decided that no one can live past the age of thirty. To disguise the grim reality a device called the Carousel disintegrates the thirty-year-olds in a colourful display of lights. People enter the carousel willingly because they've been told that the process is a form of life-renewal. Those who find this explanation unsatisfactory and take off for the hills, as 'runners', are tracked and hunted by government executioners called Sandmen. Michael York stars as Logan, a nice Sandman (a long opening sequence showing him chasing and killing a runner was cut from the film). As someone pointed out at the time, the Sandmen know that the Carousel is a big con, so what

Jenny Agutter and Michael York, the two British stars of the terrible Logan's Run.

happens to them when they turn thirty? Is there a secret retirement home for Sandmen? This is typical of the screenplay's lack of logic.

Nice Mike is ordered by the computer to pretend to be a runner in order to discover the truth about Sanctuary, the place all the runners head for. Chased by his former Sandmen colleagues, he gets involved with Jessica (nice Jenny Agutter) who is helping runners to escape. After various stunningly predictable adventures they end up at a vine-covered city which we recognize to be Washington DC in a bad state of repair. And Sanctuary turns out to be a myth. All they find is Peter Ustinov, also in a bad state of repair, and a lot of pussy cats. As he is the first old person they have ever seen they take him back to the city to prove to the others that you don't have to die at thirty but can instead grow old, wrinkled and senile. Everyone seems happy at getting this dubious news and, after Logan has zapped the computer with his blaster causing it to blow itself up along with most of the city, they all go outside to start a new, natural life. Seems there was no reason for them to be living in the domes in the first place, the atomic radiation having evaporated or something.

This is a typical sf movie made by people who care nothing for science fiction, and is pushing the same simplistic message of another such sf movie, *Zardoz*: Technology equals Bad, Nature equals Good. It looks and feels like an old-fashioned movie too, and despite a budget of over $9,000,000 the visual effects aren't very convincing. The domed city, for example, never appears to be anything other than a miniature. To add to the film's troubles, it was directed by Michael Anderson. I feel him to be one of cinema's dreariest of directors and his long and successful career in the industry is a complete mystery to me.

Back in 1981 I had the pleasure of interviewing Jenny Agutter and asked about her experiences during the making of *Logan's Run*. 'That was such a big production that you weren't involved with the crew in any way. You tend to get cut off in pictures that big. There were eight different sound stages being worked on at any one time and that went on for three to four months. I tended to lose the idea of what it was we were making. We shot such tiny sections at a time — you came on and did your bit on some huge set and then went back to your dressing room and had a long wait until they were ready for you again. I wasn't exactly stretched as an actress. On the other hand, it was fun to work on such amazing sets. We got to play with a lot of mechanical toys and props like those little trains, and it was fun filming in those futuristic buildings in Dallas and Fort Worth, though a lot of the time we were working with blue screens and having to react to wonderful scenery that wasn't there.'[14]

Despite being an expensive piece of unimaginative, badly directed rubbish, *Logan's Run* was popular with audiences and, as they say, grossed over $2.5 million within five days of its release. It proved that, unlike the fifties, there was now a large cinema audience eager for sf movies. The next year was to bear out this fact.

1977 was the year of *Star Wars*.

I'd known about *Star Wars* for some time. I mean, like other people with either an interest in the cinema or sf, I'd read that George Lucas was making a big-budget space opera called *Star Wars* for Twentieth Century Fox, but that was all I knew. Even after sneaking into one of the sound stages during a visit to the EMI studio in Elstree where the movie was being shot in the summer of 1976, I was none the wiser. All I could see were the exteriors of lots of wooden tunnels and nothing else, which wasn't very impressive (with hindsight, these probably contained the corridors of the Death Star). And even when I saw a trailer for the movie at an sf convention I wasn't very impressed. Nor were the rest of the audience who all laughed when the trailer ended with a squat little robot falling on its face. The trailer, of course, was without optical effects and also consisted just of interior sequences and gave no idea of the scope of the finished movie.

By the time of the first preview screening in London I was still prepared to be severely disappointed. The movie began. 'A long time ago in a galaxy, far far away . . .' appeared followed by the film's title exploding on the screen, accompanied by the burst of theme music and then the words of the prologue slowly rolling off into infinity. The music quietens, the camera pans down the surface of a planet and a spaceship appears in shot from the top of the screen. It's okay, I thought, but I've seen just as good on 'Space 1999' on TV, Lucas is going to have to do better than this. And he did. Following the smaller ship, and firing at it, is another one. We see its bow, then more of it, and more, and more, and more until that giant mother is filling the screen. The preview audience applauded, as I did. After that opening shot Lucas had us in the palm of his hand.

Okay, I got a bit worried shortly afterwards when, during the firefight between the ship's defenders and the invading Imperial stormtroopers, the two robots do the gag where they walk right through the fire-path unscathed. In fact, I wasn't too happy about the two robots at all, but for the most part I remained transfixed throughout the rest of the movie. It looked — almost — as good as *2001* but it was a riproaring space opera. Images that I'd previously seen only on the covers of sf magazines or comics paraded by one by one up there on the big screen. As I've mentioned elsewhere, it was a similar feeling to the one I experienced when watching *Forbidden Planet* for the first time. 'Someone's done it right at last,' I told myself. Then, afterwards, on the way out of the cinema I encountered John Baxter. 'I loved it!' I enthused, 'What did you think?'

'God, it was so *mindless*,' said Baxter. I was a bit miffed at him bringing me down like that but, on reflection, I had to admit he was right. It was mindless. But it was fun. And still is. Alas, though, I now regard *Star Wars* to have been both a breath of fresh air for the cinema of science fiction — and the potential kiss of death. With one bound Lucas had taken sf cinema out of the hands of adults and into the nursery where it has tended to remain ever since.

For Lucus this was a very clever move and one that made his fortune,

George Lucas had wanted to start Star Wars *on a Wookie planet but fortunately we only had to suffer one of the creatures — Chewbacca (Peter Mayhew wore the shag-pile costume).*

Princess Leia (Carrie Fisher) gives Moff Tarkin (Peter Cushing) a piece of her mind — 'I recognized your foul stench . . .' — while Darth Vader (David Prowse and the voice of James Earl Jones) ponders on the dark side of the Force in this shot from Star Wars.

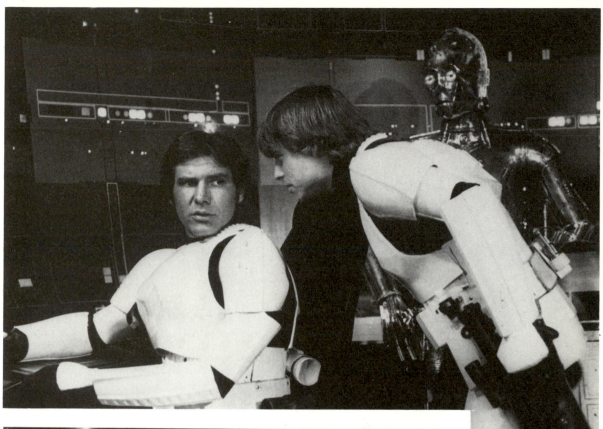

Harrison Ford as Han Solo and Mark Hamill as Luke Skywalker, with Anthony Daniels as the irritating See-Threepio in the background.

Effects supervisor on Star Wars, *John Dykstra, devised new methods for shooting miniatures.*

so no one can blame him for doing what he did. Said Lucas in a 1977 interview, 'Right after *Graffiti* I was getting this fan mail from kids that said the film changed their lives, and something inside me said, do a children's film. And everybody said, "Do a *children's* film? What are you talking about? You're crazy."'[15] But even before he made the very successful *American Graffiti* he had tried to buy the film rights to *Flash Gordon* (they were unavailable). After *Graffiti* he decided to create his own story and characters that would have the pace of the old *Flash Gordon* serials and the mood and style of Alex Raymond's comic strips. And though he went through a crash course reading science fiction he was determined that his picture would not be a science fiction one.

As Dale Pollock says in his book *Skywalking*: 'Lucas returned from the local newsstand each weekend with a large collection of science fiction magazines and comic books. Marcia [his wife at the time] wondered what was going on, but George told her not to worry, he was making a movie that ten-year-old boys would love. Lucas thought of *Star Wars* as a "tinker toy movie" set in a time that was neither future or past. It was crucial that the audience did not think it was science fiction. *THX 1138* had been hurt by Warner's sci-fi advertisng campaign [surely this is not right; I was under the impression that *THX 1138* had been hurt by the lack of any advertising campaign from Warner]. Nevertheless, he thoroughly researched the sf field from *Buck Rogers* and *Flash Gordon* to Stanley Kubrick's watershed film, *2001: A Space Odyssey*. Lucas was in awe of Kubrick's technical craftsmanship, but the movie was too obscure and downbeat for his tastes [hang on, this is the guy who made the even more downbeat *THX 1138*]. Lucas learned from Kubrick that the believability of a film set in another time and space depends on the atmosphere the writer/director creates [seems a very obvious observation for anyone to make]. Lucas thought *2001* was the ultimate sci-fi film; he had to come up with something completely different.'[16]

Well, a cynic, like myself, would say that Lucas had it both ways. Sure, the basic plot of *Star Wars* sounds like a fairy story (or *Lord of the Rings*). Farm boy sets out, in the company of a good sorcerer, a dashing outlaw and a couple of faithful servants, to rescue a beautiful princess who has been imprisoned by a bad sorcerer in his fortress. But *Star Wars* looks like a science fiction movie. It has all the ingredients of a traditional space opera

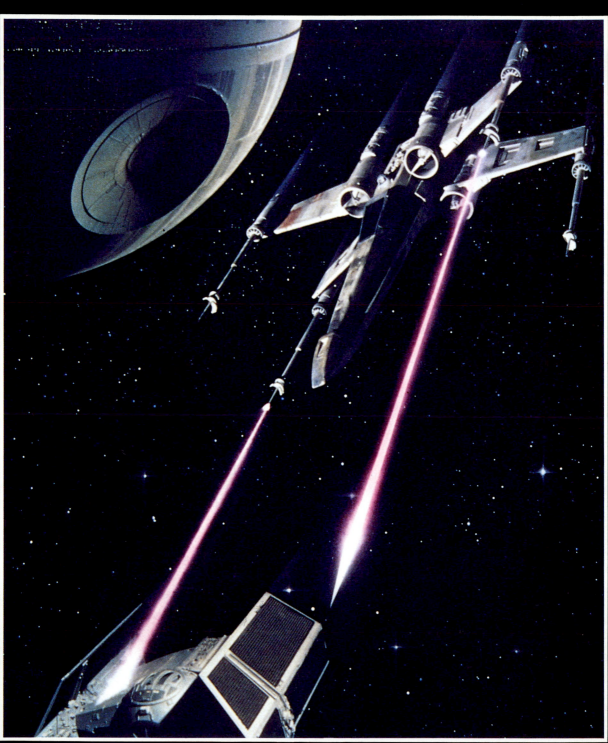

— spaceships, aliens, blasters, robots — and most of its terminology as well, like 'hyper drive' and 'tractor beam', and so to the average member of the audience *Star Wars* is science fiction. And as a result, since the success of the movie, and its sequels, science fiction has been seen, once again, as a mainly juvenile genre.

Another advantage for Lucas claiming that *Star Wars* was not sf was that he could ignore the problem of science itself. As he said, 'I had a real problem because I was afraid that science fiction buffs and everybody else would say things like "You know there's no sound in outer space." I just wanted to forget science. That would take care of itself. I didn't want to make *2001*.'[17] Yet Lucas had taken so much from sf illustrators and writers. For example, certain images in the movie seem directly based on sf magazine cover illustrations by such artists as Ed Emshwiller, John Schoenherr and Kelly Freas, and Lucas seems to have borrowed freely from Frank Herbert for his desert world at the beginning of the movie, and from Isaac Asimov for his idea of a galactic empire. As Michael Moorcock put it, somewhat more strongly, '*Star Wars* is a ramshackle collage of undigested influences which ran out of the director's control at an early stage. *Star Wars* is not so much a story as a naive compendium of other people's images used haphazardly, without grace or wit. It rips off a sub-culture and gives nothing back to it. It is an empty thing, it lacks the humour, the invention, the plot dynamics and the genuine creativity displayed in the best "Dr Who" stories . . . it is the biggest exploitation movie of them all.'[18] Well, Mike said that in 1977; he might have mellowed a bit since then. And I have to disagree with him about the humour — the film's humour is one of its saving graces (and as I loathe 'Dr Who' I can't agree with him about that either). Anyway, I wonder if Lucas would have been as successful if he had made the movie as a straight fantasy without any of the science fictional elements. I doubt it.

When I interviewed Mark Hamill some years ago he gave the official Lucas line on the movie. 'I never thought of *Star Wars* as science fiction, I thought of it as a fairy tale. One of my favourite earlier versions of the screenplay had a clever device to offset the technology of the whole thing so that audiences wouldn't think it was going to be another *2001*. It started with a helicopter shot of an enchanted forest and then they push the camera through the window of a tree and you see a mother Wookie trying to breastfeed this squealing baby Wookie and there's all this Wookie dialogue going on. She goes and points to one particular book and the baby gets all excited. She takes the book off the shelf and we see it's titled *Star Wars*. She opens the book and that's when the spaceship comes overhead and the film we know starts. Then, at the end, after we get our medals, it cuts back to the baby Wookie asleep. And the mother closes the book and puts the baby to bed, and that would have got across that it was intended to be a fairy story.' Tactfully not admitting that I thought it sounded appalling I asked him why the idea had been abandoned. 'Well, you have to go back to 1976 when we were going into production and the Fox executives were sending us memos like, "Why doesn't the Wookie have any pants on?" It's true. And we were saying, "Hey, come on guys, if you're going to ask that sort of question why are you making the movie?"'

Mark Hamill also provided an insight on working with Lucas. 'George gets very depressed when he makes movies. He's always convinced that once and for all he'll be exposed as having no talent. And he gets so disappointed with the finished product. Because before you make a movie everything is perfect in your mind but when you finally have to realize it on film it's never the same. So he gets bugged out when he's making a film. I remember when we were shooting that scene in the trash compactor. I was standing in my stormtrooper costume next to the big drop in the water and there was a scuba diver under the surface with his hands around my legs ready to pull me under. When it came to the point for me to go under I'd just tap him with my foot and he'd pull me under while I held my breath. So I was standing there waiting and I noticed George standing nearby looking really depressed and shaking his head. I just happened to catch his eye — I hadn't planned this — and out of desperation this idea came into my head. What with the monster under the water being called a Dianoga and everything, I picked up one of the little pieces of schluck, green pieces of styrofoam floating on the water, and to the tune of "Chattanooga Choo-choo" I sang, "Pardon me George, could this be Dianoga poo-poo?" And to show you how depressed he was he didn't even *smile*. I got a smile out of you — I didn't get a laugh, but I got a smile — but George just sighed, put his foot on my stormtrooper chest and I was suddenly under the water.'[19]

I suppose what really gets me steamed up about *Star Wars* (and its sequels) is its cheesy, California-style, New Age mysticism. Yes, I'm talking about the Force here, folks, Lucas's invention of a safe religion that doesn't step on any theological toes and is just as absurd as any of the existing religions in the world. As Obi-Wan Kenobi explains to Luke, the Force is 'an energy field created by all living things — it surrounds, it penetrates us, it binds the galaxy together.' Oh really? What was binding the galaxy before life evolved? And if there was nothing to keep the galaxy bound together how did life evolve? Again, all this was part of his master plan for *Star Wars*. When he was working on the early treatments Lucas said he was 'trying to get fairy tales, myths, and religion down to a distilled state, studying the pure form to see how and why it worked.'[20] Well, as concepts go you can't get more distilled than the Force. According to his biographer, Dale Pollock, 'To Lucas, the Force means looking into yourself, recognizing your potential, and the obstacles that stand in your way. He had undergone just this kind of introspection just after his car accident — it was his religious conversion, and he wanted to share it with everyone.'[21] Gee, thanks, George.

If *Star Wars* is mindless, *Close Encounters of the Third Kind* (1978) is brainless. It looks great, sure, and the shots of the mothership rising up from behind the mountain are truly awe-inspiring but like *Star Wars* it is aimed at the child within us. Admittedly these are two entirely different children: *Star Wars* appeals to the child that dreams of blowing up entire planets and shooting down an endless series of adversaries with a ray gun; *Close Encounters* appeals to the child within us that still wants to believe in

Richard Dreyfuss as Roy Neary has a religious experience when his truck is buzzed by a UFO in Close Encounters of the Third Kind.

Santa Claus and that Somebody Up There Likes Us. *Close Encounters* is the Walt Disney version of *2001*. It's spectacular, and even awesome, but totally safe. It's a giant cinematic security blanket.

Close Encounters is the sort of movie that bowls you over with its visuals while you're watching it, as does *Star Wars*, but doesn't stand up to any form of serious, or even half-serious, analysis afterwards. Firstly, it doesn't work as a piece of narrative. It is highly inconsistent, especially in the treatment of the aliens: the mischievous and even sadistic behaviour of the UFOs in the early stages of the film bears no relationship to the obviously friendly creatures who are revealed at the end. And then there's the problem of the international group of UFO hunters led by Lacombe (François Truffaut). Just how much does this group know? Sometimes they seem completely in the dark and at other times it seems as if they have already made some sort of contact with the aliens. They have the map co-ordinates for the landing and presumably that information came from the aliens. They prepare the huge landing site complete with the music-and-lightshow device with which they plan to communicate with the aliens. But how did they know such a device would be necessary? I mean, if their prior level of contact with the aliens had reached the point of dealing with such specifics then why did Lacombe and his team go over the moon when they started exchanging a few musical notes with the mothership after it has landed? Yes, I know it's one of the movie's highlights but there's no rhyme or reason behind it. Also, how did they have sufficient knowledge of the aliens to have a team of astronauts ready to go on board? None of it makes sense if you think about it, so it's probably wise not to.

Actually showing the aliens at the end was, I feel, a serious mistake. After the ethereal beauty and other-worldliness of the various UFOs the banality of the creatures that emerge from the mothership brings you down to Earth with a bump. But Spielberg had always intended to reveal his aliens: 'I never pretended that I would leave that up to the imagination of the public. But I also knew that it was the most dangerous move I could possibly do with this movie, and even Stanley Kubrick had chosen the safer course. But I just didn't want to do that, and I think especially because of *2001*, I didn't want to not show the ETs. It never occurred to me, incidentally, that it would be anything but a friendly encounter. And I was frankly amazed at the plethora of questions from the American press,

asking: "Why weren't they hostile? Why didn't they fight? Where were the tanks?" I was amazed that anyone would ask me that after seeing the movie. I never intended to make the visitors and the phenomenon anything but benign and pixie-ish. Within the UFO phenomenon there's never been a reported death among all the thousands of reports from around the world. So even that research fortified my belief that the experience would be a quantum leap for man in the sciences and humanities.'[22]

I don't know but I suspect that a species of aliens that journeys all those long light-years across the coldness of space just to play silly games with the human race hasn't got much to teach us (and nowadays, of course, they've enlarged their repertoire of pranks to include leaving funny patterns in cornfields).

Spielberg even went further with his cutesy aliens when he released, in 1980, *Close Encounters of the Third Kind — The Special Edition*. This version included material shot for the first version but never used, new footage (mainly at the beginning and the end) and also had some of the original material removed.

Part of the elaborate effects set-up for the climax of Close Encounters. *This actual array of lights in the studio would later be married into elaborate optical effects to create the complete mothership.*

183

Most of the newly shot footage is at the end of the movie, though there is a new sequence near the start when Lacombe's UFO hunters discover a ship sitting in the middle of the Sahara Desert (actually Death Valley). The extra stuff at the end shows what Roy Neary (Richard Dreyfuss) sees after he enters the mothership. The interior looks very much like the exterior — a soaring city of lights — except that we also see row upon row of little alien faces peering out of what appear to be the windows of their high rise apartment blocks. The sight reduces Neary to tears but if this was supposed to be Spielberg's quantum leap for man I was unimpressed. I feel this sequence is completely redundant — if you haven't already been awed by the mothership then these extra scenes aren't going to do the job. But then I think the whole of the *Special Edition* was a waste of space.

The importance of *Close Encounters* as cinema, for me, is the fact that it took the art of special effects up another notch. The optical effects were supervised by Douglas Trumbull and consumed $3,500,000 of a total budget of $19,000,000. Said Trumbull, 'I liked *Close Encounters* because it was a totally different look with new kinds of effects. The hardest thing about this picture was that we didn't have the advantage of being out in space creating a fantasy. We had to be down on Earth with totally believable illusions. But putting a UFO on the screen is like photographing God — people have a very abstract, mind's-eye view of what they expect to see in a flying saucer. So the general look we went for was one of motion, velocity, luminosity and brilliance. We used very sophisticated fibre optics and light-scanning techniques to modulate, control and colour light on film to create the appearance of shape when in fact no shape existed.'[23]

But as great a technical achievement as *Close Encounters* is there's no denying that it confirmed the message established by *Star Wars*, that science fiction cinema was essentially a juvenile-oriented medium, and this was naturally picked up by the imitators who were waiting in the wings. However, there was one important sf movie at the end of the seventies that went against this trend . . .

Alien.

Lost in space: space movies in the seventies and eighties

Douglas Trumbull, responsible for the brilliant optical effects in *Close Encounters*, claimed that he turned down the opportunity of supervising the effects in *Star Wars*, 'because I felt it was just another space opera, just an extension of the stuff I'd already done in *2001* and *Silent Running*.'[1] Just another space opera? If Trumbull didn't have the nous to recognize that *Star Wars* was something totally new in cinematic terms it explains why the two films he has made to date are so misjudged. *Silent Running* is an extremely dumb movie yet it has a cult following, presumably because of its right-on message, which has become even more right-on since it was made in 1972. *Silent Running* is as green a movie as you can get . . . but it's still dumb.

The basic idea behind the film is that in the future the world has become so polluted that vegetation can no longer exist. All that remains of the planet's vegetation is stored in domes attached to giant spaceships in orbit around the sun. The main plot gets underway when the order comes through from Earth that the domes are to be jettisoned and then blown up with the atomic bombs that just happen to be on board for this very purpose. On one of the ships is a guy called Freeman who is played by Bruce Dern in a typically intense manner. Unlike his ecologically unsound crew-mates, Freeman is green to his toe-nails and is horrified by the order. So, like any good conservationist, he murders his colleagues and heads off into deep space with one of the domes, accompanied only by three cute little robots named after Donald Duck's nephews, Huey, Dewey and Louie (they were played by amputees walking on their hands). His plan, presumably, is to wait out there until trees come back into fashion. But, overcome with remorse, he detaches the remaining dome, after fitting it with artificial sunlight, and blows himself and the ship up.

Now hands up those who can spot a few flaws in the scenario. First, let's take a look at the Earth itself. It's obviously in a very strange state: we are told early in the film that it has no vegetation and a uniform temperature of seventy-five degrees (Fahrenheit, one presumes). That not only means that there is nothing to replenish the atmosphere's oxygen supply but that there is no more weather. A uniform temperature across the world would mean no climatic changes. It would have been interesting to hear the screenwriters' ingenious explanation for this extraordinary phenomenon but they don't provide one. I'd also like to have known how the drastic rise in the sea level when the ice caps melted was handled — as they must have done if the temperature is seventy-five degrees everywhere on the planet. What with a shortage of oxygen, no crops, and worldwide flooding you'd have thought the human race was having a tough time of it but no, on the contrary we learn from one of the characters that human civilization is flourishing down there. There is no more disease, no poverty and no unemployment. Then the big question is: what are all the members of this utopian society eating? Here the screenwriters do provide an answer. The people all eat synthetic food. That's all right then. But what's it made out of, one wonders? What's its organic base? Maybe people, as in *Soylent Green*? We are not told.

Returning to the nub of the film, the order to destroy the vegetation-filled domes comes because the ships transporting them are needed for 'commercial' reasons. Okay, if you can swallow that piece of nifty plotting you then have to ask why there is any need for the domes to be blown up. Surely they could simply be detached from the spaceships and left in orbit around the sun. In fact, why are they attached to the damned ships in the first place? I have no idea and nor do the screenwriters, except if they didn't have the stupid things attached to the ships at the start of the movie there would be no story. For the purpose of creating a dramatic conflict they have set up a situation which is totally artificial. Like their synthetic food it has no logical basis. Just who were the screenwriters? Once again

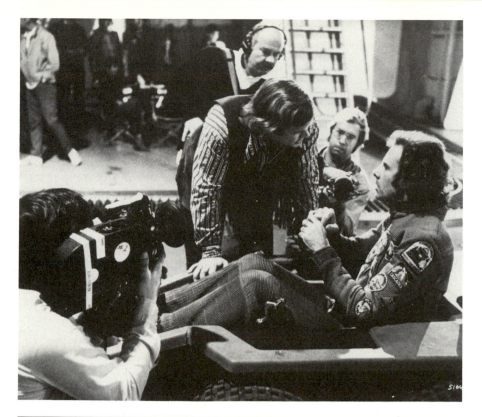

Director Douglas Trumbull tries to persuade his star, Bruce Dern, not to make a getaway from the set of Silent Running. *Just kidding really — I haven't a clue what they were saying.*

Silent Running *had impressive spaceship miniatures but a prehistoric script.*

we name the guilty men: Mike Cimono (that name rings a bell), Derek Washburn and Steve Bocho (so does that one). One final blunder they made was towards the end of the movie when Freeman, the fanatical expert on plant life, discovers that his charges are starting to wane. It takes him some time to work out the obvious reason . . . lack of sunlight.

Yes, there are some good things to be said about *Silent Running*. Trumbull manages to achieve some *2001*-like effects shots on a much smaller budget, and the relationship between Freeman and the three cute little robots is . . . cute. But it definitely does not deserve the rosy reputation it has acquired. On its last showing on British television it was described by the *Guardian* newspaper as a 'witty, elegant ecological fable.' Well, they got 'fable' right.

The following year, 1974, saw the release of a low-budget space movie called *Dark Star*, made by two people who went on to have an important influence on sf cinema, John Carpenter and Dan O'Bannon. Carpenter wrote the script with O'Bannon and also directed the movie; O'Bannon appeared in the movie and also designed the special effects. *Dark Star*, unlike *Silent Running*, is an intelligent sf movie. It's also a black comedy that sends up space movies and sf in general. The *Dark Star* of the title is the name of a spaceship in which four men roam the galaxy locating 'unstable' worlds and nuking them. Conditions in the ship have deteriorated. The computer is having difficulty maintaining the life-support system; the crew are in a state of advanced psychosis; the captain is dead but still partially conscious in the ship's freezer; and the ship's mascot — a rather nasty alien that resembles a large beach ball with claws — is

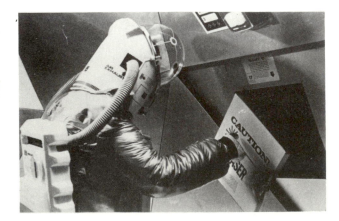

The space suits in Dark Star *may have been made out of parts of a vacuum cleaner and bits of styrofoam packing, among other household items, but the script was far more intelligent than many of the incredibly more expensive films in this chapter.*

becoming increasingly belligerent. But the most pressing problem the crew face involves one of their sentient thermo-nuclear bombs that wants to explode prematurely.

Dark Star began life as a forty-five-minute film shot on 16mm by a group of students at the University of Southern California. It was the brainchild of Carpenter, who started planning it in 1970 and who shortly afterwards interested O'Bannon in the project. For the next three years they spent all their spare time shooting the movie, financing it out of their own pocket. Later producer Jack H. Harris (who had produced *The Blob*) provided the necessary money to shoot extra footage in order to stretch the film to feature length and to transfer it onto 35mm. The extra footage mainly consists of Pinback's (O'Bannon) slapstick confrontations with the alien and his predicament with the elevator, which is where the film flags a bit. But overall it holds up very well and in spite of the limitations imposed by the circumstances of its production it is a polished and technically impressive feature debut for John Carpenter. He, of course, went on to make such movies as *Halloween*, *The Thing*, *Starman* and *They Live*, while O'Bannon was instrumental behind *Alien* and *Total Recall*. (Incidentally, BBC-TV's very funny sf series 'Red Dwarf' clearly owes a lot to *Dark Star*.)

1977 was the year of *Star Wars* and the success of this kiddie-oriented movie, good as it may be, predictably led to inferior imitations. The first wave came from Italy, in the form of the equally forgettable *Starcrash* and *Humanoid* (both 1978), while Canada gave us the truly awful *The Shape of Things to Come* (1979), produced by that old hand at exploitation movies, Harry Alan Towers. The film has nothing to do with H.G. Wells; it's just a cheapo space opera with terrible effects. The only fun is at the end where the villain, Jack Palance, has a styrofoam ceiling bounce off his head during his big death scene.

The first American imitation of *Star Wars* was a television production called 'Battlestar Galactica' (the pilot was released theatrically outside the United States) which even had special effects by *Star Wars* effects supervisor John Dykstra. Visually it was a direct rip-off of *Star Wars*, so much so that Lucas and Fox took legal action against MCA/Universal and the producer, Glen Larson, for copyright infringement but failed to win. Larson also produced an updated 'Buck Rogers' television series (again, the pilot was released theatrically in Europe and other unfortunate countries). More of the same sort of bland, production-line sf as 'Battlestar Galactica'.

The trend in kiddie-oriented space opera would lead to such movies as Disney's *The Black Hole*, *Flash Gordon*, *Battle Beyond the Stars*, *The Last Starfighter* and *Explorers*, not to mention the series of *Star Trek* movies, but thankfully, in 1979, there was another important development in the space movie genre – *Alien*, the movie that put the horror back into science fiction.

Alien, directed by Ridley Scott, is, of course, our old friend the fifties monster movie all dressed up in posh new clothes. To be more specific, it's *It! The Terror from Beyond Space* all dressed up in new clothes. A spaceship is invaded by a nasty alien life-form that hides out in the ship's ventilation system and starts picking the crew off one by one, storing their bodies in the same ventilation system. But there are several light-years difference between the two movies, despite them sharing the same plot. Not only had special effects become incredibly more sophisticated in the years between the two productions but by the time *Alien* came to be made sf movies were a serious business, with studios willing to lavish budgets on them that would have boggled the mind of fifties sf film-makers. Also the film-makers themselves cared about sf movies, thus a film like *Alien* is made with an infinite attention to detail that would have also boggled the mind of fifties sf film-makers. It may be the same old plot but it is presented to the audience in an entirely different way. Or as one of the producers, Walter Hill, put it: 'Ridley solved the problem of getting the audience to take the material seriously by laying over it this absolute veneer of technique — enormous technique. I thought the visuals were remarkable beyond my expectations.'[2]

Apart from Ridley Scott the other person who deserves credit for the visual richness of the film is the artist H.R. Giger who designed the derelict alien spaceship and the egg depository below the ship, as well as the alien itself (and the dead alien pilot in the ship). Giger's designs are disturbingly organic in style; the exterior of the alien ship resembles the pincer of a giant crab and the giant entrances into the ship are so vaginal in shape that they would have Freud coughing on his pipe smoke. And his design for the alien itself is superb, especially for the head. Unlike most movie aliens this one actually does appear alien.

By the time *Alien* was released I was writing film reviews for a genre

H.R. Giger's organic set designs for **Alien** *were instrumental in making the film visually distinct from all previous sf movies.*

The cast of **Alien** *— a truly impressive line-up of talent. No fifties sf movie was ever blessed with actors of this calibre, but then no fifties sf movie was ever blessed with* **Alien's** *budget.*

More organic **Alien** *set designs by H.R. Giger.*

magazine called *Starburst* and here is how I started my review of it: '*Alien* is a very annoying film, because on one level it is a masterpiece, and on another it's a botched job. Or to put it another way — as a science fiction film it's seriously flawed but as a horror film it works perfectly.' Do I still feel the same? Well, I don't care so much about the scientific errors that got me so steamed up back then (though I still think that a movie whose advertising slogan was 'In space no one can hear you scream,' could have been rather quieter in its space scenes), nor would I now go so far as to describe it as the perfect horror movie any more. In a less hyperbolic mode I would say that it's a very good sf/horror movie.

But one thing that still annoys me about *Alien* is the cutting of a brief but very important sequence near the climax. By removing it the cleverly worked-out life cycle of the alien species is simply thrown away. The sequence involved Ripley (Sigourney Weaver) encountering Dallas (Tom Skerritt) encased, alive, inside a cocoon. Clearly undergoing some awful metamorphosis, he begs her to kill him and she does. This sequence would have completed the circle of the alien's life cycle if left in, for it shows where the eggs come from: stage one has a face-hugger emerging out of an egg and attaching itself to a victim, impregnating said victim with a parasite that grows inside the host body; stage two has the creature erupting out of the host body; stage three is the fully grown alien who then impregnates other victims with something that cocoons them and transforms them into eggs, and away you go again. Scott said that he cut the sequence for reasons of pacing but according to O'Bannon: 'Ridley Scott did not cut the cocoon sequence; that was a decision of the studio executives (the "Company"). Ridley fought to keep it in.'[3] One person who must have been glad the sequence was cut was James Cameron, because when he came to write the script for the sequel, *Aliens*, it allowed him to create the 'mother' alien who is the source of the eggs.

Dan O'Bannon had responded to my review with a long letter which the magazine published. Apart from describing how his original script, written with Ronald Shusett, differed from that of the finished movie he said, 'I certainly agree that the script that was committed to the film was self-contradictory, confusing, one-dimensional, clichéd and bargain-basement as science fiction. I get a lot of pain from that, because it wasn't necessary. It was creative vandalism of a story that aspired to more.'[4]

To suggest that relations between O'Bannon and the producers, Walter Hill and David Giler, were acrimonious would be an understatement. For the producers, David Giler had this to say: 'Walter Hill probably had more to do with getting the O'Bannon script launched than anyone. Mark Haggard at Goldwyn Studios asked him to read it, and Walter championed the project from then on. It was a bone skeleton of a story then. Really terrible. Just awful. You couldn't give it away. It was amateurishly written, although the central idea was sound. Basically, it was a pastiche of fifties movies. We — Walter and I — took it and rewrote it completely, added Ash and the robot sub-plot. We added the cat, Jones. We also changed the characters. We made two of the crew working class, we made two of them women . . . we fleshed it out, basically. If we had shot the original O'Bannon script we would have had a remake of *It! The Terror from Beyond Space*.'[5] Which, despite all the gloss, is what *Alien* really is (I'd also heard that it owes a lot to Mario Bava's *Planet of the Vampires*, made in 1965, and I recently caught up with this stylish but tedious low-budget movie, and yes, a sequence where astronauts enter a derelict alien ship and find the body of a giant alien sitting at the controls is remarkably like the one in *Alien*, but that was the only similarity I noticed). Ironically, the producers, and Fox, were obliged to make an out-of-court financial settlement to A.E. Van Vogt, author of the 1939 story, 'The Black Destroyer' (see Chapter Six).

And now we come to *Star Trek — The Motion Picture*, and here I must declare, not so much an interest but a bias. To the Trekkies, sorry, Trekkers, who read *Starburst* magazine I am the equivalent of Salman Rushdie. I am considered to be a blasphemer against the One True Religion. It is true that, over the years, I have been less than kind to the *Star Trek* movies within that magazine's pages. When the original TV series began in the sixties I welcomed it: gosh, real (almost) science fiction on TV! Great! Admittedly the standard of the scripts declined as it went along and the third season was a bummer. Then it ended. Fine. If that had been that I would have had mainly fond memories of the series and no doubt happy to watch old episodes again when and if they were rerun. But unfortunately a terrible thing happened to 'Star Trek' — it became a cult. A cult that grew and grew and maintained increasing pressure on the NBC network to make a new series. As I said earlier, the success of *Star Wars*

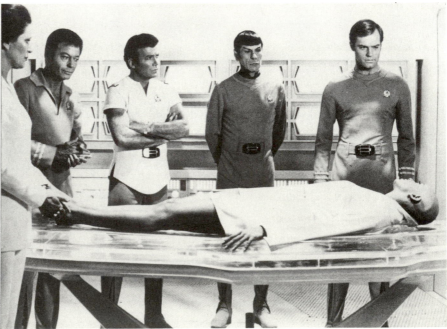

No longer actors but icons — William Shatner as Kirk and Leonard Nimoy as Spock from the cult TV series that became a cult film series: Star Trek.

A scene from the first Star Trek *movie, cunningly titled* Star Trek — The Motion Picture. *Enough said.*

was the catalyst that enabled the creator of the series, Gene Roddenberry, to turn 'Star Trek' into a 'major motion picture'. But the problem with the first *Star Trek* movie, and all the movies that have followed, not to mention the new TV series, 'Star Trek — The Next Generation', is that they are stuck in a time warp. They are recreating, over and over again, that mid-sixties TV series. For fear of offending the members of the 'Star Trek' cult everything must remain the same, and this applies to 'Next Generation', despite a new cast. The cinema of science fiction, at its best, has moved on from the original TV series some considerable distance, in terms of visual style and concepts of the future, but *Star Trek* still parades those out-dated 'sci-fi' clichés of yesteryear — the tight-fitting 'futuristic' costumes, the shiny, plastic-looking sets and props, the alien landscapes made of shiny styrofoam, and a galaxy dominated by a benign federation of worlds. *Star Trek* is really no longer part of science fiction; it's become a genre all of its own. It's marooned within its own little universe where the rules and conventions of the original series must be rigidly obeyed.

As I said in my review of *Star Trek II: The Wrath of Khan*, the second movie in the series: 'Watching it is like watching a wind-up toy go through its actions. It is a banal, unoriginal piece of work. It is a Mickey Mouse picture devoid of the merest hint of *real* life. The characters are the same cardboard entities from the TV series going through the same mechanical routines and uttering the same old clichés. Look, there's good old Dr "Bones" McCoy being "testy but lovable"; and here is good ol' Spock, all straight-faced and "emotionless" and going on about being "logical" but underneath it all you know he's really a sentimental softie; and over there is "Scottie" doing his impression of a stage Scotsman ("Hoots mon! The engines canna hold, Captain!"); and here is Kirk, a brave smile hiding his sadness while he oozes "humanity" all over the deck . . .'

One trouble with 'Star Trek', and it might be the main one, is that it is pushing a philosophy. The philosophy belongs to Gene Roddenberry and like George Lucas's, it is very Californian in nature. In fact, it came as no surprise to me to learn recently that Roddenberry and other people connected with 'Star Trek' are involved with the New Age movement and prominent supporters of Harmonic Covergence. Time and time again, in the movies and in the two TV series, the crew of the *Enterprise* encounter entities with god-like powers who put the crew through tests or play games with them but inevitably these all-powerful beings possess an Achilles heel, allowing Kirk or whoever to triumph over them. What is this Achilles heel? They . . . lack . . . human . . . emotions. Yes, seems to be Roddenberry's message (which he delivers time and time again). We human beings may have our faults but being human is awfully important. I mean, what's the point of having omnipotent powers if you can't experience . . . lurv? Yes, the crew of the *Enterprise* were all getting in touch with their feelings long before it became fashionable, even in California. Also Roddenberry seems to be pushing the idea that the human race, thanks to its essential goodness, will someday acquire a god-like status itself. I'm afraid, however, that poor Gene is going to have a long wait.

God-contact was — surprise — the theme of *Star Trek – The Motion Picture*. Kirk and team are sent out in a newly refurbished *Enterprise* to intercept a mysterious object that is heading towards Earth. They encounter it. It is very big and has god-like powers. It wants something and it calls itself *V'ger*. Finally penetrating it, going where no man has gone before, the gang discover its secret. The *Voyager* space probe. The probe had apparently encountered a machine intelligence out in space and things developed from there. Now it has come home in order to 'join' with its maker. Kirk has a bit of a problem here, knowing that *Voyager*'s makers have long gone and that *V'ger*'s arrival will wreck the Earth. But the problem is solved when a crew member volunteers to fuse with *V'ger* (it had already zapped his girlfriend so he had nothing to lose) and so back into deep space *V'ger* toddles, happy now that it has human emotions and the ability to lurv.

Despite being directed by the very able Robert Wise the movie is a turgid, dreary thing. More money was spent on its effects than on those in *Star Wars*, and both Douglas Trumbull and John Dykstra were involved in supervising them, but rather than emulate the pace and mood of *Star Wars*, it's clear Roddenberry wanted *Star Trek – The Motion Picture* to be his version of *2001: A Space Odyssey*. Whereas the images in *2001* were truly awe-inspiring all you get in *Star Trek* are lots of slow camera passes along expensive miniatures. For example, early on there's a sequence where Kirk is given a guided tour round the refitted *Enterprise* in a small shuttle craft: we see the spaceship from the front, we see it from the top, we go very slowly along the entire length of one side and then we go very slowly along the other side which, not surprisingly, is very much like the other side. At the time I wrote, '"Enough already!" I mentally protested as the sequence dragged on and on, "I admit it's a very impressive model of a spaceship but I've seen all I want to see of it!"' There's a similar and even longer sequence later on when we see the huge *V'ger* space vehicle.

However, this slow-moving, pretentious, ponderous and very expensive (it cost over £40,000,000) movie made money. No doubt the Trekkie factor was the reason for its box-office success but when Paramount came to make the second *Star Trek* movie they were determined to make it much more cheaply. By turning over the film's production to the 'television arm' of Paramount, and farming out the effects work to George Lucas's efficient effects facility, Industrial Light and Magic, they managed to keep the budget to a mere ten million. They also changed the style of the second movie, *Star Trek II: The Wrath of Khan*, making it pacier and more of a space opera. It is also more like an extended episode of the TV series, which is not surprising as it's a sequel to an episode from the 1966–67 season called 'Space Seed'. In the movie, its villain, Khan (Ricardo Montalban, acting with his brakes off), attempts to get his revenge on Kirk for marooning him and his men on a bleak, arid planet called Ceti. It's a tacky movie — though ILM's effects are okay — with a very tacky script. The guilty men behind the latter were Jack Soward and Harve Bennett, who was also the executive producer. An example of just how tacky the script was: Khan and his men lure two of Kirk's crew members, one of them being the ashen-faced Chekov (Walter Koenig), down to the planet's surface, take over their minds and use them to manoeuvre Kirk and Co. into a trap. How do the villains take over their minds? Easy, they introduce 'Ceti eels' to the ears of Chekov and his colleague. The little creatures, looking like centipedes, crawl into the ears of their victims and proceed to 'wrap themselves around the cerebral cortex', making them susceptible to 'persuasion'. Handy little creatures. But we've been informed that the Ceti eels are the only natural life-form on the planet, and we've also been told that the eel is a parasite. So how did an organism, whose only function is to wrap itself around the cerebral cortex of a human being, evolve on a planet where there were no human beings? This is not only a brainless piece of script-writing, it's also extremely patronizing. The inference one draws from it is that the writers have contempt for their audience. 'Hey, so it doesn't make sense but who will notice? They're only sci-fi fans, Trekkies. They'll swallow anything as long as it's got a "Star Trek" label on it.' They may be right. Then again, it's possible that the writers didn't even know what the word 'parasite' actually means.

As the series of *Star Trek* movies continued they became progressively more inbred. *Star Trek III: The Search for Spock* was mainly concerned with the resurrection of Spock (he'd snuffed it in *II*) and was awash with religious imagery. The fourth one, which again had a god-like entity approaching the Earth (though this one wanted to meet a whale rather than its maker), was actually directed by Leonard Nimoy (and, to be honest, wasn't as bad as the others), while the fifth, about a search for a god-like entity, was directed by William Shatner. Hopefully it will be the last, as the aging, original cast are well past their sell-by date. I think the best summing up of the *Star Trek* movie phenomenon was made by a critic on *Time Out* magazine who said when reviewing *Wrath of Khan:* 'The net effect between embarrassed guffaws is incredulity: a movie at once post-TV and pre-D.W. Griffith.'

The Empire Strikes Back, released in 1980, lived up to the expectations raised by *Star Wars* though, unfortunately, it was saddled with even more Californian mysticism than the original. Sure, the Force played an important part in the first movie but here it's moved into centre stage. In *Star Wars* there's a sequence where the Peter Cushing character, the villainous Moff Tarkin, says to Darth Vader, 'The Jedi are extinct. You, my friend, are all that is left of their religion. Their fire has gone out of the Universe.' But in *The Empire Strikes Back* we learn that the Emperor himself is a Jedi, albeit on the Dark Side. And so powerful and important is the Force that in the film's climax Darth Vader tells Luke (who has turned out to be his son) that if he joins the Dark Side they will be able to rule the galaxy together. So clearly Lucas had a change of attitude about the Force since he wrote the first script, deciding to give it even more emphasis as a plot device. And what is worse, he has come up with another guru figure to replace Obi-Wan Kenobi. And what is even worse, it is Yoda. A muppet . . .

One of my pet hates in the cinema are guru figures (scenes involving rituals of any kind come a close second; and often the two are combined). I hate it when some young adept is obliged to sit at the feet of the Master and listen to a load of mystical tosh. Those sorts of scenes were kept to the minimum in *Star Wars*, thank goodness, and as gurus go, Obi-Wan Kenobi was pretty painless thanks to Alec Guinness's amusing performance. However, I loathed Yoda on sight and he lived up to my grim expectations. The sequences involving his training of Luke to be a Jedi are tedious indeed, but at least Yoda doesn't ask Luke what is the sound of one hand clapping. Also George Lucas's home-grown religion is very inconsistent: 'A Jedi uses the Force for knowledge and defence, never attack,' the annoying Yoda tells Luke, but what about the famous sequence in *Star Wars* when Luke is completing his attack run on the Death Star and the disembodied voice of Ben Kenobi urges him, 'Use the Force, Luke! Use the Force!'

Yoda apart, there is much to enjoy in *Empire*. Its visuals are more richly textured than those in *Star Wars*, the special effects are more sophisticated and Lawrence Kasdan's contribution to the screenplay resulted in a vast improvement in the dialogue. In a daring move the film begins with a climax and then slowly unwinds from there, ending on a downbeat note. The opening sequences are set on the ice and snow world of Hoth where the rebels have established a base. The base is detected by an Imperial spying device and the Empire moves in, attacking the rebel with giant, four-legged walking machines.

The Norwegian location that stood in for the ice planet of Hoth for the opening sequences of The Empire Strikes Back.

These sequences are a breathtaking mixture of different techniques. The Walkers, for example, were animated in some scenes by the traditional stop-motion photography technique perfected by Ray Harryhausen but some scenes involved shooting the model in real time, thanks to a new process that the ILM technicians dubbed 'go-motion'. This involved using the same sort of computer system that controlled the effects cameras that are required to make numerous, precise passes over the spaceship miniatures; in this case the computers controlled rods fitted to the feet of the Walkers and operated them like puppets. Again, a computer is necessary as precisely the same movements must be repeated again and again in order to fit all the various image components seamlessly together on each frame of film. Go-motion, or 'motion-control', animation results in a much smoother look to the model's movement – stop-motion animation tends to create strobing, which accounts for the often-noticed jerkiness. But it can only be used in specific set-ups, which is why the Walker sequence required a combination of the different techniques. Brian Johnson, the British effects expert who supervised the effects on *Empire*, told me that even with go-motion, the sequence took a long time to shoot. 'Each shot of the Walkers wasn't very long compared to the screen time that one of Harryhausen's models tends to receive but even so we weren't working any quicker than Ray. And sometimes, because of the motion-control process, our shots took longer to line up than his. Altogether it took quite a few months to get that stuff done. The models of the Walkers, incidentally, ranged widely in size — from tiny little ones for the long shots to ones that were about four feet tall. And we built a full-size section of one for the sequence where Mark, doubled by a stunt man, goes up on a wire and tosses a bomb inside.'[6]

Johnson said that the Hoth sequences, filmed in Norway, were the most difficult to shoot, especially the shots involving the Taun-tauns, two-legged animals that Luke, Han and the other rebels use as steeds. 'Tying together some of the animated Taun-taun stuff with the original live action was very difficult,' he said. 'I went through every reel of location footage and selected the background plates to go with the animation and to try and match from one scene to another. I did a rough selection and George made the final selection out of the ones that I gave him. Then we said, this is the background that the Taun-tauns run through — are we going to use the original plates or are we going to build a three-dimensional set that matches it exactly and put the animated Taun-tauns in the middle of it and hide the aramatures and control mechanisms? So some shots were done against a blue screen and some were done in a three-dimensional set. We did have full-scale Taun-tauns but they were very difficult to operate because it was so cold. Everything froze solid. In fact, the only shots of the full-size animals that worked were the close-ups. All the other shots of them didn't get into the movie. I enjoyed the Norway location but then I wasn't there for the full six weeks. I came back and carried on with the live-action shooting at EMI-Elstree but my crew were there for the full time and got frostbitten. I think for them it was the toughest shoot they'd ever been on; they were six thousand feet up a glacier and were always short of breath apart from being frozen.'[7]

Other than the battle with the Walkers the film's other effects tour de force occurs when Han Solo and friends are in Solo's ship the *Millennium Falcon* being chased by the Imperial fleet. They seek to shake off their pursuers by flying into an asteroid belt. It's a remarkably spectacular sequence, even when viewed on video, and has never been equalled, even in the third *Star Wars* movie which has space effects sequences that are more ambitious but don't have the same impact as the asteroid one. Again, as with the snow battle, this takes place in the first half of the movie and nothing that follows is as visually spectacular. Interviewing the producer, Gary Kurtz, at the time of the film's release I asked him if they hadn't got their storyline back-to-front with the Big Scenes at the beginning instead of at the end. He, not surprisingly, didn't agree. 'No, because the whole focus of the story is Luke's personal confrontation with Darth Vader. That had to be the end. It's true that if you were looking at this story from the conventional point of view and asking what is the best way to sell it to the audience then it wouldn't be structured the way it is. And that's part of the gamble we're taking, I admit. It would have been easier to just remake *Star Wars* and hope that the audience would come back and see it again — and probably a certain amount of them would — but the original concept was to tell a continuing story and have it all fit together. It is a gamble, yes, we didn't want to get into the trap that the James Bond films did, making the same story over and over again while limiting the whole focus of the story to a few special effects.'[8]

The gamble paid off and *Empire* was a financial success, much to the relief of George Lucas who, unusually for a film-maker, had put all his own money into the procution. If the film had failed Lucas would have been made bankrupt. The making of *Empire* was a stressful period for Lucas, particularly as he had handed the directorial reins to someone else, Irvin Kershner. While Lucas spent most of the time in California dealing with his bankers, Kershner and Kurtz were in Britain making the movie — and the movie went over budget and behind schedule. When the production was only half completed Lucas's bank, The Bank of America, refused to loan him any more money. Another bank stepped in but as filming costs continued to rise he exhausted that source of credit too and was obliged to renegotiate his agreement with Fox in order to secure enough money to finish the film. By the time it was finished it had personally cost Lucas $33,000,000 including interest (he recovered that amount within three months of *Empire*'s release and went on to make a huge profit, the film becoming one of the all-time top money-makers). According to his biographer, Dale Pollock, 'Lucas takes responsibility for the near fiscal disaster on *Empire*, though at the time he blamed Kurtz and Kershner for going $10 million over budget. A lack of communication was the real villain — Lucas couldn't be in two places at once and wherever he wasn't, problems inevitably arose. "Gary did the best job he could, he made enormous contributions, but he was in over his head," Lucas says. "If anybody is to blame it's me. Because I was the one who knew and I stayed over here (in Marin County where his organization is based) until was too late.'9

Significantly, Gary Kurtz wasn't involved with the third, and to date, final movie in the series, *Return of the Jedi*, which is also the least satisfactory of the three. Lucas seems to have been determined to play it very safe this time. While it does continue the story and provide a climax it is very much what Kurtz said, with justification, that *Empire* wasn't — a remake of *Star Wars*. There's even another Death Star in it, which blows up at the last crucial moment all over again. And to play it even safer Lucas stepped up the kiddie appeal factor by introducing the Ewoks, insufferably cute teddy bear creatures (this is a recycling of an idea from one of Lucas's early versions of *Star Wars* which involved a visit to the world of Wookies). Even the production qualities are a disappointment in some areas. The standard

A meeting of helmets frames Billy Dee Williams as Lando, who figured prominently in The Empire Strikes Back *after it had been pointed out that there were no black actors in* Star Wars.

Luke battles it out with Darth Vader prior to discovering that he should be calling Darth Dad.

of the special effects remains as high as ever, the best effects sequences being the chase through the forest on the Speeder bikes and the battle against the two-legged Walkers (much of the latter footage was added to the movie later).

But some of the make-up jobs on the various creatures are inferior, especially in the first section of the movie dealing with Jabba the Hut (himself unconvincing) and his various minions — the pig creatures are especially embarrassing.

The plot too shows sign of strain. Much of the film deals with the rebels' attempt to blow up a generator on the Ewoks' world which is providing a defensive force-field around the unfinished and unoperational Death Star Mark 2. They finally succeed in their mission but at the end of the movie the Emperor reveals that Death Star was fully operational all the time and it duly proceeds to start zapping the attacking rebel fleet. But if it was fully operational why couldn't it generate its own protective force-field?

And there is the usual inconsistency when it comes to the Force. The big climax, apart from the space battle, involves the Emperor trying to seduce Luke over to the Dark Side of the Force. The implication is that if Luke loses control and tries to kill the Emperor then the Emperor will have won and Luke will be lost. Yet when Darth Vader, Luke's Dad, snaps and throws the Emperor to his death down a conveniently close-by shaft this act of violence redeems him from the Dark Side. And what a disappointment it is when Luke removes his Dad's helmet and we finally get to see the dreaded visage — who would have suspected that Vader was in reality Humpty Dumpty, complete with a cracked eggshell for a head? The benign-looking Sebastian Shaw, an elderly British character actor, seems an odd casting choice for the villain who has been such a malign presence in all three films (though he doesn't really do anything villainous in *Jedi*). It would have been best never to have seen his face at all (it's interesting that once the helmet comes off we also lose the distinctively rich tones of James Earl Jones's black voice; Vader's last words are spoken in a nondescript white voice). And as for the revelation, coming after the one about Luke being Vader's son, that Leia is Luke's sister — oh, come on! And if they are brother and sister how is it that she's of royal blood? Does this mean she's not a real princess, or does it mean that Luke is actually Prince Luke? And does this also mean that being a Jedi is a hereditary complaint? These galaxy-shattering questions have given me many a sleepless night.

Speaking of Princess Leia, her character suffers a strange change in *Jedi*; from being the tough and abrasive woman-of-action in the first two movies she's rather wishy-washy in this one, and her lowest point comes when she seems to meekly accept being a nearly-naked plaything of Jabba the Hut. Carrie Fisher wasn't happy about this. 'Absolutely not! I was crazed that day when I came in and saw those pages of the script for the first time. George was off ill that day but I said to the others, "Excuse me, but you guys want me to take my clothes off and then chain me up. After two films where I'm not afraid of Vader or Tarkin, why should I be afraid of a slug?" In the scene where I'm tied to Jabba, Han comes in and says "Where's Leia?" And I say, "I'm here!" and he asks how I am. I answer, "I've been better!" Even that line was cut from the finished movie. I think we wrote that, Richard (Marquand, the British director of *Jedi* who, sadly, has since died), Dave Tomblin and I. Then, as the others are led off to be fed to the sand monster, leaving me sitting there, Leia doesn't say, "Well, good luck in the digestion process!" as I said in rehearsal. I was amazed that Leia would just sit there, in those skimpy clothes, saying practically nothing. The only way they could justify that, I told them, was if Jabba pulled my chains real tight so I couldn't speak. I couldn't see my character *not* talking.'[10]

Return of the Jedi was another big money-earner for Lucas but since then he has stayed away from the sf genre, instead making outright fantasies like *Willow* and *Howard the Duck* (why, oh why, George?). The only movies he's been involved with since *Star Wars* that have come close to duplicating their success has been the *Indiana Jones* series, though their director, Steven Spielberg, can lay claim to the lion's share of the credit. For years there have been rumours of a fourth *Star Wars* movie (there have been some spin-off TV-movies set on the Ewok world but we'll ignore them) but I have my doubts it will ever happen. Coming up with an entirely new concept for a new cast seems insurmountably difficult — I've never really believed the story that Lucas had a nine-part saga all mapped out from the very beginning. My guess is that if he ever does a fourth movie it will feature as many of the old characters as possible as well as some new ones. After all, the Emperor may be dead, most of the Imperial fleet zapped and the second Death Star in little pieces but what about the rest of the Empire?

Surely a galaxy-wide power structure consists of more than just an Emperor and some spaceships. There must at least be thousands of Imperial garrisons on all the occupied planets, and surely more than one candidate for the job of Emperor. Anyway, I'd welcome a fourth, more mature *Star Wars*, just as long as it was minus Yoda and those bloody Ewoks.

John Barry, the art director on *Star Wars*, was going to direct the Second Unit on *Empire* when the opportunity arose for him to direct an sf movie of his own. It was called *Saturn 3* (there's more about it in Chapter Eleven), starred Kirk Douglas, Farrah Fawcett and Harvey Keitel and was based on an idea for a low budget sf story that Barry had told director/producer Stanley Donen (*Singin' in the Rain*, *Charade*, *Bedazzled*) in the early seventies. The original idea might have been a good one but by the time it reached the screen it had become one of those sf films made by people who don't know anything about sf. As I've said before, they know what an sf film should look like and so they conscientiously put in what they consider to be the proper ingredients — the spaceships, the robot, the laboratory — but they don't know what the film they're making is actually about. The idea seems to be that if you make a movie that looks like an sf movie then it automatically becomes one. There are some scientifically ridiculous scenes in *Saturn 3*, my favourite being the Harvey Keitel character flying his little spaceship into the rings of Saturn. There seems to be no logical reason for this other than the fact that someone on the production team had figured out how to do a neat ring effect (with, it appears, coloured water). What's even more absurd is that, judging from the size of the ship compared to Saturn itself, the planet must be a mere four hundred feet in diameter. It's surprising to see Martin Amis receiving sole responsibility for the screenplay of this silly movie but it's no doubt the usual Hollywood Writers Guild story that the first writer on the project gets the sole credit. I'm sure many others worked on the screenplay after Amis turned it in, including, it is said, Frederick Raphael.

Anyway, Barry happily went off to direct his first feature and lasted only three days on the job. According to Donen: 'It was my fault, not John's. The truth is that John had hardly ever been on a set, which I didn't realize. He was such a terrific talent, but he'd spent most of his time in an office. He knew next to nothing about staging a scene, or handling actors. And since nature hates a vacuum, the actors jumped on him. The film started floundering. Finally I had to tell him, "It's not working. I'll have to be on the set with you." But when I turned up on the set, John said he just couldn't work like that, so he left. There was no question of his being fired.'[11] Oh no. But admittedly, it must have been tough for a novice director to have to face both Harvey Keitel, who has a reputation for being difficult (his voice in the finished movie is dubbed by someone else) and Kirk Douglas who has a . . . reputation. It is rumoured that Martin Amis based the character of the aging film star Lorne Guyland in his novel *Money* on Douglas. Significantly, *Saturn 3* is conspicuous by its absence from Douglas's autobiography, *The Ragman's Son*, though practically all of his other films receive a mention.

Donen took over the direction of *Saturn 3* and Barry returned to *Empire*, and then, two weeks later, tragically died of a brain haemorrhage. Said Mark Hamill, 'He'd started working on *Empire* on the proviso that if he got the chance to direct *Saturn 3* he would leave and do it. And he did get the chance so he left, but then all that junk happened to him — he had such an awful time on *Saturn 3* — and he came back to us. He was all excited at getting into directing the Second Unit and then suddenly we lost him. It was a horrible experience for all of us because he was such a nice guy.'[12]

In a sense George Lucas was making the kind of movies in the seventies that the Disney studio should have been making if they'd moved with the times instead of being stuck in the past. And their attempt, in 1979, to jump on the *Star Wars* bandwagon with a space movie proved the point. It was an expensive, beautiful-looking relic. It was *The Black Hole*.

The plot concerns the crew of a spaceship that accidentally find another spaceship that has been missing for twenty years, the *Cygnus*, in the close vicinity of a black hole. They go on board and encounter its only human occupant, Dr Hans Reinhardt. It soon becomes clear that Reinhardt is your archetypal barking mad movie scientist, and playing him Maximilian Schell consumes more of the scenery than the black hole itself. He is supposed to be a cross between Captain Nemo and Captain Ahab, a man who has cut himself off from humanity in order to feed his obsession about the nature of the black hole. He's turned his fellow crew members into cyborg slaves and has a small army of robots to protect himself, including one very large one called Maximilian.

The sets and costumes in
Saturn 3 *were great . . .*

*. . . the script and direction
were not, though the cast
— and here are two of its
unfortunate members, Kirk
Douglas and Farah
Fawcett — tried hard.*

The problem — the *main* problem — with the movie is that it has no plot. Even though it should have been obvious to them from the start that ol' Hans is a ranting flake it's not until they discover the fate of the other crew members that the visitors try to escape. The film is then padded out with fights between them and robots, and between robots and robots, until the inevitable happens and the *Cygnus* gets sucked into the black hole. The surviving visitors briefly visit a Disney heaven before ending up back in their own ship while Hans ends up in a Disney hell, trapped in the body of Maximilian (pretty heavy symbolism here, folks). This was the climax that the studio claimed was so audacious and mind-boggling that the leading players weren't permitted to know about it until the last minute.

The lowest points in the movie involve two cute robots clearly inspired by the ones in *Star Wars* but much more disagreeable. One is called VINcent and has Orphan Annie's eyes, plus pupils, and Roddy McDowell's voice — not a pretty combination. VINcent meets up with a similar robot who has the voice of Slim Pickens! The scenes between these two are designed to have you chuckling but are more likely to have you chucking up instead. The scenes of destruction at the end are spectacular, and the design of the *Cygnus* — it resembles a vast Victorian glasshouse — is interesting, but otherwise the movie fails on every level. The guilty men: the director was Gary Nelson and the screenplay was by Jeb Rosebrook and Gerry Day from a story by Jeb Rosebrook, Bob Barbash and Richard Landau. Hang your heads in shame.

Roger Corman, naturally, jumped on the *Star Wars* trend and came up with the stunningly exciting idea of remaking *The Magnificent Seven* as a space opera. *Battle Beyond the Stars* (1981) could have been a total disaster but the screenplay by John Sayles and the visually inventive direction by Jimmy T. Murakami, better known as a cartoon animator, provide some incidental pleasures as the plot unwinds along its predictable path. Richard Thomas (from 'The Waltons') plays Shad, the hero who rounds up a bunch of mercenaries to protect his home planet from a bunch of nasty space pirates led by John Saxon. Among the hired guns rounded up by John Boy is Gelt, played by Robert Vaughn who reprises his character from *The Magnificent Seven* complete down to the same costume and the price for his services: 'A meal and a place to eat.' It's hard to tell if Vaughn's world-weary performance is acting or a reflection of his genuine boredom with

Sybil Danning poses as a Valkyrie space warrior from Roger Corman's space opera remake of The Magnificent Seven, Battle Beyond the Stars.

the whole thing. The most amusing individual among the motley bunch of humans and aliens that Shad takes back to his planet is St Exmin (played by the statuesque Sybil Danning in a variety of startling costumes), a member of a tribe of warrior women known as Valkyries. Her main ambition is to die a glorious death in battle. 'You've never seen anything until you've seen a Valkyrie go down,' she proudly tells Shad.

Around the same time Peter Hyams, who had previously made the sf-ish *Capricorn One* and the unintentionally hilarious Second World War romance *Hanover Street*, had the stunningly exciting idea of remaking *High Noon* as a space movie. The result was *Outland*, a more 'serious' and expensive movie than *Battle Beyond the Stars* but much less fun. Sean Connery stars as Marshall O'Neil, the security chief at a mining installation on one of Jupiter's moons. Investigating a surge in suicides among the workers, he discovers that someone is supplying the miners with a drug that increases their work rate while giving them a high but has the drawback of inducing suicidal tendencies. O'Neil tries to expose the situation but discovers that the Company is behind the scheme, and when he proves incorruptible the Company send in the hired guns. Doin' what a man has to do, Marshall O'Neil faces them alone, though he is given some moral support from an alcoholic woman scientist, played by Frances Sternhagen. As I pointed out earlier, this is a prime example of a *fake* sf movie; the sf element is completely extraneous to the story. You could remove all the sf paraphernalia and still shoot exactly the same movie. And, like *Battle*, because it is a remake of another movie the plot is ploddingly predictable. The sets, however, are impressive, having the functional future look established by *Alien*.

Dino de Laurentiis, who in the seventies did to sf cinema what Irwin Allen did to it in the sixties, gave us *Flash Gordon* in 1980, causing much distress as a result. You may recall that young George Lucas wanted to buy the film rights to the character in the early seventies but was unable to because they were then held by Federico Fellini. Fellini sold them to Dino who hired the idiosyncratic British director, Nicholas Roeg (*Don't Look Now, The Man Who Fell to Earth*), to make the movie. 'I love the *Flash Gordon* books,' Roeg said, 'and gradually came to the conclusion that Alex Raymond was a genius, an absolute genius.'[13] But it seems a strange choice of director for the subject matter concerned and eventually Dino came to the same realization and told Roeg that they had two entirely different movies in mind. Roeg left and another British director, Mike Hodges (who Roeg introduced to Dino) took over.

So presumably the *Flash Gordon* that reached our screens is Dino's version, and no matter how off-beat or weird Roeg's version might have been, it couldn't help but have been a tremendous improvement on this garish, crass and patronizing effort. Visually it has nothing to do with Alex Raymond's beautiful artwork but seems more inspired by the cheap look of the old *Flash Gordon* movie serials. If its vulgar, kitsch visuals and heavy-handed humour seem reminiscent of another sf movie, *Barbarella*, then it should come as no surprise when one recalls that Dino produced that as well. In fact, there is little to distinguish between the two movies — same pantomime sets and costumes, same crummy special effects. It's as if *Star*

Wars and *Superman*, another movie based on a comic-strip hero, had never happened. And if the movie's camp attitude also seems reminiscent of the 'Batman' television series, step forward Lorenzo Semple Jnr, the script editor on 'Batman'.

The cast is a mixed bag, including Max Von Sydow as Ming the Merciless, Topol as Dr Zarkov, Timothy Dalton as Prince Barin (who, by playing his role straight, comes off best), Brian Blessed as the leader of the bird men and the bland and unknown Sam Jones as Flash himself. The women don't have much to do except look decorative in their various costumes: Melody Anderson is okay as Dale Arden but Ornella Muti, as Princess Aura (Roeg was going to cast Debbie Harry in this part) wins the prize for being the most decorative hands down. In the overracting stakes Blessed beats Topol by half a length.

No, *Flash Gordon* is a sorry mess. Another send-up of the serials, a soft-porn version made on a small budget, *Flesh Gordon* (1972) was not only much funnier it also had much better special effects.

A depressingly juvenile space movie is *The Last Starfighter* (1984) which

Another dangerous woman: Ornella Muti as Princess Aura, one of the few good things in the ghastly Dino De Laurentiis production of Flash Gordon.

owes much of its storyline to *Star Wars* but any resemblance ends there. The script is witless and banal and the film lacks the visual richness of *Star Wars* (to be explained shortly). It begins with a neat idea. Alex Rogan (Lance Guest) is a teenager living in a trailer park managed by his widowed mother. The only thing he is good at is playing video games and when he beats the top score on one particular machine called 'The Last Starfighter', he discovers he has qualified to become a space pilot. He learns this from an alien in human form (Robert Preston) who then whisks him off into space in his car-shaped space vehicle. It seems the galaxy is under attack from evil aliens and Our Side needs every good pilot available to prevent the disaster. All the outer space stuff becomes pretty tedious; more interesting is what is happening back on Earth where the alien has left an android double of Alex to take his place. Amusing as it is, the full potential of this aspect of the story isn't realized, nor is the alien hit-man sent down to kill Alex. But at least the ending works; it's a nice scene when Alex lands his spaceship in the trailer park to pick up his girlfriend.

I mentioned the film's lack of visual richness. This arises as most of the special effects are computer-generated instead of achieved by the animation of models. On one level the computer graphics are very impressive and just about acquire a three-dimensional look . . . but not quite. There's a certain flatness, a cartoon animation quality, to the spaceships, space stations and asteroids in *The Last Starfighter*. Also the computer visuals are rather bland and lacking in texture compared to conventional model animation — just compare the sequence where Alex flies his spaceship through a tunnel in an asteroid to the similar sequence in *The Empire Strikes Back* to see the difference.

A much better juvenile-orientated space movie is *Explorers* (1985), written and directed by Joe Dante, whose previous movies include *Piranha*, *The Howling* and *Gremlins*. Dante had graduated from Roger Corman's unofficial college for young film-makers, first working in Corman's trailer department. One trailer he did was for *The Final Programme* (see Chapter Nine) which Corman had bought, cut and retitled *The Last Days of Man on Earth*. Dante's radio spot for the film began with a nuclear alert siren and a voice announcing grimly, 'These are the last days of man on Earth.' 'The radio stations were furious,' said Dante. 'People were calling up in a panic. It was like Orson Welles's *The War of the Worlds*. So we had to take it off.'[14]

Explorers concerned every young sf fan's dream — that of being able to make a do-it-yourself spaceship in your own backyard and go soaring off into space. The three young teenage boys in Dante's movie, very well played by Ethan Hawke, River Phoenix and Jason Presson, do just that after Hawke receives highly sophisticated electronic information in the form of dreams that turn out to come from aliens. Yes, this is a definite nod to the beginning of *This Island Earth*, and clips from that and other sf fifties movies, such as *The War of the Worlds*, figure prominently in *Explorers*. He passes the information on to his young genius friend, Phoenix, who, with the aid of a computer, creates a spherical force-field. As there is no intertia within the field they realize they can use it as a form of transport, so they construct a vehicle out of bits and pieces from a junkyard, encase it in the force-field and off they go.

Their first test flight includes an amusing sequence at a drive-in that happens to be showing a tacky space opera. Hovering in front of the screen they are taken to be just another bad special effect by the audience, until they zoom out of control over the cars and total the drive-in's snack bar. Later, they get more ambitious and head off into space to meet whoever has been sending them messages. Hawke, the most idealistic of the three in terms of being a committed sf fan, is convinced they are going to meet god-like aliens who will unlock the secrets of the universe. On the contrary, they encounter, in a giant spaceship, two ridiculous-looking aliens who constantly repeat dialogue and routines they've picked up from watching American TV shows and movies. What's even worse is that the two aliens are actually just kids who have stolen the equivalent of Dad's car. Dad turns up in the end, in an even bigger ship, very angry, and our three heroes have to return to Earth, losing their own vehicle in the process.

I think it's a lovely movie, though I think the design of the aliens was a serious miscalculation. It was clearly a labour of love for Joe Dante. As John Baxter wrote in an article on Dante: '*Explorers* betrays Dante's scepticism about childhood and the nuclear family. Each of the three kids is, as he was, a loner. And like him, their leader, Hawke, subsists on a personal mythology of comic books and old sf films. There's a healthy dose of irony in the idea that aliens may not be superbeings but creatures as unsure of themselves as we are.'[15]

Alas for Dante, the movie was not a success. It was anything but a success.

'It was a disaster,' he said. 'Nobody had a good word to say about it and nobody went to see it.' Dante knew at the one and only preview of the movie that he was in trouble. 'It was going all right until we got to the aliens. When the boy walked up to the alien and asked him to speak, and the alien said, in a perfect imitation of Bugs Bunny, "What's up, doc?" I could tell that the audience did not get it.'[16]

Before I talk about *Dune* (1984), another Dino De Laurentiis harpoon driven into the cinema of sf, I must make the confession that I have been unable to penetrate Frank Herbert's novel about the coming of a messiah to a planet riddled with giant worms and suffering from a severe water shortage, or any of the countless sequels he wrote. Similarly, I have never managed to get very far with *Lord of the Rings*. I may have been put off by the cult status that surrounded both these books during the sixties, the suggestion that they were somehow required reading. Anyway, that is why I cannot discuss the movie version of *Dune* in comparison to the novel. But then, I doubt if anyone can. Someone once described *Dune* as a very long trailer for a movie that never got made (actually, it was me). To say that it is disjointed is putting it mildly. There's an apocryphal story told about many Hollywood directors and producers, how when a movie is going over budget or over schedule, this or that director or producer has taken the script and ripped out several pages. That story has also been told about Raffaella De Laurentiis, Dino's daughter who produced *Dune*, but in her case I don't think the story was apocryphal. Watching the movie you do feel that every second page in the screenplay has been ripped out.

If Nic Roeg was an odd choice to direct Dino's *Flash Gordon* then David Lynch was an even odder choice for Dino's *Dune*. But whereas Roeg got the heave-ho, Lynch did actually end up directing *Dune*. Perhaps, since *Flash Gordon* did dismally at the box office Dino this time decided to trust his initial instinct. And it proved wrong. Lynch and *Dune* made unhappy bed partners and from his other films one can see that he had no affinity for the subject matter. Presumably he saw it as a challenge but the result was a movie that was simultaneously too complicated and too simplistic.

There are some things to admire in *Dune*, such as the majestic sets and Ruritanian costumes, both of which broke with design tradition established by *Star Wars*, *Alien* and *Blade Runner*. The Sand Worms are impressive — at first at least, though there's just so much you can visually do with a giant worm. It's a case of once you've seen one giant worm emerge from the sand then you've seen them all. And let's face it, the shots of Paul Atreides (Kyle MacLachlan) and his men riding to the attack on the backs of the worms are fairly ludicrous. Ludicrous is, in fact, the best word to apply to the movie. So much of it is ludicrous; the wildly rampant mutant eyebrows worn by Freddie Jones, Brad Douriff and Dean Stockwell; the way that so many of the characters talk to themselves a lot in a vain attempt to explain the plot to the audience; the scene where Patrick Stewart (later to become the new captain of the starship *Enterprise*) charges off into battle with a small dog tucked under his arm; and most ludicrous of all is the scene where the smirking Sting models his iron cod-piece.

I liked the movie when it was at its most grotesque: I thought the Guild Navigator was interesting and I enjoyed Kenneth McMillan as the repulsive — in terms of gravity as well as looks — and thoroughly evil Baron Harkonnen, though fans of the novel tend to violently disagree with me on the latter. Fans of the novel, I've found, have very mixed feelings about the movie and for good cause. I remember coming out of the London preview screening of *Dune* and bumping into Frank Herbert's British publisher. He looked ashen-faced. I asked him if it had been faithful to the novel and he replied bitterly, 'Well, I'll tell you one thing — it doesn't rain at the end of the novel.'

Finally in this chapter we come to *2010*, the sequel to *2001*. It was directed in 1984 by Peter Hyams and thankfully it's an improvement on his *Outland*. Hyams also wrote the screenplay which was based on Clarke's novel of the same name. Roy Scheider plays Dr Heywood Floyd (the William Sylvester role in the original film) who joins a Russian mission to Jupiter to find out what happened to the previous expedition. Yes, this belongs to that already out-dated species of cinema — the Cold War movie. Much of the plot is concerned with a growing tension between the United States and the Soviet Union, which is mirrored in the microcosm of society within the Russian ship with its mixture of Russians and Americans.

They rendezvous with the *Discovery*, the spaceship from *2001*, in orbit around Jupiter, and enter it, reactivating its systems, including HAL. Bowman (Keir Dullea, from the first film) makes an astral reappearance to warn them to leave the vicinity of Jupiter within two days, and the famous black monolith also reappears, though this time it's two kilometres long. Symbolically joining forces, the Russians and the Americans succeed in beating the two-day deadline and head for home while the black monolith starts to multiply and consumes Jupiter, turning it into a new star.

I like *2010*. It makes a respectable stab at being a sequel to *2001* and, rare for a movie of the post-*Star Wars* era, it also attempts to depict space travel as realistically as possible. It also features some very good special effects. Like *The Last Starfighter*, it makes use of computer-generated visuals, but these are used sparingly and much more successfully, creating images of Jupiter's swirling surface, based on artistically enhanced photographs taken by the Voyager probe. They also create the scenes of the black monoliths replicating and changing shape. My chief quibble on the technical side is the arbitrary treatment of zero gravity and artificial gravity within the two spaceships. For example, it wasn't made clear that the purpose of the rotating sections on the Russian ship was to create artificial gravity within the ship by means of centrifugal force. And, in fact, the layout of the Russian ship's interior is never made clear and you never see how the crew transfer from the rotating sections to the zero gravity part of the ship.

Another example, there's that marvellous, vertigo-inducing effects sequence when the John Lithgow character and one of the Russian astronauts make the transfer from the Russian ship to the *Discovery* which is tumbling, bow over stern, at a fast rate. They land on the middle of the ship then make their way along it to the spherical bow; but surely when they reached the bow they would have been flung off it by the strong centrifugal force? And once they were inside, shouldn't 'down' have been in the direction of the front of the ship and not the floor? Maybe it's just my faulty sense of wonder again.

The problem with *2010* is that *2001* doesn't need a sequel. After all, the movie ended with the human race on the verge of cosmic transcendence — the next stage of an evolution engineered all along by the mysterious, god-like aliens. And how do you show something like that? The answer is that you can't. Clarke even ignored all the implications of *2001*'s ending in his novel of *2010*. What we get instead in *2010* is Jupiter being turned into a second sun. Ordinarily enough an event that would deserve a degree of comment but after what *2001* has led us to expect it's a bit of a damp squib.

One must remember that the origins of the two movies were very different. *2001* came from a collaboration between Stanley Kubrick and Arthur C. Clarke whereas *2010* is based on a novel by Clarke alone. And the novel wasn't written because Clarke had a burning desire to write a sequel to *2001*. Clarke had actually announced, after writing *The Fountains of Paradise*, that he'd retired from writing fiction. What happened was that Clarke's American agent called him in Sri Lanka and said that if he wrote a synopsis for a sequel to *2001* he, the agent, could sell it for a million dollars — it was back in the seventies that sf suddenly hit the bestselling lists and a lot of the old dinosaurs of sf were lured back into the fiction market, producing longer, less interesting versions of their old classics. It was an offer Clarke couldn't refuse and he duly produced the synopsis. And then, while the wheeling and dealing was going on over the hardback and paperback rights, it was suggested by an interested party that Kubrick was sure to want to make the movie of the novel. I was marginally involved in the whole circus at the time (I worked for the publisher) and said that I was sure that Kubrick wouldn't be interested in any such thing, and I was proved right but by the time this became common knowledge the *2010* project was snowballing and his involvement no longer mattered. So there you have it: *2001* came about because Kubrick wanted to make a new and ground-breaking type of sf movie (and succeeded), while *2010* had its origin in the mind of an agent. I rest my case.

11

Rogue robots, angry androids and crafty computers

One thing that has always annoyed me about most robots, androids and computers in sf movies is the way in which they are anthropomorphized. Take See-Threepio, the prissy robot in the *Star Wars* movies (yes, take him, *please*), for example. He is just a man in a metal suit, capable of a whole range of human emotions (his droid companion, Artoo-Detoo behaves more like a child wearing a tin can). Even HAL, the computer in *2001*, is more human than machine in his emotional outlook, even *more* human than the bland astronauts on board the spaceship. Yet it has always seemed to me that if we ever succeed in developing an Artificial Intelligence, i.e. one as self-aware as we are, it will be very different in essence from human intelligence. Just because we have a 'thinking' machine does not automatically mean that this machine will have emotions as we recognize them. Our emotions are biological characteristics, having evolved over millions of years, and are also closely tied in with our development as a highly social animal. A machine intelligence — a 'pure' mind — would be totally neutral and have nothing in common with us. It would lack even the fundamental organic urge to survive. Its programmers could inscribe all manner of commands in order to have it simulate a human personality, as they can do to some extent with computers today, but as human as a computer mind might appear, it would still be a fake, mere camouflage over a mind that we wouldn't be able to empathize with.

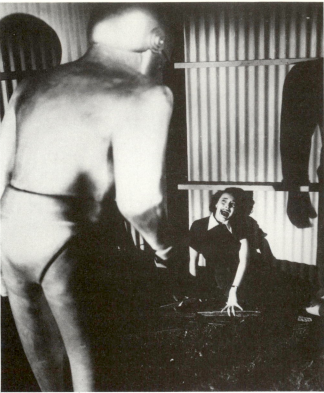

(Above) Robots don't get much more anthropomorphic than these two tinny twits, See-Threepio and Artoo-Detoo.

(Above right) Gort, the rubbery robot from The Day the Earth Stood Still, *had a humanoid shape but remained an unknown quantity in terms of its mental processes. Patricia Neal certainly had misgivings about him.*

The robot in Colossus of New York *possessed a human brain but, having lost his soul, was soon up to no good.*

Very few film-makers have touched on this aspect of Artificial Intelligence, but then so have very few sf authors.

Curiously, the word 'robot' originally didn't apply to mechanical humans but artificial men of organic origin, and was first used in the 1921 play, *R.U.R.*, by the Czech playwright Karel Capek. Probably the first movie robot, and certainly the most famous one of the silent era, was the female one in *Metropolis*. Alas, she is only briefly seen in the movie, spending most of her screen time covered in a layer of flesh in order to impersonate that saintly Maria (see Chapter One). After that robots were treated as jokes in the cinema and remained relegated to the kiddie-oriented serials such as *Flash Gordon* until the fifties when they started coming out of the closet. Gort, the robot in *The Day the Earth Stood Still*, is certainly intended to be taken seriously. And so, to a latter extent, is *Gog* (1954), though to my disappointment, when I saw the film as a boy, the robot is only incidental, being just one of many scientific marvels in a top secret installation that run amuck due to foreign, or alien, interference with the computer, NOVAK, that controls the installation. Unusually for a movie robot of that period, Gog, and his companion, Magog, are not humanoid in form but shaped like large pepperpots, with spherical heads and several mechanical arms (yes, I suppose they do bear a vague resemblance to Daleks).

The Robot Cause took a step backwards with *Torbor the Great* (1954). Aimed very much at the kiddie audience, it was directed by Lee Sholem and was described by *Variety* as 'melodrama awkwardly clothed in pseudo-scientific trappings, overlooking the original but brief scientific theme for cops and robbers hokum.' I can't verify this opinion as I've never seen the movie. In fact, I can't even recall ever seeing a still of Torbor himself. But I did recently catch up with another rarely seen fifties robot movie, *Colossus of New York* (1958). Directed by Eugène Lourié on an obviously restricted budget, it's a bit of a hoot though it does have its unsettling moments. Martin Ross plays a scientific genius who wins the Nobel Prize for Peace; no sooner does he return to New York with it than he's hit by a truck outside the airport. Luckily, his father happens to be a brain surgeon and he secretly whips out the relevant organ and keeps it alive in a glass tank in the accepted sf movie manner. Another scientist, Carrington, is horrified when he learns of this. He tells the brain surgeon that his son's soul departed his body at the moment of death and that a brain without a soul is automatically evil but the surgeon refuses to accept this, saying that 'the brain is all there is.' Easy to see who's on the shaky moral ground here.

The surgeon's other son just happens to be a mechanical genius and he follows Dad's instructions and builds a giant robot body to house his brother's brain. The robot is finally revealed. It's big, with a bald head and fixed facial expression, and appears to be wearing a costume made of window drapes. Then comes the moment when the robot is activated, and this is quite effective, aided by an unpleasant-sounding electrical crackle which is present whenever the robot is operational. Speaking in a distorted, and tortured, voice, the scientist wants to know what has happened to him. His father's answer isn't very comforting, not to mention an understatement. 'You've been ill. Very ill.' We then get a subjective shot from the robot's point of view and it's as if he's perceiving the outside world through a badly tuned TV screen (similar shots were used years later in *Robocop*). And when he lurches heavily to a mirror and sees himself he collapses with a cry of 'Destroy me!' It's a genuinely moving moment and you really do get an impression of his horror at finding himself trapped in this crude, unpleasant and no doubt extremely uncomfortable body. Dad is of no help, saying he understands how he feels: 'No more family life or the normal life of a man.'

The scientist allows himself to be talked into finishing his work for the benefit of mankind, and at first he stays in the lab but that crucial lack of soul soon starts causing problems and his personality changes. The film rapidly deteriorates after this but there's a truly weird ending, in what is supposed to be the lobby of the United Nations building, with the robot standing on a balcony and zapping to death people with beams fired out of his eyes. A last shred of humanity leads him to allow his young son to switch him off by means of a handle on his chest and he topples from the balcony to his death. After the surgeon has admitted to Carrington that he was right about the lack of soul there's a final shot of the robot's head with a small puddle of blood forming beneath it.

The robot character who most symbolized screen robots of the fifties was Robby the Robot from *Forbidden Planet*. Robby has his anthropomorphic moments but much of the time he behaves as he should do — as an intelligent machine without feelings. And he was designed by someone who knew his science fiction — probably Irving Block — as Robby incorporates

Everybody's favourite robot from the fifties, Robby, seen here with his Forbidden Planet *co-star, Anne Francis.*

Isaac Asimov's 'Three Laws of Robotics', which prevent him from any action that may cause harm to a human. When given a direct order to kill Robby starts to short-circuit instead; this is cleverly used near the end of the film when Morbius orders Robby to kill the approaching invisible monster — the fact that Robby freezes indicates that he senses that the monster is Morbius.

In 1957 a kind of sequel to *Forbidden Planet* appeared, but the only thing the two films had in common was Robby the Robot, apart from the same producer, Nicholas Nayfack, and screenwriter, Cyril Hume. In *The Invisible Boy* Robby is much more anthropormorphic but then the film is very much more of a children's picture than *Forbidden Planet*, though in no way a patronizing one. I know I really enjoyed it when I saw it at the time. I loved the idea of the boy putting the robot together himself and later made several vain attempts to build a robot out of bits and pieces I found in the garage at home. The boy in the film, Timmie (Richard Eyer), has an advantage as the robotic bits and pieces that he finds in his garage have come from the future. They had come from a scientific colleague of his father who claimed he'd travelled to the year 2309 and returned with the robot. The scientist had dismantled Robby to see how he worked then died before reassembling him. Until Timmie managed it no one had been able to put the robot back together.

The movie also has a super-computer for a villain, and I was very impressed by that too at the time. This was another crucial moment of cinematic imprinting for me. As Bill Warren said in his book *Keep Watching the Skies*, it's probably the first film to deal with a super-computer as a threat to the world. Using Robbie as its mobile tool (the computer has neutralized Robby's Asimovian inhibitors), the computer has inserted miniature controlling devices into the brains of most of the scientific and military personnel at the research base where Timmie's father works. The computer's plan is to rule the world from orbit in space but everything goes wrong for it when Robby, at his most anthropormorphic moment, rebels against a command to harm Timmie and finally ends up destroying the computer himself. Phew. I haven't seen this for years but I suspect I would still enjoy it.

There was a dearth of sf movies featuring either robots, androids or intelligent computers during the sixties. One major exception was *2001* with its famous talking computer, HAL. As I said at the start of the chapter, HAL is very emotional for an intelligent computer, even though Douglas Rain, as his voice, keeps his vocal range very limited (but without making HAL sound like a speak-your-weight machine... or a Dalek). The sequence where Bowman enters HAL, after getting back on board the *Discovery*, and methodically proceeds to deactivate him while HAL argues and pleads with him in that eerily flat voice is very affecting. The reason for his emotional breakdown, which leads him to murder the crew, is not too clear in *2001* though in the sequel, *2010*, Clarke explains that it was caused by the National Security Council meddling with his programming and causing a conflict with his essential truthfulness.

An intelligent computer of a very different type to HAL was the subject of *Colossus: The Forbin Project* which Universal 'released' in 1970; originally they had big plans for the movie but along the way someone at the studio must have lost faith in the project and its existence was effectively kept secret from the public. Maybe it was the same person at Universal who lost faith in George Lucas's *THX 1138* at the same time. Based on a novel, *Colossus*, by the British sf writer D.F. Jones, it's an unusually intelligent sf movie in that the screenwriter, James Bridge, has reproduced the consistent internal logic of the novel. Colossus is a giant computer designed to take control of the United States defence network, since it has been agreed that the decision to launch, or not launch, a nuclear strike is too important to be left to mere fallible humans. But when activated the computer reveals personal ambitions of its own, and these far from coincide with either the interests of the American government or with those of its creator, Dr Forbin (Eric Braeden). When the authorities fail to give in to its demands the computer takes direct control of all the country's missile bases and threatens to destroy American cities. The film is basically a battle of wits between Colossus and Forbin. The computer doesn't kill Forbin, because he holds his creator in high regard, but instead attempts to isolate him completely from the outside world and keeps him under constant electronic surveillance.

As intelligent super-computers go, Colossus nearly fulfils all my criteria for Artificial Intelligence, but though he's supposedly emotionless, isn't lust for power an emotion, along with the will to survive? And he seems to develop an unlikely awareness of human nature. There's a very amusing moment when Forbin, in order to have a channel of communication with the outside world, tells Colossus that his woman assistant, Cleo (Susan Clark), is his lover and for the sake of his sexual well-being she must be allowed to visit him. 'How many visits from her a week will you need?' asks Colossus. 'Oh, at least five,' replies Forbin. 'I said *need*, not want,' says Colossus.

Despite all of Forbin's ingenuity Colossus continues to extend his power and then links up with his Russian counterpart and the two computers have the entire world at their mercy. An attempt is made to render them toothless by secretly removing all the warheads from the missiles under the cover of routine maintenance but Colossus discovers the ruse and has all the ringleaders executed, again sparing Forbin. The film ends with Colossus still firmly in control and promising that a new age is about to begin on Earth. He will end all wars, all disease, all poverty — but on his terms. Forbin declares his continuing defiance but you get the firm impression that the omnipotent computer is here to stay. The film is really an elaboration on the famous short story by Frederic Brown which ends with a group of scientists asking their first question to the super-computer they've just activated: 'Is there a God?' 'There is now,' it replies.

Looking back at the movie from over twenty years later it's interesting to see the ways in which it's become dated. It's not just the Cold War scenario, it's also that Colossus is so big. In the opening sequence we see Forbin activating the computer section by huge section — in shots reminiscent of those of the giant Krel machine in *Forbidden Planet* — before it is irreversibly sealed off within the bowels of the Rocky Mountains, and it's obvious that Forbin has never heard of the silicon chip. If you remade the film today Colossus would probably fit inside an attaché case, in which case it would have to be retitled *Colossus: The Compact Version*.

The robots in *Westworld* (1974), though humanoid in shape, aren't very anthropormorphic. In fact, to my satisfaction, you never really know what's going on in their minds, or in the mind of the computer that is controlling them, or even if they or the computer possess Artificial Intelligence at all. Michael Crichton, the writer and director, has suitably left everything rather vague. The only explanation we get for the robots going haywire and slaughtering the paying customers in the futuristic Disneyland called Delus is that a 'virus' has got into the electronics (was this the first time that the term 'computer virus' was used?).

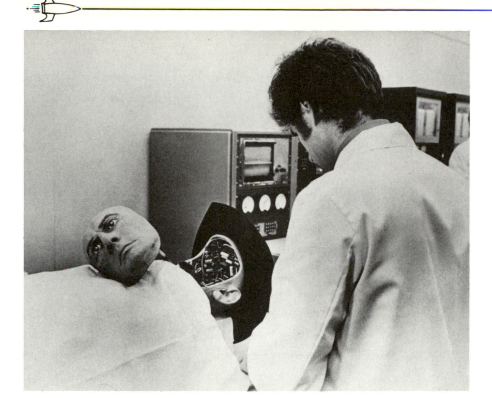

Anthropomorphic in appearance, the reasons for the lethal actions of the robots in Westworld *remained an enigma.*

Westworld marked Crichton's debut as a feature film director (he had directed a TV movie, *Pursuit*, the previous year) and a very fine debut it was. It's a pity that all of the movies he's made since have failed to equal it, with the exception of *Coma* (1978). *Westworld* works on more than one level; it's an exciting sf thriller but it also works effectively as social comment on how Hollywood fantasy and reality are becoming more and more interwoven. The Wild West theme park that our two heroes (Richard Benjamin and James Brolin) visit is not based on the real Old West but Hollywood's version of the West (a point emphasized by the fact that Yul Brynner, as the unkillable robot gunman, wears the same black costume that he wore in *The Magnificent Seven*). The film is primarily about two men who discover, one fatally (it's interesting that of the pair the one who most looks like a Hollywood hero figure, James Brolin, is the one to be unexpectedly shot dead by the robot gunman), that their machismo fantasies, nurtured by movie and TV westerns are somewhat redundant in the face of grim reality.

In *Westworld* there's a sequence where the two men sleep with a couple of robot saloon girls and I thought at the time that the idea wasn't very appealing. I mean, from what we see of the robot innards in the underground repair room, for a man to have intercourse with one of them would be the equivalent of putting his member into a kitchen blender. But I appear to be in a minority for *The Stepford Wives* (1975) sees a whole townful of men eagerly replacing their flesh-and-blood wives with robots full of electronics. When, on learning the awful truth, the heroine, Joanna (Katharine Ross) asks the mastermind behind the scheme, Dale Coba (Patrick O'Neal), a former Disneyland technician, the reason why, he simply replies, 'Why? Because we can do it?' Not a very satisfactory answer as the robot wives appear a rather unappetizing lot, and that's leaving out the problem of their internal workings.

All was made clear by the scriptwriter, William Goldman, who in his book *Adventures in the Screen Trade* revealed why the women look, behave and dress as they do. Goldman's original idea was that the robot wives of Stepford would look like *Playboy* models walking around the town in tight t-shirts and summer shorts but what we get in the movie are women swanning around in full-length dresses and floppy sun hats. As Goldman said: 'Look, this movie is about insane men . . . so frightened of women, so panicked that their wives may begin to assert themselves, that they resort to murder. And if you are so insanely desperate, so obsessed with women being nothing but sex objects that you are willing to spend the rest of your days humping a piece of plastic . . . well, that plastic better goddamn well be in the form of Bo Derek. You don't commit murder and make a new creation to have it look like Nanette Newman.'[1] Nanette Newman? Well, she's the wife of the film's director, Bryan Forbes, and she is definitely not a tight t-shirt and shorty shorts type of woman but one more suited to full-length dresses (the floppy hat is optional). When Forbes suggested to Goldman that his wife should play one of the Stepford wives Goldman says he knew then, long before shooting had started, that the project was doomed.

So rather than create perfectly formed sex objects the Stepford husbands seem to be turning their wives into perfect imitations of the stereotype of the ideal housewife featured on TV commercials. In this respect Ms Newman is perfect, and whenever I see her on TV these days doing one of her commercials for a washing-up liquid I experience a frisson of unease. And despite the creative tensions between the screenwriter and the director the movie is rather good. On the credit side are the performances of Ross and Paula Prentiss who establish a convincing rapport as the only two women in town who don't want to spend all their time in the kitchen. The film's one big failing is that it doesn't exploit the fear of possession. The Stepford wives are not turned into something else against their will, they are simply being replaced. Yes, being murdered is definitely worth getting het up about but, for example, the sequence where Joanna discovers that the Prentiss character has become a typical Stepford wife would have had greater impact if it was the woman herself who had been irreversibly changed rather than just replaced with a robot replica.

From men who want to have sex with machines to a machine that wants to have sex with a woman. This is the theme of *Demon Seed* (1977), directed by Donald Cammell, a superior sf movie that was unfairly treated by the critics on its release. Many dismissed it as just another rape fantasy where a woman is exploited and degraded in order to provide titillation but Cammell, and his screenwriter, Robert J. Jaffe, are clearly more interested in ideas rather than sensationlism. Julie Christie stars as Susan, the wife of Alex (Fritz Weaver), a scientist who has been supervising the construction

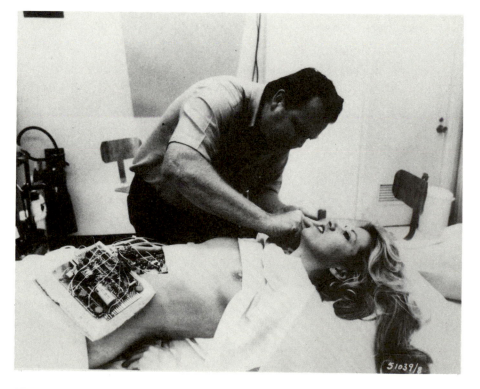

In both Westworld *and* The Stepford Wives, *men are keen to sleep with robot women but as this shot reveals such sexual activity might prove hazardous for the men concerned.*

229

of a super-computer, Proteus, at a nearby research establishment. The switching on of the computer coincides with the collapse of their marriage, which had been mainly caused by the death of their young daughter from leukaemia. The scientist has retreated into his work while she has become increasingly distrustful of science and technology.

Like Colossus, Proteus soon displays a will of its own; it doesn't want to conquer the world, however, but to become a part of it. 'When are you going to let me out of this box?' it asks Alex (in the voice of Robert Vaughn). This is one of the interesting aspects of *Demon Seed* — the movie attempts to ask what it might be like to be an Artificial Intelligence. And the answer is that it wouldn't be much fun, which raises the question of whether it is morally right to create a thinking entity that would be trapped within a computer system. Of course, this returns us to the problem with Artificial Intelligence that I pointed out at the start of the chapter, and that's our tendency to anthropomorphize our concept of it. We automatically assume, as did the makers of *Demon Seed* that an Artificial Intelligence would have feelings like ours. Proteus, like Pinnochio, wants to be real flesh and blood, but there's no reason to assume that it would care, or be capable of caring, one way or the other.

Anyway, Alex, who chooses to ignore any moral responsibility for Proteus's predicament, attempts to restrict it even further by shutting down the number of terminals available to it. But he has forgotten the terminal installed in the basement of his own house — a house that has been outfitted with a sophisticated, though not intelligent, computer system called Alfred that is capable of various domestic tasks as well as controlling the security devices. Proteus invades Alfred via the basement terminal and then reveals itself to Susan, whose first reaction is to get out of the house but finds she is trapped. Proteus now has total control of the house and her various attempts to outwit the computer and escape fail completely. Proteus finally tells her what he wants of her — he wants her to have his baby (no, don't ask me why Proteus, a sexless entity, presumes he is male). Susan isn't too keen on the idea and Proteus forcibly impregnates her with his own electronically generated genetic information, delivered by a rather uncomfortable-looking metallic phallus (this is the scene that gave the film its bad reputation but, as scenes of robotic rape go, it's all very tastefully done).

Susan swiftly gives birth to a hideous 'thing', a monstrous baby covered with what appears to be metallic scales. Horrified, Susan wants to destroy it but Alex, who has finally put two and two together and arrived on the scene, prevents her. He then peels off the thing's scales to reveal a human child who is the exact image of their dead daughter. Only when she opens her mouth and says, in Proteus's voice, 'I'm alive,' do we realize that Proteus has succeeded in getting out of his box and fusing with humanity in a very novel way. Susan's reaction to this revelation appears ambiguous, understandably so. She's got her daughter back but the little girl has the mind of a super-computer and the voice of Robert Vaughn.

It's a shame that this ending tends to produce guffaws from audiences as the movie really was a brave and genuine attempt to make a serious sf movie and for the most part is successful. Typical of its intelligent touches was the sequence where Proteus attempts to convey to Susan what seeing is like when your 'eyes' — radar scanners and radio telescopes — are sensitive to the whole range of the electromagnetic spectrum and you are being bombarded by an awesome sensory input.

In *Saturn 3* we have a robot that wants to make love to Farrah Fawcett, though there's no mention of it wanting her to have its baby. As I said in the last chapter it's a bad sf movie but at least there is a kind of logical reason why a robot would have sexual desire — its brain has been imprinted with the thoughts and memories of its human controller, but as the controller is also a crazy psycho this leads to problems.

It's set inside one of Saturn's moons where, in between making love, Adam (Kirk Douglas) and Alex (Farah Fawcett) are working on creating an efficient hydroponic food system to feed the starving masses back on Earth. For reasons connected only to the plot, the Powers That Be decide that things could be speeded up if an efficiency expert and his robot, Hector, are sent to the installation. Aha, but the expert has been murdered and the deranged Captain Vince (Harvey Keitel) has taken his place (what use would a great, lumbering robot like Hector be in a fragile, food-growing laboratory? Don't ask.) As soon as he arrives and gets a look at Alex he demands that Adam hand her over. Adam refuses and Vince's growing frustration, which is communicated to the robot, is what sets Hector off on his rampage. It kills Vince and from then on it's a battle of wits between it and Adam and Alex. To save her, Adam is finally obliged to sacrifice his own life.

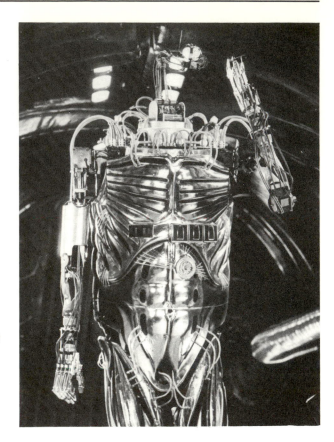

Hector, the homicidal robot in Saturn 3, *had an excuse for his activities, having been mentally linked to Harvey Keitel.*

The latter stages of the movie — when it stops being pretentious — are reasonably exciting and the robot itself is well designed and operated; the film as a whole looks very good indeed (production designer was Stuart Craig, formerly John Barry's assistant) but it's a case of a lot of expensive gloss covering a brainless script. But before we leave it here is a piece of trivia: on its release the image that featured on all the advertising was a shot of Farah Fawcett standing with legs apart and wearing what appeared to be a kinky set of black and silver underwear. You will search in vain through the movie for this shot; apparently it was part of an erotic dream sequence that got dropped completely in post-production. I don't know which character had the dream — probably the robot.

The androids in Ridley Scott's *Blade Runner* (1982) very clearly possess human desires and emotions but that's okay because they're not machines but genetically engineered human constructs. The movie was based on the novel *Do Androids Dream of Electric Sheep?* by Philip K. Dick and, in the time-honoured tradition in such matters, there is a big gulf between the novel and the movie. The novel is set in a future where the majority of the population has emigrated to the 'colony planets' after an atomic war has poisoned the Earth and killed off almost all the animals. The few animals that still exist are worshipped by the remaining humans and those who can't afford to own a genuine one make do with robot replicas. The novelist's protagonist, Decard, is a policeman who spends his time hunting down renegade androids and dreams of the day when he will be able to afford to own the animal of his dreams — a real, live sheep. When he's assigned to hunt down six special androids that have escaped from the grim Martian colony it seems that he will be able to realize his dream because the bounty on them will make him rich. But as the hunt progresses, with many twists and turns and typical Dickian reality shifts — at one point the androids convince Decard that they are the police and that he is an android with an artificially implanted memory — he starts to have second thoughts about what he's doing. Then he's seduced by a female android called Rachel who is one of the six. She believes that he will now be incapable of killing any more of her companions but to their mutual surprise he continues on and eliminates them all.

The point Dick is making in the novel is essentially a religious one. Dick was basically a religious writer and most of his work deals with a search for the meaning of reality, for God, and towards the end of his life he believed he had found Him. Likewise *Do Androids . . . ?* had a religious message: no matter how human the androids appeared they lacked souls and were therefore evil. Hardly a new concept in sf cinema; you can trace it back through films like *The Colossus of New York* to the 1918 film *Alraune*. Said Dick, 'To me, the androids are deplorable. They are cruel, cold and heartless. They have no empathy — which is how the Voight-Kampff test catches them — and don't care about what happens to other creatures. They are essentially *less* than human.'[2] Dick told this to Ridley Scott when the director screened twenty minutes of the film for him during the production. Scott replied that he, 'considered it to be an intellectual idea and he was not interested in making an esoteric film.'

The androids in the movie — called replicants, because they are no longer androids — are very different from Dick's version. They appear fully human (apart from their lack of empathy for animals), outfitted as they are with false memories of past lives that never existed. They are

Two of the deadly Replicants who featured in Blade Runner, *Pris (Daryl Hannah) and Batty (Rutger Hauer), who were genetically engineered creations rather than robots or androids.*

certainly capable of murder and what could be more human than that? But they are essentially victims, custom-made organic slaves created to do the dirty work on other worlds, mainly as disposable soldiers. And they are smarter, faster and stronger than ordinary humans, which is why their manufacturer had built into them a shelf-life of only four years. When they reach that age they self-destruct. And this is the reason why the renegade replicants have come to Earth. They want to see if their built-in obsolesence can be altered, allowing them to live a normal life span. Even Dick thought this was a good idea.

Dick was originally hostile to the production, especially after he had read an early draft of the screenplay by Hampton Fancher, who had approached him back in 1974 about the possibilty of making a movie out of *Do Androids . . . ?* (even earlier, in 1969, Martin Scorsese had considered the idea). 'Fancher's screenplay was terrible,' said Dick. 'Corny and a maladroit throughout. It was on the level of *Philip Marlowe Meets the Stepford Wives*. I did not approve of what it tried to do, and I don't think it accomplished what it tried to do. In other words, it aimed low and failed at what it aimed at.' Dick mellowed when screenwriter David Peoples joined the project and rewrote Fancher's screenplay. 'Peoples did a first-class piece of work . . . he transformed the screenplay into a beautiful, symmetrical reinforcement of my original work.'[3]

Dick tragically died in 1982 and never had the opportunity of seeing the finished movie. It's likely he wouldn't have been as approving of it as he had been of the final screenplay because adverse reactions at various preview screenings led to last-minute cuts and other changes being made. The main alteration was the ending: originally the film ended with Deckard and Rachel entering the elevator after Deckard has picked up a tiny unicorn made of tin-foil. The significance of the little unicorn, deliberately dropped there by the unpleasant Gaff (Edward James Olmos), relates to an earlier, deleted sequence, where Deckard thinks about a unicorn, the implication being that Deckard too is a replicant with implanted memories and, like Rachel, has only a short time to live. The new ending has the pair of them flying in a spinner through bright sunshine over beautiful countryside (it is said this background is unused footage from the prologue of Kubrick's *The Shining*) while Deckard's voice-over informs us along the lines of: 'Hey, it's all okay, folks — Rachel isn't like those other replicants after all. She's a special model, and doesn't have a built-in shelf-life. She could possibly last for years and years . . . ' And, of course, without the unicorn sequence, the tin-foil unicorn has no significance and the suspicion that Decard is also a replicant no longer exists. This clearly tacked-on ending cynically negated much of what the film had been about, such as the immutability of the replicants' fate. In a key sequence, when the leader of the replicants, Batty (Rutgar Hauer), confronts Tyrell (Joe Turkel), head of the Tyrell Corporation that manufactured the replicants (Batty is literally meeting his maker), Tyrell makes it absolutely clear that there is no way that what has been built into the replicants' cells can be undone without killing them in the process. So convinced is Batty that Tyrell is telling the truth that he kills him.

But Scott was unrepentant about changing the ending. 'I think it will be better accepted than our first choice,' he said shortly before the film's release. 'Which was too ambiguous — European, if you will. I should think that our alternative ending will be better accepted.' By young American audiences, he no doubt meant. Scott seemed anxious that the movie should

In the original version of Blade Runner it was strongly suggested that Deckard (Harrison Ford) was a Replicant too but this ended up on the cutting-room floor.

not be perceived as being about something, even though it clearly was. 'I must say I'm not comfortable with these issues of morality. There is simply no intentional message in this film, although people will read all sorts of things into it. Basically, I see film-making as creating entertainment.'

He, however, did regret losing the direct implication that Deckard was a replicant. 'I think it worked wonderfully. Deckard was sitting, playing the piano rather badly because he was drunk . . . and there's a moment where he gets absorbed and we went into the shot of the unicorn plunging out of the forest. It's not subliminal, but its a brief shot. So the origami figure of the unicorn at the end tells you that Gaff has been there, but how would Gaff have known that a private thought of Deckard's was of a unicorn? That's why Deckard shakes his head like that when he picks it up.' But even with the shot of the unicorn cut Scott thought that 'The innuendo is still there. The French get it immediately. I think it's interesting that Deckard could be a replicant.' Oh, those French! How European of them.

Scott also said at the time: 'In *Blade Runner* I would go so far to say that the design is the statement . . . the design of a film is the script.'[4] In his case this is very true. A strong narrative drive is not his strong point as a director (I haven't seen his more recent crime thrillers so this may no longer be the case). A former art student, he became a designer for BBC TV before he started his own production company and began making commercials. This background is often held against him with critics saying that his feature films are just long, glossy commercials with the plot of the film acting as the 'product' and camouflaged as much as possible. I suppose one could say with some justification that the lavish visuals of *Alien* are being used to 'sell' a hoary old sf plot but it's not the same with *Blade Runner*, as the story and the visuals really are one and the same thing.

Surprisingly enough, *Star Wars* was Scott's blinding light on the road to Damascus, and led to him switching over to the road to Hollywood. '*Star Wars* is a great movie. It's absolutely extraordinary. Completely turned me about. I thought, "What the hell am I doing?" It's just the idea of taking that as a subject and doing it in a particular way was absolutely incredible. I never go to a film twice but I saw *Star Wars* four times, and I just thought that all the detail was incredible. The film I'd done at that time was *The Duellists* and I was then preparing, would you believe, *Tristan and Isolde*, which is pretty bloody highbrow, and I decided not to do it. *Star Wars* was one of the reasons I went for *Alien*. I just found the whole premise of Lucas's thinking — because he had a real vision of a world — was great.'[5] So, thanks to Lucas we were spared Scott's *Tristan and Isolde*. I'm certainly grateful — I actually went to sleep during *The Duellists*. This also explains why he feared that the original ending of *Blade Runner* was too European. He must be worried that a director of European arty moves still lurks within him and that one day he'll wake up and find he's directing *Tristan and Isolde* after all.

And like Lucas, and Kubrick before him, he became an all-round director. In the old days a director would leave specific sections of a movie to the respective departments dealing with them — the art department, the second unit, the special effects department — and just concentrate on shooting the actors, but with the increasingly visual sophistication of movies, especially genre ones, the director must have a proficient knowledge of all aspects of the production. As he said in 1982, 'The film directors of the eighties and nineties will have to do everything, and special effects and computers are going to become as much a tool as the Mitchell camera.'

But, and here we come to the important part; what did I think of *Blade Runner* when I first saw it? Well, I liked it very much (sighs of relief all round) despite the obvious flaws. I knew it had been buggered about because there had been a preview of the original version in London some months before. Not that I got to see it — the editor of *Starburst* magazine had given my ticket to John Baxter, and I've never forgiven either of them ever since — but people had told me all about it. One of the biggest flaws was the Marlowe-type voice-over done by a bored-sounding Harrison Ford. It had always been intended to use some narration though very sparingly, but the final version of the movie has too much narration, a lot of it stating the obvious. Said Scott, 'I think with hindsight, I would like to have redone the voice-over, and I think Harrison would as well.'

A smaller flaw, but still an irritating one, is that unless you've read Dick's novel you wouldn't understand why animals are held in such reverence by the people in the movie. I thought this was due to cuts but subsequently found out that this was a fault in the screenplay. David Peoples said: 'Scott had always felt strongly about Dick's original animal theme, that a holocaust had wiped out most of the real animals and that it was an incredible status symbol to have one. But we just never licked that, other than inserting the short Animoid Row scene, and the bit about the owl in Tyrell's office.' And there was the scene where Deckard, posing as an official, asks the replicant stripper (Joanna Cassidy) if the snake she uses in her act is real and she replies that she's not rich. Pity this interesting theme is so neglected.

But overall one must regard *Blade Runner* as a classic of sf cinema, up there with *Forbidden Planet*, *2001: A Space Odyssey* and *Star Wars*. Ridley Scott's main contribution to the genre was with his representation of a city of the future. As one critic rightly said of *2001*, it was the sf equivalent of seeing the first western to use real exteriors; so with *Blade Runner* you feel you are seeing for the first time a real city of the future. The opening shots are breathtaking. With the huge pyramids and skyscrapers, and the towers belching fire and smoke, it's like an aerial view of hell after the property developers have moved in. Amazingly, though it seems to appear to stretch forever the miniature set of the city was only thirteen feet deep and eighteen feet wide. And only the model buildings in the foreground were constructed in any detail; the ones in the rear simply consisted of rows of brass silhouettes in diminishing scale to force the perspective and hence fool the camera and the human eye. At street level, the viewer is overwhelmed with a barrage of visual information, the strange and unfamiliar being cunningly mingled with familiar images from our own time, such as the Coca-Cola logo, all of which creates a future city of convincing reality that no other sf film has yet managed to repeat. The effects supervisor, incidentally, was Douglas Trumbull.

Finally, something for you trivia-collectors: carefully compare the fight scene between Deckard and replicant Pris (Daryl Hannah) and the fight scene in *Diamonds Are Forever* between James Bond and the two female minders and count up the number of identical shots. It's both instructive and a lot of fun.

Where innovative film-makers go Roger Corman is sure to follow and that same year, 1982, he rushed out his production of *Android*. Actually it's a witty movie, made on a slightly bigger budget than most New World pictures at the time, and well-directed by Aaron Lipstadt from a screenplay by James Reigle and Don Opper. Opper also starred in the movie, as Max 404, an android who 'lives' on a space station with the resident mad scientist, Dr Daniel (Klaus Kinski who, for the first time, actually appears to be enjoying himself in a movie). Max 404 would fail the Brosnan Test for Artificial Intelligence as he is highly anthropomorphized — he models himself on James Stewart as he appeared in *It's a Wonderful Life* — but who cares, Max is an endearing creation. He is living a pretty boring artificial life on the station, either watching old movies or playing video games, until the day he picks up a distress call from a spaceship and gives it permission to dock, not realizing that the crew are escaped convicts who have taken over the ship. One of the three new arrivals is a young woman (Brie Howard), much to Max's delight, and Dr Daniel is equally delighted. It turns out that he has been trying to create a new android that will be the perfect woman and in one amusing sequence he tries to persuade the female convict to let herself be wired up during a 'sexual experience' in order to imprint his android with female sexuality. She reacts by saying, 'I've heard a lot of weird stories from men trying to get into my pants but that beats them all.'

Things go wrong for the convicts when they attempt to steal Dr Daniel's secrets. He strikes back by removing Max's inhibitor and turning him into a killing machine, but the mad doctor gets a rude surprise when he finally activates his perfect woman, Cassandra (Kendra Kirchner) only to have her turn on him. All ends happily for Max as he sets off for Earth, in the company of the beautiful Cassandra, in his best James Stewart mode. One can only hope they don't encounter any blade runners down there. A small gem of an sf movie (and it is said that Lipstadt and his team deliberately made the film so tight — it only runs eighty minutes — that there was nothing for Corman to cut out and spoil).

Robots were apparently anthropomorphized into the ground in the 1981 movie *Heartbeeps*, directed by Alan Arkush. I can only judge from stills from the movie, and what I've read, as it was never released in the United Kingdom after rusting solid at the American box office. It's about a family of robots, including a baby robot who seems to have inspired the makers of the much more successful *Short Circuit*, who go AWOL from their factory or whatever and wander off to explore 1995 California. Sounds absolutely appalling and I'm not sorry to have missed it, even though it did

A cutesy-wutesy widdle robot from Heartbeeps.

star Bernadette Peters as one of the robots. Interestingly, the gooey, over-cutesy robot make-up was designed by Stan Winston, who was to design a very different kind of robot in *The Terminator* (1984).

The robot in *The Terminator*, the Terminator itself, passes the Brosnan Test for Artificial Intelligence with flying colours. It is a pure machine intelligence that inexorably follows its programming, which is to hunt down and kill a young woman in the twentieth century before she can give birth to a son who will grow up and prove a threat to the robot's super-computer masters, formerly Defence Network Computers who had set off a nuclear war in an attempt to exterminate mankind (admittedly these machines fail the test). In a masterpiece of casting, Arnold Schwarzenegger is perfect as the robot when in barely human guise, and when its outer layer of flesh and blood has been burnt off the Terminator is Stan Winston's brutal skeletal robot (there was both a full-scale version and a smaller model animated by stop-motion photography). The film itself is also a masterpiece, with a beautifully plotted script by the director, James Cameron. The rest of the cast is good too: Linda Hamilton is Sarah Connor, the Terminator's target who ends up defeating him/it in the final battle in an automated factory and Michael Biehn is Kyle Reese, the warrior from the future who has come to protect her and dies in the attempt, but not before he had made her pregnant with the fateful child . . .

My only criticism is that there seems to be one car chase too many, and I also think it was a narrative error to abruptly drop the police presence in the movie after the Terminator's ('I'll be back.') attack on the police station — The police are everywhere during the first half of the film and then you don't see a single one after the massacre. You'd think that the deaths of some thirty cops by one homicidal maniac would provoke quite a bit of police activity. And I would have preferred it if Lieutenant Traxler (Paul Winfield) had survived the massacre, not only for the pleasure of seeing him have to eat his words but also for the fun of seeing him placed in the same position as Reese, that of trying to persuade his police colleagues that the man they're after is no ordinary man. But these are only minor quibbles and don't really detract from enjoyment of the movie.

According to Cameron, *The Terminator* came about because 'I'd never really seen a good robot in a movie, ever. Not a really great one the way

Before and After: two shots of Arnold Schwarzenegger as the killer robot in Terminator. *Note how much wider his head is in the second shot.*

they used to be portrayed on the covers of *Analog* where robots had a waist like an insect so you knew it could not be a guy in a suit.'[6] Yes, unusually for an sf film-maker, Cameron actually used to read the stuff as well as just watch it in cinemas or on television. That's why *The Terminator* is so full of clever sf references as well as having the well-constructed internal logic of a good sf story (for its time travel aspects see Chapter Fifteen). Much of the situation in the sequences set in the future, for example, points to Philip K. Dick's famous story, 'Second Variety', where automatic factories keep producing ever more human-like killer-robots designed to fool their way into the bunkers where the remnants of humanity huddle after a nuclear war. But there are also many references to previous sf movies, such as *Alien* and *Mad Max 2* (aka *The Road Warrior*) and Cameron has expressed his admiration of both the directors of those movies. (Harlan Ellison took legal action against Cameron and the film's production company, Hemdale, claiming the film borrowed too freely from a number of his works, including his story 'I Have No Mouth and I Must Scream' and an episode of the 'Outer Limits' TV series called 'Demon With a Glass Hand'; the claim was settled out of court in Ellison's favour.)

James Cameron is very much in the mode of the 'all-round director' described by Ridley Scott earlier in this chapter. He received his background training, like so many others, at the Roger Corman College of Film-Making, otherwise known as New World Pictures. While working there he got his training in art direction and special effects as well as developing his directing skills. It was also at New World that he met Gale Anne Hurd, who co-wrote the script and also produced *The Terminator*. She had acquired her organizational and budgetary skills by working with Corman on such movies as *The Lady in Red* and *Alligator*. Both Cameron and Hurd worked on *Battle Beyond the Stars* (see Chapter Ten); he was the art director and special effects photography director while she was the production manager. After *The Terminator*, by which time they were married, they made two other movies together, *Aliens* and *The Abyss*, but have now gone their separate ways, both professionally and personally. On her own, Hurd produced the wretched *Alien Nation*, which was directed by the British director Graham Baker, but redeemed herself later by producing the marvellous *Tremors*.

With *The Terminator*, and the subsequent *Aliens*, Cameron established himself as an equal to Lucas, Spielberg and Scott in terms of importance to the sf cinema genre; it's true that for all its technical brilliance, his third sf movie, *The Abyss*, was a disappointment (see next chapter). As I write Carpenter is at work on *The Terminator 2: Judgement Day*. The relatively small budget of the first one, $6.5 million, has been expanded to a whopping $60 million, but then it is said that Cameron's salary alone is in the multi-million dollar area, while Schwarzenegger's fee came in the form of a $14 million aeroplane (admittedly, this didn't come out of the film's budget but was a gift from the production company, Carolco Productions, who also made *Total Recall* and who bought the *Terminator* rights from the original company, Hemdale). It is also said that Schwarzenegger is playing a nice Terminator this time. An appalling idea but apparently true because Big Arnie wants to maintain his new, softer image and refrain from playing any more heavies. Tsk, tsk. Though he's the same physical type as the one in the first film the humans in the future have reprogrammed him and sent him back to protect Sarah Connors (Linda Hamilton again) and her son from another assassin sent by the computers to kill them. This new android Terminator, called Key 1,000 (Robert Patrick) is a newer, more sophisticated model which means that Big Arnie will face stiff competition. On top of that the $60 million budget also provides us with a chance to see that nuclear holocaust unleashed by those humaphobic computers.

1984 saw the release of *Runaway*, another movie about rogue robots but far inferior to *The Terminator*, and also far inferior to Michael Crichton's previous *Westworld*. But at least the robots here are anything but anthropomorphic (with the exception of the boy's robot nanny); instead of homicidal robot gunfighters, Crichton this time gives us homicidal household appliances. He also throws in some homicidal farm and building machinery too, not to mention acid-injecting mechanical spiders. Tom Selleck stars as Jack Ramsay, a cop in the not-too-distant future who has to deactivate any microchip-controlled equipment that has gone out of control and is behaving dangerously. The opening sequences make it plain that such occurrences are pretty common when Jack is sent into a house to deal with a mechanical babysitter that has flipped its lid and is wandering about with a .45 automatic. Crichton sets up this interesting situation rather efficiently and at first makes it almost seem credible. But then the plot rapidly goes out of control and inconsistencies abound. For example, a gun that can shoot round corners is introduced; we are told that the rocket-propelled bullets will only hone in on a specific target but later we see it being used as an ordinary gun on a random target. Things go seriously wrong with the introduction of a comic-book villain, Luther, who has some crazy plan to flood the world with psychotic microchips. The fact that he's played by rock musician Gene Simmons who only has one expression in his facial repertoire — glowering — only adds to the character's lack of credibility. The plot soon collapses completely but there is some fun to be had from the action set-pieces, especially the vertigo-inducing climax on top of an unfinished skyscraper, and also from the presence of Kirstie Alley.

I was rather surprised by *D.A.R.Y.L.* when I first saw it back in 1986. I knew it was about a young boy who turns out to be a robot and I expected the worst, but while it has its saccharine moments, and is a glowing commercial for the American nuclear family, it is intelligently thought out. Yes, the robot has emotions but Simon Wincer, who wrote and directed it, makes the very acquisition of these human characteristics the crux of the movie. The kid isn't really a robot, he has a human body with a synthetic brain — he's part of some nasty military project — and his human sensory input has had an effect on his computer-like mind, making him think like a human (well, it kind of works logically). It's the realization that D.A.R.Y.L. (I forget what it stands for) has become human that leads one of the scientists on the project to smuggle him out of the secret base and set him free. The scientist is assassinated shortly afterwards while D.A.R.Y.L. is taken under the wing of a local family and learns what life is all about. The nasty military people locate him and send in a couple who masquerade as his 'real' parents. He's taken back to the base but again the same things happens — one of the scientists realizes he's now human, and when the order comes through to terminate the project, he sneaks D.A.R.Y.L. out, losing his life in the process (it's interesting that the one woman scientist toes the official line on D.A.R.Y.L.). Commandeering a jet plane, the little cyborg makes a clean getaway, fakes his death and rejoins his adoptive family. Call me mad, call me an old softie, but I like this movie.

There is no logic at all to the acquisition of human emotions by the robot in John Badham's *Short Circuit* (1986). One bolt of lightning and this mindless robot suddenly has the full range of human emotions, ranging from an empathy with living things to a sense of humour. As I wrote at the time, if a burst of electricity can do that to mindless morons we should be wiring English football hooligans into the mains. *Short Circuit* is really a robotic imitation of *E.T.*, with the robot, called No 5, and as cute as anything, being mistaken for an alien when it invades the home of Ally Sheedy, a devout Greenie and technophobe. The plot is also similar to that of *D.A.R.Y.L.* with the robot being hunted by nasty military types who want their war toy back, and with one of the scientists from the project, played by Steve Guttenberg, becoming sympathetic and helping the robot to escape. Both films end with a faked death to solve everything and both films are really children's films (the child in me preferred *D.A.R.Y.L.*).

Though non-anthropomorphic in shape the robot in *Short Circuit* has more humanity in his little pincer than the robot in *Robocop* has in its entire body, which is strange because the latter houses a human brain, not to mention a human face. After being shot to pieces by a vicious gang in a near-future Detroit, a cop called Murphy (Peter Weller) is transformed into the ultimate policeman by scientists working for a corrupt corporation that is trying to take over the city. The cyborg is regarded as a machine but buried within it is the ghost of the former man, haunted by memories of his wife and son. Only his former partner, policewoman Lewis (Nancy Allen), realizes that there is still a human side to him. He does become more human as the movie progresses but that makes his awareness of his situation only more painful. As he tells Lewis towards the end of the movie, after she has sustained a number of bullet holes, 'They can fix you. They can fix anything.'

Robocop was directed in 1987 by Paul Verhoeven who had previously caused a stir with such idiosyncratic movies as *The Fourth Man* and *Flesh and Blood*. He said he took on *Robocop* because he liked comic books (it was noted on the film's release that there was a certain similarity between the Robocop character and the British comic character *Judge Dredd*) and also he was attracted by the 'beyond this life' feeling to the story. 'This guy is completely robotic, and starts to realize that there was something else. He starts to remember. That was for me the emotional level and the reason I wanted to do the picture. Sf for me always has a philosophical level. It's a way of expressing something you can't express otherwise. Sf should always be poetic. It has to do with the divine, and with God, or other levels of

Another Before and After situation: this time it's Peter Weller who got the treatment in Robocop.

paradise, or other worlds that you want to believe in . . . '[7]

Hmmm, doesn't sound like the kind of director who would provoke this response from a member of the audience: 'I want my money back, I want my time back — and most of all I want my innocence back. There are some things I can live without knowing, and one is what it looks like when someone has his hand shot off at close range in full colour on a large screen. I made the mistake of paying £4.50 to see just that, among other grotesquely violent images, in a widely advertised and seriously reviewed film. Twenty minutes after handing my money over I was back out on Leicester Square feeling shaky and tearful from being subjected to the undiluted nastiness that is *Robocop*.' That was journalist Maggie Anderson writing in the London *Evening Standard* in 1988 (curiously, her piece went on to also condemn the film's ending — 'Should we really praise creativity that comes up with plunging a human being into toxic waste as a way of dispatching the villain?' — but how did she know that if she'd left after only twenty minutes?) She wasn't the only one to condemn the film's violence. And, admittedly, *Robocop* is violent, but the violence is so exaggerated you can't really take it seriously. Also it's presented with a large amount of dark humour. *Robocop* is in fact a very funny movie with a strong satirical sub-text, especially at the expense of American television, but many, like Maggie Anderson, didn't get the joke. Another was Harlan Ellison who wrote in his review: 'It is a film about, and intended for, no less than brutes,' though he neglects to mention whether it left him feeling shaky and tearful.[8]

One who did see the joke was actor Dan O'Herlihy, who plays the Old Man, the head of the corporation. He took the part on the strength of one line. 'Oh, yes, it was a very great line, the best I've ever had in a movie. I'm sitting at this table and they bring in this enormous robot, and tell one of the vice-presidents to demonstrate how it works by pointing a gun at it. The thing responds by saying that he has fifteen seconds to drop his weapon. Ronny Cox, who plays Dick Jones, a corporation hot-shot, says to him, "Do it!" So the fellow drops the gun but the robot then says "You have ten seconds to comply." The vice-president protests that he has dropped the gun but then the robot's arm cannons go *Boom! Boom! Boom!* and he's splattered all over the place, on the ceiling and the walls. The Old Man is the only one who hasn't left the conference table so Ronny Cox

Paul Verhoeven, director of Robocop *and* Total Recall, *in action. Here he is no doubt demanding bigger bullet holes in the actors.*

comes to him looking apologetic. And I look at him and say, "Dick, I'm very disappointed."

'There was another good line at the end of the movie. Dick has the Old Man around the neck with a gun at his head. Robocop has just said he's programmed not to attack any member of the corporation, so I say, "Dick, you're fired!" which releases Robocop, who goes *Boom! Boom! Boom!* and Dick is blasted out through the window and falls forty-seven stories.'[9] O'Herlihy is clearly an actor who enjoys his work.

The original cast appeared in the sequel, *Robocop 2*, which was released in 1990. As with the original it displays brilliant special effects and the stop-motion animation sequences (supervised by Phil Tippett) are simply mind-boggling, but though it has a screenplay by the top comic-strip writer Frank Miller (and Walon Green) it is inferior to the original. One problem is that it's just a rerun of the first movie with more spectacular effects and even more violence. There is no attempt to develop Robocop's situation from the original film and take it a step further — if anything he has regressed from the character he was at the end of the first movie. An interesting sub-plot involving his wife and child disappears along the way and the Nancy Allen character is completely wasted.

As the director this time isn't Paul Verhoeven but Irvin Kershner, who made the sequel to *Star Wars*, it's not surprising that there's a different feel to the movie. He tries to reproduce Verhoeven's style and does get the surface right but the black comedy doesn't come off this time and as a result the film's mega-violence is literally overkill. Not surprisingly, it was nowhere as financially successful as *Robocop*.

Incidentally, Jon Davison, who produced both the *Robocop* films, and is another graduate of the Roger Corman school, New World Pictures, had long been fascinated by screen robots. He even named his production company Tobor Productions in tribute to the director of *Tobor the Great* which Davison says was 'the best robot movie ever shot in five days.'[10]

Where does the robot movie go from here? Well, at the moment it appears to be going backwards if the British production *Hardware* (1990) is any indication. This is a movie that has no originality whatsoever, being a collection of visual borrowings from *Demon Seed*, *Saturn 3* and *The Terminator*. And it also bore an uncanny resemblance to a short comic strip story that had appeared in a *2000 AD* annual in 1980. Both movie and strip

feature a woman sculptor who lives on the top floor of a tall building; her lover (husband in the strip) is a space pilot who brings her a sack full of bits and pieces of a killer robot for her to use in her sculptures; the robot partially reassembles itself and proceeds to chase the woman around the flat after screwing up the automatic security system and sealing all the doors and windows; and there's a scene where the woman attempts to confuse the robot's infra-red sensors by opening a freezer door. 'I know he didn't do it intentionally,' said the film's producer Joanne Sellers, referring to the film's writer and director Richard Stanley, after her company had been obliged to give Fleetway, owners of *2000 AD*, and the writers of the comic strip, a credit on the movie. 'It most probably stuck in his mind as a young boy.'[11] Yeah, I know the feeling.

12

The good...

This chapter takes a look at the nice, or if not necessarily nice, at least the neutral, alien visitors to Earth courtesy of Hollywood during the seventies and eighties. Actually, until Spielberg's *Close Encounters* in 1978 alien visitors had been thin on the planet during the seventies but one exception was Thomas Newton in *The Man Who Fell to Earth* in 1976. Directed by Nicolas Roeg, from a screenplay by Roeg and Paul Mayersberg, it was based on the 1963 novel by Walter Tevis. This superior sf novel is highly evocative and almost impressionistic in style and tells of an alien who comes to Earth to use the planet's resources to build a spacecraft large enough to save most of the inhabitants of his dying world (presumably Mars), only to fall foul of mankind's xenophobia. It was transformed by Roeg and Mayersberg into a confused and self-indulgent film that alternates between pretentiousness and moments of cinematic brilliance. Yes, as I may have intimated by now, this movie did irritate me.

Why in particular? Well, the relatively clear-cut narrative of the book has been replaced by a non-linear structure that swings back and forth in time in a manner that has become Roeg's stylistic trademark as a director. It worked marvellously in *Don't Look Now* and *Bad Timing* but not on this occasion. Elements of the novel which were perfectly straightforward, such as the reason for the alien's visit, have been needlessly obscured. Other changes are simply illogical. In the novel Newton tries to resist having his head X-rayed because he knows that his ultra-sensitive eyes will be

Candy Clark is less than happy to discover that David Bowie is an alien, something we've long suspected.

permanently damaged but in the film the X-rays, for some inexplicable reason, merely fuse his contact lenses to his eyes. Various unnecessary characters and incidents have been added, including some embarrassing sequences set on his home world where his wife and children totter about some sand dunes in what appear to be up-market Buck Rogers costumes.

Clearly, like other film-makers before him who have had no interest in or knowledge of sf (such as John Boorman with *Zardoz*), Roeg seems to have felt that he was slumming by dealing with an sf subject and so was obliged to wrap the subject up in a pretentious disguise. As Paul Mayersberg wrote in *Sight and Sound* magazine: '*The Man Who Fell to Earth* is an extravagant entertainment. It has dozens of scenes that go together, not just in terms of plot, but also like circus acts following one another: the funny, the violent, the frightening, the sad, the horrific, the spectacular, the romantic and so on. We have clowns and lions and trapeze artists and dancing elephants and performing seals and ladies fired from cannons . . .' Bloody hell. But no, it's not as bad as all that; Mayersberg was speaking a mite metaphorically here (unless the dancing elephants etc. were cut from the print I saw). Earlier in the article he had given the game away when he wrote: 'When Nicholas Roeg first showed [the novel] to me the adaption looked like being a relatively simple matter, at least from the point of view of a screenplay. That's to say there didn't seem to be any major obstacles in the development of the plot. The characters looked essentially right, the mood was coherent, and so on. Later, as I wrote the first draft, I became aware that the eventual film was not going to be at all easy. Slowly I began to see why the book had not been filmed before. In an odd way it was *too much of a good thing*.'[1] (My italics.) But, alas, this realization didn't stop him and he went ahead and wrote his silly screenplay anyway.

The film, though, has its moments of visual brilliance and David Bowie looks convincing as the frail, ethereal and terribly vulnerable alien. It's just a pity he's not much of an actor. The rest of the cast is fine, particularly Candy Clark as Mary-Lou, the crude and boozy girl who loves Newton no matter who or what he is and also introduces him to alcohol, and Rip Torn as the scientist Nathan Bryce who becomes the Judas who finally betrays Newton. But the longer the movie lasts the more incoherent it gets and the last half hour is really tedious. Twenty-three minutes was cut from the film when it was initially released in the United States which is presumably why the reviewer on *Time* magazine could describe it as 'pretty straightforward science fiction.' I'd like to have seen that version. Whoever did the cutting must have done a hell of a job.

The year that *The Man Who Fell to Earth* was released was the same year that George Lucas was making *Star Wars*, the movie that was to have the biggest influence on the commerical cinema since *Dr No*. In the last chapter we saw the effect it had on one film-maker, Ridley Scott, and there's an indication it might have had a similar affect on Roeg because at that time he became involved in Dino de Laurentiis's *Flash Gordon* project. It's a shame we never got to see what Roeg would have made of it, or whether or not he would have reflected a *Star Wars* influence because he left the project and Dino went on to make the abomination described in Chapter Ten. Roeg's next movie, *Bad Timing* (1980), definitely had nothing to do with *Star Wars* or sf. I'm glad he made it as I think it's one of his best movies but then came *Eureka* in 1981 and while, like all his movies, it has things to admire, it also makes *The Man Who Fell to Earth* seem simplistic in its structure (and I'm talking about the full-length version). After a limited release the studio promptly put it on the shelf where, apart from some sporadic attempts at distribution, it has tended to remain ever since. His latest film to date is the very commercial children's fantasy, *The Witches*, which he made for the late and greatly lamented Jim Henson.

It might appear that George Lucas's decision to make a big sf movie influenced Steven Spielberg's choice of genre for his next movie after *Jaws*, which was *Close Encounters of the Third Kind* (1977), but he had actually been working on an idea for a UFO movie for several years, and in fact had been fascinated with UFOs since the age of six. He maintains, however, that he is a UFO agnostic. 'I'd *love* to believe. I haven't seen one — not for want of trying.' He maintains, rightly, that *Close Encounters* isn't a science fiction film ('My father was into sf but I've never cared for it much.') Instead: 'It's a UFO movie. It's about what people believe is happening. Sixteen million Americans believe that UFOs are visiting us. That we're under some sort of close scrutiny and have been for many years. And, yes, I believe that the government is covering up, doing everything in its power to pooh-pooh the UFO controversy.'[2] Thankfully, he also rightly separates the UFO phenomenon from science fiction though naturally the two can't help but overlap in the mind of the public. But I think you can safely say that most sf writers and fans, while willing to believe that intelligent life (whatever that actually means) probably does exist elsewhere in the universe, or even in this galaxy, do not believe that UFOs are alien spaceships, while most UFO enthusiasts do believe just that. That is a generalization, folks; if you happen to be an sf fan who does believe that UFOs are spaceships please don't write to tell me. Also if you are a UFO enthusiast who happens to believe that UFOs are entities from the astral plane, please don't write and tell me either.

In Chapter Three I mentioned the widespread belief in flying saucers during the fifties. While the phenomenon has never really gone away there seems to have been a resurgence in the seventies which is continuing to this day. *Close Encounters* certainly served to fan the flames. I, as you might expect, do not believe that UFOs are space vehicles from other worlds. As it is seems likely that no other life exists within our solar system our alien visitors would have to come from another star and even the nearest star is an awfully long way away. An awfully long way. A lot of people just don't seem to appreciate the cosmic distances between stars, and I admit that's

In Close Encounters
aliens have travelled vast
distances across space in
order to play silly games
with a young mother and
her son.

The man who gave us
friendly aliens galore:
Steven Spielberg at work
on Close Encounters of
the Third Kind.

The strong religious
element in UFO movies is
evident in this shot from
Close Encounters.

the fault of sf writers and the makers of sf movies and TV shows. Especially the makers of the latter. It all seems so simple: 'Warp factor one, Mr Sulu,' says the captain on the old 'Star Trek' and all those stars go whizzing by on the view screen (the new series is just as scientifically loopy; I saw one episode where the *Enterprise* goes very, very fast indeed and ends up on the 'edge' of the universe!). It may sound like sacrilege coming from an sf writer but I seriously doubt interstellar voyages will ever be possible. Yes, I know that sounds like one of those arrogant types who once claimed that the human body wouldn't survive speeds of thirty miles per hour, that the sound barrier would never be broken or that man would never land on the moon, but this is rather different. Einstein's law governing the speed of light isn't going to be revoked and I doubt if scientists are ever going to invent the equivalent of a hyperdrive to get round that annoying law. Oh sure, one day we'll no doubt be technically capable of putting a load of people in a big spaceship and shunting them off in the direction of a 'nearby' star and many years later the grandchildren or the great grandchildren, or the great, great, etc. grandchildren of the original passengers will get there (either that or the original passengers will make the journey in suspended animation, another sf device that we haven't quite got the hang of yet) but interstellar travel like that commonly shown in the movies and on TV will never happen.

I could be wrong. Only recently I heard a British flying saucer buff on the radio plugging his new book. He said that he had been assured by scientists that hyperdrive was technically feasible. But then he also said that the nearest star to Earth that had planets was nine light years away. Either he's coming from the Twilight Zone or the scientific magazines I read are way behind in reporting the latest developments. So let's say I am wrong and these members of much superior civilization have got a hyperdrive and the capability of visiting the Earth regularly — you're telling me they come all the way out here just to leave corn circles in fields and probe the bodily orifices of people like Whitley Strieber? These are the actions of a superior race? Okay, to be fair to Strieber he doesn't say that the entities he described in his bestselling 'true' book are aliens from outer space, he only suggests they might be, along with providing a whole string of other suppositions about their nature, but many other people have claimed to have undergone similar assaults from aliens.

One of the linchpins of UFOology is the belief that a flying saucer crashed in Arizona in 1947 and that the United States Air Force grabbed the wreckage and have been hiding it ever since. Whitley Strieber (for it is he again) wrote a 'novel' about the event called *Majestic*, which he said was based on thorough research. I heard him being interviewed on the radio when he was in Britain to flog his book (if you put all the books on UFOs end to end you'd be mad). He said that the intelligence officer who investigated the crash site knew it was wreckage from a UFO because the metal he found was as thin as the tin-foil in a cigarette packet but could not be bent or even dented with a sledgehammer. The Air Force, said Strieber, collected three truckloads of this wreckage but after calling a press conference to announce the find of the century they had an abrupt change of mind and displayed to the press the remains of a weather balloon. The Great UFO Cover-Up had begun, and goes on to this day. But why? Why would any American government want to keep the existence of wreckage from a flying saucer a state secret? Well, according to Strieber in the interview I heard, it's all the work of Christian fundamentalists in the CIA who are afraid that the religious faith of America would be undermined if the public got wind of the alien visitors.

I find that explanation just a little difficult to swallow but my real difficulty lies with the idea that the official lid has successfully been kept on the cover-up ever since 1947. We're talking about the country that gave us Watergate, the country where model versions of its super-secret Stealth bombers were sold as toys long before the government officially acknowledged the aircraft's existence. No, if in the real world the United States Air Force had got its hands on a genuine alien spacecraft made of an ultra-light but super-strong alloy in 1947 you can bet your bottom dollar that in 1948 Air Force planes would have been constructed of the same material.

I don't know if it figured in Strieber's novel (look, I read *Communion*; enough is enough) but a major part of the legend surrounding the UFO crash of 1947 is that the bodies of the alien crew were also found and have been on ice in some secret base ever since. They do feature in the movie *Hangar 18* (1980) which is an updated version of the 1947 'incident'. Here a flying saucer is sent plunging to Earth after being hit by a satellite launched from a space shuttle. Recovered by the Air Force, it is taken to a base to be checked over by a team of scientists. Complete secrecy has been imposed, simply because a presidential election is imminent and the President's advisor, played by Robert Vaughn, thinks that the President's chances of re-election could be damaged if he was associated with a flying saucer. Doesn't seem too logical; in fact as so many appear to believe in UFOs it should have enhanced his popularity. Anyway, Vaughn starts going to extreme lengths to supress any word of the saucer getting out while the investigators are making some important discoveries, including the dead bodies of the alien crew and an Earthwoman who has been stored alive in a chamber. They also make the connection between the alien alphabet and ancient symbols found on prehistoric ruins. Erich Von Daniken rides again. Finally they deduce that the aliens plan to conquer the world but the President's advisor now arranges for a bomb-laden plane to crash on the base, killing everyone (the voice-over at the end that announces there were survivors after all was added for the TV version). It's competently made but really only for UFOologists and conspiracy buffs. The director was James L. Conway.

Another government conspiracy involving aliens featured in *Strange Invaders* (1983), and a strange mish-mash of a movie it is. Written and directed by Michael Laughlin, it's an only partly successful homage to the sf movies of the fifties (it even has Kenneth Tobey in a small role). The ambiguous aliens have taken over a small town in Illinois, replacing the original inhabitants with themselves in human disguise, and it's all part of some 25-year deal they've made with the United States government. Paul Le Mat plays Charles Bigelow, who uncovers the truth when he goes to the town in search of his estranged wife Margaret (Fiona Lewis) and his daughter. It turns out that Margaret is an alien herself who disobeyed the rules and went off to have a baby with a human. The aliens are also searching for the pair and Charles has to contend with both them and government agents who are anxious to keep the lid on the conspiracy, as government agents tend to do in films like these. Charles is aided in his quest by a newspaper editor, played by Nancy Allen, who has made a speciality out of such roles in sf films where she lends lone support to a man who is misunderstood or disbelieved by everyone else (e.g., *The Philadelphia Experiment*, *Robocop 1* and *2*). For all its mood of menace and paranoia the movie ends happily with the town's original inhabitants being brought back to life after spending the intervening twenty-five years as blue, glowing spheres. Quirky, off-beat and fairly entertaining but just not quite right in the plotting department.

In 1982 the man who doesn't care much for science fiction, Stephen Spielberg, gave us another movie about alien visitors: *E.T. — The Extra-Terrestial*, and proved again that he knew how to deliver exactly what people, and children, wanted. *E.T.* became the all-time box office success.

When I first went to see this I went prepared to sneer but instead came away impressed. As I wrote at the time, Spielberg doesn't put a directorial foot wrong. *E.T.* is maybe no more than a reworking of an old *Lassie* movie — *E.T. Come Home, Lassie Phone Home?* — and is made with a skill and conviction that places it light-years beyond the old-fashioned Hollywood tearjerkers of that kind. And, most importantly, it possesses a marvellous sense of humour that saves it, in the main, from becoming unbearably sentimental.

The plot, as you surely must know by heart, concerns this little alien who gets left behind on Earth after his fellow E.T.s are obliged to make a hasty take-off in their spaceship to avoid being caught by the sinister Man With the Keys (Peter Coyote, whose character seems the reverse side of the one played by François Truffaut in *Close Encounters*, though in the end he turns out to be an okay guy). He is accompanied by his government henchmen (though I still can't understand how they missed spotting the alien spaceship, which looks like a hundred foot tall Christmas decoration covered in bright lights while they were chasing E.T. about in the shrubbery). Poor little lost E.T. (sniff) hides out in the garden shed of an all-American family (but one lacking a Dad). In a beautiful little sequence the alien makes contact with the youngest son, Elliott (Henry Thomas) and soon all three of the kids are involved in a conspiracy to keep E.T.'s existence a secret from their mom (Dee Wallace) and the community at large. But apart from The Man With the Keys, E.T. has another problem: he won't be able to survive on Earth unless he can contact his fellow aliens and have them pick him up (yes, here comes the classic line: 'E.T. phone home.') And when the Man and the other government agents do succeed in capturing him and submit him to a medical examination the little alien actually snuffs it.

It is here, and with the scenes of E.T. coming back to life, that Spielberg does cross the line between pathos and bathos (and the shots of a very

More pseudo-religious awe in E.T. *as the children behold the form of the little alien.*

rubbery-looking E.T. receiving heart massage are regrettably ludicrous). Amusingly, E.T.'s resurrection suggested to some American critics that the film should be interpreted as a Christian allegory (as *The Day the Earth Stood Still* was years before). 'I never anticipated,' said Spielberg, 'religious parallels with the Immaculate Heart, which people find E.T.'s glowing chest to be. Or the fact that E.T. comes back to life . . . I'm a nice, Jewish boy from Phoenix, Arizona. My mother would not, I think, be giving me my mozah-ball soup ration if I came out and admitted there was any kinda Christ parallel! It was never my intention to draw myself into sainthood.' Maybe, but the protracted farewell sequence where all the humans are staring in reverence at the alien reminded me of similar sequences in those old Hollywood religious epics where people encounter Christ. And as for Spielberg's famous statement, 'I thought I was making a little film, my most personal film, that only a few of my closest friends would enjoy.'[3] . . . well if you believe that then you'll believe in all those fundamentalist CIA agents of Whitley Strieber's.

But I did believe Spielberg when he said: 'If there's any parallel with *E.T.* and any movie I saw as a child it's *The War of the Worlds*. I remember the one moment in that film when Gene Barry and Ann Robinson were trapped in the wrecked house and Gene destroys the probe that has come through the window to seek them out. Then the Martian hand comes out of the side of the frame and grips Robinson's shoulder. She screams, he throws something at it and the Martian goes running off with his little hands in the air. That was supposed to be scary — terrifying — but I thought it was delightful.'[4] So much so that Spielberg repeats part of that sequence in *E.T.* when E.T.'s hand appears from out of frame and grips Elliott on the shoulder in a scene in his bedroom.

No matter what other movie Spielberg makes during the remainder of his career, it seems more than likely that *E.T.* will be the one to be regarded as his finest achievement, the one where he out-Disneyed Disney at capturing and recreating the magic of childhood fantasies. But before we move on, a word of praise also for Melissa Mathison who wrote the screenplay. The film has plenty of great lines, one of my favourites being when Elliott's older brother asks him if he's explained school to E.T. and Elliott replies, 'How do you explain school to a higher intelligence?' Another one occurs at the end of the movie when the brothers are about to spring the revived E.T. from the government agents and Elliott is telling his school friends that E.T. is a man from space and that they're going to take him to his spaceship. 'Why doesn't he just beam himself up?' asks one of the kids. 'Forget about all that stuff,' cries Elliott, 'this is reality!'

John Carpenter, no doubt rather fazed by the failure of his nasty alien movie, *The Thing* (1982, see Chapter Thirteen), unwisely decided to make a nice alien movie, which turned out to be a slightly more adult version of *E.T.* It was called *Starman* (1985). Now I had sat impressed but completely dry-eyed throughout *E.T.* while stronger critics than me sobbed into their Kleenex but I must admit that *Starman* had me close to bawling my heart out. As I said at the time, to describe *Starman* as a science fiction movie is like calling a sinking ship a submarine. Okay, I may be overreacting — it's only a movie, for God's sake! — but this one hit me hard. Not because of the direction, or the photography or the acting, with one exception, but because of the stupid script. Step forward writers Dean Reisner, Bruce A. Evans and Raynold Gideon and face the charge of bringing science fiction into disrepute.

Right, we shall now observe how the guilty men named above distorted, bent and in other ways abused the rules of science fiction in order to fit the demands of their screwy plot. The movie starts okay with a shot of the

Voyager probe (yes, that probe again — the one that caused all the problems in *Star Trek: The Motion Picture*) cruising through space to the accompaniment of the Stones's 'Satisfaction', a recording held on the probe along with the metal plate that has the illustration of a man and a woman and the probe's point of origin. And then the probe encounters what I originally thought to be a planet but is actually a giant spherical spaceship. After absorbing the probe the alien ship sends out a little ship which whizzes away and reaches Earth before you can say Albert Einstein and is promptly shot down by the United States Air Force.

The craft crashes in a forest near the rural residence of one Jenny Hayden (Karen Allen) who is drunkenly mourning her dead husband, recently cut down in his prime, who, by the photographs we see, bore a startling resemblance to Jeff Bridges. The disembodied alien, a ball of glowing light, enters the house and proceeds to create a human body from the genetic information contained in one of Jenny's dead husband's hairs. Now this is a nifty idea but it's the only original one in the entire movie. So a shocked Jenny is faced with the resurrected body of her husband but knows for certain that it's not really her husband because he's acting in a pretty weird way. Jeff Bridges may have got an Oscar nomination for his performance in this but I thought his version of an alien inhabiting a human body was something of a tired cliché — stiff-legged walk, face alternating between blank and funny expressions, and those inevitable gaps between the words. But despite his imitation of Jerry Lewis, with a touch of Stan Laurel and Robin Williams also thrown in, he does get the message across that he has only three days to reach the big meteor crater in Arizona. Why? Well, that's where and when he's due to be picked up by his mothership. And if he misses the boat he's in trouble because he can only survive for three days on Earth? Again — why? He's got a perfectly good body, freshly cloned and all that. The only alien thing about him is his mind so why can't he live longer than three days? Because the writers have seen *E.T.* and maybe even *The War of the Worlds*, and know it's traditional for alien visitors to come over all poorly after a stay on Earth. No particular reason, it's just an accepted thing.

And if the human body the alien has grown is only good for three days why bother growing it in the first place? Why didn't the alien use one of its magic balls (yes, he has several magic balls) to call home and say, 'Hey,

The alien in Starman *has Christ-like characteristics too; here Karen Allen and Charles Martin Smith regard him with reverence.*

sorry guys, I missed Arizona. I ended up in Wisconsin. Come and pick me up here instead. I'll pay the difference in the fuel bill out of my own pocket.' True, the alien doesn't appear to have any pockets in his disembodied form but he must have carried the magic balls in something.

The other big question is why he came to Earth in the first place. The suggestion is that the visit is a response to the message plaque on the *Voyager* probe and that the alien has come to study humanity, but if that's the case why was he heading for a hole in the ground in the middle of Arizona? Of course the real reason he came to Earth was to be cute like E.T., charm the pants off Jenny Hayden and ultimately give her a baby. All the other elements in the movie are arbitrary plot devices that exist merely to set up the central love story and have no logical meaning. Take the last-minute arrival of the mothership — how did it manage to penetrate America's air defences when the much smaller alien craft at the beginning was easily detected and intercepted? And what of the illogical behaviour of Richard Jaeckel's military character who wants to submit the alien to vivisection? He's already been told that the alien is an exact genetic duplication of a dead man so cutting him up, alive or dead, wouldn't provide a scrap of information about the actual alien. The Jaeckel character is there, and behaves the way he does, simply because it's another tradition that nice aliens are always hounded by nasty military types, as in *E.T.* (and just like *E.T.* there's a Christ reference when the alien first brings back to life a deer and then later Jenny herself).

Starman is yet another of those fake sf movies I keep talking about. The Jeff Bridges character doesn't have to be an alien from outer space. You could remove all the sf elements and the main story wouldn't be affected in any way. For example, he could be an escapee from an oppressive mental hospital suffering from the after-effects of an unnecessary brain operation — a lobotomy would be ideal — foisted upon him by the nasty hospital authorities. This scenario would not only provide a better explanation for Jeff Bridges's performance but would allow the relationship between him and Karen Allen to develop in the same grindingly predictable way as she drives him across the country to escape the pursuing authorities.

But there is a happy ending to all this: *Starman* crashed at the box office and John Carpenter went back to making nasty alien films.

I got similarly incensed a few months after the release of *Starman* by another incredibly dumb alien movie, *Cocoon*. This was directed by Ron

The cast of Cocoon, *a film I loathe even more than* Starman.

Howard, the former child actor who had previously directed the charming and amusing fantasy about a mermaid, *Splash*. *Cocoon* is a fantasy too but someone decided to give this whimsical, mawkish fable a science fictional rationale. It seems that ten thousand years ago a bunch of aliens landed on Earth and set up a base. Their leader had the choice of either the North Pole or Atlantis and chose the latter (which, according to this movie, was located just off the coast of Florida). The inevitable happened: Atlantis sank and the aliens had to leave Earth in a hurry (why? why didn't they just move to nearby Florida?). In so much of a hurry, moreover, that they were obliged to leave twenty of their companions behind. But even though they didn't have time to get their companions into the spaceship they did have time to seal each one of them into a, wait for it . . . cocoon.

So for the last ten thousand years these aliens have been lying there on the sea bed in their pods waiting for their colleagues to pull their collective finger out and return to rescue them. Why there is a ten-thousand-year wait is conveniently not explained. And what do the aliens do when they finally return? Do they use their superior technological powers to pluck the cocoons up from the sea bed? Do they hover over the ocean in their huge spaceship and use the anti-gravity beam we see them use at the end of the movie to lift up a boat-load of senior citizens? Nope. What these superior aliens do is disguise themselves as humans, go to Florida, hire a fishing boat and its captain (Steve Guttenberg), go back out to sea, lift the cocoons up by hand using scuba equipment, take the cocoons back to Florida and store them in a swimming pool next to an old people's home . . .

All this illogical plotting exists simply to provide a — hah! — explanation for the movie's central event, a group of the old people from the home who regularly use the swimming pool on the sly becoming rejuvenated, though not in physical appearance, and revert to adolescent behaviour. Surely it would have been a lot simpler to have provided a supernatural reason for the whole thing. Like, the pool was built over the legendary Fountain of Youth, or maybe a good fairy gave them a reward for freeing her from a spider web. There was no need to drag poor, innocent science fiction into these embarrassing proceedings. But without the sf elements you wouldn't have been able to have the big science fiction finish: the oldsters head out to sea, hotly pursued by the nasty authorities (why? they haven't broken any law) and down comes the mandatory giant rotating spaceship with lots of flashing lights (ILM must have a warehouse full of these things by now) which scoops them up and takes them away to alien heaven. Maybe this film has a serious sub-text about how the elderly are regarded in modern American society but all I saw was an exercise in pure bathos. The screenplay was by Tom Benedek (hiss!) from a novel by David Saperstein (I've never read this so I don't know how much blame should be attributed to the latter).

Fine cast though, including Brian Dennehy, Jack Gilford, Maureen Stapleton, Jessica Tandy and Hume Cronyn, and there were some lovely moments of visual magic, such as the evocative opening with the dolphins appearing out of the sea to squeak at the strange lights in the sky, and the scene where Tahnee Welch (Raquel's daughter) peels off her skin.

Husband and wife Hume Cronyn and Jessica Tandy appeared in another mawkish movie involving cute aliens, *batteries not included* (1988), directed by Matthew Robbins from an idea that escaped from Steven Spielberg's TV series 'Amazing Stories', and was no doubt inspired by those classics of American cinematic sentimentality, It's a Wonderful Life and Miracle on 34th Street. (There was a marvellous story in the June 1988 issue of The Magazine of Fantasy and Science by Bradley Denton called 'The Calvin Coolidge Home for Dead Comedians' which had Lenny Bruce turning up in purgatory where one of the punishments was having to watch It's a Wonderful Life over and over again — sheer hell in Lenny's opinion and mine too.) Tandy and Cronyn play an old couple struggling to preserve their apartment house and hamburger bar in a part of the Lower East Side of New York City which is being razed by a property developer (hiss! boo!). The developer has hired some young thugs, led by Michael Carmine, to terrorize the couple and their few remaining tenants (an artist, a pregnant girl and an ex-boxer) out of the building. When the thugs smash up the burger bar it looks like the end for sure but that night Cronyn prays for a miracle and it arrives — in the form of two small flying saucers. Where do they come from? Outer space? God? Who knows? The director certainly didn't. 'I'm not interested in lengthy explanations for extraordinary things,' he said. 'One line in the script goes: "The quickest way to end a miracle is to question it." I firmly believe it.'[5] How convenient.

The saucers then proceed to push the frontiers of cuteness into whole new areas of queasiness. Not only do they fly about repairing things, including the burger bar, but they also set up a nest in a shed (stable?) on the roof and proceed to give birth to three even smaller flying saucers. There's some heavy drama when one of the baby saucers appears to have kicked the bucket but all ends well with masses of saucers arriving to reconstruct the building after the evil property developer (hiss!) has burned it down. Again, the acting is fine and the special effects by, of course, ILM, are superb but this movie, concocted by *five* different screenwriters, is so gooey it would have E.T. phoning home for some bicarbonate of soda.

With *Alien Nation* (1989) we have our old favourite, the 'fake sf movie' again. At the start of the movie we are told that a vast spaceship containing 300,000 aliens has landed. The aliens are actually slaves of some other species and are genetically designed to adapt to different conditions on various planets in order to function as efficient workers. The United States government graciously lets them settle in Los Angeles where they quickly learn to mimic the human inhabitants and become a mirror image of LA society. Heavy stuff, but does the movie explore all the potentially fascinating aspects of this intriguing situation? I mean, what effect does the knowledge that there is a whole alien interstellar civilization out there have on our world? And what have we learnt from the aliens about their masters? Is there a possibility that their masters might turn up and ask for their property back? Did we learn anything technically valuable from the alien slave-ship? How come the aliens' story was accepted so readily? Why weren't they kept in quarantine for a considerable time just in case something wasn't right? And so on. But none of these areas are of any interest to the film-makers. All that sf stuff, like the sf background to *Cocoon*, isn't really necessary to the story but is there to set up a gimmicky situation, in this case to provide a twist on the old mismatched cop movie genre. You know — tough male cop obliged to team up with female cop (*The Enforcer*), white cop with black cop (*Lethal Weapon* and countless others), Russian cop with American cop (*Red Heat*), human cop with police dog (pick any title) and so on. Here we have red-neck white cop (James Caan) whose murdered partner has been replaced by one of the first of the aliens to become a cop (Mandy Patinkin). After the initial period of mutual dislike they predictably learn that they have more in common than they realize and by the end are buddy-buddies. Yawn.

There is absolutely no reason for Caan's partner to be an alien. You could do exactly the same story if the movie was set in a Chinese district and the new partner was Chinese. After all, the aliens aren't really very alien in the first place, they just have different skins and eat 'funny' foods, just like any other ethnic minority. No, this is a dumb, cynically motivated sf movie and it's a pity that it came from the team of Gale Anne Hurd and James Cameron. True, Cameron doesn't get a credit on the movie but apparently he rewrote the screenplay that had originally been written by Rockne O'Bannon, the former story editor of the eighties 'Twilight Zone' TV series (O'Bannon was not happy, it is said, about the way his screenplay was treated). And apart from the misconceived story and script, the direction, by Graham Baker, definitely lacked the zip and verve of a Cameron-directed movie.

Though Cameron and Hurd's marriage had ended they were still working together professionally at this point. I had extremely high hopes for their next production, *The Abyss*, because it combined my life-long fascination with the ocean deeps, underwater vehicles and marine technology with the theme of alien invasion. As I mentioned before, one of my favourite sf novels is John Wyndham's *The Kraken Wakes*, and I'd always wished someone would film it, and from the early pieces of information I received about *The Abyss* it seemed that James Cameron was filming, if not Wyndham's novel, a story very similar. Alas, it was not to be, for Cameron had been bitten by the Spielberg bug and what we got was *Close Encounters at Twenty Thousand Fathoms*. Yup, it was an attack of the 'cute alien saviours from outer space' syndrome. The aliens even look kind of similar to Spielberg's except they have fins and things . . .

At least, one presumes they're aliens from outer space because the movie doesn't convey much information in that area. Of course I knew they were aliens because I'd read Orson Scott Card's novelization (in an afterword, he writes: 'For good or ill, this novel is as close a collaboration between film-maker and novelist as any other since the collaboration between Kubrick and Clarke on *2001: A Space Odyssey* . . .'). But the novel contains much omitted in the movie. An important part of the original plot dealt with a build-up of tension between the United States and the Soviet Union. A nuclear war seems imminent and the aliens are aware of it. At the climax the aliens create huge tidal waves that rise above the coastlines of the

(Right) 'Life's Abyss and then you dive,' was the saying among the crew during the difficult and hazardous underwater shooting of The Abyss.

(Left) James Cameron, director of The Abyss, along with Terminator 1 & 2, and Aliens.

continents and just hover there as a demonstration of their power (just as Klaatu stopped all machinery around the world in *The Day the Earth Stood Still* forty years earlier) and the war is averted as a result. But because of the outbreak of glasnost, which occurred during the shooting of the movie, these sequences were cut by Cameron, along with the shots of military build-up. These cuts serve to unbalance the movie because now there seems to be no dramatic reason for the aliens in the story. If I hadn't read the novelization I don't think I would have grasped what was supposed to be going on in the final stages of the movie.

Cameron defended the cuts and the movie itself. 'My idea for NTI — Non Terrestial Intelligence — contact was conceived right after *Aliens*. Why should I want to make *Aliens* again underwater? I'd done *Aliens* and I was very happy with it, so why repeat it? I wanted to make the definitive monster movie with *Aliens* and I think I succeeded. The sense of disappointment some people have when the aliens in *The Abyss* turn out to be nice says a lot about the audience now for movies.'[6]

Well, that certainly puts me in my place. But there is much to admire in *The Abyss*. For one thing it was a tremendous technical achievement in terms of special effects — the miniature work in particular being of a very high standard, and there are some quite astonishing computer-generated images. The actual filming was a technical feat too, much of it taking place in very trying conditions inside the flooded reactor chambers of an uncompleted nuclear power station. The larger concrete chamber held 7.5 million gallons of water while the smaller held 2.6 million. Cameron, cast and crew spent five months in those tanks and it was no wonder that the slogan the crew eventually had printed on their t-shirts was 'LIFE'S ABYSS AND THEN YOU DIVE'. According to one actor, 'Almost every cast member knew moments of honest fright and unspeakable boredom, and most suffered at some point from ear-aches, chlorine-parched skin, poisoned hair and puckered appendages, which even professional divers don't have to contend with.'[7] Not surprisingly, some of his cast members weren't on speaking terms with him by the time the film was finished. Cameron took this philosophically, saying, 'They're not so much enemies as disgruntled people. I tend to do work at a pretty high energy level, and people aren't ready for the deleterious emotional effects at times.' Or as the film's star, Ed Harris, put it, 'I'm not talking about *The Abyss* and I never will.'[8]

Unlike many a film-maker working in the science fiction genre, Cameron does his research and gets his facts right. Having some knowledge of underwater matters, I couldn't find any fault with the technical aspects of the movie. For example, Cameron has his underwater oil drilling rig and his divers working at a feasible two thousand feet below the surface, unlike the makers of the other underwater sf movies that were rushed into production as soon as word about *The Abyss* got out (in true Hollywood feeding frenzy style), and who set their stories at truly ludicrous depths, six miles being the record in *Deep Star Six*.

All the stuff about nice aliens aside, there is a serious movie inside *The Abyss* that is trying to get out. That movie is about two primal concerns of humanity — love and death — and is carried by two of the central characters, Bud and Lindsey Brigman, played by Ed Harris and Mary Elizabeth Mastrantonio, an estranged married couple on the verge of divorce but forced by circumstances into close proximity again. It is clear, as the plot progresses, that they are still in love despite their surface antagonism. It is made most clear in one of the film's most harrowing sequences when they are both trapped on the sea bottom in a damaged submersible which is slowly flooding and there is only one diving-suit, which he is wearing. She comes up with the desperate scheme that she will allow herself to drown and he will then tow her the four hundred or so metres to the underwater drilling rig which has the means for him to resuscitate her. He unwillingly goes along with the plan and she duly drowns in a horribly convincing sequence where she at first attempts to face her fate resolutely but then gives into the inevitable panic. It is made doubly horrible by his having to helplessly watch her die in his arms. He then drags her body to the rig where he and his colleagues attempt to resuscitate her but their efforts seem futile. The others give up but he makes one last frenzied effort and more or less bullies her back to life. An emotionally powerful scene that displays the depth of his love for her.

And he too must subsequently suffer a death experience, though in his case it is symbolic; first he is obliged to 'drown' by being sealed into a helmet which is then filled with a liquid (a fluorocarbon emulsion) which will allow him to get sufficient oxygen into his lungs while enabling him to withstand greater water pressure, prior to free-falling into the abyss in

The marvellous Mary Elizabeth Mastrantonio in a close, and wet, encounter with an alien in The Abyss.

order to defuse a nuclear warhead that lies at the bottom (it's been that sort of day).

His long descent into the blackness of the abyss is genuinely disturbing. It touches several exposed nerve endings simultaneously — not least for being a visual metaphor for death itself — working on one's fear of falling, of claustrophobia, of suffocation, of extreme vulnerability and just about every other basic, primal fear imaginable. But then the movie makes a miscalculation. It should have worked. It's dramatically right and it works in the novelization but at the screening where I saw the movie it went terribly wrong. What happens is this: Bud is understandably close to mental disintegration as he continues his chilling descent into the abyss and Lindsey takes over the radio link with him in order to provide emotional support. At first she is all matter-of-fact efficiency but then her true feelings get the better of her and it all comes out, ending in a declaration that she will never leave him. Unfortunately, she begins thus: 'Bud, there's some . . . things I need to say. It's hard for me, you know. It's not easy being such a cast-iron bitch . . . But it wasn't all bad, I know that. Do you remember the bike trip . . . ?' Well, the audience I was with just roared with laughter at that and destroyed the magic. Admittedly they were a preview audience and preview audiences tend to be made up of prats, but it did seem pretty hilarious at the time, the incongruous juxtaposition between his harrowing situation and her babbling on about being a cast-iron bitch and bicycle trips.

Even so, their relationship dominates the movie, thanks especially to strong performances from Harris and Mastrantonio, and not the drippy aliens. Cameron was aware of this and said in an interview at the time, 'Their relationship worked very well. If possible it worked too well, actually, as the goals of the sci-fi aspect aren't as interesting as a result. The most emotional scene in the movie is when Lindsey elects to drown and it doesn't rely on any special effects. From an evolutionary standpoint as a film-maker I feel it's my cue to get away from effects based movies.' In the same interview he scotched a persistent rumour at the time: 'I have nothing to do with *Blade Runner II*. I wouldn't be interested and I don't want to go around cleaning up after Ridley Scott for the rest of my life! Nor will I sequelize my own films.'[9] And what did he make next? *Terminator 2*, of course.

So to sum up the 'nice alien' movies of the period, in most cases the aliens are science fictional stand-ins for what were angels, or other benign supernatural beings, who came down to Earth and sorted out someone's problems or inspired them to change their lives etc in an earlier generation of Hollywood fantasies. From *Close Encounters*, through *E.T.* and all the way down to *The Abyss* they have a definite air of religiosity (mainly of the Californian variety). Even Thomas Newton, in *The Man Who Fell to Earth*, is presented as a fallen angel. The trend appears to have ended for the time being with real angels back in film fashion (even Paul Hogan, in his last cinematic atrocity, played an angel). I can only give my approval; in my book genuine aliens from outer space tend to wield heat rays rather than spreading messages of joy and happiness.

For me, it's a case of: E.T. go home!

...The bad...

As with movies about nice aliens visiting the Earth ones concerning the nasty variety were also thin on the planet during the seventies. Almost alone was *The Andromeda Strain*, directed in 1971 by Robert Wise and based on the novel by Michael Crichton. The novel, published in 1969, had put the noses of the established sf writers out of joint. How dare this guy Crichton come out of nowhere with a science fiction type novel that has the audacity to become a *bestseller!* There were also mutters in the sf fanzines that the book wasn't any good and was full of scientific errors and so on. But I was impressed with the novel when I read it back then (I haven't read it since) and thought the scientific and medical content were its strong points, which shouldn't be surprising as Crichton had trained as a doctor (before that he had graduated in anthropology at Harvard University).

When Wise and his screenwriter, Nelson Giddings, came to adapt the novel, they wisely decided to follow it as closely as possible. As a result *The Andromeda Strain* is rare among sf films in that real science is one of the most important factors in the development of the plot — in fact the recreation of scientific procedure *is* the plot.

The movie begins with the return of a space probe that has picked up some form of microscopic alien life. (When Crichton wrote his novel there was genuine concern among scientists that astronauts visiting the moon might bring back some kind of viral or bacterial infection and they were required to spend several days in quarantine after landing.) The probe lands near a small desert town in the United States where it is later opened by the local doctor. The result is instant death for everyone in the community except for one young baby and the town alcoholic. The government acts quickly and isolates the two survivors within a huge underground laboratory complex, called Wildfire, which has been built to cope with any future outbreak of germ warfare. Experts in various specialist areas are drafted in to form a team of investigators, the aim being to discover the nature of the alien beastie, named Andromeda, and to learn what the two survivors have in common that gave them protection. As an impressive array of medical and scientific equipment is brought into action (much of this expensive machinery actually functioned, such as the microscope and television link-up system, designed by Douglas Trumbull).

And so we watch engrossed (well I was) as the scientists carry out their tests in pathology, epidemiology and clinical microbiology in a race against time. First they discover that the alien life form is a crystalline organism that has no DNA but is constantly mutating. The link between the baby

A scene from The Andromeda Strain, *Robert Wise's superior sf thriller about a killer plague from space.*

and the old drunk takes longer to determine but by that time Andromeda has mutated into an organism that consumes rubber and starts eating the seals on the doors. When Andromeda starts to spread through the complex the computer decides the game is up and announces imminent destruction of Wildfire. One of the scientists (James Olson) must make a hazardous climb up through a ventilation shaft, dodging laser beams all the way because the computer has identified him as an escaped laboratory animal, in order to deactivate the bomb. Meanwhile, in the outside world, Andromeda has mutated into something completely harmless and is dissipating out over the ocean. During the movie there are some dramatic conflicts between the various scientists but they don't make much of an impression; Andromeda and all that shiny equipment are the real stars.

Maybe Phil Kaufman's decision in 1978 to remake the fifties sf classic *Invasion of the Body Snatchers* was a reaction to the overdose of sweetness and light in *Close Encounters*. I'd like to think so. The accepted lore about remakes is that they are invariably inferior to the originals but in this case it's not so. Also Kaufman's film isn't simply a remake; he's taken the central idea from the original film and transposed it to a different setting — a city rather than a small town — with a range of different characters. San Francisco is the city concerned and Donald Sutherland plays the main protagonist, Bennell, a health inspector (we first see him discovering rat droppings in a restaurant kitchen). When his assistant, Elizabeth (Brooke Adams) tells him worriedly that her boyfriend isn't his usual self, he takes her only half seriously. And at a party hosted by fashionable psychiatrist Dr David Kibner (Leonard Nimoy) he hears more stories from people who claim that their nearest and dearest are acting strangely; Dr Kibner blithely dismisses these worries as the result of stress caused by modern city living. But friends of Bennell do take the strange events seriously; they are two alternative society types, Jack (Jeff Goldblum) and his wife Nancy (Veronica Cartwright) who run a therapeutical mud-bath parlour. Nancy, who's clearly read her Von Daniken and seen *2001*, explains cheerfully about the takeover of the city: 'It's just like when aliens came down millions of years ago to breed with apes and produce man.' Bennell is confronted with the truth when a pod of Jack is found growing in the mud-bath room. By then it's too late to alert the authorities as the city has been more or less completely taken over and it's a case of personal survival. One by one

Bennell's small circle of companions fall victim to the pods and he is left alone.

Thanks to improved effects techniques, and a much bigger budget, Kaufman is able to produce some nicely squishy scenes of half-formed pod people emerging from their pods, and even squishier scenes of pod people being destroyed. The best example of that is in the sequence where Bennell falls asleep in the tiny garden of his hillside house and is oblivious to the pods that grow, gurgling obscenely, all around him. When he wakes he messily destroys them with a garden rake but, fatally, can't bring himself to destroy his own replica. Kaufman also makes clear something that the original film never did — what happens to the original person when the pod takes over. We see that in very graphic terms when Brooke Adams's body convincingly disintegrates in Sutherland's arms.

The film ends on a very downbeat note, as the original was to have done. After Bennell successfully burns down a pod nursery in a large warehouse we see him being approached by one of the last unaffected people who thinks, as we do, that Bennell is similarly okay, but in the final shot Bennell turns and points an accusing finger at him while giving forth with the weird cry that the aliens use to alert each other of the presence of a human in their midst.

Don Siegel, director of the original version, appears in a cameo role as the cab driver who picks up Sutherland and Adams as they attempt to flee to the airport. Apparently Kaufman was in Siegel's office discussing the cameo when Kevin McCarthy, star of the original, coincidentally dropped in and immediately agreed to do a cameo himself. He appears early in the movie when Sutherland and Adams are driving through San Francisco; at an intersection they are startled when McCarthy looms up over the windshield crying, "They're coming! They're coming! You're next!" just as he did at the original end of the first movie.

The 1978 *Invasion of the Body Snatchers* marked the beginning of a whole series of remakes of fifties sf movies, most of which did dismally at the box office, but before we take a look at the second such remake, John Carpenter's *The Thing*, I want to briefly talk about the disappointing revival of another famous fifties sf character, Professor Quatermass. He returned in the 1978 production *The Quatermass Conclusion*, this time played by John Mills. It was made as a TV serial consisting of four fifty-two-minute episodes but also designed to be seen in a cut-down cinema version lasting one hundred and five minutes. Neither version is effective. As Nigel Kneale, who wrote the script, said himself, one version was too long and the other too short. The story is set in a near-future Britain fallen into anarchy, and concerns thousands of hippy types descending upon prehistoric monuments such as Stonehenge, only to be zapped into space by mysterious aliens who have been breeding us for food. Despite its ambitious scope, it doesn't work and is too diffused and unfocused. Also, as I wrote at the time: '*The Quatermass Conclusion* appears to be a bitter reaction by a member of an older generation to the younger generation whose apparently irrational behaviour makes them appear to belong to a totally different species. Naturally, in the traditions of sf, these failings are exaggerated to the nth degree. Thus muggers and juvenile delinquents become armed gangs, and the hippy movement with its emphasis on mysticism, becomes the lemming-like Planet Church (I should point out that the script was originally written for the BBC back in 1973 when hippies were still numerous). It's very much a story of Age versus Youth and significantly it's the older people who are impervious to the malign alien influence.'

Beacons, buried deep in the ground around the world by aliens thousands of years in the past, have an influence on people that, over the generations, causes these places to assume a special unconscious significance and serve as magnets to large groups of people (amusingly, one of the beacons is buried under Wembley Stadium) — the basic idea is a good one and follows in the Quatermass tradition of linking the occult sites with sf, but it needed to be handled in a different way. *The Quatermass Conclusion*, apart from looking dated even back in 1978, simply lacks the slow build-up of tension and dread that was the trademark of the first three Quatermass adventures.

And now . . . *The Thing*. Unlike the first film version, this one went back to the premise of the original story. The alien is no longer an angry carrot in the form of James Arness but a shape-changing chameleon who can imitate the bodies, and the minds, of his victims. My initial reaction to the movie was similar to the one I had to *Alien* — I thought it was great horror but poor science fiction. As I wrote in my somewhat overwrought review: 'As an out-and-out, shock-at-any-cost horror *The Thing* is a 100 per cent

Kurt Russell makes the first of many grim discoveries in The Thing.

wow, but as a new version of John W. Campbell's classic sf novella, "Who Goes There?" it's a disappointment. I was expecting big things from John Carpenter and now I feel badly let down. Even the 1951 version, as far removed from Campbell's story as it was, was better science fiction than this. But I should have known when I read in *Cinefantastique* magazine that Carpenter's screenwriter Bill Lancaster (son of Burt) found that the novella's interplay of theories about the nature of the monster, and Campbell's philosophical speculation, were "confusing" and "would have bogged down the pace".

'Despite the screenplay going through several revisions in order to clarify just what the monster was doing to whom, I still found it confusing. There seemed to be so many bits and pieces of the Thing on the loose I couldn't figure out just how many monsters there were. For example, in the sequence where we first see the Thing — after the fake sled dog has turned itself inside out (a cinematic first in blechness) — you see part of the monster grow arms, detach itself from the main body and disappear out through a hole in the roof. I spent the rest of the movie waiting for this bit to make a reappearance but it never does. As the film progressed there seemed to be so many monsters on the loose I expected there to be a surprise ending in which the survivors realize that they're all aliens and that the last real human had gone in reel two. Admittedly it's technically very impressive, and has a real nightmare quality to it, but in my opinion the Howard Hawks version is the superior of the two as sf.'

The following year I was interviewing Debra Hill, who had produced several of Carpenter's earlier movies, and asked her why the film had bombed with audiences in America, which it had, and she more or less vindicated my original view: 'John and I are very, very close but I think that the picture was just too excessive. It became more Rob Bottin's film than John's. And speaking as a movie-goer and not as a friend of John's, I would have liked to have known more about the characters. As I didn't know them I didn't feel anything for them as each of them encountered the Thing. It didn't register emotionally. John disobeyed all the rules of suspense that he'd handled so well in *Halloween*. In that we spent the first thirty minutes of the film getting to know these girls so the audience would care when they got killed. And in the end Jamie Lee beats out the Shape and wins whereas at the end of *The Thing* Kurt Russell and the other guy are just sitting there looking at each other and saying, well, it's either you or me . . . there was no sense of relief at the end.' I asked her if the rumours were true that Carpenter cut out material that provided more background for their characters. 'Yeah, he did.' I don't know why he cut it but I never saw what he cut, I only saw the finished movie. I visited him on the set a few times but that was as far as my involvement with *The Thing* went because I was shooting something else. I do know he cut some stuff and also rewrote and reshot some scenes, but I don't know why he made that decision.'[1]

By the time I came to interview Debra Hill I had revised my opinion, after viewing it again, of *The Thing* and had come to regard it, for all its failings, as a damn good sf/horror movie. I told Ms Hill this and she replied cuttingly, 'Well, *you* would. You're a writer for *Starburst* magazine. That's a real minority group, don't you think?' Ahem. But now I shall take revenge for that remark. Ms Hill went on to talk of her future production plans of the time: ' . . . Then I'm going to do *Clue* with John Landis. It's based on the game known over here as Cluedo. Jonathan Lynn who writes 'Yes Minister' wrote the screenplay and it's very funny. I've been trying to get this picture made for four years. A friend told me it was my *Yentl* . . . '[2] Her *Yentl* indeed. *Clue* did get made (Lynn ended up directing it, not Landis). Hands up who saw it? Quite.

But I digress. Ms Hill had a point about the characterization in *The Thing* — it's pared down to the point of non-existence. And apart from that, none of the characters are very likeable. There's none of that sense of camaraderie that exudes from the Hawks version, and that's odd because Carpenter has often cited Hawks as a great influence on him as a film-maker. Otherwise I now think the film works extraordinarily well, including Bottin's graphic make-up effects which nowadays appear appropriately surreal rather than shocking — the corpse consisting of two merged bodies that the Americans find at the destroyed French base at the start of the movie is like something created by Francis Bacon. And having looked again at Campbell's original, which I'm afraid has become a turgid read despite having a great basic idea, it was wise of Carpenter and his writer to ignore most of it and start afresh. Their representation of the alien as some kind of genetic pirate who hijacks the DNA from different species that it encounters on different worlds is a good one. It's a shame, though, that this concept couldn't have been delved into a little more deeply. As the creature also absorbs the personality and memories of those it absorbs, along with their physical characteristics, how influenced is it by the human emotions it picks up along the way? Does it remain your typically cold and emotionless alien of so many sf movies or is it in danger of being 'corrupted' by what it absorbs? It would have been nice to have seen a struggle between the original personality of one of the victims and its alien conqueror. Interestingly, in the scene that most people remember from the movie — the one where a head detaches itself from a body lying on a table, uses its elongated tongue to pull itself under a chair, grow legs and then scuttle upsidedown towards a doorway — the guy who stares at it in disbelief and says, 'You've got to be fucking kidding' is, by that time, already part of the Thing himself (watch the movie again if you don't believe me) which suggests that the alien has acquired a sense of humour.

Carpenter, having had a financial failure with *The Thing*, then went on to make a movie about a nice alien, *Starman* (see Chapter Twelve). This too went belly-up at the box office and Carpenter then washed his hands of the big Hollywood studios and went back to making small, independently financed movies. The first of these was *Prince of Darkness* in 1988, which was an attempt to reproduce the Nigel Kneale formula of combining the occult with science. I found the plot pretty confusing. It concerns a bunch of very unlikely physics students, led by their professor, who are called in to examine a sealed glass-like container in the crypt of a church. The container apparently contains the son of Satan, who was sent to Earth millions of years ago, and whose aim is to break out and bring his father through the barrier that separates the anti-matter universe from our world and thus deliver the world unto the Forces of Darkness. There's another narrative thread involving a warning being transmitted from the future via a tachyon beam but I was never sure what that was all about.

I enjoyed it as a straight horror movie — there are some nice shock moments in the last section as the surviving good guys battle it out with those students who have been taken over by the evil force — but Carpenter failed to successfully link the scientific elements with the occult, though it was a good try. As he explained in an interview: 'Against the background of quantum mechanics I wanted the Donald Pleasence character to confront a supreme betrayal. If quantum physics isn't rational why should anything else in the universe be? For years Christianity has characterized evil as the heart of man and I wanted to suddenly turn this on its head and say that Christianity has always known evil was a substance existing outside of man. There are two ways of looking at sf or horror — one is the right-wing idea of they are out there coming to get me, and the left-wing idea is they are me. I guess I opted for a little right-wingism.'[3] Yes, I think I follow that.

Carpenter made no secret that *Prince of Darkness* was a homage to Nigel Kneale and, in fact, credited the screenplay to 'Martin Quatermass', who, according to the production notes he issued, was 'a former physicist and brother of Bernard Quatermass, the rocket scientist who headed the British Rocket Group in the 1950s'. What a nice gesture, one thought at the time. However Kneale responded as follows in a letter to the *Observer* newspaper: 'For the record, I have had nothing to do with the film and I have not seen it. It sounds pretty bad. With homage like this, one might say, who needs insults? I can only imagine it is a whimsical riposte for my having my name removed from a film I wrote a few years ago and which Mr Carpenter carpentered into sawdust . . . ' Phew!

So what was that all about? Well, the film concerned was *Halloween 3 — The Season of the Witch*. Back to Debra Hill: 'Joe Dante suggested Nigel Kneale to do the script for it. Joe had been doing the remake of *The*

Creature from the Black Lagoon at Universal and he had Kneale over to work on the script. The movie never got made so we called Joe and asked if he'd be interested in directing *Halloween 3*. We'd been asked to do a third movie and we were stumped because the Shape was dead and Jamie Lee would never do another. So Nigel Kneale came and talked to us and went off and thought about it then came up with this sort of idea . . . ' Though I admire Kneale's early work tremendously I made the observation that he seemed an odd choice for the assignment; surely his script must have seemed, well, a little old-fashioned? 'Yes, it was too old-fashioned. It really was. But I think *Alien* ruined it for us all. When the monster came out of John Hurt's chest, audiences just went crazy and demanded more of that sort of thing,'[4] said Debra Hill.

And now for Nigel Kneale's version of the events: 'I was quite keen on doing *Halloween 3*, particularly as they wanted to take the series away from its slasher-movie origins. So I thought up a story, we had a conference, and I went off to write the full script. In the meantime Joe Dante had to pull out because he had something else on. In the end Dino De Laurentiis, who was in charge of all the money, said that it must look exactly like the other two, so Carpenter simply took the script away and ripped it to bits,

Dan O'Herlihy as the villain in Halloween 3: The Season of The Witch, *which was scripted by Nigel Kneale and later disowned by him (O'Herlihy also plays the villainous 'Old Man' in the* Robocop *movies).*

and I had nothing more to do with it. He's a talented film-maker but a very strange man.'[5] He's referring to Carpenter there and not Dino De Laurentiis, I hasten to point out. But if anyone deserves Kneale's wrath over what happened to his script it should be the deadly Dino rather than Carpenter (Dino's full-steam-ahead cruise through the film industry has left many a project floating upside-down in his wake). But actually *Halloween 3* is very different from the first two (and the fourth one): it's a weird concoction with Dan O'Herlihy playing this mysterious toy-factory owner who is using the power from one of the giant stones from Stonehenge to energize Halloween masks all over America to become magically deadly to their young wearers. I'm not sure why he's doing that but actually the movie is not at all a bad one. It's certainly not the disaster Kneale appears to think it is.

A final word on the subject from Carpenter: 'I've been a fan of Kneale's work for years and years and this (the 'Bernard Quatermass' pseudonym) was a homage to show how much I admired him. Dedicating the script the way I did was the best way I could communicate this to him. His work means a host of different things to me on a number of levels. I think his style as a writer and his power to chill are unique. I had the opportunity to work with him briefly on *Halloween 3*, which I co-produced, but at that point Nigel was very embittered about the way of the world, as was shown, I think, in *The Quatermass Conclusion*.'[6] So that settles that.

Carpenter quickly followed *Prince of Darkness* with another low-budget, independent sf/horror movie, *They Live*, in 1989. Scripted by Carpenter and Frank Armitage, it was based on a short story by sf writer Ray Nelson, 'Eight O'Clock in the Morning'. Former wrestler Roddy Piper (who also starred in the great *Hell Comes to Frogtown*) stars as the working-class hero who learns that the Earth has been colonized by aliens who conceal their existence from most of humanity through mass hypnosis by means of television signals. As the aliens resemble humanoids with faces similar to those of dead piranha fish this is a wise move on their part. It turns out we are constantly being bombarded with subliminal messages, such as 'Honour Apathy', 'Submit', 'Stay Asleep', 'Obey', and 'Watch TV', to keep us pliable while the aliens, with the help of high-placed human business-men, asset-strip the planet. But a small group of people have discovered the truth and are trying to sound the alarm by distributing special dark

glasses that reveal the aliens as they really are. Piper acquires a pair of the glasses and is soon fighting an all-out war against the aliens. At the end he manages to destroy the transmitter that is sending out the mind-sapping signals but is betrayed by the woman who had pretended to be his ally. She is played by Meg Foster and I thought she was clearly an alien in disguise as soon as I saw her because of the eerie contact lenses she was wearing, then I saw her later in another movie and realized her eyes are actually like that.

As the original story was only six pages long Carpenter was obliged to pad out the movie somewhat. The most extreme example of this is a fight scene between Piper and his black buddy (Keith David) when Piper is trying to persuade him to put on the glasses and see the truth; the punch-up goes on and on until it enters the realm of the absurd and stays there. But I like the movie overall — it is better than *Prince of Darkness*, and, unusually for an American movie these days, it contains a fair amount of sly political satire. As Carpenter described it: 'It takes the point of view of homeless Americans discovering the Reagan revolution is run by creatures from another planet.'[7] Unfortunately neither of these movies made much of an impact at the box office and at the time of writing I've heard nothing about the third film in his four-picture deal with his independent financiers.

There's a strong Quatermass influence in Tobe Hooper's way-out alien-

(Right) One of the alien capitalists from outer space in John Carpenter's low-budget They Live.

(Left) After some persuasion from Roddy Piper (which involves the longest fist fight in cinema history) Keith David graciously agrees to don the sunglasses that reveal the world has been taken over by aliens.

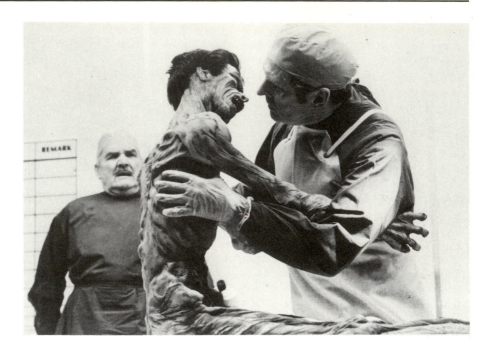

He's dead, but this victim of a space vampire in Lifeforce *refuses to lie down.*

invasion movie, *Lifeforce* (1985), but, wisely, Hooper didn't make any dedications to Nigel Kneale in the credits. It was based on the novel *The Space Vampires* by Colin Wilson and originally the movie started pre-production under that title but the distributors, Tri-Star, thought it had B-movie connotations and it was altered to *Lifeforce*. The script was by Dan 'Alien' O'Bannon and Don Jakoby and I don't how faithful they were to the Colin Wilson original as I've never read it. I did read one of his novels once, *The Mind Parasites*, and feel I've done all that is humanly possible in that area. *Lifeforce* begins with an expedition to Halley's Comet within which a massive alien ship is discovered. Also found are these perfectly preserved naked human bodies — two male and a female. They are brought back to Earth for study but before you can say 'space vampires' they revive and start sucking the lifeforces out of people, leaving withered, but still sort of alive, husks behind. The two male vampires get zapped but the female one, still naked (and played courageously by Mathilda May) walks free from the space centre and off into the night. Ms May plays almost all her scenes nude but Hooper insisted this was not a deliberate shock tactic. 'There was no way round the nudity. There wasn't anything else to do. We find these humanoids in space and I couldn't find a way to rationalize finding them clothed.'[8] Please, please, there's no need to make excuses. We understand perfectly. Situations like that can make a director's life hell.

Anyway, the hunt is on for the naked lady space vampire but she also has the power to swap bodies (aw) so it turns out to be a more difficult job than it looks. And then the big alien spaceship turns up — now looking like a giant umbrella — and starts sucking up the lifeforce from the inhabitants of London. There's a really big climax with large sections of London going up in smoke and for reasons that escape me the leader of the expedition that brought the vampires to Earth and the lady vampire, now wearing a tasteful translucent nightie, embrace in St Paul's Cathedral within the beam of lifeforce that is being sucked up into space and merge into each other. They get sucked up too and the beam stops and the spaceship heads off into space. Don't ask me to explain any of it but it was bloody spectacular (special effects by John Dykstra of *Star Wars* fame).

The movie provoked hoots of laughter from the British critics on its release in 1985, and though it has its absurd side it's also a formidable piece of work with a relentless pace and a very bleak point of view. I presume the latter has filtered down from Wilson's novel, along with a complete lack of humour in the characters, and while I suspect I would find his novel a dreary read, the transmutation of it via the screenwriters and the director has produced an sf movie that stands all by itself in the eighties — a period piece dressed up in modern high-tech clothes. It's like watching H.P. Lovecraft on speed.

I must confess I have a personal bias against the movie that Tobe Hooper directed the following year, a remake of *Invaders from Mars*. As I didn't think much of the original 1953 movie (see Chapter Five) I couldn't see the point of anyone wanting to remake it; sure, remake *The Thing*, *The Blob*, *Invasion of the Body Snatchers*, and *The Fly*, by all means, but *Invaders from Mars*? No way. Anyway, I missed it at the preview screenings and when it went on general release I had no particular urge to go and see it as friends had confirmed that it wasn't very good. But, as the time approached when I would be writing about it in this very volume I decided, in the interest of conscientious research, to hire the video of the film from my local corner store. The video had been in the shop for some considerable period and as I handed over my money I hoped it wasn't the very same copy that had been lingering on the video shelf all that time as it was sure to be in a pretty poor condition by now. Guess what — it was the same copy, because when I started to run it all I got was snow on the screen and snatches of the soundtrack. Uh oh, I thought, and quickly put one of my own tapes in, fearing the worst. Yep, the *Invaders* tape had zapped my video machine, screwing up the heads and making it completely useless. To make matters worse, it was the start of the Christmas period and, being Britain, there was no way I was going to get a repairman to come until way after New Year's Day. And to make matters even worse, there were a hell of a lot of sf films being screen on TV over the Christmas period, films that I had intended to record. All of which explains why I shall just quote from Leonard Maltin's *TV Movies and Video Guide* on *Invaders*: 'Starts fine, rapidly goes downhill toward utter disaster.' So there.

What surprised me when I saw *Predator* (1987) was that no one had had the idea before. For a movie, I mean, because I recall many old stories in sf magazines and comic books about alien hunters coming to Earth to bag human prey. Once again, I suppose it was the influence of *Alien* that inspired *Predator*'s two screenwriters, Jim Thomas and John Thomas, as it is very much *Alien in the Jungle*. Big Arnold Schwarzenegger stars as the leader of a bunch of mercenaries who are sent into a South American jungle as part of some shady CIA mission. As they hunt down their own prey, a bunch of guerillas, they are unaware they are being tracked by another, apparently superior, hunter who lurks invisible in the trees and sees by infra-red vision. After they have wiped out the guerillas and are heading back to their pick-up point, taking a lone female guerilla survivor with them, they are picked off one by one by the alien hunter who has a tendency to flay his victims and add their skulls to his collection. Okay, the dialogue is dire but the movie looks great and director John McTiernan manipulates the growing tension with a sure skill. With this movie it was clear that a major new directing talent had appeared, and of course, he went on to direct *Die Hard* and *The Hunt for Red October*. Also to be congratulated is the cameraman Don McAlpine, especially for his handling of the climactic night-time battle between Big A and the alien.

The alien's camouflage/invisibility suit is ingeniously presented — when glimpsed moving through the trees the alien appears as a shimmering heat mirage as if the suit is bending light waves around it. And the design of the alien under the suit, which we see at the end of the movie, is also interesting. The work of Stan Winston (who else), its face resembles that of a modified scorpion, and earlier in the movie we have seen the alien pick up the squashed body of an actual squashed scorpion and regard it almost reverentially, suggesting that its evolutionary origin is arachnid. I also like the idea of aliens who, despite possessing futuristic technology, are still basically ruthless hunters at heart. Such a human characteristic. And the desire to hunt provides a much more logical motive for an alien visitation than is provided by most sf films.

Then again, some aliens come to Earth just to boogey, like the alien we encounter at the start of *The Hidden* (1988). He, or it, likes heavy metal, fast and expensive cars, robbing banks, killing people and acting like an absolute pig in public places. What we have is an interplanetary psycho-pathic yob. He has the drawback of resembling a large garden slug but gets round it by his ability to enter human bodies — through their mouths — and take them over. We see this happening when a badly injured bank robber, just apprehended by the police after a spectacular car chase and shoot-out, gets out of his bed, goes to the man lying in the adjoining bed and exudes the slimy alien from his mouth which promptly slithers out of sight down the other victim's throat. The first man promptly dies while the second gets up and leaves the hospital to continue the alien's robbery and murder spree . . .

Tom Beck (Michael Nouri) is the cop with the job of finding out why two previously respectable men (the first one had been an accountant, for heaven's sake!) should suddenly turn into murdering bank robbers, but he isn't pleased when a young FBI agent, Lloyd Gallagher (Kyle MacLachlan), joins him on the case. And Agent Gallagher is also pretty strange to boot, appearing to know more about what is going on than he is prepared to divulge. If this eerily prefigures MacLachlan's FBI agent in 'Twin Peaks' at least he has a good reason for acting weird here for he too is an alien in a human body, though he's a nice alien. Actually he's an alien cop who's been hunting the criminal alien for some considerable time. And if this appears to suggest this is just another *Alien Nation*, with a human cop paired with an alien one, it ain't so. With *The Hidden* the sf elements are integral to the plot, unlike in *Alien Nation* which, as I've said, is a fake sf movie. Also, unlike *Alien Nation*, *The Hidden* is an inventive, pacy and witty movie. It was directed by Jack Sholder from a screenplay by Jim Kouf (who called himself Bob Hunt on the credits for fear of being typecast as an sf/ horror writer).

During the course of the film the alien invades a whole variety of bodies, including that of a stripper (in one bizarre sequence 'she' screws a young punk to death in the back of a car), as well as a dog's, but my favourite victim is the second one, called Jonathan Miller (no relation). As played by William Boyett, he is marvellous to watch as this barrel-chested, middle-aged businessman rips through L.A., stealing Ferraris, playing his ghetto blaster at full volume, crudely propositioning women and casually killing people, all the while trying to cope with a seriously diseased body that is slowly falling to bits thanks to the stresses the alien is submitting it to. A great performance. *The Hidden* is basically an exploitation film, but a superior one. And it even has a genuinely surprising, even touching ending.

And now we come to my favourite nasty alien movie of the eighties; in fact it's probably my favourite science fiction movie of the eighties: *Aliens* (1986). Once again the rule that sequels are always inferior is broken with this movie. I was fairly confident, after *The Terminator*, that James Cameron was the ideal choice to make the sequel to *Alien*. Ridley Scott had let it be known that he was available to direct it but for reasons known only to themselves the producers Walter Hill and David Giler didn't offer it to him. Whatever their reasons I think they were right; he had done a pioneering job with the visuals on *Alien* but the sequel required something different in terms of narrative pace. As I said in Chapter Eleven I feel that narrative drive is not Scott's strong point as a director — I feel he's a stationary sort of director; he tells his stories by means of a series of longish sequences that sometimes create a feeling of slowness in his films. James Cameron, on the other hand, is a much more kinetic director and he brought an atmosphere of charged-up pace to *Aliens*. Where Scott gives you plenty of time to look at the richness of his scenery Cameron fairly rattles along, cutting away before you're sure you've really seen what you think you've seen. Admittedly, this applies more so in the last two-thirds of *Aliens*, the first third consisting of a slow build-up, like the journey up to the top of the roller-coaster before the ride proper begins (but even so these sequences are still faster-paced than I believe Scott would have presented them).

Cameron was similarly influenced by Scott's *Alien* as Scott had been by Lucas's *Star Wars*. He said, 'I had seen *Alien* before I had got into the movie business and it had made such a strong impression on me that I had gone home and immediately started writing my own story ideas, which were heavily influenced by it. In fact the script I first wrote was called *E.T.* . . . it's true, but when some other movie came out with that title I changed it to *Mother*. Mother is the bad guy. She's the queen alien, laying the eggs. Anyway, when Hill and Giler asked me to do *Aliens*, I incorporated large chunks from *Mother*, mainly the ending and the fight between Ripley in the power loader and the mother alien. I came back to Hill and Giler with a forty-five-page treatment, single-spaced, in three days. They fell on their asses. I just felt I was working on Frankenstein's monster, sewing bits and pieces together.'[9]

Motherhood is the underlying theme to *Aliens*: when Ripley (Sigourney Weaver), and the cat, Jonesy, are picked up in their lifeboat, and she is revived, she learns that she had been drifting in space for fifty-seven years. In a sequence deleted from the theatrical print, but included in a video version, we see her receiving the requested information about her daughter — the daughter she had last seen as a little girl has died an old woman in the intervening years. This sense of her loss, and of her guilt at letting her daughter down by never returning, serves to reinforce both her attachment to the lone survivor on the colony world, the little girl called Newt (Carrie Henn), and her determination to carry out her promise at the end of the film to return for Newt after she has been carried off by the aliens. The climax is a battle between creatures driven by the maternal instinct — Ripley fighting to save her surrogate daughter, and the mother alien attempting to avenge her eggs that Ripley has destroyed.

Against her wishes, Ripley is persuaded by the slimy Company executive, Burke (Paul Reiser), to return to the planet where she and her late companions had found the alien eggs. In the years since the events of the first movie a colony has been set up on the planet in order to terraform it (change its atmosphere to make it suitable for concentrated human habitation). Her story about the alien hadn't been believed by her employers at first but now contact has been lost with the colony and a squad of space marines are sent to investigate. The marines are a rather anachronistic bunch; it's hundreds of years in the future but they talk and

act as if they're in some contemporary macho war movie. Apparently that was due to the influence of one of the producers, Walter Hill. 'Hill wanted me to do a re-run of the *Dirty Dozen* formula for the marines,' said Cameron, 'Which is certainly attractive, but in fact I was more anxious to point up the blue-collar nature of the marines — how dirty a job it is, and pretty rough.'[10]

Also in the crew is an android, Bishop (Lance Henriksen, who had been one of the cops in Cameron's *The Terminator*), of whom Ripley, after her bad experiences with another android, Ash, is naturally very suspicious. Bishop tries to convince her that he's a new and much-improved model but it's not until the end of the movie, when he's saved the day at least three times that he earns her trust, not to mention gratitude (by crawling down the conduit shaft to send the signal that brings down the spare jump ship, by flying back to pick up Ripley and Newt from the collapsing landing, and by grabbing Newt as she slides towards the open airlock bay after Ripley has forcibly ejected the mother alien). Bishop should fail the Brosnan Test for Artificial Intelligence as he's highly anthropomorphized but then he's not really a machine intelligence, appearing to be more of an organic creation. Henrikson plays him very ambiguously at first, suggesting that Ripley's suspicions might prove right but as the film progresses, and with lines like 'I may be synthetic but I'm not stupid,' he becomes a very sympathetic character.

When the marines arrive at the colony, bristling with high-tech weaponry, Ripley's worst fears are realized. The colonists are all missing, with the exception of Newt, and a huge alien nest is discovered under the fusion reactor powering the terraforming process. The marines, under the leadership of a rookie commander, enter the nest and encounter a horde of aliens. Yes, the obvious solution of how to top the original *Alien* was to have lots of aliens in the sequel. But that does have its drawbacks. The lone alien in *Alien* was awe-inspiring because it was an unkillable killing machine but the specimens in *Aliens* get blown away in the dozens. Yes, they're a disturbing sight in the shots when you see them slithering towards the camera en masse, such as in the sequence where Hicks (Michael Biehn) puts his head up through a hatchway in the false ceiling in the Ops Room and sees that the ceiling is literally crawling with the loathsome buggers, but they lack the equivalent impact of the original lone alien. (They're also

Ripley (Sigourney Weaver) and Newt (Carrie Henn) face a real mother of an alien in Aliens.

*Ripley prepares to save
Newt and slug it out with
the mother alien after
uttering her classic line,
'Get away from her, you
bitch!'*

of a slightly different design for economical reasons; the hands, head, feet
and teeth were all altered, and in some 'crowd' scenes extras merely wore
body stockings with alien parts sewn on.) It's not until you encounter the
mother alien at the end that you get the same feeling of being up against
something unkillable as well as unstoppable.

As I said when discussing *Alien* in Chapter Ten, by introducing the
mother alien Cameron had to dispense with the beautiful biological
symmetry of the original alien's life cycle. Of course, in terms of logic, there
is no reason for the mother's presence; at one point someone asks where
all the eggs could be coming from and Ripley answers that something must
be laying them, but in the first film we saw that there were hundreds of
eggs in the cavern under the crashed ship, enough to impregnate all the
colonists. But Cameron did include an element that Scott cut from his
movie, the cocooning process. Though, come to think of it, with the mother
alien laying the eggs, there is no need for the cocooning process, seeing as
its designed to produce more eggs . . .

Oh, to hell with it, *Aliens* is a great sf movie. It could have been even
better if Cameron hadn't been obliged to make cuts to his original
theatrical print, presumably for reasons of running time (even the
shortened version is one hundred and thirty-seven minutes long). Apart
from the crucial scene where Ripley learns of the fate of her daughter,
there are several other missing sequences. One is early on in the film where
we see Newt's parents make the fateful discovery of the alien ship, on a
suggestion received from Burke, which leads to the alien infestation of the
colony. Fox were to have released a complete version on video (I had the
opportunity to see a review copy) but withdrew it at the last moment,

apparently for legal reasons. There have been plans for some time to make *Aliens 3*, and various directors and writers have been involved with the project, including, at one point, William Gibson, author of *Neuromancer* which began the 'cyberpunk' school of sf writing. Gibson told me: 'Well, I was given a story outline that was reasonably good but I did have difficulties with it. It was written by Walter Hill and David Giler, two of the three producers and I worked from that. It was only about seven pages long and rather inconclusive towards the end, as those things tend to be. My contribution to their basic idea was that there was a third force out there — I suggested that it was a socialist civilization from Earth that had established itself in space, but looking back on it now it was all pretty much a pre-glasnost idea with these North Koreans and East Germans who were in competition with the capitalist companies. I had a lot of fun with it — the socialist conquest of space. I worked eight months on it but a few days after I turned in my final draft the screenwriters' strike began and when it ended a long time later the studio executives who had okayed the project were no longer with the studio. I was offered a chance by the new people to co-write another version with Renny Harlin (the new director who had been brought onto the project) but I turned it down. Harlin didn't like my script anyway.'[11]

Aliens 3 has started production in Britain and is due for release before Christmas in 1991. Its director, David Fincher, is a former rock-video director and he replaced the New Zealand director Vincent Ward who had replaced Renny Harlin (and maybe there was someone else in between whom I missed by blinking). The screenwriter is David Twohy, which brings us to the central gimmick: the second movie expanded on the first movie's concept by having more aliens so what does the third movie have? Well, according to rumour it has *combined* aliens and humans. Yes, it's miscegenation in space, people. The other rumour has it that though Signourney Weaver returns as Ripley — and writing her own dialogue — she only makes it through half the movie. I'm not sure I'm ready for this.

... And the plain old ugly

There was a dearth of good old-fashioned sf monster movies, featuring the home-grown variety type of monster, in the seventies. There was *Jaws*, of course, in 1975, which borrowed the formula of such fifties sf/ monster movies as *The Creature from the Black Lagoon*, *It Came from Beneath the Sea*, and *The Monster That Challenged the World* and refurbished it with an A-film budget and top-class direction by the young Steven Spielberg (in the days before he went all mushy on us) but it wasn't technically a science fiction movie. I mean, that shark is just supposed to be a bigger, meaner, more persistent, more intelligent, practically unkillable version of your average, everyday Great White: it doesn't look or behave the way it does because of an encounter it's had with atomic radiation. In fact, it wasn't until 1979 that an example of the genuine article appeared with *Prophecy*, and chemical pollution, rather than atomic radiation, was the culprit in this very green-spirited movie.

A socially concerned young doctor (Robert Foxworth) and his wife, Maggie (Talia Shire), go to investigate claims by an Indian tribe (I said it was green) up north in the state of Maine that the local timber mill is destroying their way of life. The doctor quickly confirms that there is substance to the claims; first he sees a salmon the size of a dolphin and a tadpole larger than a toad and is then attacked by a crazed racoon — three always infallible pointers to industrial pollution in the vicinity. He discovers that the mill has been releasing a mercury solution, a powerful mutagen, into the surrounding lake and river system which is causing these disturbing mutations within the local wildlife. His wife is shocked to learn this after they have eaten a fish dinner caught in one of the lakes, as she is pregnant (she hasn't told him that she's pregnant because he's adamant about not wanting children).

It's at this point that the film stops being a 'serious' statement about pollution and turns into an old-fashioned monster movie: a family of campers is found murdered in the woods and when the doc investigates he finds two mewling monstrosities not far from the scene of the attack. These things are really quite repulsive, vaguely resembling human babies as they might look after being beaten to a pulp and left out in the sun for a few days. One of the creatures promptly dies and the doc and his wife unwisely take the survivor back to the Indian camp. It turns out that the thing is the young offspring of the monster that killed the campers, and pretty soon Mom turns up at the Indian camp. Mom is not a pretty sight either, looking like a giant, one-eyed grizzly bear that has been flayed alive and then roasted over an open fire. It attacks the camp, killing, among many others, the rep from the mill who had turned up with some of his

Yes, it's Talia Shire but no, this is not a scene from a Rocky *movie but from* Prophecy, *an ecological horror movie.*

men. The rest of the movie concerns the efforts of the few survivors, including Rob and Maggie, to reach safety while the angry Momma monster follows them in hot pursuit. There are some good horror sequences in this section, such as the panic-stricken swim across a mist-shrouded lake with the monster gaining on them from behind, but all the problems and concerns established in the first part of the movie are simply discarded. For example, we never learn the outcome of Maggie's pregnancy despite so much emphasis on the possibility she might be carrying a mutant.

Prophecy was directed by John Frankenheimer who made some very good movies back in the sixties, such as *The Manchurian Candidate* and the sf-ish *Seconds*, about a middle-aged businessman who enters a mysterious clinic and comes out looking like Rock Hudson. Frankenheimer said it was his ambition since a child to do the world's greatest monster movie. Maybe one of these days he will realize that ambition, but *Prophecy* sure isn't it. I quite liked it at the time — it was fun to see the return of an old and familiar genre — but it's not a very good film. More typical of the critical reaction was Leonard Maltin's description: 'Classical musician and her doctor husband fight off what appears to be a giant salami in upstate Maine . . . Ridiculous horror film is good for a few laughs.'[1]

Like me, David Cronenberg had trouble swallowing the original *Fly* when he saw it as a fifteen-year-old in 1958. As I said in Chapter Six, I couldn't understand how the man with the fly's head still had his own brain while the fly with the man's head also had a human brain, but Cronenberg's scientific quibble concerned molecules. He wanted to know where all the extra molecules had come from to make the fly's head so big. He was so incensed he went and complained to a male usher in the cinema, pointing out that the scientist should have only a little fly's head and the fly should have a man-sized head. The usher told him to fuck off. Unlike me, Cronenberg eventually got the chance to make the movie he had wanted to see when he was fifteen years old, and in 1986 directed his remake of *The Fly*.

Not that it's really a remake. Only the central premise is the same, that of a scientist experimenting with a matter transmitter and getting himself mixed up with a fly in the process. Jeff Goldblum plays the scientist, Seth Brundle, who doesn't get to switch heads with the fly but undergoes a slow

Jeff Goldblum goes to pieces in Cronenberg's version of The Fly.

metamorphosis as its cells permeate his system. As this process continues he does acquire some of the characteristics of a fly, such as the ability to walk across the ceiling and the need to vomit on his food before consuming it. And he's just not changing, he's deteriorating as well; bits are dropping off him — ears and things, which he stores in his bathroom cupboard — and it's clear to him that his condition is terminal. The situation is also screwing up his love-life. No sooner has the solitary scientist encountered the beautiful lady reporter (played by the beautiful Geena Davis) and fallen in love than he starts turning into a fly. It's a cruel world. She does her best to stand by him in his predicament, though increasingly nauseated (she even dreams of giving birth to a giant maggot), but their relationship faces a dead end. Seth makes a desperate, last-minute attempt to save himself by putting himself through the matter transmitter again but ends up in even worse shape and mercifully dies.

Many if not all of Cronenberg's movies deal with forms of physical revulsion, as well as physical mutability, and *The Fly* fits comfortably within his oeuvre, even though he didn't initiate the project (originally the $9,000,000 Mel Brooks production was to have been directed by British newcomer Robert Bierman). Seth Brundle's spectacular disintegration is said to reflect Cronenberg's morbid fascination with the aging process and

I'll buy that (a glance in the mirror gives me no choice), but the critics who, at the time, said it was a metaphor for AIDS were, in my opinion, pushing it. But is Cronenberg's *Fly* more scientifically accurate than the original? Well, swallowing the unlikelihood of a working matter transmitter (the very term is a misnomer; matter can't be transmitted, only energy), I thought it was but then I saw a letter in *Time Out* which pointed out an obvious flaw in the movie. The reader drew attention to the fact that the human body plays host to a whole variety of parasites, some harmless, some not, and that a fly would be 'just the cherry on a veritable cocktail of horrors'. Finally, a piece of *Fly* trivia: it was Cronenberg's *Fly* that proved the last straw for the *Spectator* magazine's prissy-toned film critic, Peter Ackroyd, and he gave up the job, much to my satisfaction.

The fifties-style dinosaur movie made a comeback in 1985 in the form of *Baby*, directed by B.W.L. Norton and scripted by Clifford and Ellen Green. It was about a young woman paleontologist (Sean Young, typecast yet again), and her sportswriter husband (William Katt), finding a family of brontosauruses living in the African jungle. They are obliged to act as the dinosaurs' protectors to prevent a nasty male paleontologist (Patrick McGoohan) from capturing them. It did not impress me. *Baby* is one of those movies that is fascinating for all the wrong reasons. For example, I was more interested in what was going through the minds of the actors and film crew when they were shooting the scenes than what I was watching on the screen. Take the sequence where Ms Young and Mr Katt are indulging in a bit of steamy foreplay beside a jungle lake; what had Ms Young been thinking about while she disrobed seductively in front of Mr

Which one of these two figures is made of plastic? No, it's not Sean Young, who made an unwise career move by starring in Baby, Secret of the Lost Legend.

Katt and some poor sod bent double in a plastic dinosaur suit had to keep
butting into her with the creature's head . . .?

The movie *Baby* most resembles in terms of plot is *Gorgo* which also
featured a baby dinosaur that is finally rescued from evil humans by its big
mother (and both films end with an identical shot of mother and baby
swimming away side by side). Of course in *Gorgo* the whole city of London
gets tromped on by Big Momma while in *Baby* it's only a small African
village that suffers the same fate. *Baby* stands or falls on whether or not
you find the dinosaurs convincing, and I didn't. The big dinosaurs are okay
— they move more realistically than Baby and have leathery-looking hides.
Again, these were people-in-suits jobs but would have been filmed at high
speed to create the illusion of slow-moving, very large animals and there
were also some full-scale models, for stationary shots, capable of lifting
their heads or twitching their tails, but Baby, with its smooth, plastic-like
skin, just looks like what it is — a man, or a woman, in a dinosaur costume.
At times it had as much reality as a pantomine horse, which made it all the
harder for me to keep a straight face while the actors did their best to
pretend they were interacting with a real animal. I have the strong
suspicion that every time the director yelled 'Cut!' everyone, cast and crew,
fell to the ground and rolled about helpless with laughter.

Baby, I was told, was going to be the first in a whole new wave of dinosaur
movies so to cash in on this I immediately wrote a novel called *Carnosaur*,
which was all about genetically engineered dinosaurs escaping from a
private zoo and rampaging around rural England. But the big dinosaur
wave never came. *Baby* was it. Though as I write I have heard that a big
production about dinosaurs loose in the modern world is currently
underway in Hollywood. Spielberg is producing and it's based on the novel
by Michael Crichton, *Jurassic Park*, which concerns genetically engineered
dinosaurs in a dinosaur theme-park doing a Westworld on the paying
customers. Publishers please note: the reprint rights to *Carnosaur* are
available.

The Fly was a financial as well as critical success but another remake of
a 1958 monster movie, *The Blob*, came to a sticky end at the box office in
1989. I was surprised at this because I rather enjoyed it and thought the
special effects were marvellous. Produced by the producer of the original
Blob, Jack H. Harris, it was directed by Chuck Russell (who had previously

co-written and directed *Nightmare on Elm Street III*) from a screenplay by Russell and Frank Darabont. The story is very similar to that of the 1958 film, apart from one major plot twist and the fact that the Blob itself is a much more versatile beastie. As in the first *Blob* things get going when some teenagers encounter an old tramp with his arm encased in goo that he found inside a meteorite. The teenagers, Meg (Shawnee Smith), Paul (Donovan Leitch) and Brian (Kevin Dillon, brother of Matt) take the old man to a doctor's surgery where, before you can say *Yuckkk!*, the Blob is off and drooling. After consuming the old man (well, most of him), it eats Paul, which comes as a surprise as he's been set up as the film's hero. So with Paul in the belly of the Blob, the hero's mantle passes to Brian, who gets to reprise Steve McQueen's role (and with his black leather jacket and motorbike, Brian does look like something out of a fifties movie).

As in the original the local cops don't believe the teenagers' story about the Blob and accuse them of stirring up trouble. Where this version makes a major departure from the first story is when Brian and Meg, searching the woods for the meteorite, discover that it's already been found — by a group of armed men in white suits. And it's no meteorite, but a satellite, one that had been sent up by the United States government containing a deadly biological warfare experiment (no, don't ask why it was necessary to send it into space). So this version has two threats: the Blob itself and the government agents who put the town in quarantine and start rounding up the townspeople in order to transport them to some dubious destination. The eruption of the Blob right through the town's high street puts an end to all the government shenanigans near the climax of the movie and it's up to the teenagers to save the day by freezing the monster into submission, just as in the first film.

While the first Blob was somewhat limited in its movements and its form this Blob, thanks to a much bigger budget and eighties effects techniques, is much more versatile. As it grows ever bigger it becomes more like the organism in the 1965 sf novel, *The Clone*, by Kate Wilhelm and Theodore L. Thomas, spreading through the sewers and even killing one victim by sucking him down a kitchen plug-hole. And the sequence where Candy Clark is trapped in a phone box, which is being engulfed by the Blob, reminded me of that famous short story, whose name and author I can't remember — it's that famous — about the police getting a call for help

A squishy victim of the Blob in the remake of The Blob.

from a woman in a similar situation (they go to the box concerned and find it empty; turns out they've got a crossline from another dimension and have no way of helping the woman who gets consumed by the Blob, as does Candy Clark). Lyle Conway, the effects man who supervised the blob effects, said it was a nightmare to do. 'This is the only film I can think of,' he said, 'where the star of the movie arrived in a bucket. It was hellish trying to get a performance out of it.'[2]

Like the old *Blob* this new one was aimed very much at the teen audience but unlike the old one this one missed the target. I don't know why. Dialogue isn't that great but in all other respects I thought it was fine. Kids these days . . . don't know how lucky they are.

Also aimed at the teen market was *Watchers* (1989), based on the novel by Dean R. Koontz. In the novel the protagonist was an ex-soldier but in the movie he's been turned into a teenager (Corey Haim) who lives with his mom (Barbara Williams, who doesn't look old enough to be the mother of a teenage son). The film's central idea is much the same as the novel's: two genetically engineered creatures, one an intelligent dog and the other an organic killing machine (i.e., a monster), escape from one of those typical secret government laboratories where such things are done. Together they make up a military weapon; the dog will penetrate behind enemy lines and the monster is designed to follow him, killing as it goes. No, I know it doesn't make a scrap of sense but for reasons of the plot of both novel and film that's the way it has to be. So our young hero adopts the dog, or vice versa, unaware at first that the monster is zeroing in on the dog, murdering as it goes. But, as with *The Blob*, an equal threat is posed by the government agents, headed by the sinister Michael Ironside (the villain in *Scanners* and *Total Recall*, among others), who will stop at nothing to keep the experiment covered up. But the dog, who can spell using Scrabble squares, alerts our hero to the danger and he and Mom flee to a remote log cabin in the woods where the final confrontation takes place.

It's an okay monster movie, and the dog gives a great performance, but unfortunately the monster itself isn't very effective, looking like nothing more frightening than a large baboon with a lot of teeth and claws. Far more scary is the Ironside character, who also turns out to be the result of a genetic experiment, and it's a toss-up between him and the monster as to who claims the most victims in the movie. But the weirdest thing in *Watchers* is the would-be boyfriend of the hero's mom. For some reason he's supposed to be a Cockney and, just so American audiences don't miss this important character embellishment, the actor occasionally launches into an awful rendition of 'I've Got a Lovely Bunch of Coconuts!' A final bit of trivia before we move on: *Watchers* was shot in the wilds of Canada's British Columbia which was where Frankenheimer shot much of *Prophecy*. A spooky omen that was to cast its shadow over *Watchers'* box office takings.

Deep Star Six won the race between the three underwater sf movies hastily put into production in 1989 to beat the Big One, *The Abyss*, into release. It's a load of loony fun and I enjoyed it but what did annoy me was the following claim by its producer/director Sean S. Cunningham: 'We did a lot of intense research on the sets and the creature . . . we spent months going through books, films and documents from the Smithsonian and Scripps Institutes to create a world and a creature that would be completely realistic.'[3] There should be some equivalent of the Trades Description Act to prevent film producers from getting away with such waffle. Completely realistic, he says. Oh sure. Here we have a bunch of really dumb scientists who are building a secret nuclear missile base six miles down on the ocean floor. We're talking deep here. When they discover that the missile base is sitting right on top of a cavern the chief of the dumb scientists, instead of choosing a new site, orders that the cavern be blown up. This releases a monster from the cavern that is a cross between a giant lobster and a giant prawn. Then the dumbest character of all detonates all the nuclear missiles, causing a shock wave that wrecks their underwater habitat and allows the giant prawn thing to get inside . . .

Let's talk about pressure. In Chapter Twelve I said James Cameron was rare for a film-maker because he tends to get his scientific facts right, the authentic technical material in *The Abyss* being an example of this. The underwater rig in *The Abyss* is two thousand feet below the surface of the sea; it also has an internal air pressure equal to that of the water outside. This is to allow the divers, who are wearing conventional scuba-like suits, to come and go without having to depressurize each time. The only time they would have to depressurize, in a depressurization chamber, was when they wanted to return to the surface. The habitat in *Deep Star Six* also has a high internal air pressure even though its divers use 'hard' suits and therefore would be protected from the water pressure. Then again, the divers come and go through a 'moon pool'. Now a moon pool is an open, horizontal hatchway into the sea, the water prevented from coming in through it by the air pressure in the chamber being equal to the water pressure. Naturally, there's a limit to the depth that such a device can be

These men have reason to look worried, because lurking below the surface of that water is a giant killer prawn, in this scene from Deep Star Six.

used and six miles is a teensy weensy bit beyond that limit. To put it another way, to prevent the water from jetting up through that moon pool the air pressure within the habitat in *Deep Star Six* would have to be several tons per square . . . inch. Human beings in such an environment would be, well, extremely dead. And in an extremely squishy physical state.

Why did Cunningham and his writers set their story at such a ludicrous depth? I suppose because *Deep Star Six* makes for a better title than *Deep Star Two* or *Deep Star Five Thousand Feet*. Incidentally, the original title for the film was *Deep Six* but the distributors insisted that the word 'star' be included because it was a science fiction movie and, as everyone knows, sf movies have 'star' somewhere in the title.

Leviathan is very similar to *Deep Star Six* but is set a mere two miles below the sea and doesn't feature a moon pool. It's a more classy and expensive production than the other picture, and even has a star in its cast (Peter Weller, from *Robocop*), its main drawback being that it's produced by Dino De Laurentiis. It was directed by George Pan Cosmatos and the screenplay was written by George Peoples and Jeb Stuart from a treatment by Peoples (who did the version of the *Blade Runner* screenplay that Philip K. Dick liked so much). I enjoyed this movie as well but it irked me as I felt it had

Amanda Pays, an underwater astronaut, also has good reason to be concerned in this scene from Leviathan, *because that thing looming into shot in the foreground is only part of a very ugly monster.*

stolen an idea of mine. Well, to be honest, I'd nicked the idea from Carpenter's *The Thing* in the first place. It was an embellishment on the concept of a creature that absorbs the DNA of its victim. My idea, which a friend and I turned into a film treatment in 1982, had this oil rig being used for a secret genetic experiment. The result is a shape-changing monster that absorbs the personalities and memories of its victims along with their DNA and they struggle amongst themselves for control of the mutual body. A British director was interested in it but nothing came of it film-wise so we changed it into a novel, called *Slimer*, that was published in 1983 under the joint pseudonym of Harry Adam Knight.

I'm not really suggesting that Peoples got the idea from *Slimer*; he probably got it from *The Thing* like I did, or maybe from Roger Corman's fifties movie, *Attack of the Crab Monsters* — I've never seen this but read recently the monsters of the title similarly absorb the personalities of their victims. Great minds and all that. And anyway, not much is finally made of the personality-absorbing aspect in *Leviathan*, nor is the monster a shape-changer, being just a mere blob-like collection of various body parts.

As with *Deep Star Six* a mixed team of men and woman are working on the sea bottom, in this case carrying out an underwater mining operation. Everything in this area is much more technically convincing than in *Deep Star*; they work in hard suits and there's a feeling of authenticity in the early sequences that is worthy of *The Abyss*. Then they come across the wreck of a sunken Russian ship called *Leviathan* (everyone clap) that appears to have been torpedoed. In a sequence reminiscent of the one in *Alien* where the alien spaceship is investigated, two of the divers enter the wreck and retrieve the ship's safe. It contains a video log made by the captain of the sunken ship and some vodka. Naturally, someone is stupid enough to drink the vodka and before you can say DNA backwards he has turned into something nasty. It seems that the naughty Russians, back in pre-glasnost days, were carrying out a genetic experiment in order to create a breed of super-warrior. They spiked the vodka of their unsuspecting human guinea pigs — the crew of the *Leviathan* — with a drug and when things went terribly wrong they torpedoed the ship as part of a cover-up (literally a Russian Watergate — sorry).

After that it's all fairly predictable; as with *Deep Star Six* it's easy to spot the actors who are going to come out of the movie alive. In this case it's

Peter Weller and Amanda Pays — the rest of the cast are expendable as monster fodder. Pays (who co-starred in the 'Max Headroom' television series) is the token Britisher and gives a curiously embarrassing performance. Her character isn't helped by the fact that she's a trainee astronaut. Yes, an astronaut. A bit of subtle irony here from the writers, having a trainee astronaut on the ocean bottom and all that. Anyway, she and Weller make it back to the surface, along with the token black actor (Michael Carmine), but in an incredible surprise ending last seen in *Deep Star Six* the creature pops up out of the water as well! Scratch the token black actor but needless to say the creature gets zapped before it can munch on the two stars. Actually, though the concept of the monster is a good one (well, I would say that, wouldn't I?), it isn't that well executed in the movie, despite being designed and built by Stan Winston's company, and glimpses of it are wisely kept to a minimum.

Finally, the best of the bunch — *Tremors* (1990), a deliberate throwback to the sf/monster movies of the fifties, right down to the desert setting. I loved this, and most of the reviews of it that I read gave it the critical thumbs-up, but like *The Blob*, another fifties throwback, it didn't attract a big enough audience to rate it at the box office. Shame. It was written by Steven S. Wilson and Brent Maddock, the writing team who had previously given us *Short Circuit* and **batteries not included* but who redeemed themselves with this one. Wilson has said that years ago he had been sitting on a rock in a desolate area near China Lake in California when he had a chilling thought: 'What if there was something in the ground, just waiting for me, and I could not get off this rock?'[4] Like all smart writers he made a note of the idea and, ten years later, when their agent told him and Maddock that they were hot enough after their various screenwriting successes to initiate a project of their own, the idea was turned into *Tremors*.

It wasn't the first movie about a ground monster — earlier there had been *Blood Beach* in 1981. It had a great advertising slogan — 'Just when it's safe to go back into the water . . . you can't get across the beach!' — but failed to deliver the goods. *Tremors* more than delivers. As *Blood Beach* tried and failed to be, *Tremors* is *Jaws* on dry land. To the monsters the earth is a fluid medium which they can bore/swim through at tremendous speed (there is speculation about their origin but we never find out what they are or where they came from). Fred Ward and Kevin Bacon star as Earl and

Val, two down-and-out cowboys who barely make out by doing odd jobs in and around the small desert town of Perfection, population fifteen, which becomes besieged by the four mysterious subterranean creatures.

At first Earl and Val can't figure out the reason for the strange things they keep coming across in the desert, like the body of an old man they find way up a power pylon (he'd died of thirst rather than set foot on the ground again), a car they find completely buried but with its lights and radio still on, and a road-repair gang's vehicle and equipment but no sign of the road gang. (Earlier this had been the scene of an amazing effects shot — a road worker is drilling into the asphalt with a pneumatic drill and unknowingly drills into one of the creatures; the creature reacts by speeding away and the road worker is amazed, as we are, to see his drill tear along the road and then go up the side of a hill, and when his leg gets tangled up in the drill's power hose, he has no choice but to follow.)

After what appears to be a section of a large snake is found wrapped around the rear axle of a truck, the people of Perfection presume that they are being plagued by giant snakes, but then Earl and Val, with the help of student seismologist Rhonda (Finn Carter), discover just exactly what they are dealing with when one of the monsters, while chasing them, brains itself when it crashes into the side of a concrete culvert. The 'snakes' turn out to be tentacles that emerge from the mouth of the creature which resembles a giant, leathery slug with an armoured head. From then on it's a battle of wits between the dwindling citizens of Perfection and the three remaining underground beasts. Ingenuity coupled with good old human aggression wins out in the end. There's a very amusing sequence where one of the things smashes into the basement home of a couple of gun-crazy survivalists, Burt and Heather Gummer, who proceed to unleash their entire arsenal into the thing, switching bigger and bigger calibre weapons, until it calls it a day and expires.

The film is a joy in every way, with a witty script, a good and likeable cast and great special effects. What's good about the latter is that you are unaware of just how many there are in the movie. I've read some critics who have described it as having very few special effects but apart from the obvious ones involving the full-size monsters the film is packed with effects shots, many involving complicated miniatures, that you just don't notice when watching the movie, so seamlessly is everything put together (I must

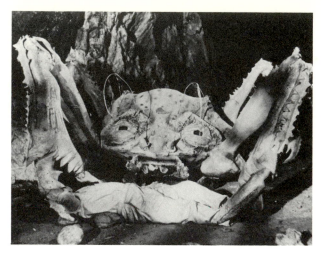

A genuine fifties sf monster — one of the mind-absorbing giant crabs from Roger Corman's Attack of the Crab Monsters.

admit it wasn't until I read an article about it in *Cinefex* magazine that I was aware of the extent of the effects work in *Tremors*).

The monsters were designed and created by Alec Gillis and Tom Woodruff Jnr, former associates of Stan Winston who had formed their own company. They had both worked with executive producer Gale Anne Hurd before on *The Terminator* and *Aliens* which was an advantage. Said Steve Wilson, who, with his partner, Brent Maddock, was a co-producer on the movie: 'Tom and Alec were excited about having a fairly big project land in their laps but their company was so new that they did not have a facility set up yet. So we met at a Marie Callander's in Burbank to discuss the script and what we wanted the creature to look like. The script had just a very few lines of description. It said that the mouth opened like some kind of grotesque flower and there were horrible spines all over the body — and that was about it. So they took that sketchy description and came back with a few drawings and they just knocked us out of our chairs! "There it is! That's the monster!"'[5]

It's a pity that this relatively small-scale, intelligent monster movie wasn't a popular success, not only for director Ron Underwood, whose feature-film debut it was, but also for us fans of the genre. What most of the films included in this chapter have in common is that they didn't do very well at the box office (with the exception of *The Fly*) which suggests this type of movie is out of fashion, and which further suggests that we fans of the genre are a dying breed and, most heartbreaking of all, that it's extremely unlikely that any of my monster novels, such as *Slimer*, *Tendrils* (about these snake-like things coming out of the ground that turn out to be attached to a huge monster that almost eats the entire population of London — it's true!), *Worm* and *The Fungus*, will ever get filmed. Yep, definitely a shame.

Time trips . . .

B ack in the early eighties — 1981, I think it was — I had a gosh-wow of an idea for a science fiction movie. It had occurred to me that time travel had yet to be properly exploited by science fiction film-makers and that there was a lot of material sitting around on sf library bookshelves just waiting to be tapped. Sure, plenty of movies had featured time travel but it had been used mainly as just a form of transportation to drop characters into an exotic location, usually the future. Film-makers had tended to ignore the paradoxical questions that the concept of time travel raises, unlike the sf writers who have long revelled in the mental conundrums that time travel produces.

A famous example is Robert Heinlein's story 'All You Zombies', a reworking of one of his earlier stories, 'By His Bootstraps', which is about a time traveller who has a sex-change operation, goes back in time as a woman, seduces his former male self, becomes pregnant and gives birth to . . . himself. The story ends with the narrator saying that he knows where he came from but what about '. . . all you zombies?' (Yes, solipsism was a consistent theme in much of Heinlein's work). Another classic time-travel story was Ray Bradbury's 'A Sound of Thunder', published in 1952, which was about hunters going back in time to shoot dinosaurs. The hunters are obliged to follow the strict rules imposed by the organizers, one being that they can only kill a specifically designated dinosaur, and another being that they must never leave the special pathway that had been laid through the prehistoric jungle. But one hunter does so, inadvertently stepping on and killing an insect. When he returns to his own time he finds it completely altered, for the worse; the implications being that even the smallest changes made in the past by time travellers, such as the death of an insect, can have tremendous repercussions up the time line (so much for the originality of chaos theory with its butterfly wings affecting weather systems).

Science fiction writers like Poul Anderson, Murray Leinster, Isaac Asimov and Fritz Leiber had written stories and novels about 'time wars' where various groups of people from the future are in conflict with each other as they either try and change the past, for various reasons, or restore things as they were. My idea was to 'borrow' from these and other sf writers, as George Lucas had 'borrowed' from sf writers and artists to create *Star Wars*, to create an epic time-travel movie script. And I had a great title for it — *Time Wars* (I said it was great, I didn't say it was original). Apart from the title all I had was a vague idea of the background to the action. It would be a struggle between 'time warriors' from two different futures — one good, one bad — who need to control past events in order to ensure the existence of their respective future societies. I had an opening sequence as well: there's this attractive young woman hitching along some desert road in America. A strange-looking car pulls up and its handsome, male driver offers her a lift. She accepts even though the handsome driver, like the car, is a bit odd. Well, of course, the man is a time warrior, one of the good guys, from the future, and the car is a time machine . . . and the woman turns out to be an important element in the time wars thanks to something vital she is going to do in the future. He's come to make sure she does whatever it is she's going to do without interference from the bad guys . . .

And that's as far as I got. I showed the five or six pages I'd done to a screenwriter I knew, Chris Wicking (*Scream and Scream Again*, *To the Devil a Daughter*, among many others), and he was enthusiastic about the idea and expressed an interest in collaborating with me on it. Well, we never did, for reasons I can't recall, and as I couldn't come up with a suitably ingenious plot on my own *Time Wars* never got past page six. But I'd also mentioned the idea, and described the opening sequence, to John Baxter, who'd also reacted favourably. In 1982 John returned to Australia and I think it was in 1983 that, during a phone conversation, he mentioned that he and Brian Hannant (who was one of the writers on *Mad Max 2*) were writing the screenplay for an sf film called *Time Rider*. It begins, he told me, with this female hitchhiker in the desert being picked up by this guy driving a time machine disguised as a car . . . Ahem, I interrupted, and gently reminded him where this idea had come from. John was surprised, having totally fogotten about my telling him about *Time Wars*. Not that I minded one way or the other as by then I'd thrown in the towel on my project.

Time, as they say, passed, and I would get the occasional report from John on the progress, or lack of it, on *Time Rider*. One setback came when another movie called *Timerider* was released in the States. I later caught up with this on video and it's a pretty feeble affair about this champion bike-rider who, with his bike, goes back in time to the days of the Old West and ends up, if I remember correctly, screwing his great grandmother. Good cast though, including Fred Ward, Peter Coyote and L.Q. Jones. Anyway John and Brian Hannant were obliged to change the title of their movie which became *Time Guardian*.

Then *The Terminator* came out and I thought it would automatically mean the end of *Time Guardian*. It certainly ended any lingering urges I may have had about persevering with *Time Wars*. At first I thought it was uncanny that *The Terminator* was so close to my basic idea for *Time Wars* then I realized that writer/director James Cameron had probably read the same sf novels and stories that had given me the idea in the first place. Also he'd gone and licked the plot problems: for example, I was never able to come up with something for my woman character to do that would be so goddamn important to the future dwellers but Cameron has the perfect solution — she becomes pregnant and gives birth to the man who will eventually save the human race from the machines. She becomes the mother of a virtual Messiah. He even has the right initials, his name being John Connor. Nor would I have ever had the great idea of including a killer android disguised as Arnold Schwarzenegger . . .

Ironically, the success of *The Terminator* didn't mean the end of *Time Guardian*. On the contrary, it provided a major boost to the project because the producers of *The Terminator*, Hemdale, became interested in producing what they saw was a similar movie. Of course, they wanted the script

Big Arnie in one of the best of all time travel movies, The Terminator.

entirely rewritten but that is only to be expected. *Time Guardian* chugged slowly onwards and, after many more setbacks, shooting on it actually began in September of 1986. In the meantime *Back to the Future* had come out in 1985. What a great idea, I'd muttered sourly to myself as I watched it, using a car as a time machine. I knew from John that *Time Guardian* no longer had a car-shaped time machine in it, instead it was a whole city that went time travelling . . .

But before we take a closer look at time travel movies of the eighties — and I tell you how *Time Guardian* had a dire effect on the Australian film industry — let us go back ourselves in time and take a look at time travel movies of the fifties.

Actually there weren't that many of them during the sf movie boom of the fifties. Practically none, in fact. The theme of time travel didn't begin to interest film-makers until the end of the decade when George Pal produced and directed his version of Wells's *The Time Machine*. But one film-maker was ahead of his time and made his own version in 1956. He was Edward Bernds, former sound effects man for *The Three Stooges* and the film, which he wrote and directed for Allied Artists was called *World Without End*. It was about four astronauts returning to Earth from a mission to Mars in 1957 (something of an optimist was our Mr Bernds) and going through a time warp, though they don't realize it at the, er, time. They encounter this strange planet and land on it, not recognizing it as Earth (as Charlton Heston would do in *Planet of the Apes*). They find the surface crawling with hairy-looking monsters while under the surface, in tunnels, exist normal-looking humans. To the dismay of the astronauts they learn that they are back on Earth but hundreds of years in the future. An atomic war back in 2188 had devastated the planet and the creatures on the surface are mutants. Resigned to the fact that they are stuck in the future the astronauts help the underground people regain control of the surface by reinventing the bazooka.

Yes, Bernds had simply reversed the situation in *The Time Machine* by putting his version of the Morlocks on the surface and the humans underground. This didn't fool anyone and several law-suits were filed against Allied Artists for plagiarism, one coming from the H.G. Wells estate. I've never seen the movie but according to Bill Warren in his book *Keep Watching the Skies:* 'While hardly in the first rank of 1950s sf films, *World Without End* is better than a curiosity piece, and a good example of an above-average try by a minor company.' But, as Warren noted, it established the formula for time-travel movies that would last well into the sixties. Ironically, Rod Taylor, who was to star in *The Time Machine*, was one of the astronauts in *World Without End*.

Time travel played a small part in *The Invisible Boy* in 1957 (see Chapter Eleven) and a bigger part in *Terror from the Year 5000* in 1958. This was an AIP cheapie produced, directed and written by Robert Gurney, about a scientist who has built a 'time vault' which can materialize people and objects from the future. His bent assistant is secretly experimenting with the device, plucking things from a future world that has suffered in the inevitable atomic war, such as a four-eyed radioactive cat. The time vault also materializes an evil and disfigured woman from the year 5000 who is anxious to breed with an uncontaminated man . . .

I haven't seen this either but according to *The Great Science Fiction Pictures* by James Robert Parish and Michael R. Pitts, 'this is a nicely made little

Rod Taylor played H.G. Wells's time traveller as man-of-action in George Pal's version of The Time Machine.

thriller but upon original release had the misfortune to share a double-bill with a horror clinker called *The Screaming Skull*. Today the film has a minor cult following because of the presence of Salome Jens in her screen debut.' Enough said.

Then, in 1960, George Pal came out with his *Time Machine*. Our Rod stars as the Victorian inventor who builds a time machine (beautifully designed by the film's art directors, George W. Davis and William Ferrari) and zooms off into the future — pausing along the way to watch London being destroyed in, yes, an atomic war – before finishing up in the year AD 802,701. As in the H.G. Wells story he finds a world divided into two distinct groups: the childlike Eloi who spend all their time playing games, eating and drinking, and the monstrous Morlocks who live and tend their machines below the ground and are, in reality, breeding the oblivious Eloi for food. But Pal, and his screenwriter David Duncan, have shorn all the social and political implications from the original and what we have left is a simple tale of how a two-fisted macho man snaps the Eloi out of their fatal apathy by demonstrating that a good punch on the jaw will solve everything. Inspired by his example, the up-to-then terminally effete Eloi are quickly kicking Morlock ass. With their assistance, the time traveller sets fire to the Morlocks' subterranean complex and destroys them (it seems that the world's entire populations of Eloi and Morlocks exist only in this small, localized area — a common failing with many sf movies set in the future).

The film may be simple-minded but it looks nice, and the time-trip into the future is well-done, with alternating bouts of light and darkness to suggest days and nights speeding by, and the clever use of a shop window dummy to show the years flashing by as the fashions in womens' clothing rapidly change. It's probably, after *The War of the Worlds*, Pal's best movie and he periodically announced that he was to make a sequel, but it never happened.

But alas, more inferior time-travel movies set in post-atomic war futures continued to appear, such as *Beyond the Time Barrier* (1960). In it a test pilot, played by Robert Clarke, is catapulted into the year 2024 and finds the usual desolation, the result of a nuclear war in 1971. The usual mutants are roaming about above ground while the usual humans huddle underground etc. I haven't seen this either but I do know that it was shot by director Edgar G. Ulmer in eleven days simultaneously with his *The Amazing Transparent Man*. Ulmer, who used to be Fritz Lang's assistant, and is quoted in Chapter One, made Roger Corman look like a slow-poke.

A more inventive treatment of time travel, dealing as it does with a paradox, was to be found in Chris Marker's short 1962 movie *La Jetée (The Pier)*. Set after the Third World War (of course), a group of French scientists working in their underground bunker (of course) send a man back in time using drugs. A particularly vivid childhood memory acts as a catalyst for the time traveller — it's of a day when, as a small boy, he had been watching a particularly beautiful girl at Orly and then seen a man, running nearby, shot dead. The time traveller meets the same girl again and falls in love with her. He decides to abandon his mission and stay in that prewar era. When he attempts to run away with her he is shot dead by another traveller from the future and we realize that, as a child, he had witnessed his own death that day. An unusual feature of this twenty-nine-minute film is that it is composed almost entirely of stills, the one exception being a brief moment when, in a close-up, the girl's face suddenly comes to life.

Back to the old formula with *The Time Travellers*, directed by Ib '*Reptilicus*'

Melchior in 1964. Four scientists go through a 'time portal' that they'd accidentally manifested in their laboratory and find themselves in a future where — surprise — the world has been ravaged by an atomic war and the surviving normal humans are being bothered by restless mutants. There's an interesting twist in that one of the scientists, at the end, gets trapped in a perpetual time loop. No, I haven't seen this one either but the *Monthly Film Bulletin* liked the ending; 'Bold and not without irony,' is what they said about it. The other thing that I know about the movie is that Forrest J. Ackerman, the man who invented the term 'sci-fi', has a small part in it.

I did once see on TV, in the seventies, a curious movie, made in 1966, called *Cyborg 2087*, and maybe James Cameron did too, because it's about this cyborg (part-machine, part-human) from the future who comes back to 1966 to prevent a scientist from building a device that will later be used as a mind-control weapon by a totalitarian government in the year 2087. And sent back to stop him from doing just that are two blank-faced government cyborgs with orders to kill him. Yes, this was a movie ahead of its time all right, and a rare one that exploited the paradoxical properties of time travel to the full. With the assistance of the scientist's attractive assistant, Sharon (Karen Steele), the cyborg, Garth (Michael Rennie), persuades the scientist to abandon his invention even though Garth knows that if the device is destroyed its disappearance will eliminate the possibility of his own existence. And that's what happens. Garth vanishes and all memory of his visit is eradicated from the minds of everyone concerned, including Sharon who'd fallen in love with him.

Unfortunately, though well plotted, the screenplay, by Arthur Pierce (who also wrote the script for *Space Invasion from Lapland*) is mediocre and the direction, by Franklin Adreon, is in the same category and the film has the flat, textureless look of a low-budget TV movie. But it does have its clever moments, such as the representation of the two government-issue cyborgs who act more like machines than men. As they track Garth through the town with their instruments they never deviate an inch from the invisible trail, even if it means pushing cars to one side or running straight through a houseful of party guests. It's worth a look if it ever turns up on TV again.

I was highly impressed when I first saw *Time After Time* back in 1979 but having viewed it again recently I find it's one of those movies that time has

Malcolm McDowell as the young H.G. Wells himself in Time After Time.

In his time machine H.G. Wells heads off to 1977 San Francisco to track down Jack the Ripper and fall in love with Mary Steenburgen.

not been kind to. It's still okay but it looks rather slapdash now and also seems an awfully slow movie. I think what won me over so totally back in 1979 was the sheer audacity of the idea of having Jack the Ripper (David Warner) steal a time machine from the young H.G. Wells (Malcolm McDowell) and end up in modern day San Francisco with Wells hot on his heels. And the film's other strength is the performance by Mary Steenburgen as the young female bank clerk who befriends, and then falls in love with, the oddly dressed and confused H.G. Wells who comes into her bank to change gold sovereigns into dollars. Steenburgen creates a wholly believable, and appealing, character even though the script doesn't give her much to work with. McDowell is passable as Wells, though he seemed miscast to me, and makes the best of the early sequences in San Francisco where he is understandably suffering from culture shock. McDowell and Steenburgen work well together and the intensity of their relationship is convincing (it should be, as they got married shortly afterwards), which makes the ending, where Wells must tearfully beg the Ripper for her life, quite moving. Less successful is David Warner, as the Ripper, who gets the bare bits in a very patchy script.

Time after Time was written and directed by Nicholas Meyer, who had previously written the script for another movie where a fictional character interacts with an historical figure, *The Seven Per Cent Solution*, which had Sherlock Holmes getting it on with Sigmund Freud (it was based on Meyer's own novel). One wondered who would get the treatment on his third outing — Einstein meets Fu Manchu, perhaps? — but Meyer gave up mining that particular creative vein and turned to directing *Star Trek* movies (not a fate I'd wish on anybody). Despite my enthusiasm waning somewhat for *Time after Time* one must give Meyer credit for doing something inventive with the time-travel genre (though, surprisingly, it wasn't a financial success). And he even managed to introduce and solve a couple of paradoxes: one occurs when Wells takes Steenburgen forward one day in the time machine and she reads in a newspaper that she will be the Ripper's next victim; and the other one involves Wells taking her back to his own era without altering history.

The Final Countdown (1980) promised one hell of a paradox but failed to deliver. The idea must have seemed a good one — let's send a modern aircraft carrier back through time so that it ends up in Pearl Harbor on the day before the attack, and have it within striking distance of the Japanese fleet! (I understand that the original idea was to send a modern tank back to the First World War, but someone obviously got carried away.) So this aircraft carrier, the USS *Nimitz*, goes through this time warp and ends up back in 1941. Right, now what? Well, not a lot. The writers at this point realized they couldn't have their modern carrier sink the Japanese fleet because then history would have been changed and how would they get around that? Well, a good sf writer might have had a try at coming up with some clever way to allow the *Nimitz* to zap the Japs and yet, in the end, not really change anything, but the four screenwriters on *Final Countdown* — David Ambrose, Gerry Davis, Thomas Hunter and Peter Powell — were not good sf writers. Or good writers, period. Their solution was to pad out the movie like crazy with lots of loving shots of the *Nimitz*, its fighter planes, its weaponry (at times you feel like you're watching US Navy recruiting film) and then, when the Captain finally decides to unleash his fighters onto the Jap fleet, along comes that sneaky old time warp again and whisks the *Nimitz* back to 1980. It also whisks back the squadrons of fighters on their way to the Jap fleet, which I thought a bit odd seeing as they were by then some considerable distance from the carrier. Hey, but you never can tell with time warps . . .

There is some contact with the Japanese forces; when two Zeros are seen strafing a yacht they are shot down by two F-14s, and a rescued Zero pilot later causes problems on the *Nimitz* but that's it. The yacht incident also introduces another sub-plot: a woman (Katharine Ross) from the sunken yacht is brought on board and a romance develops between her and a naval officer (James Farentino) who elects to remain with her in the past. In a surprise ending we see them, covered in latex wrinkles, waiting in a limo on the dockside as the *Nimitz* returns to port.

Kirk Douglas, who plays the captain of the carrier, recounts in his autobiography that he had a thrilling three weeks filming on the *Nimitz*, and even had the opportunity of going up in one of the jets, but seems puzzled as to why the film (produced by his son Peter) didn't do well at the box office. He thinks the special effects might be to blame — it's true that they weren't very good — but what doomed the movie from the start was the screenplay. With all his lengthy experience in the film industry it's clear, like so many other actors, that he still can't spot a dud script.

I shall quickly pass over another 1980 time travel movie, *Somewhere in Time*, a sentimental, mawkish romance based on the sentimental, mawkish novel, *Bid Time Return*, by the once great Richard Matheson. Christopher Reeve plays a playwright who falls in love with the seventy-year-old painting of an actress (Jane Seymour . . . zzzzz) and wills himself back in time to order to have an affair with her. But he can't sustain himself in the past and is reluctantly pulled back to the future where he has an encounter with the actress as an extremely old woman (Jane Seymour and a lot of latex wrinkles). Then after they're both dead and in an ending that even Barbara Cartland might sneer at they meet up in heaven and she's young again. It's all beautifully photographed but that's the best you can say for it. The director was Jeannot Szwarc, whose previous film was *Jaws 2*, and who went on to make *Supergirl*. There's a moral there somewhere.

In 1984 came *The Terminator*, the best time travel movie made up until then (see Chapter Eleven) but that same year saw the release of another time-travel movie, *The Philadelphia Experiment*, that deserves an honourable mention. Now if I tell you it's about an American Navy ship being propelled through time don't jump to the conclusion that it's another *Final Countdown* — it isn't, thank goodness. As I understand it was based on Charles 'Bermuda Triangle' Berowitz's 'true' book about an experiment carried out at the Philadelphia Naval Yard in 1943 where a destroyer was supposed to have been made invisible by some new secret device but things went terribly wrong and the Navy and the government have been covering it up ever since (the destroyer is probably being stored in the same warehouse as the pieces of UFO wreckage and the bodies of the aliens I talked about in Chapter Twelve).

The screenwriters, William Gray and Michael Janover, use this supposedly actual event as the launching pad for their story. The experiment causes the ship, the USS *Eldredge*, to go ripping through the space-time continuum. Two young sailors, played by Michael Pare and Bobby di Cicco, jump overboard and find themselves in 1984. The di Cicco character is in a bad way and, after being taken to hospital, literally fades out of the picture, much to the amazement of the medics. Eluding the authorities, Pare makes a break for it and is befriended by a young woman motorist (Nancy Allen, who's very good in this) who comes to believe his weird story and helps him find out the truth of what happened. He later confronts the

Michael Pare as the time-displaced Second World War sailor in The Philadelphia Experiment.

scientist who was in charge of the original experiment and learns that an attempt to repeat the experiment has created a giant time vortex above the research establishment that is sucking in the atmosphere at an increasing rate. Pare must enter the vortex, land on his old ship and turn off the power generator that is causing this catastrophic cosmic plug-hole. He succeeds in doing this and the warship returns to 1943, and in a bizarre image we see that many of the surviving members of the crew, horribly burnt, have merged with the metal of the ship's superstructure.

All this is very spectacular, if absurd, thanks to some impressive special effects (the vortex, looming malignly over the base and spitting lightning, is suitably apocalyptic) but it's the human element in the story that makes the whole thing work. Pare, not usually a better-than-average actor, convinces as a man coming to terms with the realization that he is forty-one years from home and trapped in a disturbingly unfamiliar, and hostile, new world. As in *Time After Time*, some fun is to be had with his reaction to television, and there's a good moment when he learns that a B-movie actor from his time is now president. And there's an interesting sequence when he and Allen track down his old shipmate who had initially travelled into the future with him, but the, now, old man, severely traumatized by those events of forty years ago, refuses to admit his existence.

Despite being a New World Pictures production, and based on a loony premise, the movie, directed by Stewart Raffill (originally it was to have been written and directed by John Carpenter in 1980) has a core of intelligence in the script that is enhanced by its cast. I like it.

A brief mention of a time-travel movie directly inspired by *The Terminator*, *Trancers* (1985 — title later changed to *Future Cop*). This was a Charles Band production, but unlike most Charles Band productions it's pretty good, thanks to a witty script (Charles Band was the low-budget equivalent of Dino De Laurentiis and, like Dino, finally went bust, though I've heard that he's making a comeback). Comedian Tim Thomerson plays Jack Deth, a tough cop who is sent back in time to 1985 to inhabit the body of one of his ancestors in order to combat the evil Whistler, who is inhabiting the body of one of *his* ancestors. Whistler is killing the ancestors of people who will oppose him in the future, and has a small army of zombies to aid him in his dirty work. It's very amusing at times, like in the sequence where his abrasive chief from the future comes to 1985 and inhabits the body of a small girl to give him new orders. Very inventive. And it even had a great advertising slogan: 'Jack Deth is back . . . and he hasn't even been here before.'

And now for the *Back to the Future* series that exploits to the full the paradoxical potential of time travel, especially in the second movie, but keeps everything within a basically humorous and entertaining context (though *II* does have its unusually dark moments). What director Robert Zemeckis and his co-writer Bob Gale had the courage to do was have their characters succeed in changing the past and therefore change their present. By doing so they dally with that marvellous old sf concept — the possibility of different time lines and parallel worlds.

In the first movie Marty McFly (Michael J. Fox) is accidentally sent back to 1955, and to a crucial day which led to his very existence. Originally his father-to-be, George McFly (Crispin Glover), had been knocked down by his mother-to-be's father's car and this was the catalyst that led to their eventual marriage, but now Marty pushes his father-to-be out of the car's path and is knocked down in his place. So it is Marty who is now nursed by his mother-to-be, Lorraine (Lea Thompson) and as this development puts in jeopardy his own future existence, as well as that of his brother and sister, he must contrive to repair the damage and ensure that they do fall in love. But in arranging for this to happen in circumstances completely different from the original, he also manages to change his father's attitude to life, transforming him from a wimpish nerd into a confident, positive-thinking type of man. The results of this change Marty discovers when he returns to 1985. His father is not only a successful businessman, he's a successful sf writer to boot (wow, talk about wish-fulfilment!) and the lifeless relationship between his parents has been transformed into a happy marriage (a side-effect of this is that his mother is no longer a dowdy alcoholic) and even his brother and sister appear to have changed for the better.

Another important change is the role reversal between his father and Biff Tannen; originally George McFly had been the intimidated butt of Biff's bullying but now Biff is the subservient one in the relationship. And the last important change: in the beginning we had seen the inventor of the time machine, Doc Emmett (Christopher Lloyd, his performance helping to sustain the old Hollywood belief that scientists are both absent-minded and barking mad) machine-gunned to death by Libyan terrorists — Marty had later attempted to tell the 1955 version of Doc of his fate but Doc, following the established sf precepts about time travel, refused to acquire knowledge that might alter future events — and when Marty returns to 1985 several minutes before he originally left, he sees Doc gunned down again before his past self zooms off in the De Lorean time

The start of one of the most successful and ingenious time-travel movies, Back to the Future, *with Michael J. Fox and Christopher Lloyd. It led to an even more ingenious sequel.*

machine. Ah, but Doc is not dead, he is wearing a bullet proof vest, having pieced back together the warning letter from Marty that he had refused to read and had torn up in 1955. All neatly thought out, but for this to be a logical solving of a paradoxical situation you have to invoke the existence of diverging time lines. Because clearly Marty has not returned to his own world but one that has been altered in all sorts of ways (for example, the original Doc obviously didn't remember Marty's 1955 visit).

Zemickis and Bob Gale take this world-altering ability to dizzy lengths in the second movie; in fact, some said they took it too far, and admittedly when you have to have one of the characters, Doc, explain what is going on in the plot by drawing a diagram on a blackboard it's a sure sign that your plotting permutations have become a mite too ambitious. But personally I felt it was the first real time-travel movie, in the same way that I reacted to earlier milestones in the cinema of sf.

In *Back to the Future II* Doc takes Marty and his girlfriend, Jennifer (Claudia Wells in the first movie, here a virtually wasted Elizabeth Shue who spends most of the movie unconscious) to the year 2015 in order to prevent Marty's son from becoming a criminal. While there Biff (Thomas F. Wilson again), now an embittered old man, steals the De Lorean and goes back to 1955 where he hands to his younger self a sports almanac which will provide the younger Biff with the results of all the future major sporting events for years to come. This has the effect of drastically changing the local area, as Marty discovers when he returns to 1985. The town is a hellish mess and dominating everything is Biff's Las Vegas-like gambling and pleasure palace. What's even worse is that Biff had murdered his father and is now married to his mother (Lea Thompson) who has become an alcoholic with surgically-enhanced breasts (once again, as with the first movie, the Oedipal element is strongly suggested but carefully handled).

To restore things as they were Marty and Doc return to 1955 to try and prevent the young Biff from getting his hands on the almanac, and here the plotting becomes truly mind-boggling as the Marty and Doc of this movie interact with themselves and the events of the last section of the first movie. The visual effects involved are breathtaking, some sequences seamlessly combining footage from both movies. They succeed in their main mission but with Doc trapped back in 1890 and Marty, time machine-less, in 1955 but a telegram delivered to Marty from the Doc gives him the information he'll need to save the situatuion, which leads directly into the third film . . .

But before discussing that I want to backtrack to what is a major flaw in the logic of the second movie: from the moment when the old Biff has handed over the almanac to his younger self he has altered the future, putting himself on a different time line to the one from which he came in the stolen time machine, therefore he wouldn't have been able to return to the same 2015 from which he came, and Marty and Doc wouldn't have got their time machine back and the movie would have come to an abrupt halt. Zemeckis and Gale were apparently aware they had a problem here because originally there was a scene of the old Biff fading away after he has got out of the car but this was later cut, no doubt because some pedant like me would ask why the car didn't fade away as well.

The third film isn't anything like as ambitious as the second and I was disappointed with it. It's really just an amiable spoof western with time-travel trimmings. In the telegram that Marty receives at the end of the second movie, Doc explains that he couldn't repair the De Lorean because the parts he needed wouldn't be manufactured for another fifty years after

Doc Emmett Brown at the climax of Back to the Future — *in the third film of the series he too would fall in love with Mary Steenburgen, clearly an occupational hazard for time travellers.*

1890. He has hidden the car in a cave, and gives Marty directions to the cave in the telegram. Marty repairs the time machine and travels back to 1890 to pick up Doc, but Doc has found true love in the form of a pretty school teacher (Mary Steenburgen, from *Time After Time*). There are the usual run-ins with Biff, or rather his ancestor — here a bullying gunslinger — lots of references to Hollywood westerns, and the usual problem of getting the De Lorean up to speed so that Marty can return to the future (on this occasion a steam train is used) and pick up Jennifer from the porch swing where he left her, asleep, in the last movie. And there's a final surprise when Doc and wife turn up in an H.G. Wells-style, steam-powered time machine to say hello before heading off into space. This one was the least successful of the three at the box office, though really only number one was a true financial blockbuster (the last two were made back-to-back as an economy measure). It's unlikely there will be any more in the series.

Back to 1986 for awhile to look at a charming, if seriously flawed, time-travel movie, *Flight of the Navigator*. Like Dante's *Explorers*, it is very much concerned with the fears and dreams of pre-adolescent boys while centring on every young sf fan's dearest wish — to have a spaceship of your very own. The film begins in a nightmarish vein when, one night in 1978, a twelve-year-old boy (Joey Cramer), sent to fetch his younger brother, falls down a small canyon in a heavily wooded area near his Florida home. He loses consciousness for a time, then wakes and goes home, only to discover that there are strangers living in his house and there is no sign of his family (a classic childhood fear). He is taken to a police station where a check is made to see if he's been reported missing. And he has been, except the report was made eight years before in 1978. The police take him to the house where his family has moved to in the intervening years and he gets another severe shock when he sees how they've aged in the short time, from his point of view, since he last saw them. And later, after he's been taken to hospital, he is again shocked when he is visited by his 'younger' brother, now a cool and confident teenager. All this is handled straight, and Cramer convincingly portrays the boy's distress and fear at finding himself in what seems to be an episode of 'The Twilight Zone'.

What's happened is that eight years before he was picked up by an alien spaceship that took him to a planet light-years away and has now brought him back (the logic behind this piece of tortured plotting does not withstand any degree of scrutiny). The ship, meanwhile, has hit an electricity pylon (another strained piece of plotting) and is now in the hands of a team of NASA scientists who are unable to penetrate its seamless surface. When the boy is found to have complex computer information in his brain, including the specifications of the alien ship, he is taken to the NASA base for further tests. He manages to sneak into the hangar where the ship is being kept and the ship opens to receive him. The ship is controlled by a robot device consisting mainly of a talking sphere on the end of an articulated arm. To begin with, the robot isn't too cute but after a mind-link with the boy it becomes as anthropomorphic as hell, and completely insufferable (and the fact that its voice was provided by Paul Reubens, the dreaded Pee Wee Herman, complete with nerve-grating laugh, makes it even worse).

From then on nothing much happens in the movie. The boy has fun flying around in his shiny spaceship while the NASA people vainly try to track him down, and the robot's chatter becomes increasingly inane. And things aren't helped by the introduction of some alien muppets . . . I mean, creatures . . . specimens that the ship is returning to their home worlds. The ship, incidentally, is beautifully designed and the visual effects, which included some computer-generated imagery, are impeccable without being too flashy. Finally, the boy has the ship head for home in Florida but when they arrive they find the place crawling with NASA people and police so he requests that the ship take him back to 1978, despite the potential risk to his life this presents. The ship does so; he wakes up back in the canyon and returns to his family as he remembers them, leaving his distraught mother and father in that other time line even more depressed now that they've lost their son for the second time running. But this is not the sort of film that is capable of addressing that type of problem. Anyway, it's a pleasant, good-looking movie that could have been a lot more if the script hadn't taken the easy way out. The script was by Michael Burton, from a story treatment by Mark Baker. The director was Randal 'Grease' Kleiser. Like *Explorers*, it was not a popular success.

Another time-travelling flop was *Biggles* in 1988. Biggles is the fictional flying ace created by Captain W.E. Johns when Britain still had an empire. He started life as a pilot in the First World War, was still going strong after the Second World War and was immensely popular with generations of young boys in Britain and the Commonwealth. I read and enjoyed *Biggles* books when I was a boy (but I much preferred the series of juvenile sf novels that Johns wrote concerning the adventures of Professor Brane and his chums in outer space) and I'm sure that some *Biggles* books, jingoistic and racist as they would seem by today's standards, still reside in the children's sections of many libraries and elsewhere but I'm equally sure that a lot of young boys today have never heard of him. And as far as America is concerned, I'm sure the character is completely unknown. So why would a film-maker think that an expensive movie about *Biggles* had any chance of being a big popular success with today's young international audience? You've got me. But *Biggles* was indeed made into such a movie and predictably crash-landed at the box office.

It's obvious that the writers, John Groves and Kent Walwin, knew that they would have to come up with a clever and very cunning plan in order to hook the American audience. But failing to do that they instead simply concentrated the film on a young and handsome contemporary New York advertising executive (Alex Hyde-White) who, for no particular reason, starts to flash back through time to the First World War where he keeps encountering Captain Bigglesworth (Neil Dickson). Biggles is busy trying to track down a new German secret weapon — a heat ray — that could win Germany the war and with the assistance of the American yuppie he, and his chums Ginger, Algy and Bertie (have I missed one?), finally succeed in finding and destroying it. Hooray.

Watching this weird movie you wonder just what was going on in the minds of the people who made it. I mean, why call it *Biggles* and then relegate the title character to a minor supporting role in his own movie? It could have been anyone back there on the Western Front that the yuppie was drawn back to. But, as I said earlier, why would anyone want to bother making this movie at all? However, it does have a couple of funny moments involving the unpredictability of the hero's jaunts through time. On one occasion, in a London hotel room, he takes the precaution of equipping himself with the uniform and all the gear of a First World War British soldier and sitting there waiting for a jaunt that never comes, he is discovered by a highly amused hotel maid. In another sequence, one moment he and his girlfriend (yes, she gets to go back as well) are shooting at a line of attacking soldiers on the Front and the next moment find themselves standing on a bridge in London's dockland and spraying a row of police cars with machine gun fire. But otherwise it's a complete waste of time, technical talent and money. It was directed by John Hough.

Biggles avoids any of that complicated paradoxical stuff but our next movie, *Millennium* (1989), is all paradox. If anything, it's more complex in its time-travelling plot than *Back to the Future II*, but far less satisfying as a movie. It began life back in 1978 when that very good sf writer John Varley wrote a story called 'Air Raid'. It was an ingeniously plotted piece about time travellers from a future war-and-plague world materializing inside contemporary passenger planes some minutes before they are due to crash and swapping the people on board for 'wimps' (mindless bodies grown in tanks). This way desperately needed healthy people could be hijacked into the future without creating any dangerous 'temporal dislocations', because the passengers were destined to die anyway. The story attracted the attention of a Hollywood producer, John Foreman, who commissioned Varley to write a screenplay based on it. Varley did so but, as is so often the case in the film industry, the project was shelved. So Varley then expanded his screenplay into a novel, *Millennium*, which was published in 1983. And five years later the film project was revived by producer Douglas

Leiterman and it was all systems go.

I had high hopes for this movie – after all, it's rare for a top sf writer to have the opportunity to write a screenplay based on one of his own works – but then I heard who the director was and I immediately got a sinking feeling. The director was Michael Anderson. As I've commented elsewhere in this volume, he has made some of my least-favourite genre movies. I don't think he's a very good director, period, and it's a shame that over the years he's frequently been handed sf projects, one of which was the TV series based on Ray Bradbury's *The Martian Chronicles*. Bradbury was unhappy with the result: 'It was the director, Michael Anderson. His pace was all off. I saw a couple of his other films right after that, with Michael Caine and Orson Welles, and he managed to make them boring.'[1]

The preview screening of *Millennium* confirmed my misgivings. It starts okay with Kris Kristofferson (in neutral acting mode) as Bill Smith, ace air-crash investigator, checking out a recent plane crash in which there are a number of peculiar anomalies, such as the co-pilot's recorded voice crying out that the passengers are horribly burnt before the actual crash, while becoming romantically involved — okay, having a one-night stand — with attractive but odd Louise Baltimore (Cheryl Ladd, giving an excellent performance) before she apparently vanishes. Later, when Smith is examining an unfamiliar object from the wreck, he gets a paralysing shock. While lying there immobilized on the hangar floor he sees Louise materialize, dressed in a strange costume. She retrieves the object and disappears back through her time gate and at this point the film's point-of-view switches over to her. We follow her into the future where we learn that, from her point of view, that was her first encounter with Smith. Then, because she hasn't retrieved all of the missing device from the future, a stunner that had been left behind on a plane, she must go back and have a second encounter with Smith, though from his point of view it will be the first time he's seen her. And so we once again repeat the events we've already seen: their 'first' meeting, their subsequent trip to the restaurant, the night they spend together in the hotel room and so on, except this time round we're seeing it all in a different light, knowing what we do now about Louise. Interesting idea and in the hands of a good director it might have worked but in the hands of Anderson it just brings the film to a dead halt. We sit there watching again what we've just seen before and the film never recovers from this hiatus.

Also there are signs that somebody with a screw loose has been meddling with Varley's screenplay, but maybe Varley himself is to blame. He certainly screwed up his own novel of *Millennium* with a tacked-on epilogue that made nonsense of much of what had occurred before. But whoever's to blame, there are several major divergences between the film and Varley's novelization of the original script. One example is Louise's personal robot, Sherman. In the novel he's a faceless 'fluid-moving' creation who is also, literally, her love machine — a walking sexual aid. The way he appears in the movie he could only provide sexual aid to a bulldozer. He's your typically clunky, old-fashioned Hollywood robot complete with jerky movements and funny walk (there's no hint of any sexual relationship between him and Louise, however this was probably written into Ms Ladd's contract). But then the movie itself, despite Varley's involvement, is your typically clunky, old-fashioned Hollywood sf movie, complete with jerky movements and funny walk.

To end this chapter I return to *Time Guardian*. Yes, the movie did get made and was even sort of released though no one was very happy with it. John Baxter said, 'It's hard to believe that one film can have so much wrong with it. Abysmal isn't the word . . . about half the script survives but that's so garbled I can hardly believe I wrote a word of it, and you can't imagine the hopelessness of the special effects. The time-travelling city looks like a drawing covered with chicken wire.'[2] (See Chapter Eighteen for more on this great movie.)

More importantly, no one else thought much of it either. The film had a very limited run in the United States and flopped badly. Its failure had further reaching repercussions: it turned out that *Time Guardian* was the flagship in a ten picture deal set up between American distributors and an Australian movie mogul called Antony I. Ginnane and which had absorbed $40,000,000 of Australian investors' money. As one Australian film-maker said, 'This funding disaster threatens to set back the Australian film industry ten years.' And to think it all stemmed from my casual mention to John Baxter years before of an idea for a time-travel movie. Maybe there's something to the 'Chaos' theory after all.

...And mind trips

The title of this chapter is something of a cheat, being the means by which I can group together films that don't easily fit into other categories. Then again, I think most, if not all, the films in this chapter deal with the inner space of the mind.

The first is a good example: *Slaughterhouse Five* (1971), which could conceivably have been included in the last chapter on time-travel movies but I really do think it is more of a mind trip than a time-travel story. What it is is a laudable attempt to bring Kurt Vonnegut Jr's best-known novel, which he would deny is science fiction at all, to the screen. Scripted by Stephen Geller and directed by George Roy Hill, it concerns a middle-class, middle-aged American man, Billy Prilgrim (Michael Sachs) who, increasingly alienated from his family and his everyday life, starts to experience sudden shifts back in time to when he was a prisoner-of-war in Dresden, the German city that was subsequently firebombed on a massive scale by the Allies. He then experiences shifts forward in time to the future when he has become the prisoner of an alien race who keep him in a zoo on their planet of Tralfamador and provide him, for company, with the presence of Hollywood starlet Montana Wildhack (Valerie Perrine). But while the juxtaposing of the horrors of Dresden with the fantasies of Tralfamador worked in the novel, the contrast in the movie between the Second World War sequences, which are effectively done, and the sequences on Tralfamador, which are embarrassingly misjudged, are fatally jarring. But

Michael Sachs is very good in the lead role, convincingly portraying both a gawky adolescent of unusual naiviety, and a balding, pot-bellied middle-aged man.

And now we come to two films by a film-maker who is perhaps beyond the proper scope of this book, being, as John Baxter points out in our conversation in the final chapter, that rare animal, a maker of adult science fiction films, while most of the films covered in *The Primal Screen* are intrinsically juvenile. The film-maker concerned is, or rather, was, Andrei Tarkovsky, and his two sf films are *Solaris* and *Stalker*.

Solaris was a 1972 Russian production, based on the novel by the Polish sf writer Stanislaw Lem, and like *2001: A Space Odyssey*, though without that film's lavish visual effects, it deals with an encounter between mankind and an alien entity that has god-like powers and is totally enigmatic. A research station has been placed in orbit around the planet Solaris to study the strange, oceanic mass that covers its surface. This mass is believed to be sentient but the scientists on board the station have failed to find a way of communicating with it. When it becomes apparent to the project controllers back on Earth that all is not well on the station another scientist Kris

Kris Kelvin (Donatas Banionis) has learned why things have seriously deteriorated on board the research station observing the planet Solaris.

Kelvin (Donatas Banionis) is sent to investigate. He discovers that the station is being 'haunted' by corporeal phantoms, products of the scientists' innermost desires, given substance by Solaris, but like Morbius and his monster from the Id, the scientists have no control over their creations. Kris is soon plagued with a creation of his own, in the form of his late wife (Natalia Bondarchuk) who committed suicide some years before. For me this section of the movie was the most interesting with Kris, tortured with guilt over his dead wife and with increasingly conflicting feelings about her replica, tries to cope with the artificial creature who, though she possesses some of the original woman's personality traits — provided by his memories of his wife — is a totally alien being. He attempts to destroy her but fails, and even when he succeeds in trapping her in a rocket and firing her off into space, a duplicate soon manifests itself in his room. And when 'she' begins to realize her true nature and attempts suicide (by swallowing liquid oxygen) to spare him any more pain, she still cannot die.

By the very nature of its theme there can be no satisfactory resolution to the questions that the movie raises. *Solaris* doesn't really have an ending but simply winds down and then comes to an enigmatic halt, something else it has in common with *2001*. But whereas *2001* was a secular approach to the concept of God, *Solaris* reflects the spirituality of its maker, as Tarkovsky was an intensely religious man. This is even more evident in *Stalker*, a film I like less than *Solaris*. I admire it, certainly, but I'm afraid that, given the choice of running it or *Aliens* through the video machine, I'd go for the latter. But that's my problem.

However, in order not to do a disservice to an artist who will no doubt be revered long after many of the other film-makers mentioned in this volume are forgotten, I will quote from a colleague of mine, the sf writer David Wingrove, on the subject of Tarkovsky and *Stalker*: 'What is the Zone? Is it merely an acausal pocket left after the visit of an alien spacecraft to Earth? Or is it, in the scheme of Tarkovsky's movie, the heartland of the imagination itself? . . . His film does not merely transform its original source (the novel *Roadside Picnic*, by Arkady and Boris Strugatsky) but transcends its terms of reference. *Stalker* is, ultimately, pure cinema — a wonderful succession of multiple expressive images which accumulate in the viewer's mind and attain deep significance . . . Thus the Zone becomes the spiritual heartland, the imagination, life itself in the midst of non-life;

the colourful inner self denied in 'real' life. The Strugatskys' book reflects a similar concern to Tarkovsky's own, but the film allows far subtler suggestion than print and here, with no special effects whatsoever, Tarkovsky implies that the Zone is something wholly alien and almost incomprehensible. This is the science-fictional level: the journey by the guide, Stalker (Alexander Kaidanovsky) into the Zone with the Scientist and the Writer to find the elusive "Wishing Room" at its heart. The acausality of the Zone and the nature of the mysterious central artefact (which can grant whoever penetrates it their heart's desire) mean they must approach it, indirectly, almost *intuitively*. What would, in another's hands, have been a rather dull section of the film, in Tarkovsky's proves one of the most genuinely tense sequences in cinema, a tension created not through over-the-top Hollywood special effects but by tapping some level of ourselves which is universal and unchanging. It is a sequence which, in its final stages, is almost unbearable — the journey down the tunnel which leads to the Wishing Room is not matched in cinema, even by Hitchcock, for its creation of an intense, almost nightmarish sense of anticipation. It is, in a very real sense, both the entrance to Hell and to Heaven. Abandon hope all ye who enter here is a literal necessity for admittance to the Zone and the Wishing Room at its heart. Going into the Zone is a gamble which can lead to sudden death unless those venturing there place their utter trust in the Zone and do no try to manipulate it. Thus the Scientist and the Writer have reached a point of spiritual vacuity — an absence of hope — and can survive in the Zone. As for Stalker, he is the eternal Divine Fool, perhaps Intuition itself, unbridled by Intellect: acting upon what feels right and what seems right rather than by what he *thinks* to be right . . . *Stalker* is not merely an exceptional science fiction film, it is a great work of art, and perhaps the most memorable experience in sf cinema.'[1]

Perhaps, perhaps . . . but it's the film's religiosity that puts me off. And as for Stalker, the Divine Fool 'unbridled by intellect, acting upon what feels right and what seems right rather than by what he *thinks* to be right', I am uncomfortably reminded of another Divine Fool in another movie advising his young acolyte to 'Let go of your conscious self and act on instinct . . . your eyes can deceive you — don't trust them. Stretch out with your feelings.' In my opinion, it's been mankind's habit of acting upon what feels right and seems right, acting upon its instincts, rather than thinking, that's been a root cause of most of humanity's problems down through the ages.

If Tarkovsky was a film-maker who could create a mood of profound unease without ever showing anything explicit we come now to a film-maker who takes a very different approach: David Cronenberg. He, like Clive Barker, believes very much in showing you what's really on the end of your fork — all the blood, vomit and worms. It is very unlikely that Tarkovsky would have shown someone's head exploding but that's what Cronenberg did near the start of *Scanners* (1981). *Scanners* was his most overtly science fiction movie up until that time. The ones before that, with perhaps the exception of his two experimental films made when he was a student, *Stereo* and *Crimes of the Future*, were very much in the horror genre: *Shivers* (also known as *They Came from Within*), *Rabid* and *The Brood* (his version of *Kramer vs Kramer* and far superior to that over-rated movie). However I think that *Scanners* is the less successful of all his films and also the most atypical. For one thing there's no sex in *Scanners*, or rather Cronenberg's highly individual interpretation of sex; one that is permeated with self-loathing and physical disgust. As I touched on previously when discussing his *Fly*, what is it with Cronenberg and his obsession with physical decay? Well, as the man himself said in a *Starburst* interview: 'I suppose it's a mediaeval preoccupation. Although I'm not a Catholic,

This can only be a scene from a David Cronenberg movie and it is — the famous exploding-head sequence in Scanners.

maybe this is my version of Original Sin. Basically, it's the idea that you are born having to face your own death, and death is very physical, not abstract. It's the spectre of having a mind that feels it ought to be able to live for another two thousand years but having to watch the body that supports it, or is somehow inexplicably linked with it, slowly age and die. That's true horror for me. When I'm feeling more cosmic about it, it's quite wonderful and miraculous and marvellous and I don't mind. Other times it's totally unbearable.'[2]

His next film, *Videodrome*, was to be his most visceral, squishy movie until *The Fly* and that surgical horror story *Dead Ringers*, but apart from the exploding head and telekinetic duel at the climax of the movie, the yuck-factor in *Scanners* is remarkably low. *Scanners* also lacks much in the way of originality, being very similar to George Pal's *The Power* in plot. Both movies begin with a super-mind revealing his existence during an ESP demonstration — in *The Power* the manifestation of mental force is a piece of paper twirling on a pin while in *Scanners* it's that lovable old exploding head — followed by a middle section where the nasty super-mind eliminates his enemies one by one, and finally the big mental duel between the good super-mind and the bad one (and, of course, the latter sequence in *Scanners* is considerably more graphic than the Pal version, thanks to the physical grotesqueries — exploding eye-balls, exploding veins and arteries — provided by ace make-up man Dick '*The Exorcist*' Smith).

There are other problems with the movie apart from its lack of originality. The overall construction of the screenplay is slipshod and there are several clumsy lapses in narrative continuity. Apparently this is because Cronenberg had to start shooting, due to various financial reasons, before he had even finished writing the script. 'There was a time,' he said, 'when no one knew what was going on, times when everyone went to lunch and I sat down and wrote the scene that was coming up.'[3] This may explain why pieces of the story seem to have been left out completely but it doesn't explain the many lapses of logic within the story. For example, the point is stressed that the 'scanners' are unable to block the thoughts from other people, unless they take a special drug, and yet they are continually being caught unawares by people sneaking up on them (I lost count of the times the scanner hero was surprised by the villain's non-scanner gunmen). Probably the film's biggest problem is the lack-lustre performance given by

*James Wood as a mad
Max, with Debbie Harry
on the box, in Cronenberg's
mind-boggling*
Videodrome.

*Max's relationship with his
TV set becomes increasingly
unhealthy.*

the actor playing the lead role, the aptly named Stephen Lack. Lack's lack
of acting talent is quite embarrassing, particularly in the scenes where he
was up against the formidable Michael Ironside playing the villain.
Cronenberg said he cast Lack on the strength of his unusual eyes — and
they are unusual; sometimes they appear to be pointing in two different
directions — but this is on a par with the producers of the Bond series

claiming, as they did, that they cast George Lazenby as James Bond because of the way he walked.

Cronenberg didn't make a similar mistake with the lead actor in *Videodrome* (1983) — he cast the charismatic and frenetic James Woods as Max Renn, the owner of an 'adult' cable TV company whose video-induced hallucinations take on a physical reality. If you need to show a character going crazy you can't pick a more suitable actor than Woods. With *Videodrome* we are in Philip K. Dick territory where reality is plastic and keeps changing into something else the moment your attention wanders. And here it's not just the situation and the surroundings that have acquired a disturbing plasticity but the physical self as well. During the film Renn undergoes several bizarre and queasy physical changes, the most bizarre involving a vagina-like opening that appears in his stomach and then swallows the revolver he's probing it with (the revolver later reappears as part of his arm). These were the creations of make-up expert Rick Baker.

It's difficult to describe the plot of *Videodrome*, as you can't tell what is real and what is purely happening inside Renn's head, and sometimes it seems to be both cases at the same time, but it begins with Renn looking for some hard-hitting exploitation material for his cable company. This leads him to discover 'Videodrome', a fairly explicit sex and masochism show that is being transmitted, apparently, from somewhere in the Far East. While he tries to find the owners of the show he becomes increasingly obsessed with the copies of the 'Videodrome' show that he's taped. Then he becomes involved with Nicki Brand (Deborah Harry), a psychologist whom he meets, ironically, when participating in a television talk show on the subject of 'TV and Social Responsibility', and who turns out to be into masochism herself (being burnt with cigarettes is one of her many turn-ons).

Renn eventually learns that 'Videodrome' isn't simulated sex and sadism but for real — it's snuff television — and it's not being transmitted from the Far East but from less exotic downtown Pittsburgh. And what he doesn't know yet is that prolonged exposure to the 'Videodrome' signal causes a tumour to grow in the viewer's brain that causes the viewer's fantasy to take on a subjective physical reality. It is then that the slit in his abdomen first appears, the first of the many surreal experiences that Renn must endure. It turns out that Renn has fallen into the clutches of a sinister, right-wing organization who want to use the 'Videodrome' brain-bending signal to wipe out the sort of perverted person who watches the sort of porn that Renn transmits on his cable station. And after that the film gets really confused as Renn, who has become a living weapon, is shunted back and forth between the factions who want control of the organization and the powerful 'Videodrome' device. The film climaxes with some stomach-churning visuals; one of the villains is shown bloodily disintegrating as erupting tumours tear him apart, and in one of the most surreal shots in the film, a huge mass of blood and guts explodes gruesomely out of a TV set . . .

I was very impressed by much of the film but it is confusing, even after several re-edits following preview screenings that showed audiences had trouble following the plot. It died at the box office but has since become a cult movie by way, appropriately enough, of the home video market. It is undoubtedly Cronenberg's most complex and ambitious film to date, an attempt to seriously confront a number of thorny subjects, including voyeurism, pornography and censorship. Asked if he identified with Max Renn, he said, 'The most obivous thing we have in common is that I too have been attacked by talk-show hosts for the films I've made that are violent or disturbing. I've been asked why I don't make nice, happy things and if I don't think I'm contributing to "a social climate of malaise". And I might well have responded similarly to Max — talking about catharsis as a necessary part of life — but my view of him is different. There is an undertone there in the film that implies he's not really sure of his own relationship to what he shows on his TV station, how he relates to his own sexuality and so on. Being a human being who's as sensitive to himself as anybody else, I suppose I have similarities to Max at that point, but then we really start to diverge. That isn't to say that I haven't noticed that I can be attracted to images of sexual violence, and wonder what that means about myself. But I'm *not* Max Renn.'[4]

A brief look at another sf movie that concerned a sinister organization using a TV signal to control people's minds — *Looker* (1981). This was written and directed by Michael Crichton and it represents the low point in his screenwriting career as the plot makes absolutely no sense at all. Albert Finney plays a successful Beverley Hills plastic surgeon who notices that some of his ex-clients are being murdered. What these ex-clients all had in common, apart from being his ex-clients, was they were all beautiful young models or actresses and that their plastic surgery involved only minor modifications to their faces and bodies but the modifications had to follow very precise specifications, which were provided by the clients. As he naturally falls under police suspicion for the murders the surgeon decides he'd better find out what's going on. This he does by sticking close by his last such client (Susan Dey), who is still alive, and as a result learns that an advertising corporation, headed by a villainous duo (James Coburn and Leigh Taylor-Young) used the women as the basis for computer-generated replicas. These replicas were put into TV commercials and by some means or other — something to do with the eyes of the replicas — a subliminal message was implanted into the minds of viewers. The villains plan to use the system to control politicians as well as make themselves even richer.

Now there are two ideas here. One is the interesting concept of computer-generated imagery that is so realistic you can't tell it from reality and the implications of such technology, which is going to arrive sooner or later, are quite staggering. The other is the old and tired one of mind-control by means of hidden electronic signals. The trouble is that Crichton has failed totally to link them together. I mean, he hasn't even provided a badly contrived reason. Why are computer-generated images of the women necessary for the mind-control device to work? Why do the original women have to conform to such precise physical specifications? It would be a simple matter, once all the data gathered in the full-body scan of the live subject is in the computer, to make any modifications required to the computer-generated image. That's what computer-generated imagery is all about, for goodness sakes! You can make it do whatever you want. But the biggest question of all is why the women have to be killed after their vital statistics are in the corporation computer? I've watched *Looker* twice on TV (it never got a theatrical release in Britain) and I've never picked up on this rather important plot pivot. Maybe it ended up on the cutting-room floor. Maybe it never existed. Maybe Crichton hoped that, with all the technological sleight-of-hand he hits you with, you just assume that the motive for the murders is in there somewhere.

But I did like one of the movie's gimmicks, a time-lapse gun that, when fired at someone, causes them to lose several seconds. Crichton pulls off some good visual gags with this, and he also has fun with the film's climax. This takes place when Coburn and Taylor-Young are staging a presentation of their commercials to a group of dignitaries; bare sets are being filmed backstage while the computer inserts its generated images of the actors into the footage. As a result of this, Finney and the bad guys stalking him backstage keep popping up in the adverts being watched by the audience. The high point of this comes in a commercial for breakfast cereal with the chirpy family pushing the product appearing quite oblivious to the dead body of a thug sprawled across their breakfast table.

And now, two movies that attempt to tackle the Big Questions: What's It All About? Is There a God? And, the old favourite: What Happens When You Die? One of the movies, *Altered States*, I thought very good when I saw it in 1981, and the other, *Brainstorm*, I thought very bad when I first saw it in 1984. I haven't been able to see *Altered States* again so I don't know if my original high opinion of it would still stand; however I have recently viewed *Brainstorm* again and my opinion that it's a stinker is unchanged.

Altered States, directed by Ken Russell, was remarkably faithful to the original novel by Paddy Chayefsky, the highly-regarded TV and movie screenwriter (he wrote, among other things, the scripts for *Marty*, *Hospital* and *Network*) who claimed it had nothing to do with science fiction. It follows the cosmic odyssey of a young scientist, Dr Eddie Jessup (excellently played by William Hurt in his movie debut) who is obsessed with discovering nothing less than the Meaning of Life. He begins experimenting with a sensory deprivation chamber and is convinced that the hallucinations he experiences inside the chamber are evidence of untapped reservoirs of primal knowledge within the human consciousness. But his experiments reach a temporary dead end and a number of years pass before he is able to continue. In the meantime he meets and marries, almost off-handedly, a beautiful anthropologist, Emily (Blair Brown, also excellent and also making her film debut). They have two children but Emily comes to realize that Eddie's obsession consumes him totally and that she and the children are mere phantoms to him. They break up, amicably, and she goes off to do field work in Africa for a year or two. During this period Eddie goes to Mexico where he experiments with an Indian hallucinatory drug. He believes the drug has the power to unlock the eons of history locked in the atoms of every one of us. He hopes that it might eventually enable him to journey back in time to the very moment of the creation of the universe.

After obtaining access to another isolation tank he continues his experiments with the drug, aided by colleague Arthur Rosenberg (Bob Ballaban) but against the advice of another colleague, Dr Parrish (Charles Haid, later one of the stars of 'Hill Street Blues'). Very strange things start to happen to Eddie during his sessions in the tank and he comes to the conclusion that the changes in his consciousness are being externalized — his body is physically regressing along with his mind. And what's more, these manifestations begin to occur even when he's not in the tank, along with increasingly disturbed visions. His two friends are not convinced of this at first but when Jessup regresses one night into an apeman and escapes from the lab and goes on a spree through the city which ends in the local zoo, they are obliged to face the truth. By this time Emily has returned and Eddie is beginning to appreciate just how much she really means to him but the Great Obsession draws him on. Finally, in a truly spectacular and disturbing sequence, he is sucked back along the neural pathways of the universe to the moment of the Big Bang and comes face to face with the Absolute itself. The confrontation almost destroys him but he is saved when Emily makes a courageous plunge into the physical vortex that has manifested inside the laboratory and brings him back by the sheer strength of her love for him.

So what's the Answer to the Big Question? 'The Final Truth is that there is *no* Final Truth,' a devastated Eddie tells Emily. And having faced the Absolute and found nothing but a terrible void Eddie fears that he can never become part of the real world again. But once again Emily saves him: during a final metamorphosis, which this time occurs inside his apartment, she forces him to choose life and her, rather than the infinite by putting her own life in danger. My reaction at the time: 'You can interpret *Altered States* in several ways — as a modern reworking of *Dr Jekyll and Mr Hyde* or a story about a woman who triumphantly competes with the ultimate/ the Universe or whatever for the love of her man . . . but whether or not you agree with whatever point you believe Chayefsky was trying to make, or even if you think Chayefsky was talking a load of old rope, you have to admit that Ken Russell has made a stunning piece of cinema out of the original material. It would have been too easy to make it all seem

William Hurt is wired up for the ultimate primal experience in Ken Russell's Altered States.

Hurt goes back in time to discover the secret of the universe, but doesn't like the answer he gets, nor the side effects of the trip.

infuriatingly pretentious or simply ludicrous but Russell avoided all the pitfalls, even during the apeman sequence that could easily have drifted into absurdity. *Altered States* is a dazzling torrent of light and sound that succeeds in being intellectually stimulating and rather disturbing all at the same time. Russell presents Eddie's hallucinations so skilfully that they hit you with the force of a punch in the stomach, particularly if you are sitting in the front row as I was. The sudden shifts in reality — like the moment when Jessup steps out of the bathroom and finds himself on the brink of a cliff above the depths of Hell itself — become increasingly unsettling and by the time I left the cinema I was feeling distinctly shell-shocked. I never thought I'd live to see the day but I've got to admit that Ken Russell — *Ken Russell* — has made what will probably rank as one of the all-time great science fiction movies. The mind boggles.'

Serves me right for sitting in the front row. I don't know if I would still regard it as one of the all-time great sf movies — I suspect that seeing it on video would dimish its mind-boggling capacity substantially — but someone who disliked it intensely was Paddy Chayefsky, and he even had his name removed from the credits as the author of the screenplay. I had read his novel and thought, as I said earlier, that Ken Russell, of all people, had been remarkably faithful to it. Later I learnt that Chayefsky and Russell had fallen out on the first day of shooting (Russell had been practically a last minute choice as director after the original one, Arthur Penn, had been dismissed from the production), and the producer, Howard Gottfried, calmed matters down by making the two men come to an agreement: Chayefsky would not interfere with Russell's direction if Russell promised not to change a word of the script. Russell kept to his side of the bargain but when it came to the editing he very much did his own thing and this is when Chayefsky disowned it.

Brainstorm (1983) also ends with a man encountering the Absolute but is drawn back to the land of the living by the love of a good woman, but that's about all it has in common with *Altered States*. I'd hoped that the movie was going to be much better than it turned out to be because you had to admire Douglas Trumbull's tenacity in getting the highly troubled production (among other things the actress Natalie Wood died during the shooting) completed and the film released, but there was no denying that *Brainstorm* was, and is, a mess.

The film's central idea, though not a new one, is the invention of a device that records a person's physical and emotional sensations and plays them back in the mind of someone else. The idea has a lot of potential and the movie does explore some of the more interesting aspects of such a device (there is inevitably a sequence where someone records an orgasm and then runs the tape on an endless loop — and fries his brain as a result). But then Trumbull had to go and get all Serious and Significant by having the plot take a turn for the metaphysical. One of the scientists working on the project has a heart attack (this is set up for us by having the character, played by Louise Fletcher, be a ludicrously heavy smoker) and manages to put the thought-recording helmet on before she dies. The device's inventor (Christopher Walken) is eager to try out this recoding of the Death Experience but his first attempt nearly proves, rather appropriately, fatal for him. His second attempt succeeds, despite the efforts of his employers and, another inevitable ingredient, sinister government agents to stop him. In a climax almost as banal as that in *The Black Hole* Walken 'dies' and goes up to, one presumes, heaven after a short detour through hell. Hell here resembles a room party at a science fiction convention while heaven, or God, is represented by a glowing white light surrounded by lots of flapping pillow cases.

I'm not sure what conclusion we are supposed to draw from these experiences. Walken appears to find death a positive experience and is unwilling to respond to his wife's pleas to return (a horrible irony here in that she was played by Natalie Wood) but finally his love for her triumphs over the lure of the Absolute and he returns to his body. But is he downhearted at still being alive? No, on the contrary, he's very excited and starts babbling on about the stars and the Wright Brothers (this sequence is significantly staged in front of an exhibition commemorating the brothers' first flight). The message I got from all this was there was some connection between the death experience and aeroplanes. Or was Trumbull trying to say that dying could prove to be the technological breakthrough that would enable Man to reach the stars? One suicide pill and — bingo — you're an astronaut! (This positive and downright queasy atittude towards the death experience, I have learnt since writing the above, was the contribution of the writer of the screenplay, Bruce Joel Rubin. He later wrote the screenplay of another death-celebrating movie, the immensely popular *Ghost*, and also scripted the darker, but still with a 'death is a positive experience' theme, *Jacob's Ladder*. Amusingly, Rubin disapproved of another recent 'death experience' movie, *Flatliners*, which featured a group of young doctors deliberately stopping their hearts under controlled conditions. Why did he disapprove? Because 'it depicted the departure from this world in every single case as a terrible experience. This is irresponsible of the writer, and frankly, I don't think he took the notions he was planting in the public mind seriously.'[5] And this piece of claptrap comes from the man who gave the public mind *Ghost*! Queasier and queasier.)

Brainstorm's biggest handicap, apart from Rubin's screenplay, is a technical one. The film is all about a device that can transfer emotions and sensations but, of course, the film can only provide images. So all those subjective shots of rollercoaster rides remain just familiar movie images, even in the form that I originally saw *Brainstorm*. This was in a cinema where, whenever the 'brainstorm' sequences appeared, the cinema screen widened and the film went from 35mm to 70mm. All very impressive but it still didn't give you the sense of heightened reality that Trumbull was after. I gather he had originally planned to shoot these sequences using his 'showscan' method where the film is projected onto the screen at sixty frames per second instead of the usual twenty-four, but this didn't prove feasible (for one thing all the cinemas screening it would need special equipment).

Tron (1982) could easily have fitted in my chapter on robots and computers, as the film's excuse for a central plot involves a sentient, anthropormorphic computer trying to take over the world, but the film's central idea is the visualization of what it might be like inside a computer. In a sense you could say the movie pre-dates the creation of sf author William Gibson's cyber-space, but where Gibson's concept is a perfectly reasoned possibility of what the visual 'reality' might appear to be like, in a direct interface between a human consciousness and a highly sophisticated computer network, the visual computer world in *Tron*, though spectacular and cleverly presented, is ludicrously illogical and unscientific. What the makers of the movie, Donald Kushner and Steven Lisberger (who also directed) have done is to deliberately confuse the visuals of video games with computers. True, video games are controlled by computer chips, but that is no reason to suggest that the internal workings of a computer would be visually analogous to those of a video game, but that is what *Tron*'s makers establish early on in the movie. The other really big scientific absurdity is the device which they use to get their hero, Flynn (played by Jeff Bridges), inside the computer, some kind of laser mechanism used to reduce solid objects into 'molecules' which can be stored within a computer for a time and then be reconstituted in the original form. Molecules stored inside a computer system? Were Kushner and Lisberger patronizing their mainly young audience (it was a Disney production) or were they simply ignorant about computers?

Anyway, that's the crux of the plot. Flynn gets trapped inside this computer system which has been taken over by the nasty Master Control Program. Created by the villainous Dillinger (David Warner), managing

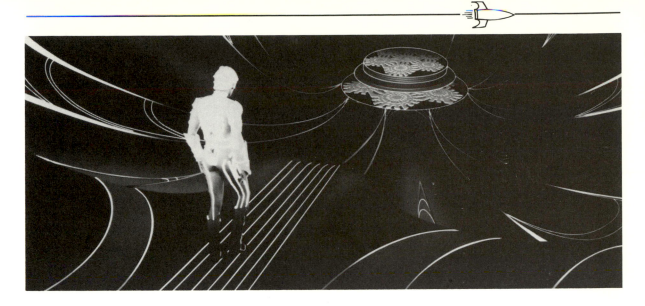

director of the computer company, the MCP is gobbling up smaller, weaker progs as its influence spreads. Flynn discovers that computer users that he knows from the real world have their program 'doubles' inside the computer system, and that even pure computer programs come complete with personalities, little bodies and are even of mixed sexes. This is anthropomorphism gone mad. And if you start asking yourself what use sex would be to computer programs then the *Tron* virus has entered your neural system and your brain has started to rot. Press the 'Abandon Edit' button immediately.

Tron had great visuals but that's all.

But, yes, yes, *Tron*'s abstract visuals, created by a mixture of actual computer-generated graphics and traditional animation methods, are very impressive (it was designed by Syd Mead, who worked on *Blade Runner*, comic artist Jean Moebius Giraud, and Peter Lloyd). But as is the case with so many sf movies with state-of-the-art special effects, the gap between the look of the finished film and its content is depressingly huge.

I'm closing this chapter on an up-note by discussing an sf movie I personally like; a small-scale film that not only looks good but has a streak of intelligence running through it. I'm talking about *Dreamscape* (1984). Its background plot, the one that provides the impetus for the foreground action, concerns the American President (Eddie Albert) whose recurring nightmares about nuclear warfare and its devastating aftermath so upset him that he intends to sign a disarmament treaty with the Russians. This so alarms one of his top advisors (Christopher Plummer) that he suggests

A memorable sequence from **Dreamscape** *when Dennis Quaid finds himself in the nightmare of a man with vertigo.*

The lizard man seizes his young victim within his nightmare in the impressive **Dreamscape.**

the President check into a special clinic at a certain Thornhill College. And here's where we get to what the film's central theme is all about, for the clinic is doing research into recurring nightmares and bad dreams by using telepaths to enter the dreams of the troubled sleeper and sort out the problem by confronting the source of the trouble.

Now the idea of person entering the dream of someone else and manipulating it is not new in written sf. At least two top sf writers have explored the theme: John Brunner with his novel *The Whole Man* in 1964 and Roger Zelazny with his novel *The Dream Master* in 1965, but as far as I know *Dreamscape*, based on a script by David Loughery and with rewrites by the producer Chuck Russell and the director Joe Ruben, was the first sf movie to venture into this area. Dennis Quaid plays Alex, formerly the clinic's ace telepath but who, at the start of the movie, is having more fun as an amoral gambler. It is gambling losses that force him back into the clutches of the clinic and its icy director (played by icy Max Von Sydow) against his wishes. But his initial hostility starts to thaw thanks to the influence of the director's female assistant (Kate Capshaw) and his genuine sympathy for one of the clinic's patient's, a small boy who suffers recurring nightmares about being trapped in a gloomy house with a terrifying lizard man. Alex, by entering the boy's dream, helps him overcome the monster despite his own profound fear of the thing (this springs, I think, from a phobia he has about reptiles). This and the other sequences where Alex enters the dreams and nightmares of the patients are extremely well done and capture perfectly the dreamlike quality of dreams. And no, that comment wasn't as dumb as it might seem; a lot of movies with dream sequences fail to get them right — often they're too obviously dream sequences with weird lighting and strange music (all my dreams have perfectly normal lighting and come without a music track) whereas the dreams in *Dreamscape* have a disturbing surface look of normality about them, even when they're shocking. I was particularly impressed, and disturbed, by one of the film's early dreams that Alex entered, the one being dreamt by a man suffering from a fear of heights (a fear I share). I think, also, the fact of Alex's presence provided the audience with an extra, objective, viewpoint of the dreams that added to the verisimilitude of the experiences. Also interesting, partly because of its moral ambiguity, is the sequence where Alex enters a dream being experienced by the Kate

Capshaw character and proceeds to seduce her (this was drastically trimmed in the British release print, and another sequence, where Alex joins in the dream of a man who suspects his wife of infidelity, was missing altogether).

The dream at the film's climax is more traditional — cinematically speaking — in its nightmarish appearance but it's still an impressive set-piece. This is when Alex enters the President's usual post-nuclear holocaust nightmare to prevent another psychic, Tommy Ray (David Patrick Kelly) acting on orders from the President's creepy advisor to scare the President to death while he sleeps. The duel between the psychics is visually inventive with Tommy Ray finally transforming himself into the lizard man from the little boy's nightmare, but seen nowadays appears overly familiar thanks to countless similar sequences in the apparently endless *Nightmare on Elm Street* series. (It's interesting to note that at one point in the battle Tommy Ray turns the fingers of one of his hands into steel knives. *Dreamscape* and the first *Nightmare* movie both have the same 1984 release date but I wouldn't mind betting that the former provided the inspiration for the latter; after all, the script for *Dreamscape* had been in circulation for some years before the film was made.) It's a shame that *Dreamscape*, a relatively intelligent, witty and relatively morally sound movie that, alas, didn't make much impact at the box office, should have paved the way for the morally unsound, and hugely successful, *Nightmare On Elm Street* movies.

Hello again, dystopia

I could be wrong but I believe it was Fritz Leiber, the sf and fantasy author, who wrote the first stories set in an inhospitable post-nuclear holocaust world thinly populated by hardened and extremely ruthless individuals who would happily kill each other for a can of beans. I remember reading, a long time ago, one such story by Leiber, the title of which escapes me, where two such people have a wary encounter in the barren landscape, one a man and the other a woman. Slowly they each divest themselves of their large variety of weapons, undress, make love, re-arm themselves and go their separate ways, blood enemies once again (or does one kill the other? I can't remember). Harlan Ellison's *A Boy and His Dog* is set in such a milieu and I suspect that the movie version of his novella (see Chapter Nine) provided part of the inspiration for the Australian movie *Mad Max 2*, also known as *The Road Warrior*, which hit me right between the eyes when I first saw it in 1982 and which I still greatly admire — I rate it among the top ten of my favourite sf movies. Of course, the post-apocalyptic setting is only there to provide an excuse for a modern western using vehicles instead of horses. The future for the human race is clearly a bleak one here but we're too busy enjoying the exhilarating action to dwell too much on the darker aspects of the situation.

I had earlier enjoyed the original *Mad Max* back in 1980. It had come as a surprise as I knew little about it when I went to see it. Dubbed American voices but it was clearly set in Australia, and it was unlike any

Australian movie I'd seen before. Its director, George Miller, clearly didn't come from the *Picnic at Hanging Rock* school of Australian film-making. It was raw-edged, highly energetic and very violent with some amazingly spectacular, and destructive, car stunts. It was also science fiction, though marginally so, being set in a near future world where the centre was clearly no longer holding. Only a few highway cops were preventing the collapse into total anarchy, one of those cops being Max Rockatansky, played by the young Mel Gibson.

Max goes Mad when his wife (Joanne Samuel) and baby are run down and killed by a gang of psycho bikers, the same sadistic loonies who had earlier burnt his closest buddy, another cop, to death. Max himself has become emotionally burnt out and, after once again donning his police uniform (he had retired from the force after the death of his friend) he sets out after the gang and kills them one by one. The final death, involving the leader of the gang, is particularly sadistic — Max leaves him handcuffed by one wrist to the wreckage of a petrol-soaked car, his only chance of survival being to cut through his own wrist with the hacksaw blade, that Max has left with him, before the petrol ignites. He doesn't make it. The film ends with Max alone and in pretty bad physical shape — the bikers had run over him a few times — facing what seems to be an empty future.

The movie had a lot of rough edges, some of the performances weren't too hot (but then the silly dubbing didn't help) and the violence was probably too excessive in places (though the British film censors had already been at work in that area) but I felt that the movie was definitely out of the ordinary and even recommended it to John Baxter who was, then, usually pretty scathing about all Australian movies, and was relieved when he confirmed my opinion. I therefore had high hopes for the sequel, *Max Max 2 — The Road Warrior*, when it turned up two years later and it was immensely satisfying, at the preview screening, not just to have my expectations confirmed but actually exceeded.

Mad Max 2 is a much more polished piece of cinema than the first film and has the advantage of a classical plot that seems to be the perfect distillation of so many other films about the lone hero emerging out of the wilderness to protect the members of an ungrateful community from their enemies (the film's strong whiff of mythology is due to the fact that, like

The young Max (Mel Gibson) in Mad Max.

By the end of third movie Max Max: Beyond Thunderdome, *Max was looking somewhat older and ravaged.*

George Lucas, both the producer and director were strongly influenced by Joseph Campbell's *The Hero With a Thousand Faces*). In *Mad Max 2* the semi-urban setting of the first film has disappeared; the collapse of civilization has been complete and the film is set in the Outback where the survivors are battling it out over the remaining supplies of petrol. The last remnants of law and order are gone. Max, as we see him at the beginning of the movie, seems perfectly suited to this world — he is a cold-blooded loner, still emotionally burnt out, though he does have a dog as a companion. And at first, when he helps out the community being besieged by a horde of punk nomads — the community's camp contains an oil well — he does it simply for the petrol, but by the end, when he volunteers to lead the group that will decoy the nomads in the wrong direction while the others escape, it is an act of pure altruism. He has regained his humanity. This final action sequence, incidentally, remains as one of the longest and most exciting road chase sequences ever filmed with car, bike and truck stunts that are simply astonishing (amazingly, only one stunt man was injured, and that happened when a camel stood on his foot during a break in the shooting).

As *The Road Warrior*, the movie was a popular hit in America and made an international star out of Mel Gibson. It also led to Hollywood roles for Vernon Wells, who played the craziest and most fearsome of the punk nomad baddies (he even got to be Arnold Schwarzenegger's chief foe in *Commando*). And as it was a financial hit for its distributors, Warner Brothers, it was decided to make a third film with a bigger budget — this became *Mad Max: Beyond Thunderdome*. And it proved to be a big disappointment to me. It has an okay beginning, with Max's arrival at Bartertown — a neutral territory that provides creature comforts for the hard men of the Outback, and ruled over by the splendid Aunty Entity (Tina Turner) — and there's an action-filled climax (though nothing like as impressive as the one in the second film), but the middle of the film consists of a long and tedious section where Max, an outcast, encounters a bunch of children living in an oasis in the desert. They are survivors of a plane crash and are waiting for their saviour who, according to their legend, will come and take them back to civilization. Naturally, they assume Max is that saviour and, naturally, he doesn't want the job. Soggy, predictable stuff — *Lord of the Flies* out of Spielberg — and it stops the movie in its tracks.

Vernon Wells gave a memorable performance as a juiced-up, post-apocalyptic punk in Mad Max 2, *also known as* The Road Warrior.

I asked John Baxter why he thought the first two movies were so good and the third such a disappointment. He said, 'Well, because Byron Kennedy, the producer, was dead by then. Kennedy was the motivating force behind it all. He had gone to Hollywood years before on a scholarship and spent the time studying the business structure of Hollywood. He'd come back and his advice to George Miller was so good that it sustained the release of the first movie and the great success of the second. By the time of the third one Kennedy had been killed in a helicopter accident and the motivating force was gone. I had all the drafts of *Max Max 2* right from the very first outline and it was very clear that Kennedy's intelligence was motivating much of what went on in that film and it's fascinating to see how much of the second film's early draft has been carried through into the third film rather than any new material. What had basically happened was that Miller had gone back to the early drafts and picked out certain sequences that he hadn't used and put them in the third; like the feral children living by the plane wreck, that was a left-over from No 2, though originally it hadn't been a plane but a school bus, and he used this idea as the whole skeleton of the third film. It simply lacked that fixing vision that Kennedy had. I went on the set when they were shooting *Beyond Thunderdome* and it was really evident that it had got out of hand and the main motive force now wasn't Miller but Terry Hayes, who was the co-writer of the script and by then one of the major people in the Kennedy-Miller organization. And though Hayes is a fairly skilful, ex-tabloid journalist and quite good at putting together certain sorts of screenplays, I don't think he was equal to the challenge of *Beyond Thunderdome*.

'Miller and Kennedy were like Michael Powell and Emric Pressburger. Powell used to do all the directing but Pressburger used to do most of the writing and a lot of Pressburger's influences can be seen in the movies. In the same way Kennedy was the motivating and creative force for Miller. Miller has this phantasmagoric vision — a wonderful eye, I mean, his eye is really the eye of a painter or a photographer rather than a director's. His ability to compose and frame things is absolutely razor sharp. Brian Hannant (co-screenwriter on the second film) told me that during the making of *Mad Max 2* Miller would never cut to a shot that was not the equivalent of an image that the main character might be seeing. For instance, near the beginning when Max is up on that hill and looking down at the besieged camp for the first time — normally a director would go for a long shot with a zoom down into the centre of the camp but Miller didn't. What he did was show Max taking a large telescope out of his bag, opening it out and looking down through it, and then Miller cuts to a close shot of the camp. And Brian said this was not a joke, this was Miller's absolute fidelity to the point-of-view of his main character. If Max couldn't see it it was not happening. And the result is that I think his films are uniquely personalized — in all that genre his are the lone movies where you really start to feel part of that mythical character a little. But for all that he still needed that creative force that Kennedy provided. That was what *Beyond Thunderdome* needed, a totally new idea, and what you got was warmed over ideas from the second film plus a lot of rather trendy and expensive costume stuff put in at the behest of the distributors to make it a splashier film. I think the lack of Kennedy's input is the reason why Miller has made so little since then . . .'[1]

The year before *Mad Max 2* was released saw the release of a vaguely similar movie, except that it had an urban setting instead of a desert one and it wasn't very good. I'm referring to John Carpenter's *Escape from New York*. It's set in a future America (1997) where things have got so bad the entire island of Manhattan has been turned into one large prison camp holding millions of offenders who run it themselves. The President of the United States has had the misfortune to crashland on the place and is now being held by the inmates at a secret location. So the authorities send in the hardest dude they can find, Snake Plissken (Kurt Russell, doing a curious imitation of Clint Eastwood), who has twenty hours to rescue the

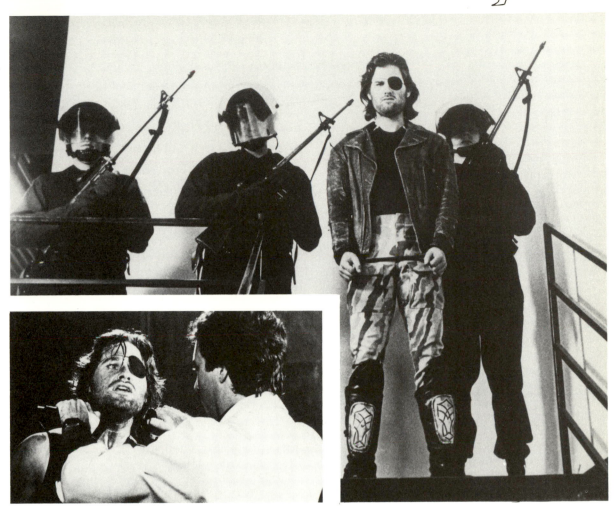

president before the explosive charges planted in his neck by the authorities go bang . . .

Escape certainly begins well, Carpenter skilfully sets up an interesting situation but it rapidly becomes clear that he can't deliver the goods. He even wastes the film's central premise, absurd as it may be — here is Manhattan Island as one vast prison but apart from a few intriguing sequences when Snake first arrives, such as the visit to the theatre (a direct lift from a similar sequence in *A Boy and His Dog*), and the attack of the 'crazies' who erupt up through the floor of a shop, we see very little of what life is like in this bizarre, pressure-cooker of a society where women are scarce and anarchy rules. Instead, Carpenter lets the movie degenerate into a fairly routine chase-thriller which becomes increasingly devoid of

Kurt Russell as Snake Plissken in John Carpenter's Escape from New York.

(Inset) Snake is implanted with miniature time-bombs to ensure his co-operation.

originality as it progresses. At the halfway point the plot simply falls to pieces, suggesting that Carpenter and his co-writer Nick Castle ran out of ideas. The way in which Snake and his companions, including the President (Donald Pleasence), escape from the villain (Isaac Hayes) and his men in the lobby of the World Trade Centre is particularly ridiculous. First they incapicitate a veritable army of thugs with a feeble cloud of steam and then limp their way outside to be saved by a cab driver (Ernest Borgnine) who drives them away. As this is the second time that Borgnine and his cab have appeared at an opportune moment to get Snake out of trouble it's a sure sign of creativity burnout.

The subsequent chase across the George Washington Bridge, mined to keep the prisoners from escaping, is also a feeble affair. For some reason the villain forgets to bring his army with him, and by the small size of the explosions, the mines don't look as if they would have served as an effective barrier to some three million hardened criminals. I also couldn't understand how the map showing the location of the mines came to be in the hands of those back on the island when we were told that the man who drew it had got shot by the police after crossing the bridge. Did the police obligingly post it back to Manhattan?

Back in 1981 I wrote: '*Escape from New York* is basically a badly thought-out piece of work which, for all its technical virtuosity, is inferior to the two movies it most closely resembles, *The Ultimate Warrior* and *A Boy and His Dog*. Carpenter is an adept visual technician but weak in the areas of plotting and dialogue. The latter in *Escape* seems to consist of nothing but homages to various Howard Hawks movies — after a while you wish the characters would stop being cute and actually say something.'

In the early eighties, with the year 1984 fast approaching, someone naturally had the idea of remaking a film version of George Orwell's *1984*, the mother of dystopia stories. The first version had been made in 1956 by my least-favourite sf film director, Michael Anderson, and while it's not as bad as some of his movies it's not that hot either. And it wasn't helped by the miscasting of Edmond O'Brien as Winston Smith, the clerk in the Ministry of Information who, inspired by his lover, Julia (Jan Sterling) decides to rebel against the totalitarian nightmare of 1984 and create a private world away from the ever-present gaze of Big Brother. Strangely enough, two different endings were shot: the American one faithfully followed that of the novel with Winston and Julia successfully broken and declaring that they love Big Brother while the British version, incredibly, had them overcoming their brutal conditioning and dying, hand-in-hand, in a hail of bullets while defiantly shouting 'Down with Big Brother!' Needless to say, the latter completely vitiates Orwell's theme about the absolute power of a state that *is* absolute power.

The 1984 version of *1984*, written and directed by Michael Radford, is a much better movie than the first. For one thing, the second film could be much more explicit, both sexually and in the scenes where Winston Smith is brutally broken down. In that crucial moment when Smith cries, 'Do it to her, not me! Do it to her!' you have to first believe how important Julia was to him and, secondly, accept that what is being done to him is so terrible it will cause him to betray his love for her. The film is helped by its excellent cast: Suzanna Hamilton gives a fine performance as the vital, sexual Julia, a life-force that invades Smith's drab existence and turns his own life upside-down; John Hurt is fine in the latter sections of the film — no actor could better portray a man crumbling from within though unfortunately he looks much the same in the early sequences and one isn't quite sure what Julia saw in this man. And, surprisingly — in the light of many of his previous film performances in recent years — Richard Burton is very good as O'Brien (it was to be his final role: he died shortly afterwards). It is a calm, matter-of-fact performance, heavy with menace but also suggesting that O'Brien knows he's trapped in the system, the difference being is that he accepts it totally and considers it his tedious, messy but necessary duty to convince doubters to do the same. Thus in the scenes where he's torturing Smith, O'Brian makes it clear that there's nothing personal in what he's doing; these atrocities have to be committed because that's the way it is and the system can never be changed. And this makes O'Brien's behaviour all the more disturbing — if Burton had played him as a leering, sadistic type the effect wouldn't have been as chilling. For me, the worst moment in these sequences is when O'Brien shows Smith his shattered reflection in a mirror and then casually pulls out one of Smith's loosened front teeth in a demonstration of the state's total power over him and his body.

So *1984* is a good and honourable stab at filming Orwell's novel but the trouble it has as a piece of cinema is that the story is so well known that

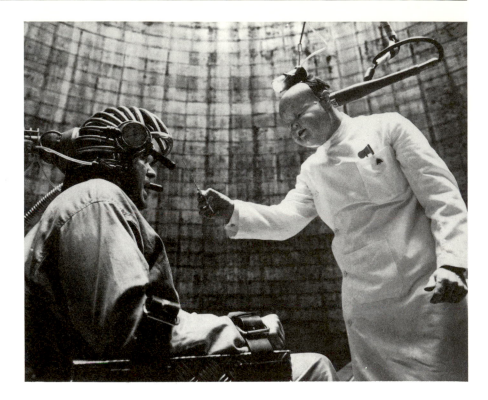

The climax of Brazil, *Terry Gilliam's 1984 version of* 1984.

the audience knows there can be no surprises. As much as you want Smith to somehow escape and be reunited with Julia you know there's no hope — the ending is as inevitable as death and taxes. However, Terry Gilliam kind of got round this with his own unofficial version of *1984* (also made in 1984), *Brazil*. When his protagonist, Sam Lowry (Jonathan Pryce), has been captured and is being tortured (by a cheerful Michael Palin) there comes a marvellously carthartic moment when a horde of freedom fighters, led by Robert De Niro as the legendary Harry Tuttle, storm into the cavernous torture chamber. Sam's torturer is shot dead, the guards are killed and Sam is carried off to be reunited with his version of Julia, Jill (Kim Greist), whom he had been told was dead, and off they go to live the rest of their lives in a rural idyll. Then Gilliam cuts to show Sam still sitting strapped in the torturer's chair — it had all taken place in his mind. And yet, in a sense, he had escaped after all. From the expression on his face Sam had parted company from the real world and wasn't coming back.

Ironically, this ingenious ending — letting us have our cake and eat it too — did not go down well with the executives at Universal, the film's American distributors, who considered it much too downbeat and insisted that the final bit be chopped off to give the movie a straightforward happy ending. They also wanted a number of other cuts in the movie, saying it was too long and too confusing. Gilliam resisted and battle was joined, Gilliam receiving the support of many American critics and film-makers. Unusually, the director won out over the might of the Hollywood studio and it was his cut of the movie that finally got released. However, despite all the critical praise, it was not a box-office success.

I myself have mixed feelings about the movie, as I usually do with any movie made by Gilliam. He can create marvellous visual set-pieces — and *Brazil* is full of them — and I love his basic pessimism about the human condition, as well as his laudable desire to expose the messier side of life that many would prefer to be kept discreetly hidden. But his films always seem to be unfocused with too much packed into them for their own good, and this is certainly the case with *Brazil*. Also, while he has the advantage over Radford's version of *1984* in that he is not under any constraints to be faithful to the novel and can go freewheeling off into bravura fantasy sequences one moment and into black satire the next, he is still handicapped by that overly-familiar *1984* scenario. And, it is too long. Where sf movies like *Blade Runner* and *Aliens* suffered from the cuts the studios imposed upon them I'm afraid I have to side with the Universal execs on this one and say that *Brazil* could do with some judicious pruning. Still, there is much to admire in *Brazil*, such as the stunning aerial sequences where Sam dreams that he is soaring through a magical sky on artificial wings, and the sequence concerning his first day on the job at the absurdly bureaucratic Ministry of Information which deftly combines Orwell with Kafka.

A more appropriate title for *Slipstream*, said one critic, would have been *Slipshod*. A glib comment, perhaps, but I'm afraid slipshod perfectly sums up *Slipstream*. It's one of those movies where all concerned weren't sure exactly what kind of movie they were supposed to be making and ended up with a disaster. It's set in your standard post-apocalyptic world, though the apocalypse wasn't a nuclear one but of the now more fashionable environmental variety. Whatever it was it broke civilization up into small communities and the only form of transport between these communities is by means of lightweight aircraft within the slipstream of the title, another legacy of the catastrophe. The plot concerns two law officers (Mark Hamill and Kitty Aldridge) who have captured a mysterious fugitive (Bob Peck) and are taking him back to their home base. You can tell there's something mysterious about the Peck character because, while the others are dressed in your standard trendy post-apocalyptic gear, he is wearing a pin-striped suit. A Han Solo type of adventurer (Bill Paxton) kidnaps the prisoner in order to collect the reward and a game of cat-and-mouse begins between the four characters as they chase each other down the slipstream, encountering various weird communities along the way. It transpires that the Peck character is actually an android and a potential Messiah for the rebirth of a new and better world thanks to the knowledge he carries within him.

Big Arnold again, in The Running Man, *based on a Stephen King novel.*

Yaphet Kotto and Arnie discover there's no business like show business.

A hodge-podge of science fiction, green politics and Californian mysticism, it really is an embarrassingly bad movie, which was a serious setback for its producer, Gary Kurtz, who I know had worked for a long time to put the project together. Since splitting with George Lucas he had not enjoyed much success in the film industry (and a costly divorce settlement ate up most if not all the money he had made out of the two *Star Wars* movies he had produced). He had been involved with such movies as *The Dark Crystal* and *Return to Oz* which had not been overly popular with audiences. It's a mystery to me how *Slipstream*, produced by Kurtz and directed by Steven M. Liseberger (who made *Tron*), based on a script by Charles Pogue (who co-wrote *The Fly*), Tony Kayden and Liseberger, could have turned out to be such a mess. It probably has something to do with what John Baxter said of the Kennedy-Miller partnership and the *Mad Max* movies: there has to be someone involved in any film production who has a strong, overall vision of what the film is they're making, and this was obviously not the case with *Slipstream*, despite the long gestation period. (Pogue had written a screenplay several years previously and according to Liseberger the final script was something 'completely different to the Pogue original, which was based on an outline from another producer's ramblings back in the early eighties about a fourteen-year-old's encounter with an android as he journeyed in the future, a coming of age saga mixed with sci-fi.[2] Curiously, at the same time, Kurtz said that Pogue's script was 'intended to be something of a *Mad Max* rip-off set in the Australian desert.'[3] In addition, there was extensive reshooting that took place after the film had been completed. The cast is okay though, especially Hamill who is playing against type. But when in Britain to promote *Slipstream* he revealed to the *Starburst* interviewer that he was as in the dark as anyone as to what the film was about. 'Your guess is as good as mine!' he replied in answer to the question. 'It's funny to me, it's pretentious, it's stupid, it's very important. It reminded me of an Italian western.'[4]

1988 saw Big Arnie Schwarzenegger (who by then had become synonymous with sf cinema) playing a cop in totalitarian future America in *The Running Man* (directed by Paul Michael Glaser). He rebels when he's ordered to machine a protesting crowd from his helicopter. 'I won't kill innocent women and children!' he cries, innocent men still apparently being fair game. So he ends up in prison, escapes and almost manages to get out of the country before being betrayed to the authorities by the woman (Maria Conchita Alonzo) whom he is forcing to accompany him as cover. As a result he is obliged to take part in the nation's top rated TV show, 'The Running Man', where the contestants, mainly people the government wants to eliminate, are hunted down by murderous hulks, called Stalkers, flourishing a bizarre array of weapons, and are killed in front of the cameras while the audience, both studio and national, goes wild with delight. Well, of course, with one or two bounds, Big Arnie turns the tables on his persecutors, kills lots of people, restores democracy to America and gets the girl. All very different from the original Stephen King novel (originally published under his Richard Bachman pseudonym) it was based upon: not only does the hunt in the novel range right across the country rather than be restricted to one small area near the TV station, it was much darker in tone, ending with the dying protagonist, his entrails tangled around his feet, piloting an airliner into the side of the TV Games Building.

The Running Man, scripted by Stephen E. De Souza, is mixed up on every level. We, the audience, are supposed to be disgusted by the rampant blood lust being displayed by the 'Running Man' audiences in the movie and yet we are expected to cheer on Big Arnie in a similar fashion when he starts splattering the pursuing Stalkers one by one. Okay, he is given one little speech to make when he refuses to finish off a disabled Stalker in cold blood which is supposed to indicate to us that he is a different kind of killer to the Stalkers but this isn't very convincing. And as he is in the habit of making James Bond-like quips whenever he despatches a baddie you are given the impression he doesn't take killing people all that seriously. The film is also confused psychologically: the audiences are shown to be rooting for the grotesque and heavily armed Stalkers when surely, in real life, it would be the unarmed contestants who would attract audience sympathy (well, I hope it would be the case).

The Running Man tries for *Robocop*'s mixture of satire and black humour amid the gore but can't pull it off successfully. Still, some of the jokes do work (the intentional ones, that is; I'm not referring to the embarrassing theme song we hear being played at the end of the movie as Arnie and the girl go into a victory clinch). My favourite moment of intentional humour came when the man in the business suit enters Arnold's cell and informs him that he is his legally appointed theatrical agent. As Arnold is escorted to the TV studio the agent reads out the terms of his contract in the tones of a priest reading from the Bible as he escorts a condemned man to the execution chamber.

Before we engage with Big Arnie's biggest sf movie, a brief look at a feminist dystopia movie, *The Handmaid's Tale*. I've never read the novel, by Margaret Atwood, but I am reliably informed that this movie does not do it justice (however, when the film was released in Britain, Ms Atwood strongly defended the film in radio interviews she gave). It's set in a future America where, due to environmental disaster, most women have become infertile and society has succumbed to the rule of Christian fundamentalists who have set up a totalitarian state. Women have been sent back into the kitchens where they belong and minorities, such as unbelievers and gays, have been sent to work camps (or executed). Ah, but how to celebrate and reinforce the ideal of the nuclear family, which is the cornerstone of Christian fundamentalist ideology, if most women can't have children? That's where the 'handmaids' come in; they are young, unmarried women who happen to be fertile and are required to join what is a kind of pseudo-religious order. But despite their nun-like clothing they are not obliged to be celibate; on the contrary their duty is to have sexual relations with the men of the ruling party and bear them children. And does this sexual servicing take place under furtive conditions? No, it takes place in the marital bedroom with the wife present as well.

A good novelist, and I'm told that Ms Atwood is one, could probably make the reader accept all of the above but presented coldly and clinically on the big screen one's only reaction is a guffaw of disbelief. There are good performances all round, especially from Natasha Richardson in the title role (which originally was to have gone to Sigourney Weaver) and the film is visually striking, but the basic story material, as handled by director Volker Schlondorff and screenwriter Harold Pinter, simply becomes a tall tale that is too big to swallow.

I recently reread, after seeing *Total Recall*, the 1966 story it was based on, Philip K. Dick's 'We Can Remember it for You Wholesale', to see how much of the story had been incorporated into the movie. Surprisingly, much of what must rate as Dick's most mindbending, and amusing, short

It's that man again, in Total Recall.

story, made it into *Total Recall*, though, of course, the gap between the two is as wide as Arnold Schwarzenegger's shoulders. The story and movie do share a common beginning, with a clerk, Douglas Quail, who is troubled by persistent dreams about Mars. Interpreting these as part of a deep desire to go to Mars, but unable to afford an actual trip he instead visits Rekal Incorporated to have artificial memories implanted so that he will be under the impression that he has visited Mars as a secret agent working for the Interplan organization. But when the Rekal people start to administer the treatment they discover that Quail really was an Interplan agent who had been sent on a mission to Mars and his previous personality, and memories, have been buried beneath a new, artificial set of memories as part of Interplan's cover-up operation, which they've unwittingly blown.

Several plot convolutions later, when Quail has remembered the details of his mission to Mars — it was to assassinate a political leader, which he did — he makes a deal with the Interplan bosses to provide him with yet another new personality rather than eliminate him, but to ensure that his old memories don't break through once again he suggests they base his new self on his most powerful wish-fulfilment dream fantasy. Interplan agrees and when their psychs probe Quail they find that his most powerful fantasy involves him encountering some mouse-like aliens in their tiny spaceship when he was nine years old. They were the vanguard of an invasion force but because of the kindness shown to them by the young Quail they made a covenant with him not to invade the Earth as long as he lives. So it seems that Quail's deepest fantasy is to be the most important man in the world. But, of course, as they attempt to implant this 'fantasy' as a false memory they discover a real memory of the event. Quail actually is the most important man in the world . . .

For a start, Quail's name has been changed to Quaid in the movie (Big Arnie playing a guy called Quail? No way, man! Actually it was changed to avoid unwanted connectuions with Vice President Quayle). He is no longer a clerk but a construction worker, but the movie does follow the story to the point where Quaid has to go on the run to get away from the secret agents who are out to kill him, then the action switches to Mars and the movie goes its own way, admittedly producing some clever plot twists en route before letting itself down with a truly absurd ending — Mars receiving an instant atmosphere from an alien artefact (and the shots of Quaid's and the girl's heads expanding like balloons, and with their eyes bulging like fried eggs, from the lack of air pressure, go beyond being merely absurd). It is even more ridiculous than the shower of rain at the end of *Dune*. And yes, there are definitely no sentient alien mice in the movie. It's kind of hard to believe that Dick's modest little story should end up as this $60 million blockbuster (estimates of the true cost vary: one goes as high as $73 million while the director says it was only — hah — $49 million) with breathtaking visual and physical effects, and bone-crunching action sequences (sixty-six stunt people were used). It doesn't do to wonder what Dick would have thought about it but one thing is certain — he wouldn't have liked the way they misspelt his name in the credits.

Total Recall had a gestation period that was even longer than the usual Hollywood one. Ronald Shusett, who later co-wrote the original *Alien* screenplay with Dan O'Bannon, had been keen to turn Dick's story into a movie since the mid-seventies. After the success of *Alien* he and O'Bannon had enough clout to approach Disney with the project and the studio initially took it on (yeah, it's hard to imagine now *Total Recall* as a Disney movie, even from their Touchstone division) but then expressed dissatisfaction with the last third of the screenplay and passed on it in 1980. In 1982 the dreaded Dino De Laurentiis entered the frame and he brought in David Cronenberg to direct it. Richard Dreyfuss was to star in this version but Cronenberg had a similar experience with Dino that Nic Roeg had with him over *Flash Gordon*; after Cronenberg had spent some considerable time developing the project Dino informed him that his version of the movie was not the one that Dino wanted to make and they parted company (also the distributors thought Cronenberg's version of the screenplay was 'too intellectual'). After that, in 1986, the Australian director Bruce Beresford was brought in and he cast Patrick Swayze in the lead role. Beresford's production, which was going to be made in Australia, was close to the shooting stage in 1987, with something like $6,000,000 already spent, when Dino's De Laurentiis Entertainment Group went belly up, pulling the plug on that movie and others. Enter the Terminator himself, Schwarzenegger, who had seen the script when working with Dino and liked it. He persuaded Carolco Pictures, a company in which he has an interest, not to mention an influence, to buy the rights to *Total Recall* which it did in 1988. Schwarzenegger was also instrumental in bringing in *Robocop*'s director, Paul Verhoeven, into the project. The combination of Schwarzenegger and Verhoeven was to guarantee that any touch of subtlety in the movie was going straight out the window.

When I reviewed the movie I said, '*Total Recall* is the story of some poor sod caught up in a terrible conspiracy, but as the poor sod is none other than the Terminator himself you feel more sympathetic for his enemies than you do for him. You know from the beginning that they don't stand a chance. Arnie is the celluloid equivalent of a black hole; just as the incredible mass of a black hole's singularity bends time and space around it, Big Arnie has a similar effect on any movie he's in — because of the sheer physicality of his screen presence the movie kind of wraps itself around him. Verhoeven wisely went with the flow and made *Total Recall* an out and out vehicle for the Big Guy.'

That said, I enjoyed it a lot. Considered purely as an sf movie it's well above average and, as I noted earlier, in spite of all its excesses, especially in the area of the violence, it does remain remarkably faithful to Dick's perennial theme of 'how can you tell the difference between the real and the unreal?', much more so, in fact, than *Blade Runner*. One of my favourite sequences in the movie is quintessential Philip Dick, though I hear it was one of David Cronenberg's contributions to the script from way back. It's the moment when the Rekall psychiatrist and Quaid's fake wife, Lori (the excellent Sharon Stone), appear in Quaid's Martian hotel room and try to persuade him that he is stuck in Rekall's memory-implanting machine and that none of what he is experiencing is real. Quaid is almost convinced. After all, as Lori asks, in the movie's best line: 'Which is more likely? The explanation we've just given you or the idea that you're an invincible secret agent who is the victim of an interplanetary conspiracy to make you think you're a construction worker?' This suggestion that Quaid's experiences might actually be the simulated Martian fantasy/adventure that he originally paid Rekall to implant in his mind is maintained throughout the film, right up to Quaid's final line, 'Maybe it *is* all a dream.'

I agree with what Dan O'Bannon said about it (though he was highly critical about many aspects of the film, such as the violence, and had parted company with Shusett when his original ending was changed to the one we see on the screen). 'This movie is something very rare. It's an actual science fiction movie. Most sf movies are really something else in disguise.'

Hear! Hear!

Space, time
and the nerd factor

It seems only fitting that this final chapter should centre on John Baxter, without whom this volume wouldn't exist. John was born in Sydney, Australia in 1939, and began writing, and selling, sf stories in his early twenties (it was a pretty rare achievement for an Australian writer to be published in any of the US or UK sf magazines in those days). He sold his first sf novel, *The God Killers*, at the age of twenty-six and since then, apart from writing a number of non-sf novels, has edited several anthologies of Australian sf stories, the first being *The Pacific Book of Australian Science Fiction* in 1968. John and I never met in Australia, though I did know of him by reputation, but coincidentally we both left Australia for the United Kingdom around the same time, though he made the journey sensibly by ship while I travelled by double-decker bus.

Shortly after arriving in London in 1970 I came across John's book *Science Fiction in the Cinema*, the first of its kind, and I was greatly impressed by it, not to mention highly influenced. With writing ambitions of my own, I was inspired to approach John's then publishers, the Tantivy Press, with an idea for a film book. As John had written about sf movies, and Ivan Butler had written a fine book on horror movies, my other cinematic love, for the same publisher, all I could think of was a book about James Bond movies. While waiting for the publisher's reaction I happened to meet John himself: I was standing in line at the National Film Theatre in London when I heard a man, who was picking up tickets at the box office, identify himself as John Baxter. I introduced myself and he generously said he would do all he could to assist a fellow Australian (struggling) writer. And he was as good as his word, recommending my idea to Tantivy Press (the result was the publication *James Bond in the Cinema*), and later introducing me to the editor at his new publishers, Macdonald and Janes (now just Macdonald), who became the publishers of my first book on sf cinema, *Future Tense*, in 1978. John also contributed to the Epilogue of that book, reinforcing the theme of his own *Science Fiction in the Cinema*: that sf films have little in common with written science fiction. 'It certainly applies to the films I was writing about then,' he said in 1978. 'Whether films have changed since then and come closer to science fiction I don't know. I don't think they have. Special effects are what obviously dominate sf films today and that wasn't true of the movies I was writing about. But I still don't think sf film-makers these days are very interested in content — they're more concerned with setting and back-ground. They're becoming obsessed with it, they're not really concerned with ideology; they're making these big, expensive movies tucked away in factories and concentrating solely on getting the background right. Nobody making sf films is really addressing themselves to the issues of the day . . .'

I thought it appropriate that this book should also end with an interview with the man who started it all but before I asked him if his opinion about sf films had altered during the intervening years, I had to ask him about his own personal involvement, as a screenwriter, with a big-budget sf movie, *Time Guardian* (see Chapter Fifteen) . . .

John, when did you realize things were going wrong with the project?

'I suppose I realized things were going wrong from the very first moment when we tried to get some interest in it from potential producers and distributors — it was extremely easy. In fact, we were fighting people off. People were eager to option this science fiction outline about a time-travelling city that travels up and down the time lines, stopping occasionally in central Australia — it should have warned me that the sort of people who were interested in making sf films, especially in Australia, were not interested in it for the same reason as myself and my co-writer and director Brian Hannant. Brian had just come off from being a co-writer on *Mad Max 2 — The Road Warrior* and was extremely hot so when we put this idea around people were eager to put money into it — when the project was

A scene from Mad Max 2, *co-written by Brian Hannant, co-writer and director of* Time Guardian.

finally acquired by a small production company called Chateaux Productions and they issued the necessary prospectus to find public investors, the budget of $8,000,000 plus was raised in one morning.

'That should have been our real warning — everybody said, "Time-travelling city? Wow! Nobody has ever done that! Let's have it!" No one sat down and said, "Just exactly how do we do this time-travelling city? And are the special effects available in Australia of an adequate level and standard to achieve the city and other elaborate effects sequences?" We had not thought any of this out. In Hollywood, I realized later, it wouldn't have been done that way — the outline that we put around, and the first draft script, would have been just the first step in an elaborate process of examination, of rewriting, of budgeting and of finding out if the required effects were achievable.'

*Presumably there wasn't much choice for **effects companies** in Australia?*

'We had no choice at all. There was only one special effects company operating. Called Mirage, it had mainly done effects for TV commercials and had never done anything on this scale before, though they were very good when it came to creating rubber creature masks — they were quite clever at that sort of thing but they weren't really able to come up with the necessary high-tech stuff. We had problems right from the beginning just trying to achieve the simplest effects. Our robot cyborg characters, the Jinn-Diki, had very large aerials sticking up from the backs of their necks and were supposed to be receiving antennae for the messages being sent from their central intelligence. Unfortunately, whenever the Jinn-diki moved, these antennae waggled around vigorously because they had not been made of a sufficiently hard substance, and then snapped off. Also the original Jinn-diki consisted of a total body suit — they built the suit and it looked very good, but when an actor got into it he couldn't move, he could only stand there in it. He looked good all right, but he was totally immobile. So that had to be changed. And one of the major effects problems was that there was no one in Australia who could do adequate blue-screen work, certainly nothing like the quality we required.

'But the effects weren't the only drawback. There were fundamental difficulties, for example, with the casting. The original prospectus said that the main male character, Ballard, would be played by an American actor like Scott Glenn. He was our first choice: we wanted a very tough, very hard, dangerous-looking man who might conceivably be sent back from the future as a kind of trouble-shooter, a time guardian essentially. For a lot of complicated reasons we ended up with the Australian actor Tom Burlinson and his main problem is that he's always going to look eighteen. He was delighted to play the role because he saw it as an opportunity to play a mature persona, and he loved the thought of having an action role, but no matter how much you blacked up his face and put fake scars on him he still looked like Audie Murphy. He carries no conviction in the role but it's not his fault — he's a perfectly good actor. It was gross miscasting. The two major names in the film, Carrie Fisher and Dean Stockwell, were brought in for international appeal. Neither were our choices and neither of them really knew what they were doing there, except that they figured it was money and a holiday in the sun. Neither were well used, in my opinion, in the movie . . .'

Why was that? Carrie Fisher, for example, spent most of the movie lying on her back after being zapped by a cyborg.

'Well, her role wasn't very important. The main female part is that of the contemporary girl that Ballard meets in Australia. We were looking for a major American star to play Ballard, a less well-known Australian actress to be his helper/friend from the future, and the girl he meets in Australia — who, in fact, in the original draft, was going to be the main character rather than Ballard — to be played by some fairly well-known American actress. We needed an international presence for her part but it got completely turned around; her part was played by a little-known Australian actress who didn't add anything to it, and the nothing role of Ballard's female colleague was given to Carrie Fisher. A total waste. I would have preferred her to have been the captain of the flying city rather than Dean Stockwell.'

So why wasn't she?

'We weren't given that option. Anyway, at this stage of the film my association had become peripheral because, as everyone knows, the writer gets automatically pushed out. All they were thinking about by then was the special effects — could they get enough effects together for the million dollars they had to spend on them. Chateaux and Hemdale had really ceased to worry about the cast. As long as they had some names that looked good on the marquee, that was all they were really concerned about. They had really ceased to worry about the content of the story, they were much more concerned about big explosions.'

How did your relationship with your co-writer, Brian Hannant, change as he became involved with the pre-production of the movie and then the actual direction?

'The truth is that he and I fell out over the film, and later on he also fell out with the producers and was fired from the film. The essential problem between us was that I wanted to stick as close to the original story as possible. I was not terribly interested in getting a lot of special effects because it seemed obvious to me that you weren't going to be able to make the equivalent of *2001* in Australia. *Time Guardian* was never going to be *Blade Runner*, it was always going to look a little bit cheap so we should go with the characters and story and to hell with all the explosions and stuff.

We all went over to Adelaide to look for locations — the company had received a very good offer from the South Australian Film Corporation to let us use the Corporation's studio, so it was increasingly felt, against the will of almost everyone, we should make the film in and around Adelaide. Quite close into Adelaide, in fact, rather than going out into the Outback and shooting at the original location, which was a natural ring valley called Wilpeena Pound. (There is one very brief shot of the place in the movie, an aerial shot, that I gather Brian put in at a later date, paying for it out of his own pocket.) So when it was decided to shoot around Adelaide a group of us went out to look at a series of locations that would stand in for the ring valley. And the first one we looked at was a rock quarry. And I said, "It's a rock quarry!" And Brian said, "Oh no, it will be great . . . we'll shoot across there and that becomes the edge of the ring valley . . . " And I said, "It's going to look like a rock quarry! All science fiction films are shot in rock quarries! It's going to look like 'Dr Who' . . . !" But all these technicians, the pyros who do the physical effects, explosions and light effects, were all getting very excited and saying, "Yeah, what we can do is jump off there and follow up with another big one over there . . . !" And you could see Brian loving it, and the producers were looking very happy and I was saying, "But it's just a rock quarry." And increasingly I was isolated until there was just me and Geoff Burton, the cameraman, who had doubts about it, and as the others walked ahead dreaming up more and more beautiful explosions, he said to me, "Welcome to the film industry, John."

'And so it got to the point where Brian rang me from Adelaide about three days before the film was due to start shooting. He was very agitated and said that it'd been decided that the big climax of the movie was going to be the total blowing-up of the town of Midas — the town built for the movie — so we'd got to lose I forget how many minutes of dialogue and character. And I said, no, I don't want to cut anymore, and I don't want to work on it anymore. And he said, "We've got to do it! We've got to do it!" And I said, "No, I'm not coming over and I'm not going to do yet another rewrite and eviscerate the thing still further." And that's the last time I talked to Brian. I gather that the film just went from bad to worse. There were increasing difficulties with the technical end of things, culminating with Brian himself becoming disenchanted with the production and leaving. So the final version was put together by the editor and, to my mind, it is a total disaster. In fact, when I was working in Hollywood the year after I went to see a time-travel movie made by Corman's company, Miracle Pictures, called, I think, *The Future Hunters*. Anyway, it was incredibly cheap; it was set in Arthurian England, represented by these very nasty painted cheese-cloth backdrops and a lot of people wandering around in costumes from a cheap revival of *Camelot*. And I was thinking, this is *awful* — this is the cheapest, nastiest film I've ever seen. So when *Time Guardian* had its one-week release in the USA it was double-billed with this awful movie.'

Which leads us neatly to Hollywood and the new generation of sf film-makers. What is your opinion of them and the movies they make?

'Well, I had a really interesting time in Hollywood because one automatically gets into the company of people like Joe Dante, Robert Zemeckis and Jon Davidson, the producer of the *Robocop* movies, and it's fascinating to meet someone like Davidson and have him say straight off, "Are you the John Baxter who wrote *Science Fiction in the Cinema?*' And I say, "Yeah, sure," and he says, "Oh, gosh, I read that, and I loved that about it but I didn't agree with you on this" and so on. This happened a lot. I commented to another film historian, Bill Warren, that I couldn't get used to the fact that these people had read my book and he said, "You've got to remember these guys were kids and fans when that book came out, and it was the first book that actually took seriously something they already liked. It gave legitimacy to something that until then had just been a kind of enthusiasm for them, and an illicit enthusiasm at that." He was right, and what it dramatized to me was that the new generation of film-makers — and it's not just the people who make sf films like Dante and Davidson but people like Scorsese and Tavernier — grew up with the sf film of the fifties and it's part of their mental landscape. For me, it was something I came to in adulthood. I learned to enjoy sf films intellectually — it was never part of my adolescent landscape.'

Are you sure about that? What age were you when you first saw them?

'Okay, I saw them when they came out in the fifties. I was born in '39, so I was in my teens but these guys saw them when they were eight and ten and even younger because a lot of them saw them for the first time on TV when their parents were out. By the time they were fifteen they already knew more about early sf movies than most of us do after studying the

A movie that has been a primal influence on a wide variety of film-makers, The Incredible Shrinking Man.

subject forever. And don't forget those movies were easier to come by in the States whereas for us in Australia they were hard to dig out. Incidentally, to prove my point, in the French *Vogue* this month Martin Scorsese and a number of other film-makers, like Lucas and Tavernier, were asked to list their ten favourite movies and it's extraordinary how, in the middle of a list of movie titles directed by the like of Bresson and Truffaut you find *The Incredible Shrinking Man.* A lot of these sf films had a profound effect on these kids when they first saw them and they absorbed them in the same way that they absorbed, say, Bresson, and it's all part of the same landscape for them.'

But how many of them do you think actually read science fiction when they were young?

'Oh, hardly any, I'd think. It seems to me that one thing you can be sure of in Hollywood is that nobody reads anything. Even producers only look at a couple of pages of outline given to them by their development people.'

But when I was discussing Back to the Future 2 *in Chapter Fifteen I pointed out it was the first sf film, with the exception, maybe, of* The Terminator *that properly exploited the full potential of the ideas contained in time-travel literature.*

'Well, I can't believe that Bob Gale and Bob Zemeckis have read a lot of sf. They would have seen a lot of sf on television, like 'The Twilight Zone' and 'Outer Limits'. As everyone would acknowledge, Harlan Ellison's episode of 'Outer Limits', 'Demon With a Glass Hand', was very influential. It essentially plays with the same ideas as *Back to the Future*. Television sf was the main influence on these guys, not the literature.'

I quote you earlier in the book about that preview screening of Star Wars *we both attended and your comment afterwards about how mindless it all was. Did* Star Wars *set the agenda for what has followed?*

'Yeah, sure. As I've said all along, it's always been my thesis that written and film sf have nothing in common and the contact between the two can at best be only peripheral. You go to Joe Dante's house for example. There isn't any sf there, but there are a lot of comic books and a lot of comic-inspired puppets and dolls. He's a very serious scholar of comic books — he's a great fan of Herriman, he's got original comic artwork on the walls, but he's not a science fiction fan in any sense of the word. He's not interested in it. He told me about *Inner Space* [a rather good sf comedy movie that Dante made in 1987 starring Dennis Quaid and Martin Short]. The script had been kicking about for years and he'd read it and didn't like it, saying it was just a lot of scientific stuff and effects, until someone said to him that they thought of it as a Dean Martin and Jerry Lewis movie, with Dean Martin inside Jerry Lewis, and Dante loved that idea and did the movie.

'I'd have to rummage around in the conversations I had with these people but the thing that keeps coming back to mind in a general kind of way is that these people don't know anything about science fiction, and have no interest in sf, but they are encyclopaedic in their knowledge of sf movies. And also peripheral horror and splatter sf stuff. Dante for years would hire a cinema every Sunday morning, rake out 35mm prints of rare and early sf and horror movies and show them to a little group of people who were really keen on the stuff. You can't win in a conversation with Joe Dante on the subject of fifties sf movies because he's seen them all, but I'd be astonished to learn that he's read more than four or five of the basic science fiction novels.'

So you don't see any chance of an improvement in the sf cinema in terms of content?

'All I can do is point to the record: nothing has happened between *Future Tense* and now to disprove what I said back then. Science fiction films are becoming increasingly technically sophisticated and increasingly mindless. The peak is surely *Blade Runner*, which to me is ravishingly visual — a wonderful film to look at, and I run it over and over again — but the ideas are really aboriginal . . .'

Well, I disagree there. I think Blade Runner *is full of good ideas but I don't think they're properly exploited — the idea of implanted fake memories, for example. Okay, they're Philip Dick's ideas and they're there in the film but the screenwriter and the director didn't know how to use them.*

'Sure. Well, the story of how that script was written is a book in itself. I mean, endless guys worked on it and David Peoples's script was the final version but I didn't get the impression from Peoples that he was very interested in sf. Most of the time, as you say, these ideas are planted in the movie but then just left. They're of very little interest. What matters are the visuals and the action, which is where someone like James Cameron really comes through.'

Okay, what about James Cameron? I get the impression that he's pretty familiar with

Pris the Replicant (Daryl Hannah) from Blade Runner, *a movie that John Baxter considers to be one of the few bright spots in recent sf cinema.*

written sf. I mean, with The Terminator, *not only is there the 'Outer Limits' influence but, as I pointed out in Chapter Eleven, the sequences set in the future seem to have been inspired by, among other literary sources, Phil Dick's story 'Second Variety'. Cameron seems, to me, to be very good at exploiting sf ideas in a visual way.*

'I think I'd prefer to say that he makes very good visual sf movies into which he puts a little intellectual content as well.'

Hmph. Okay, what about Dan O'Bannon? He seems to know his written sf. He certainly knows his Philip K. Dick.

'Dick is the one sf author that people outside the sf readership tend to know about, in the same way that Tolkien is the one fantasy author that people have heard of. In the case of Dick I think he's not regarded as an sf writer by many people because he never wrote hard, technological sf, it was more sociological, state-of-consciousness sort of stuff. He had a cult following that extended beyond the purely sf crowd.'

I give in. What did you think of The Abyss?

'I think *The Abyss* is great. But that said, I saw it in Hollywood under the most perfect circumstances with some of the best stereo sound I'd ever heard, and in an almost empty cinema, which is probably ideal. I had the same sort of frisson as I had with *Blade Runner* the first time I saw it at a preview screening in an empty Warner West End cinema.'

I've already told the readers how you got to see the original version of Blade Runner *at that one-off screening and I didn't so let's not dwell on that. What particularly impressed you about* The Abyss?

'I loved the callous technical brilliance of *The Abyss* in the same way that I loved the callous technical brilliance of *Blade Runner*, but it doesn't seem to me to be about technology at all, it's about marriage, and for that reason I find it very interesting. It's what used to be called a "woman's picture", but one with an elegant surround, a Joan Crawford movie with an elegant, technical surround, a frame of technical detail. Who cares about the silly aliens in *The Abyss*? The film is filled with detail that amplifies the marriage element, like the thing that stops the door from closing at a crucial moment is the wedding ring on his finger. He throws the ring down a toilet at one point then gets it back again. All of it is just about love and marriage.'

So you're saying it's basically a small movie about marriage embedded in this huge technological surround?

'Sure, but you might say the same thing about most sf movies. *Blade*

The Abyss, *a small movie about marriage set in a huge technological frame, or a genuine sf movie?*

Runner is the same. And *Aliens*. That's a story about a mother and child, which is why I was so disappointed that they cut out the one sequence that so amplifies the point.'

But don't you think Cameron is rare for a Hollywood sf film-maker in that he makes an effort to get his scientific facts right. As I pointed out in Chapter Twelve, of all the directors who made underwater creature movies recently, he was the only one who set his story at a reasonable depth.

'Yes, that's true, I suppose.'

I mean, since Kubrick no other director has seemed to give a shit about getting the science right.

'I've never talked to Cameron about it but I don't think he does either. I think he wants a certain feel for his films and to that end he tries to make them as authentic-looking as possible but I'm sure, for instance, that you could find a scientific justification for that tentacle of water that forms into a face, though it's the most visually interesting idea in the movie.'

Well, I could have a good stab at it, but I won't; instead let's finish with a summing-up of the situation as you see it. Do you think Star Wars *has been the main influence on the sf cinema since its release in '77?*

'No, I don't think that *Star Wars* has been that much of an influence because the truth is that you can't replicate what *Star Wars* did. *Star Wars* was just too expensive to reproduce, just as *2001* was too expensive to imitate. You can't really take *Star Wars* and scale it down. Well, okay they did with *Battlestar Galactica* but . . .

Yes, they did, but what I'm talking about is the effect that Star Wars *had on attitudes towards sf; it reinforced the idea that sf cinema is very much a juvenile-orientated genre.*

'Yes, but it had always been aimed at children in the main. Joe Dante said of his film *Explorers* that it was crucial that kids understand what it was about and he knew at the preview that they didn't. But for him it was the kids that mattered. He also told me a story about *Gremlins* — that he was worried that it might be too violent for the kids. And at a preview, when he saw a screaming kid being carried out of the cinema by his mother, he thought to himself that maybe it was too violent until he realized that the kid was screaming because he was being dragged out against his will. The kid loved it; his mother didn't. Dante talked a lot about how great it was to work with the three kids in *Explorers*.

'A lot of these directors, you know, have no family. They're real loners and they're trying to recreate their childhoods. Spielberg with his company, Amblin' Films, and his obsession with small animals and children, his inability to really lead a properly adult life. Joe Dante is a nice guy but he's a big kid really. Lucas is the same. They make these little enclaves for themselves, they build little private worlds and confect fantasies of childhood. They're basically lonely kids. They're *nerds*. They're nerds who grew up, were given a camera, fifty million dollars and told to make movies. Of course, they love it but they're still nerdy kids. They're still the kids who never got picked for the baseball game, they're still the kids who had pimples when they were eighteen. That's their problem and they're acting out these fantasies of gigantism, force and superheroes in their movies, but really they're still just nerdy kids. And the first time an adult starts making sf movies you'll probably get something very interesting, but so far it's not happened, with the exception of someone like Tarkovsky.'

But weren't sf movies in the sixties and seventies much more eclectic in their subject matter until Star Wars *came along and restricted sf movies to purely juvenile themes in the main?*

'Well, in the sense that after the success of *Star Wars* young nerds could get movies to make. I have the feeling that if someone like Barry Levinson, a major adult director, wanted to make an sf movie he wouldn't get the money, because they'd say that it's young nerds who make the sf films

Aliens — *does it prove that its director used to actually read science fiction?*

that'll bring in the kids, so we won't give the money to this guy because it will be too intellectual. Films like *2001* and *Blade Runner* don't prove anything because they don't start anything in the way of trends, they're one-offs. You have to look at the flow, at the ten or fifteen sf movies made every year and at who makes them, and they tend to be the likes of Zemeckis, Dante, Lucas and Spielberg, those sorts of people who are basically the movie nerd generation.'

But weren't the original literary sf fans also nerds? The ones who edited and produced their fanzines before going on to write the real stuff themselves? I mean, your archetypal male sf fan is still a nerd (I suppose the female equivalent is a 'nerdette'). I speak from personal experience. And the sf conventions are full of them.

'Oh yes, sure . . .'

At the start of the book I've quoted that famous saying, 'The Golden Age of science fiction is twelve.' Isn't that true of written sf as well as sf cinema?

'No, I don't think so. It's true of a certain kind of sf. When I was twelve I really loved reading *Startling Stories* and the like, but I'm not sure that at twelve I could have made much sense out of Philip K. Dick. I think Dick was an adult writer. I think William Gibson is a serious writer, I think Iain Banks is a serious writer. I read him like I ready anybody — I can read him and then William Boyd and they're all writing the same kind of fiction as far as I'm concerned, but certainly the science fiction that is the basis of sf movies is around the twelve year age level.

'I think what will happen with sf cinema in the future will be the same thing that has been happening for the last twenty years — which will be that the main thrust of sf movies will be dumb, mindless plots dignified by elaborate special effects ever more dazzling. And maybe, every now and then, there will be some small sf movie made by some German or Finn, or maybe by a serious American director, that will be interesting to us aficionados and fascinating in the same way as *Blade Runner*. But it will be a total financial disaster and the person concerned will never make another one again.'

*

I suppose I must agree with John; at the end of *Future Tense* I wrote: 'Science fiction films that are both intellectually satisfying and visually evocative, such as *Forbidden Planet, 2001: A Space Odyssey, Quatermass and the Pit*, and *Dark Star*, will remain the occasional happy accident,' and that still

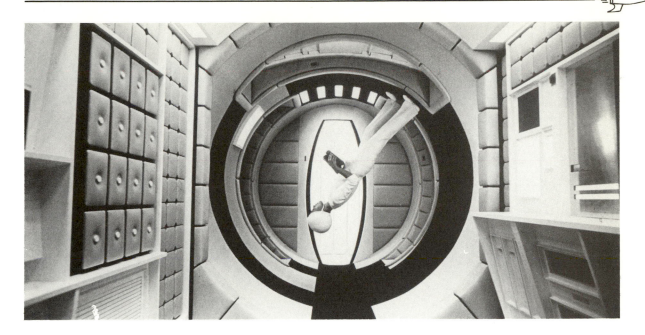

seems to be true. In the thirteen years since then there have only been a small handful of sf movies that I rate especially highly, and admittedly few, if any, of them are 'intellectually satisfying'. They are *Mad Max 2*, *Blade Runner*, *The Thing*, *The Terminator*, *Aliens*, *Back to the Future 2*, *The Abyss* and *Total Recall*. (Yes, I am well aware that Tarkovsky's *Stalker* is rated by many as one of the best sf movies ever made, but not by me. Besides, it would look very out of place in the above line-up. It doesn't even star Arnold Schwarzenegger.)

Still, to paraphrase another famous saying about sf, by Theodore Sturgeon: 'It's true that ninety per cent of science fiction films are crap but ninety per cent of everything is crap.'

2001, a genuine landmark — and one-off event — in the cinema of sf.

References

Chapter One

1 *Kinematograph Weekly*, 21 June 1923.
2 Charles Flynn and Tod McCarthy, *The King of the B's*, Dutton & Co, 1975.
3 *Sight and Sound*, Vol 36 No 3 1967.
4 *The Bioscope*, 5 June 1919.
5 J. E. Williamson, *Twenty Years Under the Sea*, Bodley Head, 1935.
6 *Ibid*.

Chapter Two

1 *The Bioscope*, 14 August 1929.

Chapter Three

1 John Baxter, *Science Fiction in the Cinema*, Tantivy Press, 1970.
2 *Ibid*.

Chapter Four

1 *Astounding Science Fiction*, July 1950.
2 *Cinema Papers*, March-April 1975.
3 *Cinefantastique*, Vol 4, No 1, 1975.
4 *Ibid*.

Chapter Five

1 *Cinefantastique*, Vol 4, No 4, 1976.
2 *Ibid*.
3 *Cinefantastique*, Vol 13, No 1, 1983.
4 *Photon*, No 22, 1974.
5 *Cinefantastique*, Vol 5, No 4, 1977.
6 *Ibid*.
7 *Interzone*, No 43, 1991.
8 *Interview with author*.
9 *Ibid*.
10 *The Dark Side*, January 1991.
11 *Interview with author*.
12 *Ibid*.
13 *The Dark Side*, January 1991.
14 *Cinefantastique*, Vol 2, No 3, 1973.
15 *Interview with author*.
16 *New York Times*, 1960.

Chapter Six

1 *Interview with author*.
2 *Cinefantastique*, Vol 3, No 4, 1974.
3 *Interview with author*.
4 *Ibid*.
5 *Ibid*.
6 *Fantascene*, Vol 1, No 2, 1976.
7 Bill Warren, *Keep Watching the Skies*, McFarland, 1982.
8 *Fangoria*, No 25, 1983.
9 *Interview with author*.
10 *Fantastic Films*, No 16, 1980.

Chapter Seven

1 *Variety*, 1958.
2 *Interview with author*.
3 Alexander Walker, *Stanley Kubrick Directs*, Abacus, 1973.
4 Julian Smith, *Looking Away: Hollywood & Vietnam*, 1973.
5 *Interview with author*.

Chapter Eight

1 *Fangoria*, No 25, 1983.
2 *Interview with author.*
3 *Cinema Papers*, March–April 1975.
4 *Interview with author.*
5 *Playboy*, 1968.
6 *Psychology Today*, 1968.
7 *Castle of Frankenstein*, 1969.
8 *Interview with author.*
9 *Interzone*, No 43, 1991.

Chapter Nine

1 *Films and Filming*, November 1977.
2 *Time Out*, No 1007, 1989.
3 Alexander Walker, *Stanley Kubrick Directs*, Abacus, 1973.
4 *Time Out*, No 1007, 1989.
5 *Interview with author.*
6 *Interview with author.*
7 *Interview with author.*
8 *Interview with author.*
9 *Cinefantastique*, Vol 5, No 1, 1976.
10 *Cinefantastique*, Vol 5, No 2, 1976.
11 *Ibid.*
12 *Ibid.*
13 *Ibid.*
14 *Interview with author.*
15 *Rolling Stone*, No 246, 1977.
16 Dale Pollock, *Skywalking*, Ballantine, 1983.
17 *Rolling Stone*, No 246, 1977.
18 *Interview with author.*
19 *Interview with author.*
20 *Skywalking*, Dale Pollock, Ballantine, 1983.
21 *Ibid.*
22 *Cinefantastique*, Vol 7, Nos 3–4. 1978.
23 *Filmmakers Newsletter*, Vol 11, No 2, 1977.

Chapter Ten

1 *Filmmakers Newsletter*, Vol 11, No 2, 1977.
2 *Cinefantastique*, Vol 9, No 1, 1979.
3 *Starburst*, No 19, 1979.
4 *Ibid.*
5 *Cinefantastique*, Vol 9, No 1, 1979.
6 *Interview with author.*
7 *Ibid.*
8 *Interview with author.*
9 Dale Pollock, *Skywalking*, Ballantine, 1983.
10 *Starburst*, No 61, 1983.
11 *Fantastic Films*, May 1980.
12 *Interview with author.*
13 *Starburst*, No 23, 1980.
14 *20–20*, No 4, 1989.
15 *Ibid.*
16 *Ibid.*

Chapter Eleven

1 William Goldman, *Adventures in the Screen Trade*, Macdonald, 1984.
2 *Cinefantastique*, Vol 12, Nos 5–6, 1982.
3 *Ibid.*
4 *Ibid.*
5 *Starburst*, No 51, 1982.
6 *Cinefantastique*, Vol 15, No 3, 1985.
7 *Cinefantastique*, Vol 18, No 1, 1987.
8 *The Magazine of Fantasy and Science Fiction*, December 1987.
9 *Starburst*, No 147, 1990.
10 *Cinefantastique*, Vol 18, No 1, 1987.
11 *Starburst Year Book*, No 7, 1990–91.

Chapter Twelve

1 *Sight and Sound*, Autumn 1975.
2 *Cinefantastique*, Vol 7, Nos 3–4, 1978.
3 *Cinema*, No 9, 1982.
4 *Ibid.*
5 *Video Now*, January 1989.
6 *Starburst*, No 135, November 1989.
7 *Los Angeles Times*, 1989.
8 *Ibid.*
9 *Starburst*, No 135, 1989.

Chapter Thirteen

1 *Interview with author.*
2 *Ibid.*
3 *Starburst*, No 117, 1988.
4 *Interview with author.*
5 *The Dark Side*, January 1991.
6 *Starburst*, No 117, 1988.
7 *Ibid.*
8 *Cinefantastique*, Vol 15, No 3. 1985.
9 *Time Out*, No 834, 1986.
10 *Ibid.*
11 *Interview with author.*

Chapter Fourteen

1 Leonard Maltin, *TV Movies and Video Guide*, Penguin, 1988.
2 *Cinefantastique*, Vol 19, Nos 1–2, 1989.
3 *Deep Star Six* production notes.
4 *Cinefex*, No 38, 1990.
5 *Ibid.*

Chapter Fifteen

1 *Interzone*, No 43, 1991.
2 *Interview with author.*

Chapter Sixteen

1 David Wingrove (ed.), *Science Fiction Film Source Book*, Longman, 1985.
2 *Starburst*, No 36, 1981.
3 *Ibid*.
4 *Cinefantastique*, Vol 14, No 2, 1983–84.
5 *Cinefantastique*, Vol 21, No 5, 1991.

Chapter Seventeen

1 *Interview with author.*
2 *Cinefantastique*, Vol 19, No 5, 1989.
3 *Ibid*.
4 *Starburst*, No 127, 1989.
5 *Cinefantastique*, Vol 21, No 5, 1991.

Index